# TRANSITIONS
## IN LAND AND HOUSING:

# BULGARIA,
# THE CZECH REPUBLIC,
# AND POLAND

**Ann Louise Strong, Thomas A. Reiner,
and Janusz Szyrmer**

ST. MARTIN'S PRESS
NEW YORK

*333.309*
*892t*

Library of Congress Cataloging-in-Publication Data

Strong, Ann L. (Ann Louise)
    Transitions in land and housing in Bulgaria, the Czech Republic,
  and Poland / Ann Louise Strong, Thomas A. Reiner, and Janusz
  Szyrmer.
        p.   cm.
    Includes bibliographical references (p.      ) and index.
    ISBN 0-312-15906-4
    1. Real property—Bulgaria.  2. Real property—Czech Republic.
  3. Real property—Poland.  4. Privatization—Bulgaria.
  5. Privatization—Czech Republic.  6. Privatization—Poland.
  7. Bulgaria—Claims.  8. Czech Republic—Claims.  9. Poland—Claims.
  I. Reiner, Thomas A. (Thomas Andrew), 1931-   . II. Szyrmer,
  Janusz.  III. Title.
  HD816.S77   1996
  333.3'0943—dc20                                              96-17339
                                                               CIP
*JK*

*Book design by Digital Type & Design*

First Edition: September 1996
10  9  8  7  6  5  4  3  2  1
ISBN 0-312-15906-4

# CONTENTS

# LIST OF MAPS

# PREFACE

This study of changing patterns of ownership in land and housing and the formation of real estate markets in Central and Eastern Europe during the post-1989 "transition" focuses on three nations: Bulgaria, Czechoslovakia and the successor Czech Republic, and Poland. Field trips to the region by each of the authors during 1992, 1993, and 1994 contributed to on-site understanding of the process and the local environment. Numerous interviews with national and local government officials and with developers, attorneys, architects, and other professionals working in the field, as well as researchers, enriched our knowledge of a complex and rapidly changing process. (A list of our informants is included with each of the country chapters.)

Our research began with reference materials; for current and recent developments periodicals and wire services were a major source. Wide-ranging interviews with state and local government officials, private-sector planners and economists, foreign specialists working in the country, real estate practitioners and lawyers, and individuals directly involved in property privatization were critical in learning what actually was transpiring. Many of these people were able to provide us with technical documents and copies of legislation so that we could describe with reasonable accuracy the framework for privatization, the steps being taken, and the results achieved. Some people have been exceptionally helpful, commenting on drafts of our work and updating information.

The present study has benefited from the help of many in the United States as well as in Europe. We wish to recognize the help of in-country collaborators of the project in Bulgaria, the Czech Republic, and Poland, though of course responsibility for the contents of this book lies with the authors alone. We particularly want to thank Diana Kopeva and Alexander Bozhkov (Sofia), Jaroslav Macháček and Luděk Sýkora (Prague), and Jacek Szyrmer and Hanna Matras (Warsaw). Andrian Pervasov and Ivan Sariev provided essential local support in Bulgaria, Dr. Dominika Winterová in Czechoslovakia, and Hanna Szyrmer in Poland. Dorothy Ives Dewey, Ph.D. candidate in planning at the University of Pennsylvania, assisted with information acquisition and documentation in the United States. Jan Urban, then editor of *EKONOM* magazine (Prague), prepared a briefing paper in 1992 while on a research visit at the University of Pennsylvania. Martin Aschenbrenner, a legal intern at White and Case (Prague), translated and summarized pertinent Czech legislation. Kim Cherry prepared the maps.

Each of the authors brings to this project work in closely related fields. Thomas Reiner has studied local planning in the Soviet Union, and land and housing changes there during the perestroika years. Ann Louise Strong has written extensively on how law and government land policies in the United States and Western Europe influence urban development and more recently has worked with Chinese scholars on ways to establish urban land markets in China. Janusz Szyrmer recently has conducted in-depth research of investment, growth, and planning in the Soviet Union and has been involved in the analysis of economic and social indicators in Central and Eastern Europe. We believe that our different disciplines—planning, law, economics—strengthened the work.

We wish to acknowledge support from several sources. At the University of Pennsylvania, we have received assistance from the International Research Fund, the Research Foundation, and the Grosser Research Fund in Urban Land Use. The Soros Foundation has provided research and field support through the Central European University Privatization Project. The Federal National Mortgage Association ("Fannie Mae") helped fund participation in the "Designing Markets" session at the 1993 conference of the Association of Collegiate Schools of Planning. Fannie Mae and the Soros Foundation East-East Fund made possible a seminar held in Prague in 1994 where preliminary findings of the project were presented and discussed.

# 1

# INTRODUCTION

In all of the countries of Eastern and Central Europe, the power of the many actors in the private sector to make decisions over use, acquisition, and disposition of real property is increasing. Whether the shift in power from public to private has been planned or spontaneous, incremental or sudden, limited or radical, consensual or challenged, varies from country to country and is related both to the scope and pervasiveness of public power under communism and to the strength of current commitment to a market economy. All the nations, however, are in transition. The process of change involves relinquishing some degree of public control over property, whether that control was achieved through ownership, regulatory fiat, and/or allocation of funds. Concurrently the process involves rebuilding information and credit systems and local planning systems necessary for the fluid functioning of markets.

Privatization is at the heart of turning from a Communist to a market economy. Privatization in its various forms reduces the scope of the state and disperses decisions. It is the strengthening of private-sector control of types of real property—a blast furnace, a beer garden, or a high-rise apartment building—and is likely to encompass restoration of ownership rights to people or institutions whose property was taken by the Communists. Ownership of property is converted from the state sector to individuals, institutions, or legal entities, such as corporations. In the process, some or many of the socialist restrictions on use or transfer of property are removed. The rationale is twofold: Owners with a substantial measure of control over their property will husband this asset and, when they wish to transfer it, a market economy will stimulate efficient allocation. A related notion is that a society is strengthened when the state's role is diminished.

When looking at privatization, most economists have focused on enterprises and their restructuring and transformation into corporations, partnerships, or other forms of private entities. That is not the focus of this book. We examine the crucial role played by land and housing in the transition of three countries—Bulgaria, the Czech Republic, and Poland—to a market economy. We are concerned primarily with the shifts in ownership and control of a country's land (its fields, forests, and urban plots) and its housing (its rural cottages, city houses, and apartment blocks) from public to municipal or private, including voluntary cooperative enterprise and individual hands—and how these shifts are altering property markets. Since enterprises, small and large, occupy land and structures, we also look, to a lesser extent, at their privatization and its impact on property markets. In addition, we examine changes in the institutional infrastructure introduced to foster free market exchange.

De-etatization, or denationalization, is at the core of reform. Privatization is a means of transferring power from the state to the voters, the consumers, the producers—companies, cooperatives, family businesses—and to organizations—political, religious, and social. Privatization must be viewed in the context of political changes, the level of effective democracy, and changes in economic and social policies. Thus, in the introductory sections of the three country chapters we seek to describe the broader context in which the privatization processes are occurring.

## TRANSITION

The World Bank defines the three main pillars of transition as macroeconomic stabilization, microeconomic liberalization (de-etatization and decontrol of prices, and institutional reform), privatization, creation of new legal and banking infrastructure and so on. Those denominated shock therapists, including Jeffrey Sachs and Leszek Balcerowicz, favored rapid liberalization and deregulation, with institutional transformation to follow. Balcerowicz, as deputy prime minister of Poland, applied his approach and found it both politically and socially costly. In Czechoslovakia and then the Czech Republic, Prime Minister Václav Klaus emphasized institutional transformation via privatization. At the fall of communism he inherited a relatively stable economy, and he sought to build upon it. Both Balcerowicz and Klaus stressed the importance of macroeconomic stability. Bulgaria lagged behind Poland and the Czech Republic in strengthening all three pillars.

The process of de-etatization in all three countries, while different in nature depending on the structure under communism, has included: transfer of state properties to municipalities, giving the municipalities both title and effective control; corporatization of state enterprises, making them one-person partnerships under the state treasury, and providing for greater control over the real property in their portfolio, including some rights to buy and sell; de-etatization of institutions that had been formally autonomous but in reality were tightly controlled by the state, including cooperatives, political organizations, labor unions, and the church; and leasing of major portions of state-owned lands to private individuals.

The institution of private property stimulates domestic and foreign investment, expansion of successful businesses, and contraction or disappearance of less successful businesses and improves resource allocation. Combined with a stable and predictable economic environment, protection of fundamental political and economic freedoms, and reliable institutional infrastructure, the institution of private property will lead to economic growth as well as fundamental changes in land use patterns. These changes include more reconstruction and rehabilitation and less new construction; more office building and less residential construction in large cities; more service activities including hotels, restaurants, small shops, large shopping centers, and gas stations; and dramatic improvement in the urban and transportation infrastructure. All of this will stimulate more real estate activity as ownership of land and buildings changes.

## THE MEANING OF PRIVATIZATION

A host of legal and definitional questions regarding the meaning of privatization exist. To what extent is privatization shackled by the wish of those in power to retain their power? To what extent is it subverted by illegal diversion of assets? Who can participate in privatization and to what extent?

The word "privatization" assumes a process that reduces the level of state control of property. Under Communist ideology, social ownership of property was the preferred, preeminent form. Yet the lines between social and so-called private were blurred, and thus there is no one formula for privatization. In theory, property was held for the benefit of all, managed by the state or its component enterprises. Sometimes title was formally registered in the name of the state. Often, as in the case of many farm cooperatives, farmers were forced to contribute their property, including land, buildings, equipment, and livestock, but no formal transfer of ownership occurred. Private ownership existed in different forms in different countries, but always subject to severely restrictive state control. Housing, for instance, might have remained avowedly private, yet constrained by rigid controls on who might occupy it, what rents might be charged, and how it might be transferred.

Control of use of property was all-encompassing; the formality of transfer and registration of title was of less consequence. One outcome has been that, in many areas, cadasters and land records have not been maintained, which vastly complicates the task of re-creating boundaries. Whatever the form of future ownership, other than as indivisible state assets, public records showing property boundaries, ownership, and restrictions on alienation of title are an essential step toward privatization, subsequent sale or transfer, and development of an effectively functioning market.

Of course, market societies also have a spectrum of ownership and use rights, embedded in a set of traditions and beliefs as to which activities are better carried out by the public sector and which by the private sector. Privatization does not suggest that all public rights and controls will be relinquished. Attitudes toward ownership and use of property are formally expressed in the new constitutions and laws, now in place throughout Eastern and Central Europe. Newly enacted constitutions frequently list categories of resource lands that will remain public, such as parks and historic sites, and specify forms of public control of other valuable resources, such as agricultural lands. Public ownership might be retained for sites of future airports, autoroute corridors, and urban centers. By statute, rent controls may be continued and tenants' rights of occupancy may be assured. Land use plans may set forth the goals to be implemented by statute.

The process of privatization of assets and the institutionalization of private property, specifically of real estate, may take several forms. Each has profound impacts on the form that transition from communism takes and the extent to which the goals of this transition are met.

Restitution seeks to return property acquired by the state in the process of socialization to previous owners or their heirs. The aim is to rectify the abuses of the seizure, and also to assure widespread ownership of property in the new environment. Privatization also is achieved through lease, sale, or gift, effected through negotiation, tender, or auction.

## PROPERTY PRIVATIZATION THROUGH RESTITUTION

Restitution—the return of state-seized property to its prior owners—has proven the thorniest problem of privatization. The pattern of deprivation and abuse of property rights varies in pervasiveness and profundity from country to country. Everywhere, however, many people's rights, usually guaranteed by a national constitution, were violated. Other people were placed in possession of lands and houses that had been seized by the all-powerful state. Decades passed, and many or most of those wronged died. What course should a post-Communist government take to right old wrongs wrought by a different government? What is fair? Attitudes may be shaped by the context of seizures of large chunks of a nation by an occupying force, as the removal of 750 square miles of Estonian territory when it became a Soviet republic in 1940, or the cession of 69,000 square miles of prewar Poland to the Soviet Union as part of the post–World War II settlement.

A country may finesse the question of how it acquired property and move to privatize it without regard to claims of the dispossessed. Or the country, for reasons of morality, politics, or rule of law, may decide to honor claims for property taken without compensation and/or in violation of law. This decision to restitute property presents a host of subsidiary questions of immense complexity. These questions concern: law at the time of the taking and today, eligibility, proof of prior ownership, the nature of property to be restituted, and limits on amount or value of property to be restituted.

### Violation of Rights at the Time of Taking

In determining who should have the right to become an owner of property being privatized, a government may look at state property as falling into two categories: that acquired illegally and that acquired by the state under color of law. Here, too, there are gradations. Property may have been taken under sanction of a law that provided for compensation, and some compensation may have been paid. Whether it was fair compensation and, thus, whether the law was legal in its administration can affect whether the prior owner has a right to recover the property when it is privatized.

## How Long Ago Was the Taking
A cut-off date usually is set before which property seizures will not be considered. Will it be set so that the seizures are within living memory of a sizable share of the population? Is the Russian revolution of 1917 too long ago? How about land reforms of the 1920s or the 1940s? How about German seizures of Jewish properties in the early days of World War II? And Soviet occupation of Eastern Poland initially in 1939? A country's history and current complexion affect how it arrives at a cut-off date.

## Who Is Eligible to Claim
The choice of a cut-off date reflects a conscious choice as to who will be included in the category of eligible restitutees. So does specification as to whether people must have been citizens of the country at the time that the property was taken, whether they must be citizens of the country at present, whether they must reside in the country, and what degree of relationship they must have to the person who lost the property. Will the son of a Jew who fled Czechoslovakia before the arrival of Hitler's forces and who now lives in Israel be eligible to claim his father's former home? Will a German who lost his farm when it was incorporated into Poland as part of settlement of boundaries after World War II be entitled to claim compensation? If so, from whom? Why should Poland pay for a decision that it did not make? And what of corporations and institutions that lost property? Which of them will be eligible to claim and what are the grounds for distinguishing among them? Are Catholic institutions to be treated differently from Jewish ones? Orthodox from Muslim ones? With the enactment of new constitutions and the appointment of new constitutional courts, legislative decisions on these issues will be subject to review and may be upset.

## Proof of Claim
What must potential restitutees demonstrate to prove that they or their ancestors lost property and what that property was? The absence of or gaps in land records and cadasters complicates the matter of proof. Deeds or shares of stock may have been lost or destroyed. Boundaries of rural properties were obliterated when those properties were amalgamated into state farms or when the land was converted to urban development. To what extent will oral testimony from elderly people with a memory of who owned what suffice to establish a claim?

## Form of Property Restituted

What form will restitution take, and will the restitutee have a choice in the matter? The possibilities are to return the actual land and/or house that was taken, to return property of equivalent value, or to pay compensation in cash, shares, or vouchers. Even if the restitutee wants to recover the actual farm that belonged to the family, is this fair if another family has occupied the land and farmed it for forty years under a law that prevailed for all that time? What if the government seized a house, paid no compensation, and then sold it to another family? Should that family be dispossessed? What if a farm's productivity has declined due to bad land management? What if a former farm now is the site of high-rise apartments? If, in principle, the actual land taken is to be returned, but its former boundaries cannot be determined, how should land be allocated? If equivalent property is to be restituted or compensation is to be offered, how is the value of the property that was taken to be established?

## Amount of Property Restituted

Are there social, political, or economic reasons for limiting the amount of property that should be restituted to a single claimant? Should the family of a Polish aristocrat who owned vast estates receive all of the land taken, or only a stated maximum amount? Alternatively, should there be a minimum tract size for restitution to reduce the inefficiencies of splintered holdings?

# PRIVATIZATION THROUGH LEASE, SALE OR GIFT

If a country elects to restitute property, restitution would preferably precede other actions, so that its resolution does not impede other privatization by lease, sale, or gifts. One means of privatization, however the country acquired the property, is by gift or nominal sales to those who have occupied the property or worked on the premises. A tenant in a city apartment or a farm cottage may be offered title for a price only a fraction of the market value. Employees of a state shop may be allowed to take it over whether this is authorized by law or not. Workers on a cooperative farm who never actually lost their titles may be authorized to develop a plan under which they establish rights to various components of farm property—land, buildings, machinery, livestock—and then lease their rights back to the cooperative. Properties may be sold at auction, sometimes with current occupants or workers given preferential opportunities in the bidding. Often this has been the path chosen for small businesses.

Large enterprises are likely to be examined for their future viability before decisions are made as to the form of privatization. Whether the enterprise should be split into subsidiary businesses, whether it may offer an opportunity to attract foreign investment, and whether its current management and employees have an interest in becoming owners are among the factors that influence decisions.

The company may be liquidated or may be restructured and offered for sale by bid or at auction or through a public offering of shares. Only when a choice has been made and executed does the enterprise's property have the prospect of coming on the market.

A country may choose to establish a voucher program to foster individual private investment in the economy. Vouchers may be given away free or may be sold for modest sums. Some companies or shares in them may be offered for purchase by voucher, as may apartments. Some restitutees may receive vouchers as compensation for property that was taken.

## THE CHOICE NOT TO PRIVATIZE

In examining its stock of property, a country will determine that some properties should remain in public ownership. Military bases, parks, historic and archeological sites, and key natural resources are usual candidates for continued public ownership. Land may be held for future development, as for a right-of-way or a suburban center.

State or state enterprise housing may be given to the municipality in which it is located. Then the municipality may decide whether to privatize none, some, or all of the stock, a decision likely to be influenced by policy on continuing protection of the tenancy of disadvantaged residents. There also is likely to be a fiscal weighing: Is it preferable for a municipality to seek current cash through property sale or to look to future return on a well-located building?

## PRIVATIZATION AND THE MARKET

Markets existed under communism. As Prime Minister Václav Klaus of the Czech Republic has observed: "I agree with Friedman (1984) when he argues that in a socialist economy 'it is a very distorted market, but it is a market nonetheless.'"[1] Some private citizens retained some property rights; the extent to which this occurred varied from country to country. Their ability to transfer these rights, however, was severely constrained by such regulations as price controls, restrictions on size of property that could be sold, limits on the amount of property that any person might own, restrictions on who might buy, and requirements that property first be offered to government. These were the legal markets. In other markets, under-the-table deals more closely reflected a market in which a willing buyer and a willing seller agree on a price.

With privatization of substantial stocks of land and housing and repeal of all or most of the earlier restrictions on transactions, a real estate market as known in capitalist countries can be expected to develop. What impediments to such a market will slow and shape its development? The necessity of updating and modernizing cadasters and land records can be foreseen, but, until the actual state of these records is determined, the difficulties and cost cannot be determined. There is an obvious need to train appraisers to assist buyers and sellers in value determination. Probably less anticipated are delays in recording property transfers, because the structure for such a system has fallen into disuse. While not unexpected, unwillingness to share transaction information or to report actual transfer prices after decades of use of fictional prices affects market patterns. The wariness of some people to obtain title to restituted property, because of possible tax consequences, or because of ensuing liability for upkeep while the property remains subject to rent controls, may be another brake on the formation of the market.

Lack of credit is a serious impediment to the real estate market. As property ownership and property development rights become widespread, what systems will be put in place to enable builders and buyers to finance acquisition and development? With state farm and housing subsidies greatly reduced, how will farmers be able to buy machinery, livestock, and seed, and how will prospective homeowners buy apartments or houses?

Under communism, land use planning had little role in deciding on location of activities, nor did land prices reflect land scarcity. Central organs of state government allocated space, often based on preferences of the Communist Party leadership. Since there were no market prices and no property taxes, there was no incentive to use space efficiently. However, as local governments regain powers and also financial responsibilities, they can be expected to turn to property as a source of revenue. Entrepreneurs can be expected to recognize the relative desirability of one site over another and bid a price reflecting this. Would these market prices, reflecting location, become the basis for property taxation? Would planning be used to constrain market forces in an effort to conform land use to a definition of public good?

With privatization decisions not fully implemented, what differences in the structure of the property market can be discerned? Would the market be similar to property markets in capitalist systems?

## COUNTRIES STUDIED AND RESEARCH STRATEGIES

Keeping in mind the issues just outlined, what countries best afforded an opportunity to examine how these issues are being resolved? It seemed desirable to choose countries with disparate histories of property ownership and disparate experiences affecting people and property during World War II and the forty-five years of Communist control, since this history would be expected to influence strongly the decisions made about privatization of land and housing and the country's ability to implement them. We chose Bulgaria, Czechoslovakia, and Poland for the following reasons.

Over many centuries Bulgaria had looked principally to the East. Before World War II it was a poor, agricultural country. Farmers owned and farmed very small plots. When the Communists took over, they nationalized farms and forests as well as industries and businesses. Their dominant emphasis was on industrialization and urbanization. The economy was shaped to fit the embrace of the Russian bear. The Communists never nationalized housing, and, although much state housing was built, it usually was sold upon completion, although at heavily subsidized prices. Thus, as of 1989, most housing was privately owned, while industry and agriculture were state owned. As a result of the prior widespread ownership of farms, over half of the population were potential agricultural restitutees although many subsequently had moved to town. Because of the strong ties to the Soviet Union and the consequent paucity of Western contacts, in 1989 Bulgaria was not as well placed as Czechoslovakia, Hungary, and Poland to elicit Western aid and investment.

Czechoslovakia, as it was called when we started our research, had been an advanced, industrialized nation prior to World War II, especially in that portion that is now the Czech Republic. The capital, Prague, was not damaged by the war and remained a symbol of a gracious, cultivated past. Some rural lands had been held in large private and church estates, but more were small farms. The Communists took over farms and forests but left farm residences and secondary homes in private ownership. In cities, many single-family homes also remained private, but multifamily buildings were taken. Most new housing was retained in state ownership. Enterprises large and small were taken. Recognizing Prague's beauty as a tourist asset, the Communists made some investment in its upkeep. In 1989 Prague became a tourist mecca, where market pressures soon asserted themselves. More than elsewhere the debate between protection of long-term, poor residents and attraction of new, often foreign, investors presented itself.

Poland's people suffered terribly during World War II. The Germans and Soviets slaughtered millions of Christians and Jews, killing 90 percent of the largest Jewish population in Europe. Most of Warsaw was leveled. One-third of the country was awarded to the Soviet Union at the end of the war. The parallel award to Poland of land that had formerly been German did not fully replace this loss. Before the war, half of the farm and forest land had belonged to large estates, most of whose owners perished either at the hands of the Germans or the Soviets. Under the Communists, the land formerly in the large estates was distributed to small farmers or placed in state farms. A large part of the land taken from Germany became state farms, populated by people moved from the land given to the Soviet Union. Other farmers retained ownership of their farms. All property in Warsaw was nationalized, as were all enterprises employing fifty or more people and much property of the powerful Catholic church. Housing everywhere but in Warsaw remained private though subject to stringent regulation. Thus, in 1989, housing not built by the state or state-dominated cooperatives was private, larger enterprises were public, and the major share of farmland was private.

These three countries thus present examples of major socialization of land, housing, and enterprises in Czechoslovakia, nominally little socialization of land and housing in Poland, and an intermediate position, with socialization of land and enterprises but not of housing, in Bulgaria.

A recent survey in Central and Eastern Europe showed that, among seven countries included in the survey, Bulgaria had the largest percentage of people who would prefer a return to communism—twenty nine percent. On the other hand, in Poland and in the Czech Republic this percentage was the lowest—eight and ten percent, respectively.[2]

This book has been researched and written while many of the events described have been unfolding. In each country, we are able to recount many decisions that have been taken and some of their outcomes. Other outcomes, particularly the conclusion of the privatization process and the full development of markets, are likely to occur in the near future. However, if chaos has subsided, there is still much volatility in attitudes toward privatization, and program directions still could shift.

We have chosen to focus on the years from 1989 to mid-1995, a period when each of the three countries faced a new world of choices and opportunities. For us and others to understand the choices that were made in these past few years, we found it essential to document changes in property ownership laws and practices from the early land reforms on through the forty-five or so years of communism. Because property ownership and control are but one of the components of a country's economic and social fabric, we have set the discussion about public ownership and control and subsequent increased private ownership and control in the context of this broader fabric. It is our belief, examined closely in the conclusion, that privatization of land and housing has proven a central element in the transformation of former Communist societies to market-oriented economies.

Maps 1.1 through 1.4 show the gains and losses of territory by the nations of East and Central Europe, with particular emphasis on Bulgaria, the Czech Republic, and Poland, from 1910 to 1930, 1948, and 1996.

**Map 1.1    East Central Europe, 1910**

**Map 1.2    East Central Europe, 1930**

**Map 1.3 East Central Europe, 1948**

**Map 1.4    East Central Europe, 1996**

# 2

# BULGARIA: PROPERTY RESTITUTION, PRIVATIZATION, AND MARKET FORMATION

Bulgaria is a small, scenic country at the crossroads of Europe and Asia, of Christianity and Islam. For centuries it has been on trade routes between Greece and Turkey and Central and Northern Europe, and between Central Asia and Greece.

After gaining independence from the Turks in 1878, and until the Communist takeover after World War II, Bulgaria developed as a nation of small farms and scattered villages and towns. Unlike Czechoslovakia and Poland, as well as other countries of Central and Eastern Europe, there was neither a landed aristocracy nor a church holding vast estates.

Bulgaria is slightly smaller than the state of Pennsylvania, similarly endowed with mountains, fertile plains, and a temperate climate, but with a population of 8.5 million rather than Pennsylvania's 12 million. With two-thirds of the people living in urban areas, Bulgaria is second to the Czech Republic in level of urbanization in Eastern Europe.

Under communism, land effectively became all people's land. Farms and forests were taken by the state without compensation under the 1947 forest nationalization, the 1948 land reform, the 1950s forced joinder of the cooperatives, and the formation of collectives starting in the late 1950s. At these times enterprises became the property of the state. However, unlike the practice in most other Communist countries, almost all housing, whether single-family rural dwellings or urban apartments, remained in private ownership, subject, however, to strict limitations on sale and ownership.

This history has made housing markets easier to establish in recent years than land markets. Creation of a market for rural land is mired in difficult boundary questions, restitution challenges, and efforts to revise the rural restitution law. The immediate outcome of farm restitution will be the re-creation of a pattern of small and inefficient parcels. Urban property restitution involved relatively few claims and is largely complete.

Small privatization was plagued with problems of corruption and illegality. However, it is essentially complete. Large-enterprise privatization has moved very slowly, mainly due to political ambivalence or antagonism, but also to lack of capital and a shortage of prospective bidders for the enterprises.

World events, including the blockade of shipments to Yugoslavia, the dismemberment of the Soviet Union, the recession in Europe and North America, and the strengthening of tariff barriers by many countries, also have worked to impede Bulgaria's economic recovery and to obscure the directions that future ties will take.

This chapter opens with an introduction to conditions in Bulgaria under communism and today, with emphasis on the industrial, agricultural, and housing sectors of the economy. Next, the rights of people to claim property in restitution for prior takings and the status of the restitution process for urban property and rural land are described. Ownership transformation through privatization, and the formation of property markets are discussed in the following sections. Ancillary but critical issues in the operation of a property market are addressed next: namely, insufficient availability of credit, the necessary components for reinstitution of a property tax, and the influence of land use planning. Last are the author's conclusions about the status of and portents for property market formation.

## BULGARIA UNDER COMMUNISM; BULGARIA TODAY

Before describing the processes of restitution and privatization of urban and rural land and enterprises, the setting—political, economic, and cultural—in which this is occurring will be outlined. Since free elections were introduced in 1990, the Socialists, the party of the former Communists, have maintained control, either as the majority party or in a coalition, for all but one year. They state a commitment to privatization but have been reluctant to implement that commitment. A weak economy, suffering from poor management and inefficient use of labor, has been further hobbled by nearby wars, the Yugoembargo, and the weakening of links with former trading partners, principally the former Soviet Union.

Because housing ownership was essentially private throughout the Communist years, the housing sector then and now is discussed here rather than in the following sections which focus on restitution and privatization.

### Geography and Settlement History

The Bulgars migrated from the north of the Caucasus to what is now Bulgaria in the seventh century, after it was settled, successively, by the Thracians, Greeks, Macedonians, Romans, and Slavs. The First Bulgarian Kingdom lasted from the seventh to the eleventh century, and at its height under King Simeon the country stretched from the Black to the Adriatic seas and included what is now Serbia, Albania, and southern Macedonia.[1] The Slavs and Bulgars—kin to the Huns—made common cause against Byzantium in a series of wars that culminated in Byzantium's victory in the eleventh century. Yet another war led to

Bulgarian victory and the establishment of the Second Bulgarian Kingdom, which lasted from 1185 to 1396. This period of independence was succeeded by almost 500 years of Ottoman rule.

The area of modern Bulgaria is about 43,000 square miles (110,994 square kilometers). It is bounded on the north by the Danube River, which constitutes most of the border with Romania; on the east by the Black Sea; on the south by Greece and Turkey; and on the west by Macedonia and Serbia. Major trade routes, historic and modern, function coastwise along the Black Sea, inland up the Danube—the Danube-Main-Rhine system, overland between Vienna, Belgrade, Sofia, and Istanbul, and overland between Central Asia and Greece.

**Map 2.1    Principal Cities of Bulgaria**

Much of Bulgaria is mountainous, with a major range, the Stara Planina or Balkan Mountains, that runs east-west bisecting the country. North of this range lies the fertile Danube tableland. The Rhodope Mountains are in the southwest and the Maritsa River Basin in the southeast. Only 43 percent of the land of Bulgaria is suitable for crops or pasture. An additional 31 percent, mostly mountains, is forested with a mix of deciduous and coniferous trees, while 26 percent of the land is unproductive. The Black Sea coast is a vacation area for Bulgarians, Europeans, and Russians; it also is the location of Bulgaria's principal port, Varna.

The cities of Bulgaria retain traces of many earlier settlers. Sofia, the capital, is located in the west-central part of the country. It lies in a broad valley surrounded by mountains, including Mount Vitosha, which rises to 7,600 feet (2,290 meters) at the city's edge. Sofia has served as a center of trade and as a provincial capital for a succession of foreign rulers. It is built atop a Thracian settlement and a later Roman city, Serdica.[2] The city's name subsequently was changed to Sofia in honor of St. Sophia. Plovdiv, the second city, is located along the Maritsa River on the Plain of Thrace. It was the capital of the Roman province of Thrace.

## Government

Modern, independent Bulgaria has existed since 1878, first as a monarchy until 1945, then as a Communist state until 1990, and now as a democracy in which the Socialists hold power.

Bulgaria achieved independence as one outcome of the Russo-Turkish War of 1877. This war is known to the Bulgarians as the War of Liberation, since it freed them from the Turkish domination that had lasted from the fourteenth century. Under the preliminary Peace Treaty of March 1878, between Russia and Turkey, and the Peace Treaty of July 1878, approved by the Great Powers—Great Britain, France, Germany, Austria-Hungary, and Italy—two republics were formed, Bulgaria, with Sofia as its capital, and East Rumelia, with Plovdiv as its capital. At this time Sofia had a population of 18,000, including 5,000 Jews in a center city ghetto, Armenians in another center-city ghetto, and 1,000 Gypsies.

The Republic of Bulgaria adopted a constitution, the Trnovo Constitution, in 1879. Among other rights it assured individuals the right to own private property—but not necessarily to keep what they had. At this time there occurred the first of three land reforms, which broke up the Turks' large estates and redistributed land to the Bulgarian peasants. "[A]s a result of the Russo-Turkish wars, not only Turkish landowners but also the majority of Turkish peasants fled the country, the Bulgarian peasants were freed from the vestiges of feudal conditions and could easily acquire new plots of land. Furthermore, in the areas where the Turkish landowners did not leave their estates, the new Bulgarian state compelled them to hand their landed properties over to the Bulgarian peasants. Thus . . . in Bulgaria agrarian capitalist development rested on a base of small holdings. By 1897, 87% of farms were under 25 acres (10 hectares); these farms accounted for 49% of all farm land, with 44.5% in farms from 25 to 250 acres (10 to 100 hectares), and only 6.5% in farms over 250 acres (100 hectares)."[3]

This redistribution was not the windfall that it may seem. The Bulgarian peasants were required to pay compensation for the land taken from the Turks. They had no equipment except wooden plows, they had no way to make their farms more productive, and many ended up losing their plots to moneylenders. In fact, ". . . the peasants were victims of medieval usury that extorted payment of as much as 200 percent interest a year. According to an appraisal referring to 1200 villages of Bulgaria at the beginning of the present century, 300 were in debt for the whole, 400 for half, of the expected value of the crop. . . . Furthermore, the peasants were heavily burdened by steadily increasing taxation . . . they were compelled to pay 15 to 20 per cent of their earning as taxes."[4]

Even if a peasant managed to hold on to his land, it was probable that the small holding became even smaller on his death, since the inheritance laws provided for division among all of the heirs.

The Trnovo Constitution provided that the country should be governed by a prince acceptable to all of the Great Powers. Prince Alexander of Battenberg, a nephew of Czar Alexander II, was chosen in 1879. The Russians sent him engineers to assist in the design of town plans and the creation of cadasters for Bulgaria. "The first specialists to stay in the country and assist in the reconstruction of the towns destroyed at the end of the War of Liberation were Russian army engineers and technicians. They drew up the cadastral surveys and regulation plans. . . . In 1878-79, . . . engineer Amadier also designed a new plan for the capital, called the Battenberg Plan, drawn up in American fashion, a term then used for straight streets crossing each other at right angles, then thought very progressive. . . . Amadier retained the course of the moat around the town and of the radial streets, thus coordinating the rectangular and radial-circular street systems."[5]

During his reign, King Alexander gradually ceased acting as a Russian satrap and allied himself with Bulgarian interests. He exerted leadership in unifying the two republics in 1885, contrary to Russia's wishes, and named Sofia as the capital. The Russians responded by abducting him and then forcing him to abdicate. The Bulgarians then sought another prince acceptable to Russia and to Europe and, in 1887, settled on a Hapsburg, Prince Ferdinand, to occupy the throne.

King Ferdinand allied the nation with Germany during World War I, despite widespread Bulgarian sentiment for neutrality. After the Armistice was signed in 1918, Ferdinand was forced to abdicate and his son, Boris III, became king. As a result of its alliance, Bulgaria had lost substantial territory and its economy had suffered.

Bulgaria's second land reform occurred in 1921, after the Agrarians were elected and formed a majority government. Once again rural land was expropriated for redistribution. Some of the terms of this law would be paralleled decades later by the Communists' 1948 land reform.[6] Six percent of all farmland, or 329,000 acres (133,000 hectares), was taken, consisting of crown and church lands; holdings in excess of 75 acres (30 hectares), or 125 acres (50 hectares) in mountainous areas for peasant owners; holdings in excess of 25 acres (10 hectares) for married urban absentee owners; and holdings in excess of 10 acres (4 hectares) for single urban absentee owners with compensation paid and the land given to 173,000 landless peasants. By 1934 only 561 farms, or 0.1 percent of all farms, totalling 170,000 acres (69,000 hectares) existed that were over 125 acres (50 hectares).[7]

During World War II, the Bulgarians fought alongside the Germans in Greece and Yugoslavia. Allied forces bombed Bulgarian cities in 1943 and 1944, with the Americans inflicting heavy damage on Sofia. Then, in 1944, after the Soviet occupation, Bulgaria switched sides and ended the war fighting on the side of the Soviets. King Boris III had died in 1943, and his son, Simeon, the current pretender to the throne, fled the country in 1946.

Bulgaria's boundaries since independence have been altered as victors in each of several wars redrew the map of Europe. Access to the Aegean, with two small ports, was gained in 1913 and lost in 1920; southern Dobruja, a strip along the eastern Danube, was lost in 1920 and regained in 1940, a gift from the Axis Powers in return for Bulgaria's commitment to their side. Another lure offered by the Germans was possession of Macedonia, home to many Bulgarians. This offer never became a reality.

In 1939 there were 50,000 Jews in Bulgaria; 47,000, a higher proportion than in any other European country, survived World War II. King Boris is widely credited for his adamant stand against German removal of the Jews. Most had been active in the antifascist resistance, and many were members of the Communist Party. Between 1948 and 1957, 40,000 emigrated to Israel.[8]

After World War II, Bulgaria remained in the Soviet sphere of influence. In 1945 it elected a single-slate Fatherland Front ticket of Communists, becoming a People's Republic. In 1946 the monarchy was discarded. The Communists adopted a constitution (the Dimitrov Constitution) in 1947, creating a one-party—the Bulgarian Communist Party—state. The primary objectives of the Communists were the industrialization of the country and the creation of a system of large cooperative and state farms.

In 1971 the constitution of "mature socialism" was adopted, placing legislative power in the forty member State Council, headed by the secretary general of the Communist Party. The National Assembly continued to exist, but as a rubber stamp.[9]

The first break with forty-four years of communism was the ousting from power of Todor Zhikov, then secretary general of the Communist Party, in November of 1989. He had ruled Bulgaria for thirty-three years. In January 1990 the Communist Party's monopoly role in government was terminated, and, in June 1990, free elections were held. Zhelyu Zhelev, a founder of the Union of Democratic Forces (UDF), a coalition of sixteen small parties, was elected president. However, the Communist Party, renamed the Bulgarian Socialist Party (BSP), won a majority in Parliament.

During this first period of BSP control, a new constitution, Bulgaria's fourth, was adopted.[10] The constitution specifies how power is to be divided between the legislature, the 240-member unicameral Parliament or National Assembly; the executive, including the Council of Ministers and the prime minister, who are chosen by the National Assembly following nomination by the president of the prime minister-designate; and the judiciary, with its Constitutional Court whose twelve members are named one-third each by the president, the Parliament, and the judges of two other courts, the Supreme Court of Cassation and the Supreme Administrative Court. The president is elected to a five-year term and may be reelected to one additional term. President Zhelev initially was elected by the National Assembly in 1990, before the constitution became effective, and then was elected to a five-year term in 1992. He has announced his intention to run again in 1997. Ex-King Simeon II may run, asserting that his forced exile exempts him from the law that candidates must have lived in Bulgaria for the five years prior to the election.

The constitution also provides for the territorial division of the country. There are nine oblasts, or regions, with Greater Sofia constituting one oblast. The oblasts are governed by regional governors chosen by the Council of Ministers, although decentralizing government so that there would be elections within the oblasts has been discussed. Establishment of districts is authorized; they existed formerly but do not today. Local governments no longer are units of the state. They may own property and raise revenue. There are 5,613 units of local government, including 238 cities and towns, 4,444 villages, 278 obshtinas (the smallest unit of local government), and 653 others. Local governments elect municipal councils for four-year terms, and the councils elect the mayor. There were local elections in the fall of 1995. UDF candidates won in Sofia, Plovdiv, Varna, and Stara Zagora, while the BSP candidates won in the smaller cities and in most towns.

The elected BSP government fell in the fall of 1990 and was replaced by a coalition, still BSP-dominated, in December 1990. In the general election of June 1991, the UDF won. In October 1991, under the leadership of President Zhelev, the UDF formed a government.[11]

Privatization was an issue high on the agendas of both parties. The BSP had drafted its version of a privatization bill; when the UDF came to power, it did likewise. The two proposals varied significantly. A comment on the UDF proposal follows:

> The controversy reflected two completely different approaches to the privatization process. The government proposed to proceed on the basis

of an amendment to the existing law of July 1991 on Incorporating Sole-Ownership Companies with Limited Liability which would have empowered the ministries, on behalf of the government, to initiate, conduct, and supervise the whole privatization process. This proposal was unacceptable both to a part of the UDF parliamentary faction and to the BSP, which criticized the government bill as a palliative measure that would delegate enormous discretionary powers to state-owned enterprises and the Ministry of Industry and Trade. . . . In the spring of 1992, amid mounting political tension, the government, with some prodding from the World Bank, revised its proposed draft of the privatization law to take account of the criticisms of its earlier proposals. The new bill provided for a greater role of the Privatization Agency, although it still made it subordinate to the Council of Ministers. . . . The bill was finally passed . . . on April 23, 1992.[12]

In the fall of 1992, the UDF government fell. A coalition of the BSP and the Turkish Movement for Rights and Freedoms (MRF) took over with a narrow parliamentary majority. That government's priorities were trade reform and privatization.

The prime minister, Luben Berov, resigned in September 1994, and a parliamentary election was held in December 1994. The BSP again proved the strongest party, leading the Parliamentary Left bloc to a majority of 125 out of 240 seats. With its promise to improve the economy, it attracted the votes of the retired and the young unemployed. The party leader and current prime minister, Zhan Videnov, is a young, Moscow-educated economist who leads the social democratic wing of the BSP. He has stated that ". . . Bulgaria's transition to a democratic civil society and a market economy is irreversible."[13] In June 1995 Videnov presented his government's four-year plan. Its objectives are to develop an efficient market economy that is more competitive, to increase employment and incomes, to stabilize the institutions of government, to achieve European standards of social security, and to qualify for European Union membership.[14] Observers praise this statement of intent but note that prior governments have not kept their promises about privatization and economic reform. "The most significant question about the new government . . . is in regard to its intentions to accelerate economic reform. Robust and prolonged economic recovery will depend on determined further steps in restructuring and privatization . . . the perception of the most recent period is that the situation which characterized Bulgaria in 1993-94 favored only criminals and profiteers. The new government . . . is not drawn from the traditional element of the BSP which strives to oppose change as an assault on the well-being of its constituency."[15]

The end of communism has been marked more by a stated conversion to market principles and an acceptance of open elections by the members of the renamed Communist Party than by a total overthrow of the long-term power holders. Today there are frequent allegations that the BSP does not really embrace privatization unless it is "quiet" privatization by which those in power gain enterprise assets. Allusions to cherry-picking via quiet privatization by BSP members are common. They are thought to have access to information and funds and to have the ability to maneuver transactions to their benefit.

President Zhelev is an outspoken critic of the BSP's governance, alleging that it has delayed restitution and halted privatization.[16] His views are shared by the Agrarian Party and the Democratic Party, which, as the coalition Popular Union, holds seventeen seats in Parliament. Anastasia Moser, secretary of the Agrarian Party, alleged during her keynote speech to the 1995 Party Congress that the BSP is enacting laws that undermine democratic reforms and deny citizens rights guaranteed by the constitution.[17]

President Zhelev is a strong advocate of membership in the North Atlantic Treaty Organization (NATO) for Bulgaria, while Prime Minister Vidanov has said that Bulgaria is in no hurry to apply. The underlying and crucial question is to what extent Bulgaria should cultivate past links, political and economic, with Russia and to what extent it should reorient itself toward Europe and the West.[18]

## Population

The total population of Bulgaria, according to the 1992 census, was 8.5 million, down from 9 million in 1990. In addition, some 200,000 Bulgarians live permanently in Romania. Eighty-six percent of the population is ethnically Bulgarian; 9.7 percent are Turks, 3.4 percent are Gypsies, and 1.1 percent are others. In 1984 Turks were required to assume Bulgarian names and in 1987 about 1,000 mosques were ordered closed. Thereafter 340,000 Turks departed for Turkey. Today, linguistic and religious freedom is guaranteed, and a substantial number of Turks have returned, mostly to work in agriculture in the southeastern and northeastern parts of the country.[19] After the fall of communism, when travel became easier, many Bulgarians left the country to work abroad.

The population growth rate per annum from 1981 to 1990 was 0.1 percent; it became negative in the 1990s. The population is aging: Between 1989 and 1992, those over age sixty increased by 3.3 percent to a total of 21.1 percent, or 1.8 million people.[20] The population density in 1990 was 209 per square mile (81 per square kilometer).

Bulgaria has urbanized rapidly, with the urban population rising from 25 percent after World War II to 68 percent in 1990, followed by a slight decline to 67 percent in 1992. Bulgaria has the second highest level of urbanization in Eastern Europe, lower only than that of the Czech Republic. As of 1992, 1.2 million people, or 14 percent of Bulgaria's population, lived in greater Sofia. The next largest cities are Plovdiv, with 341,000 people, and Varna, with 308,000.

## THE ECONOMY

Prior to the Communist accession, Bulgaria was a poor, agricultural country. In 1939, 15 percent of output was attributable to industry, while 65 percent came from agriculture and the remainder from services. In 1944, over 1 million farmers were cultivating 12 million plots, with the average plot size one acre (0.4 hectares). Almost all plowing was done by man or beast. Now Bulgaria is a poor, industrialized country in which industry and services account for 92.3 percent of output and agriculture for only 7.7 percent.

In recent years the Bulgarian economy, in the industrial, agricultural, and housing sectors, has been in deep distress, due to a combination of circumstances. The principal external causes include the breakup of the Soviet Union and the shortage of funds in the new republics for imports, the United Nations–imposed Yugoembargo, and the tariff walls of the West. Internally, the economy has been affected by the heavy debt and inefficient production of state farms and factories, the lack of credit, and the large-scale quiet or illegal privatization.

Public confidence has been at a low ebb; according to a poll in August 1993, 12.3 percent of the respondents believed that Bulgarians' lifestyle would improve, 10.7 percent felt it would not change, 62.4 percent felt it would deteriorate, and 14.6 percent didn't know. [21]

The dire problems with the economy have a crippling effect on privatization, as the following discussion of the industrial, agricultural, and housing sectors demonstrates.

The struggle to move from a planned to a market economy has brought widespread hardship and anxiety. In 1993 almost 75 percent of the people were living at or below the subsistence level. Most indicators moved in a negative direction from 1989 to 1994. The rate of change in the gross domestic product (GDP) edged into the positive column in 1994, but inflation had picked up again. The private sector share of production has been rising. However, 12 percent unemployment in 1995 combined with the mandatory retirement at age fifty for women and fifty-five for men and the inability of the government to pay cost-of-living increases to pensioners, or anyone else, are far from reassuring portents.

Gross national product (GNP) grew rapidly in the early Communist period and then slowed. The average annual increase in GNP was 5.8 percent in the 1960s, 2.8 percent in the 1970s, and a mere 0.8 percent from 1981 through 1985.[22]

### The Economy Post-1989

Growth became negative starting in 1990. Gross domestic product dropped from 1989 through 1993: 9.1 percent between 1989 and 1990, 11.7 percent between 1990 and 1991, 6.3 percent from 1991 to 1992, and 2.4 percent from 1992 to 1993. GDP was $7.6 billion (183 billion lev), or $850 per capita, in

1992.[23] All sectors declined between 1989 and 1992, with industry down 40 percent, services down 20 percent, and agriculture and forestry down 7 percent from a not very robust base in 1989. From 1992 to 1993 industrial output dropped 8 percent and agricultural output dropped 15 percent. The good news is that GDP showed a 1.4 percent increase from 1993 to 1994, while an increase of 4 percent was estimated for 1994-95.[24] Between 1993 and 1994, industrial output rose 4 percent, while agriculture rose 5 percent, reflecting some recovery from the 1993 drought.[25] Finally in 1995 industrial production rose 7 percent over 1994. Pensions for the retired 29 percent of the population are a heavy drawdown on the government; in 1992, they consumed 21.5 percent of GDP.[26]

The private sector share, which had accounted for only around 5 percent of GDP in the 1970s and 1980s, rose to 22 percent in 1993, and 40 percent in 1994.[27] It is predicted to reach 60 percent by 1998. In 1993 in industry and services, the private sector contributed 9 percent, in agriculture and forestry 4 percent, and in retail trade 52 percent. The share of the private sector in employment reached 22.2 percent in 1993. There is also the second, or gray, economy, not included in official calculations. One source estimates this as running from 15 percent to 20 percent of real GDP, making the overall picture more encouraging both as to actual employment and production.[28]

In 1989, 38 percent of the labor force was in industry, 19 percent in agriculture and forestry, and 43 percent in other sectors.[29] By the first half of 1993, industry's share of the labor force had increased slightly, to 39.2 percent, while the principal shift was from agriculture and forestry, down to 10.9 percent, to other sectors, which rose to 49.9 percent.[30]

Inflation was 64 percent in 1993, down from 334 percent in 1991 and 100 percent in 1992. The introduction of the flat rate 18 percent value-added tax (VAT) in spring 1994, replacing the sales tax, as well as expansion of the money supply, led to a new jump in inflation, back to 122 percent for 1994. The rate for 1995 as of November was 40 percent.[31]

The prime interest rate, set by the Bulgarian National Bank, was 52 percent in November 1993; it was raised to 94 percent in late 1994, but was lowered several times in 1995, down to 34 percent in August. While this bank policy may stimulate exports, it also raises the threat of new inflation.

State banks are being consolidated and are planned to be privatized. United Bulgarian Bank began operation in 1993, as a consolidation of twenty-two small banks, some of which were former branches of the Bulgarian National Bank. Many small, private banks have been created. As of mid-1993, there were twenty-nine banks with a majority state interest, fourteen banks with a majority private interest, one cooperative bank, four agricultural banks, and the State Savings Bank.[32] People rail at the banks for their unwillingness to grant credit. Yet the banks, both public and private, hold large portfolios of uncollectible debts. Nine banks hold a total of $2.7 billion (71.6 billion lev) in bad debts, constituting 90 percent of such debts. Some banks are expected to stabilize, some to need extra assistance, and at least one is expected to fail.

Several commodity exchanges function in Bulgaria. The Sofia exchange opened in 1991, fifty years after it had been closed. There are fourteen stock exchanges, including the First Bulgarian Stock Exchange, the Sofia Stock Exchange, and the East-Centre-West Stock Exchange. In 1995 the government proposed a law to regulate securities and investments. It also is exploring creation of a national stock exchange.

At the close of 1993, unemployment was 16.3 percent, the highest since 1990. In 1994 it declined to 14.1 percent and was projected at 11.5 percent for 1995. Unemployment is less severe in Sofia and highest in the north and northwest of the country. The largest drop in share of the labor force has been in agriculture and forestry, due largely to the liquidation of collective farms.[33] Only about 40 percent of the unemployed are eligible for benefits. With retirement at age fifty for women and at age fifty-five for men to an inadequate pension, there are many who are out of work but not listed in the unemployment figures. "Demographic characteristics predestine the unfavorable prerequisites for the solution of economic problems in the future. The comparison of the basic population characteristics puts Bulgaria in one of the last places in Europe in this respect. It will not take long before one employed in Bulgaria will be responsible for more than one retired."[34]

The rate of rise in consumer prices has slowed, but only in 1992 was there any growth in real wages, and even then it was not enough to match the increase in consumer prices. In 1991 consumer prices rose 334 percent while real wages declined by 39 percent; in 1992, consumer prices rose 85 percent while real wages rose only 19 percent. In 1993, consumer prices rose 73 percent, while real wages declined by 9.8 percent.

As of June 30, 1993, 74.4 percent of the population was living at or below the subsistence level, compared to 38 percent at the close of 1990. The subsistence level is calculated on a market basket of goods and services and keyed to the consumer price index. The average subsistence level per person was set at $59 per month (1,456 lev), but only $50 per month (1,230 lev) for pensioners. Pensioners are particularly hard hit; there are 2.5 million of them, or 29 percent of the population, and the 1993 pension for them was $39 per month (1,037 lev), or only 78 percent of the subsistence level[35] for them and only 34 percent of the average wage.[36] The average monthly wage in the second quarter of 1993 was $112 (2,966 lev), while the minimum to meet the subsistence level for a family of four was between $189 and $227 per month (5,000 to 6,000 lev). There is a cost-of-living adjustment system (COLA), under which wages, unemployment benefits, and pensions rise to within 90 percent of the rate of inflation in the prior quarter. However, the government budget cannot accommodate these demands. Money for approved COLA of wages in state-subsidized enterprises for early 1993 had not been paid as of late 1993.

Buying food took 40.9 percent of a household's budget in 1993, leading people to buy cheaper foods. "Over the last year or two, the consumption of meat has dropped by 39.3 per cent, of fish and fish products by 73.5 per cent, of milk and milk products by over 30 per cent, and of fresh and dried fruit by 40.6 per cent. At the same time, consumption of bread has risen by 5.3 per cent, of dried beans by 3.2 per cent, of lard by 88.9 per cent."[37]

How many hours of work does it take to buy necessities? As of May 1993, it required 44 minutes to pay for 2.1 pints (1 liter) of milk, 57 minutes for 2.2 pounds (1 kilo) of potatoes, 5.01 hours for 2.2 pounds (1 kilo) of pork tenderloin, 64.90 hours for a pair of men's shoes, and 95.4 hours for a woman's dress. Bulgarian prices are higher compared with those in the Czech Republic, Poland, and Hungary. (See Table 2.1, in which Hungarian prices are held at 100.)[38]

### TABLE 2.1: COMPARATIVE COST OF GOODS

| Goods | Bulgaria | Czech Republic | Poland | Hungary |
|---|---|---|---|---|
| Milk | 314 | 129 | 121 | 100 |
| Potatoes | 633 | 133 | 100 | 100 |
| Pork | 215 | 100 | 106 | 100 |
| Woman's Dress | 211 | 81 | 64 | 100 |
| Man's Shoes | 296 | 123 | 76 | 100 |

In the energy sector, Bulgaria has few natural resources. Formerly it relied on oil and gas from the Soviet Union and now is negotiating new agreements with Russia. In 1994 the aging nuclear power plant at Kozlodui on the Danube, with six reactors, was responsible for generating 40 percent of Bulgaria's electricity, making Bulgaria third in the world in proportion of power from nuclear generation. The reactors posed safety problems, but now, with aid from Western Europe and the United States for repairs, they have reopened. Four units, however, will be decommissioned late in this decade. Westinghouse has proposed to upgrade the two newest reactors, with 85 percent of the $250 million cost to come from the Export-Import Bank. Burning brown and bituminous coal generates much power and a substantial share of the severe urban air pollution. Sofia and the nearby industrial city of Pernik suffer from frequent inversions and are the most polluted cities of Bulgaria with respect to air quality.

There is some good news on the energy front: Texaco, a licensee drilling in the Black Sea off the coast near Varna, has found a deposit of gas of unknown size. Union Pacific and British Gas are drilling for oil and gas in the same area, and several other offshore tracts will be leased.

**Foreign Trade**

The foreign trade deficit in 1993 was $1.3 billion; in 1994, it dropped to $151 million.[39]

Foreign investment in Bulgaria has been insignificant, amounting to only $800 million since 1989. In 1992 it totaled $310 million (8.2 billion lev), less than that received by Romania ($504 million), Ukraine ($670 million), or Slovenia ($830 million).[40] It declined to $105 million in 1994.[41]

Foreign debt was $9.2 billion in 1989; by the close of 1993 it had reached $13.1 billion; but, by mid-1995, it had been reduced to $10.2 billion. Much of this debt has been incurred as a result of embargoes; Bulgaria lost $2.5 billion as a result of sanctions against Iraq and Libya and, as of mid-1995, had lost $8.5 billion as a result of the Yugoembargo. This latter loss is in large measure because 60 percent of Bulgaria's exports to Western Europe, mainly fruits and vegetables, formerly were trucked via the ex-Yugoslavia.

Bulgaria successfully negotiated an agreement with the London Club of bank creditors in June 1994, reducing its $8.1 billion debt to 300 banks by 47.1 percent. However, economists were skeptical about the country's ability to handle the terms of repayment.

Government reluctance to sell enterprises to foreigners has been another obstacle to debt reduction: "the Bulgarians have failed miserably in generating some revenue from the sale of state-owned companies to foreigners . . . there are enough Bulgarian businesses (or portions thereof) which could be sold for several hundred million dollars, including Bulgar-tabac . . . , the local telecom company, some electric power stations, electric power and gas distribution networks, etc. If the Bulgarian government shows willingness to opt for this route of financing of some of the up-front payment due to Western banks, it is virtually certain that a consortium of banks could be formed which would provide a bridge loan against the proceeds from (near-term) future privatization."[42]

Bulgaria's debt to Poland was to be paid off in 1995 in electric trucks and wine. The debt to Switzerland was written off in 1995 in return for Bulgaria's commitment to invest in ecologically beneficial projects.

During the Communist period, the Soviet Union was Bulgaria's number-one trading partner, and 95 percent of Bulgaria's trade was with Comecon countries. After the dissolution of the Soviet Union and the collapse of communism in Eastern and Central Europe, Bulgaria's trade plummeted. Now it is being reestablished with several of its former trading partners, particularly Russia. Trade also is growing with the countries of the European Union, up from 10 percent of foreign trade in 1990 to 40 percent in 1995.

One of the few areas of trade to experience growth is tourism, with visitors coming to enjoy the Black Sea coast and the mountain resorts. The number of overnight stays rose from over 4 million in 1989, to 6 million in 1992, and topped

8 million in 1993. Such visits were projected to be only 7 million in 1995, as tourists from Western Europe were edgy about Bulgaria's proximity to the Croatian/Bosnian/Serbian conflict. However, Russians are coming in increasing numbers and were expected to account for 30 percent of tourists in 1995.

In 1995 oil imports were expected to reach 5 million tons. In June 1995 Bulgaria and Russia reached agreement on construction of a pipeline to carry crude oil from Russia, Kazakhstan, and Azerbaijan, shipped by tanker to the Bulgarian port of Burgas, from Burgas to ex-Yugoslavian Macedonia and Albania and thence to Brindisi, Italy.[43] Under another agreement, among Bulgaria, Russia, and Greece, a pipeline would be constructed from Burgas to Alexandroupolis in Greece. Yet another Bulgarian-Russian agreement will make Bulgaria the regional distribution center for Russian gas.

A July 1995 agreement provides for resumption of timber production by Bulgarians in the Russian Republic of Komi and for plants in Komi for bottling Bulgarian mineral water, beer, and wine.[44]

In June 1995 Bulgaria, the Czech Republic, and Slovakia agreed to establish a free trade zone. Effective January 1, 1996, 60 percent of industrial goods traded among the three countries are duty free. All such goods will be duty free within two years. Discussions are under way concerning agricultural goods, as are similar free trade discussions with Hungary and Romania.

Bulgaria has enjoyed most-favored nation status with the United States since 1991 and became a member of the International Monetary Fund (IMF) and the World Bank in 1990. IMF has lent $1.054 billion, of which Bulgaria was expected to repay $290 million in 1995. The bank had approved $620 million in projects as of July 1995 but had disbursed only from 5 to 6 percent of this. The bank has criticized Bulgaria's slow transition to a market economy, little headway on privatization, and insufficient solvency of state banks.[45] In response, the minister of industry announced his intention to close some state enterprises that have incurrred heavy losses.[46] In 1995 IMF and the bank agreed to a loan of $93 million for a pumped storage power station; a condition of the loan was an increase in the price of electricity. The government announced an increase in August 1995—a rise of 25 percent for residential users and 38 percent for industry, which is not as much as the bank sought. The bank also is providing a $95 million loan as part of a $170 million loan package to improve the rail system.

Bulgaria entered into an association agreement with the European Union (EU) in February 1995. In December 1995 the government, bolstered by a 221-1 vote of the National Assembly, applied for full membership. How eager current EU members are for expansion of membership to Central and Eastern Europe is open to question. A major concern for current members is protection of the EU's Common Agricultural Policy. A July 1995 report on the ten countries that either have association agreements or with whom such agreements are in prospect concludes that all ten countries have experienced precipitous drops in agricultural production, consumption, and exports. The report predicts that for Bulgaria in 2010 GDP per capita will be only 36 percent of the EU average.[47]

## The Industrial Sector
Industrial production dropped yearly from 1989 through 1993. The pattern changed in 1994 when there was 4.5 percent growth, followed by 7 percent growth in 1995.[48] Privatization has proceeded very slowly, though private-sector sales have been better than those of the public sector. Foreign investors have shown little appetite for Bulgarian enterprises, although, as of mid-1993, there were over 800 joint ventures.

### Industry Under Communism
The shift to an emphasis on industrial production began after World War II, with the Communists' accession to power. By 1949 production had risen to three times that of 1937.[49]

The Communists sought to foster growth throughout the country. To this end, they established economic regions in 1959, delegating much authority to the regional councils. "However, such was the degree of autonomy of the Councils that many invested in similar projects, such as meat packing and dairy product plants, regardless of facilities in neighbouring areas, and so the powers of local government were reduced somewhat during the mid and late 1960s."[50]

In the 1960s there was considerable migration within regions to the regional capitals, where industrial development was concentrated. Some cities were thought to have become too congested, and migration to them was restricted to workers offering special skills and/or correct political ties. Despite legislation, the larger cities continued to grow; by 1970 the eight largest cities housed 25 percent of the population, with 10 percent in Sofia alone.[51] In the 1970s, the government, concerned with rural depopulation, sought to invest in smaller towns, but this did little to stem the flow.

During the Communist period, industries produced primarily for the Soviet Union and East Germany, with Bulgaria in turn dependent on the Soviet Union for most of its oil and gas.

### Industry Post–1989
Industrial production declined 23 percent from 1990 to 1991, 22 percent from 1991 to 1992, and 8 percent from 1992 to 1993. The sharpest drops were in machine, electronics, textile, and food production. The sectors leading the 1994 and 1995 gains are metallurgy, chemicals, and glass, china, and ceramics. According to one respondent, "Industry is inefficient, but most of it is not outmoded. It is inefficient because it is inefficiently run. There is no good management, but there are a substantial number of enterprises in Bulgaria with

high-tech equipment, with very good quality machines, with highly skilled laborers. The big problem is that these companies have never been run properly, since their only buyer was the ex-Soviet Union who could eat anything and would accept everything. Against the products that we sold to the Russians we were getting extremely cheap fuel and natural resources which didn't really help in efficient running of these companies."[52]

Industry was the source of about 50 percent of tax revenues in 1992. It also is the nation's major debtor. As of mid-1993, debts owed by industry totaled over $4 billion (107,000 million lev). Of this total, 55 percent was owed to banks.

Losses of the 5,871 nonagricultural enterprises owned by the state, municipalities, or cooperatives totaled $1 billion (16.6 billion lev) during the first nine months of 1993—triple the loss for the same period in 1992. Officials at the National Statistics Institute attribute this perilous condition to underused production capacity, increased depreciation costs, wage increases, and high bank interest rates.[53]

## The Agricultural Sector
Agriculture, too, is a troubled sector. While awaiting the dissolution of the state collectives and restitution of state farmland, much land has lain fallow. Farmers allotted land on a one-year basis have raised a crop but not invested in land maintenance or improvement. A crippling drought in 1993, combined with lack of conveyance of title to restitutees and accompanying lack of expenditure for irrigation, led to heavy loss of crops. Lack of credit for purchase of seed and feed stocks, and lack of markets in Bulgaria or abroad for farm products are among the many burdens on farmers.

*Agriculture Under Communism*
Under communism, Bulgaria's farmland was transformed from a mosaic of tiny parcels, growing a wide variety of crops, to enormous cooperative and collective farms, growing only a few crops. There was an emphasis on export of livestock, fruit, tobacco, and alcoholic beverages. Food processing became a major industry. As in many other Eastern European countries, state farm managers were chosen more for their political contacts than for their knowledge of farming. Under this system productivity initially rose but then declined.

In 1946 there were 850,000 owners of agricultural land, and the average holding was 0.86 acres (0.35 hectares).[54] Ninety-three percent of farm holdings were 25 acres (10 hectares) or less[55]; in addition, the holdings were usually splintered so that one family might work up to 70 plots![56] (A few fruit trees, a little pasture, a vegetable patch along a river. . . .) Productivity was low, partly because farmers could not afford fertilizer, partly because the plots were too small for efficient farming. "Shortly after the Second World War it was estimated that in the U.S.A. the production of one acre of cotton absorbed fifty-seven man hours; in Bulgaria it was 605 man hours plus 405 ox hours or 262 horse hours; maize demanded thirty-five man hours per acre in the U.S.A. but 305 in Bulgaria."[57]

The few large landowners held 1.2 million acres (500,000 hectares), but constituted only 0.5 percent of the population. There also were many voluntary cooperatives, which ". . . have a long tradition in Bulgaria. The first cooperative was founded in 1890. By 1938 there were as many as 3,300 of which 1,962 were rural. They included farm production, farm inputs, agricultural processing, agricultural marketing, agricultural credit, crafts, dairy products, and lumber mills."[58] Rental of farmland was uncommon, affecting less than 10 percent of the land.

Under the Agrarian Reform Act of 1946, farmers, including those in the voluntary cooperatives, were forced to enter state cooperatives and to sell their machinery to them.

The third land reform, that of 1948, took all farmland in excess of 50 acres (20 hectares) or, in part of the country, 75 acres (30 hectares). These reforms of 1946 and 1948 are described in the section on property seizures by the Communists.

Many of the cooperatives *(kolhoz)* were merged into state collective farms *(sovkhoz)* between 1958 and 1960, during the third Five-Year Plan. After these mergers, the average farm size rose to 11,100 acres (4,500 hectares). Some of the collectives, however, were as big as 250,000 acres (100,000 hectares). During the 1970s there were further steps toward agglomeration of agriculture. The state collective farms and the state agricultural enterprises were combined into 152 agro-industrial complexes (AICs), each with an average of 5,000 workers and 58,500 acres (23,700 hectares) of land.

> The reasoning behind the reform was that horizontal integration based on similarities of climate and terrain would facilitate specialisation in agricultural production, and individual AICs were therefore meant to concentrate on—at the most—three main crops and rear only one brand of livestock. It was also planned, in the longer term, to link AICs closely with manufacturing industry and the trading associations . . . if the planned specialisation of agricultural production took place and if it were conducted on industrial lines, then in conformity with the party programme of 1971 agricultural labour would become indistinguishable from industrial . . . the homogenisation of Bulgarian society should logically lead to the withering away of the Agrarian Party, for a polity which consists solely of workers would need no other political organisation than the Communist Party.[59]

This step proved even more inefficient and, by the end of the decade, there was some subdivision of the giant complexes.[60]

During the 1980s agricultural employment and productivity both declined, with agriculture's contribution to gross domestic product dropping from 16.5 percent in 1980 to 11.3 percent in 1989.[61]

*Agriculture Post-1989*

As of 1989, cooperatives and collectives held 99 percent of Bulgaria's farmland. At this time, 62 percent of arable land was in fields, 25 percent in pasture, and the remainder was divided among meadows, artificial pastures, and orchards. Twenty-five percent of arable land was irrigated. Principal crops were livestock, which accounted for 50 percent of production; grains, particularly wheat, accounting for 12 percent of production; and fruits, tobacco, sugar beets, and wine grapes.[62]

Wages were 12 percent less for agricultural than for industrial workers. In 1989 the farm labor force was 750,000 people, over half of whom were over forty-five and many of whom were part-time or retired workers.[63]

Farm production in 1992 declined by 12.9 percent from 1991 production. Of the 11.3 million arable acres (4.6 million hectares), 4.2 percent were not planted in 1992. Although private farm production rose 13.6 percent, this did not offset the production decline of 27.3 percent by the state cooperatives and collectives.

In 1993, 9.7 percent of arable land lay fallow. For instance, 30 percent fewer fields were planted in cotton than in 1992. Only one-third of the 2.2 million acres (900,000 hectares) equipped with irrigation systems were irrigated, due to water prices that rose eight to fifteen times over 1992 prices. Lack of irrigation was particularly harmful in 1993, as Bulgaria suffered its worst drought in 100 years, leading to declines in production.

Stocks of pigs, cattle, and sheep dropped to one-half or one-third that of several years earlier. Potatoes, traditionally an export crop and plentiful enough to be fed to cattle, were imported for consumption and planting in the winter of 1993-94. Rose petals for attar of roses are a unique Bulgarian crop, with 7,400 acres (3,000 hectares) under cultivation. In 1993, 40 percent of the crop was left to rot; wages were so low that few people were willing to harvest the petals. Wine had been a leading agricultural export, with the Soviet Union, East Germany, and Poland the principal buyers. With these markets shrunken, the wineries' exports have dropped. Each year since 1990, 40 percent of the wine produced has not found buyers. Vineyards are being abandoned, and, after years of profitability, in 1993 the wineries lost money.[64] Still, in 1994 there were 275,000 acres (111,000 hectares) of vineyards, about the same as in Germany, Hungary, Russia, and Ukraine.[65]

Dairy, pig, and poultry farms, fish farms, and vegetable and flower green-houses all have heavy debt loads. Farmers do not have money to buy fodder and fuel, and prices for produce are low. Banks and other creditors have a large stock of uncollectible debts. Bulgarian cooperative and state farms owed commercial banks $246 million (6.5 billion lev) as of mid-summer 1993, with 84 percent of this debt in short-term loans.[66] The banks' unwillingness to lend to heavily indebted state agricultural enterprises is not surprising. One illustration of the out-come is the plight of the fifty-eight state-owned pig farms. The pig and poultry industries alone owe the banks $98 million (2.6 billion lev). "More and more pigs are dying for lack of funds . . . 20,000 pigs has [sic] died in the village of Rogozen and another 15,000 in the town of Levski, causing losses of millions of leva."[67] The government is covering the banks' bad debts from state agricultural enterprises incurred prior to 1993 by converting them to state debt and issuing twenty-five year bonds to the banks totaling $75.6 million (2 billion lev). This sum covers only the principal, not the accumulated interest, on the debts.[68]

Most crop harvests rose considerably in 1994: Grain increased 9.8 percent, corn 25.3 percent, and sunflower seeds 35 percent. Livestock herds, however, continued to decline, reflecting the extensive slaughtering in 1993. Significantly, private farmers including those in voluntary co-ops produced 41.8 percent of the grain harvest and two-thirds of the corn.[69] However, Bulgaria's share of the world rose oil market had dropped to 30 percent from a 1980s high of 70 percent. According to a vice-minister of industry the decline in production could be attrib-uted both to the restitution of many small plots and to people's lack of interest in growing roses.[70] A grain shortage in 1995 led to the resignation of the deputy prime minister and the minister of agriculture.

**The Housing Sector**
The major distinguishing feature of Bulgarian housing during the Communist period was private ownership, which was the norm. As in the Czech Republic and Poland, single-family homes in rural and urban areas were private, but so, too, were condominium units in apartment buildings, although there ownership did not include land. The state confiscated housing only when people owned more than one urban unit. So, unlike the agricultural sector, ownership and title are not problems in the housing sector.

In 1985 almost 85 percent of the housing stock was privately owned. Today 95 percent is private, with 92 percent owner occupied, and an additional 3 per-cent rental units. Only 5 of housing is rented from the public sector.

There are two serious housing issues today: poor quality of the stock, due to lack of maintenance, and lack of new construction due to difficulties in obtaining housing finance.

*Housing under Communism*

Land suitable for housing either was taken by the state in 1947 and 1948 or was taken subsequently as needed. If agricultural or vacant land was taken from a private owner, he or she was compensated by being given an apartment in the new building. Construction was fast and cheap, providing a large stock of apartments for people flocking in from the countryside. An apartment building might include some units built for an enterprise and some for a municipality. Regarding the construction companies, "Until 1958 the Bulgarian residential construction industry was characterized by numerous small and medium-sized firms. Beginning that year, the government nationalized the construction industry and fostered the creation of large state-owned enterprises which specialized in industrial construction processes, resulting in the large blocks of apartments which dominate the housing stock today. The investors or developers in this process became the municipalities, or the municipalities in concert with large state-owned enterprises, which were urged to provide housing for their employees. It was their task to acquire the land, contract for and finance construction, and eventually allocate and sell or rent the units."[71]

The cooperatives also were active in building housing, with the state enterprises carrying out the construction, often at a higher standard than that of the state housing. "In the 1950s Bulgaria developed a specific form of housing construction—the Residential Construction Cooperatives. The idea of the cooperatives was to engage the efforts of future owners in the construction of multi-family housing and to make them responsible for the final works, the landscaping, and the maintenance. . . . The cooperatives were usually built on land expropriated by the State and allotted to the cooperative. The former owners were compensated with apartments in the new building. The members of the cooperative acquired rights to the building, but the land remained state-owned. When construction was completed, the cooperative was dissolved and the participants became owners of individual apartments."[72]

Housing production by category of investor—state enterprise, municipality, cooperative, or private—remained quite constant from the late 1970s until 1989, with the public sector accounting for around 50 percent of the total and the remainder split between the cooperatives and the private sector. Total production in this period was in the range of 65,000 to 75,000 units per year.

New construction of single-family homes in urban areas was pretty much limited to the party leaders, who claimed sites from the collective property and had country homes built for themselves. It is said that some of these people had land records destroyed so that the earlier ownership of their properties would be muddied.[73] Private single-family housing also was built in rural areas and villages.

Space standards increased during the 1980s. In 1980 the average effective area per dwelling was 590 square feet (59 square meters), while by 1990 it had increased to 720 square feet (72 square meters). The average living space increased from 450 square feet (45 square meters) in 1980 to 540 square feet (54 square meters) in 1990.[74]

Upon completion, apartments usually were sold. However, state enterprises often retained ownership of housing complexes built for workers, many of whom had recently left their villages. State enterprise flats were not allocated unless the prospective owner could produce a certificate of housing need from the municipality in which the housing was located. In Sofia and other large cities, it was official policy that real property, including housing, could be purchased only by residents of the city in which the property was located. This was one way of enforcing the restrictions on migration to the regional centers. According to one person we interviewed, "In reality this was used as a tool to bring in people who had connections, people who were members or close to members of the Communist party, to the cities, people who would be forming the real army of the Proletariat."[75]

Housing built for municipalities might be rented or sold. Municipal flats were allocated in accord with several categories of need, with highest priority to those who were without housing or living in severely overcrowded conditions; next in priority were those waiting for a long time—even decades—on a municipal list.

Apartment units traditionally have been owned as condominiums. The owners' association representative collects fees monthly for electricity, a person to clean the common areas, for elevator and roof repairs, and for similar expenses. Heating is provided to individual units, not to the building.

Rent from flats, whether municipal or state-enterprise owned, was payable to the municipality, since the municipality was responsible for maintenance. Rents, set at .19 lev per square meter per month in 1968 and not raised until 1991, did not vary with location. As this token rent did not cover the costs of maintenance, maintenance was grossly inadequate.

The State Savings Bank (SSB) was created in 1951; in 1957 it became the sole source of mortgage funds. In the late 1980s the SSB made from 53,000 to 60,000 housing loans per year, and these loans enabled people to buy 85 percent of the housing units produced. There were two lists for housing savers, one kept by the SSB and the other by the appropriate municipality. The bank listed savings deposits, on which people formerly earned 1 percent interest. Deposits were made voluntarily on whatever basis a saver could afford, though often these were fixed monthly deposits. The deposits also earned "interest points," calculated solely in reference to the amount of money in an account. (Recently, for example, 1 point was awarded for each 0.4 lev saved, so that a saving of $38 [1,000 lev] would earn the saver 2,500 points in a year). The points were inheritable and could be applied to housing purchase in any municipality, assuming that the saver had risen to the top of the relevant municipal queue. Savers who had earned a specified number of points, sufficient for the down payment, were eligible to buy an apartment. Purchasers would then borrow at 2 percent from the SSB for thirty years to cover the remaining principal sum. Mortgages included the commitment that the borrowers' monthly payment might be deducted from their salaries and paid directly to the bank.

Resale of housing was allowed only through the municipality and at a price set by the state. Not surprisingly, an illegal market for housing existed at under-the-table prices.

*Housing Post-1989*
Since 1989 land and housing that was owned by the state has been transferred to the municipalities. Much publicly owned housing has been sold, leaving little available for those without the means to purchase. In 1990 the state authorized the municipalities to sell their stock of rental units to tenants at pre-1990 prices, far below market (prices ran from 15,000 to 20,000 lev, then worth $800 to $1,000). The sale price was set at the unindexed price of the unit as of the time of construction, a price that was usually extremely low, given the inflation in recent years. If the tenant could raise this sum—and many did—it was an excellent opportunity. If the tenant needed to borrow, however, the terms were thirty years at around 50 percent, with principal amortized. In cities, over 50 percent of the stock of rental units was sold. In March 1991 the state rescinded authorization for these sales.

Also starting in 1990, individuals were permitted to own more than the previously authorized one urban dwelling and one weekend house, and they were permitted to sell housing units privately, at market rather than state-dictated prices, to anyone regardless of place of residence. Once private sales were authorized, many illegally held units came on the market. Almost all mortgage loans in 1990 and 1991 were for these newly legal transactions.[76]

Foreigners may buy urban property and even have special protection against expropriation: Their property ". . . may be expropriated only for state's exceptionally important needs that cannot be satisfied in any other way."[77]

The data on available dwelling units show conditions to be poor: Space standards, maintenance, and availability of utilities all are deficient. There are approximately 3 million dwellings nationwide. Dwelling units per 1,000 population rose from 320 in 1980 to 404 in 1992. However, only 360 per 1,000 were inhabited, and only 337 per 1,000 met habitation standards. Comparing the 337 units per 1,000 figure to the European standard of 420 per 1,000 population, a shortage of 104 per 1,000 could be said to exist.

The 1992 census showed that "over 35.4% of dwellings have no sewerage; over 33% have no water supply; over 86.6% have no central heating; over 36.3% have no bathrooms; over 49.9% have no inside WC."[78] There are fewer units per 1,000 population in cities than in towns: 346 units per 1,000 compared to 433 per

1,000 in 1989. In the large cities housing is rented or sold for nonresidential uses; this is especially true of Sofia, where 25,000 dwelling units, or 7 percent of the housing stock, are rented for nonresidential purposes.[79] Space per person is less in cities than in towns: 150 square feet (15.8 square meters) compared to 220 square feet (22 square meters). Forty percent of households are reported to share their dwelling with another household.[80]

Maintenance of all housing, whether privately or municipally owned, is a serious problem. It often is posited as an advantage of homeownership that owners will maintain their dwellings. Two caveats apply in Bulgaria and elsewhere: The owner must have the financial resources to spend that which is needed to maintain the housing, and the owner must have the motivation. The earlier discussion about income levels addresses the first point. Since dislike of the Soviet-style high-rise apartments is widespread, many Bulgarians have hoped that the future would bring the opportunity to move elsewhere. They have doubted, as well, that there would be a market for these unappealing units, so have hesitated to spend their very limited resources to improve them. Housing construction has dropped off dramatically, the price of housing has risen, and housing financing is difficult to obtain and very expensive.

Nationally 330,000 households, with 80,000 in Sofia itself (over 20 percent of Sofia's households), are on the municipal housing lists. Yet, as of the 1985 census, there were 178,000 vacant urban units.[81] Many houses also are vacant in villages. With the number of people who have left Bulgaria, and, particularly, the inability of most people to afford the mortgages that are available, the lists may not reflect real demand but rather the desire for housing of better quality.

Starting in 1989, when 41,000 units were built, there has been a precipitous drop in construction. In 1991 only 19,000 units were built, and the share of building by cooperatives was insignificant.[82] In 1992, 18,000 units were completed, two-thirds of which were built by state or municipally owned enterprises for the municipalities. In 1994 only 8,700 units were completed. State subsidies for housing construction have been sharply curtailed. Despite apparent demand, construction is at a standstill. "Regardless some efforts made by the state, the market transition in housing sector destroyed social mechanisms for distribution. Characteristic for 1992 is an almost complete decline of social housing construction, suspension of giving municipal dwellings to families who are in need, privatization of organizations' housing stock."[83]

While awaiting privatization, the state's housing construction firms are switching some of their limited production to single-family housing. However, prefabricated apartment units are expected to continue to account for from 60 percent to 80 percent of housing construction.[84]

The few private construction companies often look for two types of partners—one with title to buildable land and one with money. The former, in return for turning over the land, receives a percent of the finished structure(s). In center-city Sofia, the going rate is 30 percent of the finished project; in outer parts of the city it is from 20 percent to 25 percent. The people with money to invest in housing construction often are those who have profited recently from very large markups on imported goods; the other principal source of housing investment is from people, often the nomenklatura, who made money illicitly and now need a place in which to invest it.[85]

Since 1989 all banks have been authorized to lend for housing construction and for residential mortgages, but so far only the SSB has granted residential mortgages. The SSB makes combined construction and mortgage loans to individuals and cooperatives for housing construction and issues mortgage loans to home buyers. As of August 1991, housing construction loans constituted 24 percent of SSB loans. The terms for these short-term loans in 1991 were 100 percent of cost for municipalities and 70 percent for other borrowers, for 2.5 years at 55 percent interest.

"Prior to the recent deregulation of housing prices, the maximum loan plus deposit was sufficient to purchase a standard state-constructed unit."[86] This has changed recently. As of mid-1993, the SSB had increased interest on housing savings deposits to 44 percent, had lowered the mortgage term to twenty years, and had raised the interest rate to 49 percent for families with a housing savings account and the minimum 30 percent of purchase price in savings and to 54 percent for others. The mortgage may be for up to 70 percent of the average market price for a similar unit in that location.

There are different guarantee requirements, depending on the nature of the loan. Loans made prior to January 1, 1991, are guaranteed by monthly deposits of salary and by a mortgage. Later loans based on a housing savings deposit are guaranteed by 50 percent of the monthly income of the household and a mortgage.

The SSB also makes short-term loans for housing improvements, requiring a mortgage for any loan greater than $370 (1,000 lev).

Few families wishing to buy a new home or to improve their present one can afford these terms. Furthermore, people are not adding to their savings for housing accounts because they can earn higher interest elsewhere.

In Bulgaria, the average housing expenditure is very low by Western standards but normal for the countries of Central and Eastern Europe, reflecting the heavy subsidies of the Communist era. In June 1993 urban residents spent 4.2 percent of their income for housing, rural residents 5.8 percent of their income.[87]

For municipal rental housing, the base rent was raised in 1991, from 0.19 lev per square meter per month to 1.65 lev per square meter per month, with adjustments for level of services and location, so that the possible range is 1 lev to 3 lev per square meter per month. Assuming a 500 square foot (50 square meter) apartment at a rent of 2 lev per square meter per month, the monthly rent equals $6.10 per month or 5.4 percent of income based on an average monthly wage of $112 (2,966 lev). "Municipal Councils can also increase the rent of their units by an additional 15%, independent of quality or location. Further, in an attempt to prevent over-consumption of housing, the recent changes in the rental regulations also imposed an automatic doubling of rent for all public units exceeding 20 square meters per person."[88]

For those purchasing housing, the average cost is highest in Sofia, at $42 per square foot (11,000 lev per square meter); the cost is $32 per square foot (8,500 lev per square meter) in the Black Sea coastal cities of Bourgas and Varna, and $19 per square foot (5,000 lev per square meter) in medium-size cities.[89] Again assuming a 500 square foot apartment, and assuming a purchase price of $25 per square foot (6,600 lev per square meter), the cost of such an apartment would be $12,500 (330,000 lev). Obviously it is impossible for most people to purchase a home. The down payment of 30 percent would require thirty-three months' salary, and the 49 percent interest on the principal balance initially would be about $162 (4,300 lev) per month. "Traditionally, the Bulgarian government subsidized the housing sector on many levels, including fuel subsidies for materials production and transportation, direct funding of materials production companies to cover operating losses, the provision of land and units at prices below the state's cost, and artificially low interest rates on construction and mortgage loans . . . no further direct subsidies for housing are being included in the state budget. . . . Nevertheless, the system still contains various off-budget and implicit subsidies."[90]

Several proposals would make housing more affordable. The National Housing Compensation Fund was established by law in 1991 to assist people who had saved for housing but whose deposits, after 1989, would not begin to cover the usual 30 percent down payment.[91] In principle, it will apply an index based on interest points to determine how much subsidy—but not in excess of 40 percent of housing cost—to provide a saver, with each municipality determining priorities. The interest would be at a variable rate, adjusted monthly, but remaining 5 percent below market. It is anticipated that the fund also would contribute from time to time to paying down the principal amount.[92]

The current government proposes a three-tier approach. The first tier, consisting of the ill, socially disabled, or large families, would be eligible for state-financed housing. The second tier would receive favorable loans for land and housing. Only the 20 percent constituting the third tier would be on their own in the private market.

The Urban Institute has developed a housing allowance system to assist needy families living in rental housing.[93] Following a 2,000-household survey in Blagoevgrad, the Urban Institute is ready to initiate a pilot project under which tenants in both municipal and private apartments would receive an allowance to cover the difference between market rents and around 15 percent of their income. The amount of the subsidy also would be tied to the tenants' space needs so that a single person would not continue to occupy a large apartment. The scheme is intended to be self-financing, with the market rents from about half of the tenants covering the cost of the allowances to the others. Since the municipal housing is in poor condition, one expectation is that tenants paying market rents will move to better housing. At present municipal units rent for around $0.006 per square foot (1.65 lev per square meter), while market rents in the 85 percent of Blagoevgrad housing that is in the private sector are somewhere between five and fifteen times this amount. Adoption of such a system would enable municipalities to charge market rents.[94]

## RESTITUTION

Bulgaria has chosen to rely principally on restitution to restore real property taken by the Communist government to private ownership. This was not a unanimous choice across the political spectrum; in fact, restitution has been and continues to be the subject of intense political discord. However, the return of property is progressing, albeit in fits and starts. To quote two respondents: "There are political barriers and polarized outlooks. The Bulgarian Socialist Party didn't back privatization in 1991, and doesn't back the return of land. From their perspective, privatization is subsidizing losing producers. The UDF is a union of groups that are neo-conservative and do favor the return of land and the restitution of firms."[95] "The BSP was totally against restitution because that would return property to people that they had taken the property from. They tried to bypass restitution by insisting on a law that would compensate with participation in privatization by some kind of vouchers instead of returning the property in its real boundaries."[96]

The Union of Democratic Forces, during its brief tenure in power in 1991 and 1992, succeeded in passing restitution laws for farmlands and for urban properties. In only a few years Bulgaria managed to restitute over 56 percent of the urban structures and enterprises that were subject to valid claims. It also has placed 62 percent of the farmlands that were eligible for restitution in private cultivation, though many without title deeds. Government predictions that restitution would be completed in 1995 were not realized, mainly due to delays awaiting judicial decisions on contested boundaries and delays in issuance of titles as well as government recalcitrance. Nonetheless, both urban and farm property restitution are signal achievements. Forest restitution will follow.

Unlike the Czech Republic, Poland, and many other countries of Central and Eastern Europe, housing restitution and privatization are not an issue in Bulgaria. Overall, only a very small proportion of urban properties were subject to restitution claims, while most rural properties were subject to such claims.

## Communist Property Seizures, Post-Communist Property Rights

To determine what property is eligible for restitution, it is first necessary to review what property was taken, when, and what laws applied to the seizures. The Communists revoked the underlying principle of private ownership with the 1947 Constitution and its successors. The 1947 Constitution: ". . . granted public property extensive protection and imposed limitations on private property. . . . The two socialist Constitutions of 1949 and 1971 defined the three main categories of ownership. 'Social' ownership—ownership by all the people in theory, by the state in practice—was the highest category of ownership and received special protection . . . this kind of property was excluded from individual transactions under the Constitution. . . . The other two forms of property were 'cooperative' and 'individual' property. Cooperative property included most agricultural land and was governed by the law on cooperatives. 'Individual' real property was limited to one residence and one vacation house per household."[97] Armed with constitutional authority, the state confiscated enterprises, shops, offices, garden plots, and, to a very limited extent, housing.[98] "[O]n 23 December 1947, trained groups seized the country's 6,109 remaining private enterprises together with all their machinery, property, stocks and accounts. . . . On the following day the Grand Subranie sanctioned the takeover and ruled that the former owners should receive government bonds in compensation for their losses but . . . the government paid out in compensation no more than a tithe of the value of the property seized, and the nationalisation of industry amounted to little else than the final destruction of Bulgaria's small industrial bourgeoisie. . . . At the same time the confiscation of large urban properties put an end to the existence of the Bulgarian private landlord."[99]

People whose property was forced into cooperatives did not lose title to their land, but they did lose the right to use it other than through participation in the co-op. Seizure of larger farms followed in 1948, with a farm expropriation program closely paralleling the land reform of 1920. As in 1920, this land reform was small in scale, in comparison to those elsewhere in Central and Eastern Europe, because most Bulgarian farms already were small. Only 2 percent of the cultivated land was affected. All farmland in excess of 50 acres (20 hectares), or 75 acres (30 hectares) of grain lands in the northeast region, was taken, with only token compensation paid. The seizure included all but 9,600 acres (3,900 hectares) of the 220,000 acres (90,000 hectares) of land belonging to the Bulgarian Orthodox Church. In 1949 the land was redistributed to 120,000 farm families, who received between 2.5 and 5 acres (1 to 2 hectares) in return for a very small sum payable over ten years. After the reform, 6.7 percent of farms were under 5 acres (2 hectares), 30.9 percent were between 5 and 12.5 acres (2 to 5 hectares), and 62.4 percent were between 12.5 and 125 acres (5 to 50 hectares).[100]

Soon after, most of these farmers—both those who had had "excess" land taken and those who received the land—were forced to enter the cooperatives. By 1952, 61 percent of arable land was held by state cooperatives; this figure increased to 92 percent by the end of the second Five- Year Plan in 1957, at which point there were 3,200 cooperatives averaging 2,500 acres (1,000 hectares) in area.[101] Until 1958 farmers received rent on the land taken for the co-ops. Farmers did retain both title and use rights to 1.2 acres (0.5 hectares) for their own gardens. These plots could not be sold or mortgaged, and people were not allowed to hire labor to cultivate them. Between 1950 and 1960, most cooperatives were merged into state collective farms, with all farmland becoming essentially state land. Consequently farmers lost private title. While they were granted private use of 16 percent of the land, they did not hold title to it.[102]

After 1989, the Communist constitution's strictures against private property rights were abolished. The 1991 Constitution asserts that "private property is inviolable" and that the "law guarantees and protects the right to property and inheritance." During 1995 the Constitutional Court issued several decisions interpreting these provisions; some of the decisions have outraged members of the BSP. The constitution further provides that, "Expropriation of property in order to meet state or municipal needs must be according to law and provided that such need cannot be satisfied in any other way. Suitable compensation must be paid in advance."[103]

The new constitution includes a strong commitment to protect the environment, preserve valued resources, and retain arable lands. Such specificity about the priority to be accorded natural resources is unusual in a constitution. Among the constitution's provisions, it specifies: "The Republic of Bulgaria ensures the protection and conservation of the environment, the sustenance of animals and the maintenance of their diversity, and the sensible utilization of the country's natural wealth and resources."[104] In addition, "All beaches, public roads, mineral deposits, bodies of water, forests, and parks of national importance remain state property."[105] "The land is a basic national resource and benefits from the special protection of the state and society. Arable land may be used exclusively for agricultural purposes. Changes in its use are permitted only when based on proven need, in accordance with conditions and procedures defined by the law."[106]

The constitution prohibits foreign ownership of land. "Foreigners and foreign juridical persons may not acquire the right of land ownership unless legally inherited. In such cases, they must transfer such ownership to someone else."[107]

Restitution to the Jews who left for Israel or elsewhere has been resolved by returning seized property to Shalom, an organization designated as the successor to Jewish interests. The value of this property is estimated at $14.2 million (1 billion lev).[108]

**Urban and Rural Restitution**

Under the 1991 Constitution and subsequent enabling laws, those who lost urban or agricultural property through Communist seizures were entitled to seek restitution. There was a dramatic disparity between claims for urban and rural property restitution: Only 55,000 claims were filed for urban property, while 1.7 million claims, on behalf of 54 percent of the population, were filed for farmland.[109]

The smooth progress of urban property restitution means that these holdings are already or soon will be part of the active urban market. However, the several roadblocks between farmland restitution and an active rural market include insufficient public funds for establishment of farm parcel boundaries, litigation over boundaries, insufficient private funds to pay for title deeds, and lack of farm credit. Fortunately, the government now has reduced title deed costs to a nominal sum. Once property is in private hands, a period of parcel turnover and consolidation to make farming more efficient is expected. So far, 91 percent of the farm parcels restituted have been under 2.5 acres (1 hectare) in size, too small for efficient production.

Farm restitution remains a contentious issue. In 1995 the BSP passed amendments to the Law of Ownership and Use of Agricultural Land that would have favored cooperatives and impeded free market transfer. However, the Constitutional Court held that all but one of these amendments were violations of constitutionally guaranteed property rights.

*Urban Property*

Eighty percent of those industrial enterprises that existed before World War II are subject to restitution claims. The restitution laws also apply to all shops, offices, and apartment buildings that were taken. "According to the Privatization Law, the owners of real estate nationalized by laws, decrees, or acts of the Council of Ministers (in the period 1946-1962, with few exceptions) have the right to regain the respective part . . . of shares and stock of the transformed into commercial partnership state enterprise, in case their property exists in real terms and represents part of the long-term assets of state and community enterprises."[110]

Several acts provide for urban restitution: the Restitution of Nationalized Real Property Act of 1992, the Urban Regulation Law, the Planned Urban Construction Law, the Urban Development Law, and the State-Owned Real Estate Law govern restitution of real property taken by the state. Restitution is provided for if the property taken was a building and the building still exists and is the same size as when taken, or, if the property taken was land, if the land is "suitable for single home construction."[111] "A lot of difficulties are encountered in the application of this law, caused mainly by the requirement for the real estate to exist physically in the size in which they have been expropriated. . . . Some buildings have been demolished and new ones have been built up on their sites. Many

additional buildings and superstructures have been added. An additional difficulty in connection with the real estate identification is created by the lack of
archives in many cases."[112]

Although most housing remained private, the Restitution of Nationalized
Real Property Act authorizes claims for seized residential property,[113] including housing taken from someone who owned more than one house or apartment. Prior to the Communist era, architects commonly claimed one unit in each
building that they designed, so their holdings were among those confiscated.
Some of the seized housing was rented, some was sold. People who received
apartments in the structure built on their land could request restitution by filing a claim with the Ministry of Finance within six months of passage of the
act. If the property had been resold or altered subsequent to seizure, the law
states that a later law is to provide for compensation. As of the end of 1993,
no such law had been enacted. Restitution in these cases usually has not presented title problems, since most claimants had kept their deeds or could rely
on testimony of neighbors.

Small shops and businesses taken by the state for which very little compensation was paid could be reclaimed in restitution.[114] However, people who had
rented from the state and made improvements to premises were entitled to be
paid by the restitutee for those improvements. Upon restitution, these contracts
with the state were terminated, and the restituted owners either ran a business
on the premises or looked for tenants ready to assume a lease. The law provides
that persons who obtained ownership of shops between 1973 and 1990 by other
than official means are subject to restitution claims, although the restitutee can't
recover lost revenue.[115]

As of June 30, 1993, almost 55,000 claims had been filed under these laws;
in comparison, there were 30,000 such claims in Czechoslovakia. There were
64 claims per 10,000 people, with the rate of claim much higher (777 per
10,000) in towns than in villages (38 per 10,000).

### TABLE 2.2: RESTITUTION OF URBAN PROPERTY AS OF JUNE 30, 1993

| Type of Site | # of Claims | # of Sites Restituted | % of Sites Restituted |
| --- | --- | --- | --- |
| All | 54,426 | 30,772 | 56.5 |
| Lots and Gardens | 25,536 | 11,090 | 43.4 |
| Dwelling Units | 11,484 | 6,775 | 59.0 |
| Shops | 9,003 | 7,452 | 82.8 |
| Various Industrial Sites | 1,563 | 1,010 | 64.6 |
| Warehouses | 1,201 | 882 | 73.4 |
| Mills, Water Mills | 1,059 | 713 | 67.3 |
| Office Buildings | 511 | 402 | 78.7 |
| Cultural Sites | 368 | 203 | 55.2 |

In cases in which property is to be returned, restitution is proceeding well; as of June 1993, over 30,000 properties had been restituted, or 56.5 percent of properties claimed. Shops, restaurants, drugstores, and office buildings were highest in rate of restitution—all exceeding 79 percent of claims filed. A report of the National Statistics Institute details number of claims and number of properties restituted;[116] table 2.2 lists only the land uses for which more than 300 claims had been filed.

As of mid-1995, 63 percent of the housing that was claimed in restitution was back in private hands. Tenants in restituted apartments were authorized to remain for up to three years—until February 1995—paying rent to the restitutee, at a price set by the Parliament that is "preposterously low."[117] In February 1995, tenants' right to remain in the apartments was extended by Parliament for three more years. The Constitutional Court subsequently ruled the extension unconstitutional.

The remaining urban restitution issues concern compensation. The law provides that a person who holds former agricultural land and who has a valid permit for construction (permits are valid for five years) will keep the land, and the restitution claimant will receive compensation. In theory, the municipality is to pay this compensation from increased municipal taxes, such as fines on illegal construction.[118]

Another situation in which compensation for taking of land has not been resolved is where land was taken for public purposes, such as airports, high-tension lines, and roads, and no compensation was paid. While there has been compensation for current takings, there has been none for past takings.

Overall, it is fair to say that "the restitution of urban property, in particular, is already having a significant impact. All of this may well place Bulgaria ahead of many other ex-socialist countries in the protection of private property, and gives it greater immediate potential for real estate investment."[119]

## Farmland

Restitution of agricultural lands is progressing, after a late and difficult start. The government's revised targets were to have 88 percent of the land restituted by the end of 1995 and to wind up the task in 1996, except for the 3.4 percent of arable land that had been distributed to individuals prior to 1989; this land will be restituted by the end of 1997.[120] By the close of 1993, almost half of the land was being farmed on a temporary basis, pending establishment of plot boundaries. Only a tiny fraction of the land to be restituted was covered by title deeds—3,500 acres out of 12,600,000 acres. Consequently, there was no market to speak of. On the positive side, much more land is being restituted through reallotment than through restoration of former boundaries, which will result in somewhat larger, more efficient holdings. By mid-1995, 43.8 percent of the land had been restituted.[121]

Two significant facts have contributed to difficulty and delay in farmland restitution: Both are political, but one is rooted in Bulgarian farm history while the other is tied to the interests of the Communists—or the post-Communists.

First, with the exception of voluntary cooperatives, farm holdings prior to the Communist seizures were very small, partly as a result of the land reforms of 1879 and 1920. Also, most farmers' land was divided into many plots. Reflecting popular sentiment, the Law of Ownership and Use of Agricultural Land (LOUAL) guaranteed that restitutees would receive their exact prior plots if the old boundaries could be reestablished. Otherwise they were to receive comparable nearby land.[122] With many land records no longer in existence and with old boundary markers long obliterated, the surveying task proved slow, arduous, and costly.

> The restoration of the small private property of the land . . . will create a peculiar situation in this country. . . . In 1945 there were approximately one million farms with a size of 4 hectares, and the land was divided in 12 million pieces of about 0.35 hectares. Now the ownership will be restored of more than 2 million owners with an average size of their property of under 2 hectares. It is undoubtedly impossible for such a great number of farms to exist due to a simple reason— the farming can not provide a normal income not only to 2 million but to 1 million people at all . . . the reform of agriculture could have taken a different more rational path. Unfortunately, political demagogy prevailed and the act was based on an extremely regressive principle— "each Bulgarian with a piece of land."[123]

The economic sense of the re-creation of minuscule parcels, many to be owned by the nonfarmer heirs of the former owners, is another aspect of this question. "Clearly the agriculture sector had to be privatized, but the process they adopted proved to be disastrous for Bulgarian agriculture. . . . In many cases, particularly where the land was divided among the descendants, these were parcels as small as (1,000 sq.ft.) 100 square meters. This is of course not a farm, but a garden and cannot be farmed efficiently. As the collectives with large amounts of livestock were dissolved, the livestock was either slaughtered or exported on the hoof."[124]

Second, BSP opposition to the LOUAL as enacted has meant that restitution has been much slower than promised and much land has been left idle. Many say that progress has been impeded by politics. An advisor to President Zhelev has alleged that the BSP is seeking to help the nomenklatura keep land that they took by failing to enforce the law requiring return of actual prior holdings and by supporting agricultural recollectivization initiated by them.[125] A former head of the Privatization Agency observed: "It is sad to say, but the political games have stopped the returning of land and the revitalizing of Bulgarian agriculture. Looking at the figures in the polls, 60 percent to 70 percent of the electorate of the Communist party is in the villages. These are people who, at age sixty or seventy, have nothing left in front of them and can live a quiet life on the quasi-cooperative farm that exists, where they can get a small rent. They are not very eager, and in this they are supported by their village Communist Party bosses, to get their land back . . . once the land is given back to the people the Communist party activists in the villages will lose their power over the people."[126]

The LOUAL created a two-level structure for administration, with a National Land Commission that oversees the work of 301 Municipal Land Commissions, responsible for 4,800 Territories Belonging to Settlements (TBS).[127] The land commissions were appointed by the minister of agriculture. The law calls for members to include a "lawyer, an agronomist, a certified geodesist or land surveyor, a representative of the Liquidation Council and of the private agricultural proprietors."[128] Due to the lack of qualified personnel, this directive could not be achieved. "Of the 1,600 people working on land ownership restitution, only 14 hold a degree in law and no more than 50 are qualified engineers and technicians."[129]

The land commission members are full-time employees, paid from the Land Fund created by the act. The land commissions work in parallel with the liquidation councils, which have been charged with dissolution of the collectives. The Land Commissions may be designated later to act as land registration agencies.

Restitution claims were to be filed with the municipal land commissions within fifteen months of passage of the LOUAL, namely by August 4, 1992. The commissions were given six months to rule on the validity of the claims, and claimants were given a right to appeal a negative decision to a district court. Claimants could include individuals, former members of cooperatives, the Bulgarian Orthodox Church and other religious groups, and municipalities whose land had been taken. People who had had land taken in 1946 or thereafter, or their heirs, were eligible to file claims. "The right of ownership is restored to the members of cooperative farms and state owned farms over their lands that were included in the farms [and] . . . on demand to persons who have voluntarily granted their land to cooperative farms or to the state."[130] Turks who left between 1985 and 1989, and who sold their homes in the mountainous southern region under pressure, have been asking for some form of compensation but are not included in the legislation.

The process followed by the land commissions consisted of determining the validity of the claim both in terms of title and of boundaries; deciding whether the old boundaries could be reestablished or whether reallotment was necessary,[131] developing a land distribution plan; pending adoption of the plan, allocating land on a temporary basis,[132] and then issuing proof of title. The most difficult and costly part of the job has been the documentation and surveying of land to establish preexisting boundaries or, where this was not possible, to set new boundaries as part of reallotment plans. Significantly, the regulations call for consolidation when reallotment occurs. The starting point of reference is the 1939 cadaster for the municipality, if it had not been destroyed. With the survey costs averaging $6 per acre (400 lev per hectare), the Ministry of Agriculture had, as of the end of 1993, allocated enough funds for land surveys to cover 38.5 percent of the claimed land. Allocations for 1994 were insufficient to complete the surveys, so this aspect of restitution could not be finished until 1995.

Initially, the maximum land to be restituted per claim was set by the LOUAL at 75 acres (30 hectares) or "for regions with intensive agriculture, as determined by the National Land Commission, not more than 20 hectares" (50 acres).[133] This provision was repealed in 1992. However, people who had owned larger tracts and had lost all but either 50 or 75 acres (20 or 30 hectares) in 1948 were given nominal compensation then and are entitled to nothing else now. People who worked in the collectives but did not contribute land are entitled to receive land, based on time worked, in compensation for their contribution. The amount varies from 3.7 to 7.5 acres (1.5 hectares to 3 hectares) per family. To meet these needs, 370,000 acres (150,000 hectares) have been earmarked. If not all of this land is requested by eligible people, anyone may apply for an allocation, paying the local market price.

Some land is exempt from restitution in the former boundaries. If the land had been built on, either equivalent land will be provided or compensation will be paid on terms set forth by the Council of Ministers.[134] Claimants to lands classified as natural reserves, archeological sites, and cultural monuments will receive equivalent quality farmland from the state and municipal reserves.

Conversely, land in environmentally polluted regions is to be restituted, and restitutees are to be paid by the state for reclamation of the land.[135] Unclaimed, low-productivity land in depopulated areas may be given to farmers who, after ten years, will be given title without any payment. Land remaining after claims are resolved remains state property.

Restitutees and other recipients of land under this act must farm the land, lease it to a tenant farmer, or sell it. The law sets standards for use of restituted lands: "The owner shall be obligated to use agricultural lands only for the purpose they were intended to be used . . . the owner shall be obligated to use them in a way which does not harm the soil's fertility, in accordance with sanitary-hygienic standards . . . and ecological norms. . . . Proprietors and users shall (1) protect farm land from erosion, swamping, salination, pollution and other deterioration, shall rehabilitate affected soils and shall improve soil fertility; (2) use only chemical fertilizers and substances approved by competent state bodies; (3) not use for irrigation purposes water containing harmful substances and wastes exceeding applicable standards."[136]

Heirs to restituted farms are not subject to an inheritance tax. No income or property tax will be levied on restituted farmland for five years after issuance of title. Subsequently, it is to be taxed by the municipality at a rate based on the value of average produce per hectare for the region or land.[137]

The act initially prohibited transfers of restituted land for three years except to family members, the public sector, or as an exchange of agricultural lands. This moratorium on transfer of restituted land was rescinded in 1992, to permit sale as soon as title has been conveyed. Foreign heirs were given three years to transfer their title to a Bulgarian citizen. Under the 1992 amendments, up to 50 percent ownership of land by foreigners became legal. Sales or transfers must be of at least 0.74 acres (0.3 hectares) for fields, 0.5 acres (0.2 hectares) for meadows, or 0.25 acres (0.1 hectare) for vineyards and orchards.[138]

*Dissolution of the Cooperatives and Collectives*

The Cooperatives Act dissolved the existing state-mandated cooperatives, created restitution rights for voluntary cooperatives nationalized after 1944, and provided for the creation of new, voluntary cooperatives.[139] Most of the 1,050 voluntary cooperatives nationalized by the Communists were agricultural in nature, and their property is held by the Ministry of Agriculture. Of 500 claims for restitution filed by voluntary cooperatives, only fifty-one claims had been accepted or rejected as of autumn 1993.[140]

The act was amended in March 1992, over the opposition of the BSP, to dissolve the state-controlled collective farms (TKZS) created in the 1950s and 1960s. The 2,093 Liquidation Councils, one per TKZS, consisting of a chairman and from three to five members, were appointed by the regional governors to develop plans for and carry out distribution of nonland assets.[141] Pending distribution, the councils are responsible for running the farms. Working in conjunction with the municipal land commissions, the councils manage the state and municipal rural lands in their jurisdiction, totalling 570,000 acres (230,000 hectares). A critical task for the councils has been determination of entitlement to shares in the nonland assets as among TKZS members who contributed land, land and labor, or labor only. Land contributions are weighted for quality of land and number of years that it was part of the collective, while labor is measured in man-days.[142]

As of December 1993, only forty-five of the councils had completed return of all of the assets for which they were responsible despite the fact that work was to have been completed by November 1, unless they were exempted from this termination date by the Ministry of Agriculture because they still had undistributed property or had accounts receivable or payable.[143] "There is ample anecdotal evidence that LC [liquidation councils] become preoccupied with their obligation to maintain agricultural production to the detriment of their main function of setting in train the liquidation process. For obvious reasons, maintaining production is a higher priority for a farm workforce which needs to make a living in the short run. Longer-term policies which involve radical economic change bring disruption and, almost inevitably, uncertain outcomes. Thus there are understandable pressures to 'make haste slowly' in agricultural reform. In the present context, this is manifested in the tendency for LC to continue in existence much longer than was originally envisaged."[144] One of the 1995 amendments to the LOUAL mandated dissolution of the Liquidation Councils; this amendment was sustained by the Constitutional Court.

The experiences of two municipalities in central Bulgaria, one in which a cooperative was liquidated and the other in which boundaries were established, offer concrete illustrations of the problems that are being faced. The municipalities of Saedinenie and Hisar are located near the city of Plovdiv, in the heart of Bulgaria's most productive agricultural area.

The Saedinenie Liquidation Council has been responsible for the liquidation of the Giant Cooperative, a co-op with 1,700 members that has farmed over 40,000 acres (17,100 hectares). Among the crops that have been grown are 7,000 acres (2,800 hectares) of rice on irrigated land, 9,900 acres (4,000 hectares) of wheat and barley, 14,800 acres (6,000 hectares) of corn, 7,400 acres (3,000 hectares) of vegetables, 740 acres (300 hectares) of lavender, 2,000 acres (800 hectares) of vineyards, and 500 acres (200 hectares) of orchards.

At the time of our visit, a group of angry farmers had prevented the Council members from entering their offices at the Giant Cooperative for a week.[145] The farmers were demanding the immediate return of their land, even though the wheat crop was nearly ready for harvest and the Ministry of Agriculture had ruled that restitution should not occur until after harvest. They also protested that the Liquidation Council had allowed 100 cows to starve to death. We listened to the charges of thirty to forty men and women before moving on to a meeting with the council members, who said that far fewer cows had died and that the deaths occurred due to lack of care because the dairy business is unprofitable.

According to Liquidation Council members, they had allowed anyone to farm land rent-free during the period of ownership determination; 9,900 acres (4,000 hectares) were being farmed on this temporary basis. These farmers could request the services of a co-op crew to bring heavy machinery to their tracts to plant and harvest the crops. The council sold them fertilizer and pesticides. The law requires that the remaining land, another 30,100 acres (12,500 hectares), be farmed by the council, which was hiring farmers to grow the crops. The council members anticipated turning a profit of $38,000 (1 million lev) in 1993.

The Liquidation Council has used the following procedures to determine the members' entitlement to shares in the Giant Cooperative's assets. An early step was setting the total value of the assets. During 1990 the Ministry of Agriculture hired an appraiser, who set the value at 250 million lev including the land, the irrigation system, the buildings, and the equipment. With inflation, the value in 1993 was around $1.3 million (500 million lev). The Council set aside 10 percent of the total value of assets to respond to unanticipated claims.

No land records were available. Old boundaries had been totally obliterated, and all the records of the former owners who joined the cooperative had been destroyed. There also was no documentation of what equipment people contributed when they joined the co-op.

Assets—land, equipment, livestock, and labor—were given values in terms of shares. The value of equipment and animals contributed forty years ago was calculated on the basis of what they were worth at the time. Since there was no record of what was contributed, the council decreed what would have been normal equipment and livestock for the amount of land that was being farmed. If there was no record of the amount of land, the council made a determination based on the recollections of those still alive who were present at the formation of the co-op. Disssatisfied co-op members could complain to the council and try to negotiate a larger share. Share units were awarded for specified values of equipment and livestock and for labor and land. The intent was to place an equal value on land and labor, with each person receiving one share for each year that 0.25 acres (0.1 hectare) of land was part of the co-op or each year that a person worked for the co-op.

Heirs of the original cooperative members were entitled to shares whether they currently work the land or not. Some people who contributed labor but not land, including Gypsies, will receive 1.2 acres (0.5 hectare) per family. On average, the plan allocates farmers 7.5 acres (3 hectares) divided into two or three plots. In this area non-adjacent plots are traditional, to reduce the risk of crop loss due to hail. Land in excess of that claimed will be ceded to the municipality, although it is unclear how there could be excess land, particularly since laborers who did not contribute land are entitled to an allocation.

The council members anticipate that problems of land management will arise after restitution. The co-op's machinery is designed for tracts of at least 250 acres (100 hectares), not the small ones that will be re-created. Maintenance of the irrigation system will require cooperation. Machinery has been allowed to deteriorate, often with parts cannibalized to repair other machinery.

A nearby village was at a standstill with its liquidation. Its initial Liquidation Council was rejected by the villagers who distrusted the members. Then, in summer 1993, the second Council was disbanded by the state due to corruption. That Council was found to be allocating the best assets of the cooperative to family and friends.

Hisar, founded by Diocletian, is a municipality of thirteen towns and villages.[146] It is a second home, retirement, and tourism center as well as a farming community. The shortage of records and of personal documents indicating what land people owned has made restitution difficult. Some old tax registers do exist. In determining claims, the commission may accept only written evidence,[147] but the court can accept oral testimony and sworn declarations of the size and location of the prior holdings. The court must compare competing claims and attempt to arrive at a fair resolution.

Farmland in Hisar varies considerably in quality and in access to water—be it dams, rivers, or irrigation systems. The municipality includes mountainous areas and arid plains. No land records exist for the plains, where small holdings—from one-third to 15 acres (0.15 to 6 hectares)—were characteristic. Out of 8,000 claims, only ten were for over 25 acres (10 hectares). However, there were more claims than land to satisfy them: 89,000 acres (36,000 hectares) in the plains were claimed, although only 79,000 acres (32,000 hectares) exist. In recalling prior holdings, memories tend to exaggerate rather than minimize.

The Land Commission, with funds from the Ministry of Agriculture, engaged a company to do the land survey, paying $420,000 (11 million lev) for this work and the design of a proposed reallotment plan. Once parcels were marked, the claimants and the Land Commission members went to the sites and sought to reach agreement on boundaries. While substantial efforts have been made to persuade claimants to accept reallotment, many people were adamant: They wanted the exact parcels that were in their family some forty years ago.

*Implementation of Farm Restitution*[148]

The first task, virtually complete, was determination of the validity of claims. Nationwide a total of 1.7 million claims were filed for a total of 13.75 million acres (5.57 million hectares).[149] This is more than the 12.6 million acres (5.1 million hectares) available. The disparity of 1.15 million acres (0.47 million hectares) was in part due to excess claims and in part to claims to land no longer in agricultural use. Of all claims, 91 percent were filed by individuals, with one claim often covering dozens of parcels. These claims are estimated to represent some 4.6 million potential heirs.[150] With a population of 8.5 million, this means that 54 percent of all Bulgarians believed that they were entitled to a piece of land. Of the other claims 1.4 percent were filed by the state, 5.1 percent by municipalities, and 2.4 percent by churches, mosques, schools, and other institutions.[151]

The 301 land commissions have made 1.6 million decisions as to the validity of claims but not setting the boundaries, representing 96 percent of restitution claims filed. The 4 percent unresolved are primarily in urban areas or involve lands held by the Ministry of Defense, which does not have deeds covering much of this land. The government is prosecuting people who made fraudulent claims, which are thought to total over 865,000 acres (350,000 hectares). Some duplicate claims for the same land were the result of honest error.

A few people—less than 0.5 percent—with valid claims want compensation, not land. As of the end of 1993, the land commissions had made 5,601 decisions on these claims.[152] In 1994, using the income approach, the value of land for compensation purposes ranged from $2 per acre (300 lev per hectare, at the 1994 rate of exchange) down to $0.01 per acre (between 20 and 25 lev per hectare). Usually when land cannot be restituted because it has been developed claimants elect to receive comparable land with the hope that it, too, will become developable. Compensation also is unpopular because of inflation, although the price offered is adjusted annually, in November. People tend to prefer to take their chances on land value appreciation rather than see their cash payment erode in value.

There is considerable disparity throughout the country between amount of land claimed and amount available. In only one-third of the 4,800 Territories Belonging to Settlements (TBS) was there equality. In 40 percent of the TBS, claims were received for more land than was available. Where this occurred, a ratio was used to match supply with claims. In northern Bulgaria, on the other hand, there were fewer claims than the amount of land available.

Of the total of 12.6 million acres (5.1 million hectares) that will be restituted, it is anticipated that 11 million acres (4.5 million hectares) will go to individuals, 690,000 acres (280,000 hectares) to municipalities, 190,000 acres (77,000 hectares) to the state, and 320,000 acres (130,000 hectares) to institutions.[153]

The second task, not yet complete, is determination of what specific tracts of land are to be restituted, whether within restorable boundaries or through reallotment.

As of the end of December 1993, 13 percent of the land to be restituted, or 1.7 million acres (0.68 million hectares), had been restituted in its former boundaries, settling 510,000 claims. Much of this land lies in rugged, mountainous terrain, where landmarks remain to make identification of former holdings possible. This part of the restitution process now is essentially complete. These restitutees are in possession of their land and have proof of title or actual title. The additional 10.9 million acres (4.42 million hectares), representing 1,480,000 claims, either had been restituted through reallotment or were in the reallotment planning process. As of August 1995, 62 percent of land had been restituted, while reallotment plans were being revised for an additional 21 percent of the land.[154] Pending final decisions, much land—3.2 million acres (1.3 million hectares)—had been granted to restitution claimants for temporary use during one crop year. Reallotment is a difficult task, because the characteristics of many small parcels are being translated into an equivalent holding of comparable soil types and productivity that consolidates plots in order to reduce fragmentation. Reallotment was proceeding under Article 27 of the LOUAL regulations for a further 34,000 claims to 350,000 acres (142,000 hectares). If prospective restitutees object to the land distribution plan, their objections are heard by a district court, whose decisions may not be appealed.[155] Finally, 5,600 claims for compensation representing 5,900 acres (2,400 hectares) had been found valid.[156]

About half of the claimants under reallotment were given proof of title, including a plan of their plots keyed to cadastral maps. Of the remainder, those wishing to farm were allocated land equal to 80 to 90 percent of their claim for one crop year.

There have been some 130,000 court challenges to the reallotments, with restitutees arguing over the boundaries and amount of land allotted to them. Since each challenge affects boundaries of surrounding parcels, this litigation delays issuance of proof of title to many restitutees. It is not clear when all of these claims will be resolved.[157]

Proof of title is the necessary precursor to obtaining a deed from a notary, and a deed is essential to land transfer or mortgage. Yet only 1,554 deeds had been issued as of the end of December 1993, covering some 3,500 acres (1,424 hectares),[158] in part because each deed cost $57 (1,500 lev), or half a month's wages. The high cost of deeds and thus the lack of clear title were deterrents to the creation of a market for agricultural lands. This problem was resolved by the Parliament's decision authorizing Land Commissions to issue title deeds directly, rather than through a notary, and for a charge of less than $1. Also, some restitutees are said to be unwilling to obtain a deed, because they fear the taxes that will be incurred starting five years after restitution.

Short-term rentals are expected to be the norm in the early years. "[B]ecause most lessors will be in towns and therefore will have no interest in rents in kind and because rents will for the next few years be short-term annual arrangements, it is likely that most will be on cash leases. Unstable economic environment in the country means that rents will vary each year. It is expected that tenants will be in a stronger position than landowners. . . . The owners will often be uninformed about farming and only have an interest in getting some payment for their land. Hence we might expect relatively low levels of rent."[159]

It is estimated that the average size of total land restituted per claim will be just under three acres (1.19 hectares). Data on the size of parcels actually restituted show 91 percent of holdings from 0.25 to 2.5 acres (0.1 to 1 hectare) and the remainder from 2.6 to 12.4 acres (1.1 to 5 hectares). A poll by the National Public Opinion Centre shows that only 2 percent of those polled expect to receive 25 acres (10 hectares) or more under the LOUAL.[160] This confirms concerns that the plots returned will be too small for efficient farming.

## Continuing Restitution Issues

For many the heady delight at the return of family lands has given way to the recognition that fractions of hectares cannot be farmed efficiently and that credit to buy farm equipment is unavailable. This has led to the formation of new,

voluntary cooperatives on some restituted farmland, replacing the forced cooperatives that the Liquidation Councils have been dismantling. At the end of 1993,
1,341 voluntary cooperatives had been established covering 2.3 million acres
(918,000 hectares). Concern has arisen about the formation of cooperatives by
people who do not have title to the land; President Zhelev commented on this
as follows:

> Regarding the land question, my position has always remained one and
> the same, namely that the land should be returned within real bound-
> aries, in cases where the old real boundaries still exist, or within new
> real boundaries, with the merging of land holdings in one location so
> as to permit modern agriculture on the plains. . . . In this context, I have
> declared my personal opposition to the farm cooperatives that are
> being set up without land titles before the land has been returned to its
> former owners. . . . All the disputes that are going on concerning the
> liquidation councils . . . miss the main issue, which is the return of the
> land to its former owners. I believe that this is of exceptional impor-
> tance, because this is what will allow the people who receive their land
> back to form true cooperatives—private cooperatives—cooperatives of
> owners, authentic cooperatives. Along with this, of course, those who
> want to acquire land in other ways will also have this opportunity. The
> way should be made clear for them, for leasing and selling land;
> Bulgaria should have a land market.[161]

Another commentator has proposed a structure for the voluntary cooperatives:
"What needs to be done so that the new co-operatives are different from the existing ones? First, a mechanism in them for direct realisation of private property by
means of rent and dividends must be provided. Second, not very large co-operatives
must be set up where people will be able to supervise both each other and their
leadership. Third, such internal organisation in the co-operatives must be in which
the labour input should be done individually or in small groups so that each persons input can be recorded. Fourth, economic (and why not also legal) independence of the groups is necessary with full commmercialisation of the relations
between them and reducing the centralisation of the income to the minimum."[162]

Farmers whose land has been restituted are having a very difficult time. Farm
credit has been almost impossible to obtain, and farmers often are unable to buy
seed and feed. Nor can they afford to pay for water for irrigation, particularly
since water prices have been raised substantially. Fertilizer and herbicide prices
also have been raised. Banks are unwilling to lend, even to farmers who have
obtained title to their land, because land taken as collateral has a very unclear
market value and because the banks don't wish to end up holding farmland.

Although the Bank for Agricultural Credit was created in March 1990, with
a capital of $10 million (264 million lev) and 20 percent foreign participation,

to provide farm loans, according to some, it has not lent at all to farmers. The government, alarmed by the sharp declines in planting and production, took action, in the spring of 1993, to make subsidized loans available for seed for planting. The Agricultural Finance Act of 1993 enabled farmers to apply for loans, pledging futures contracts for crops.[163] The law directed banks in which the state holds a majority interest to make a total of $56.8 million (1,500 million lev) in secured loans to farmers, cooperatives whose members hold deeds to the land in the co-op,[164] and Liquidation Councils, for autumn and spring planting, including seeds and fertilizer, and for irrigation. The interest rate was 3 percent above the Bulgarian National Bank's base interest rate, but two-thirds of the interest was covered by the state. The loans fell due in autumn of 1994 or in spring of 1995 for tobacco growers. In cases of default, the Ministry of Finance is responsible for 50 percent of the amount due and the lender bank for the remaining 50 percent. The Economic Bank, Bulgaria's second largest bank— and its bank with the largest debt, at almost $700 million (18.4 billion lev)[165]— was the first to be charged with granting these loans.

In the fall of 1993, the government adopted a new law that continued the short-term credit with the state subsidizing two-thirds of the interest.[166] State-dominated banks are no longer obliged to extend credit, and state responsibility for 50 percent of default amounts also has been removed. Banks may ask for property as well as crops to be provided as collateral—and banks are requesting collateral of 200 percent to 300 percent of the amount borrowed.[167] All of these measures will lead to less credit being extended.

An Agricultural Credit Center was established in early 1993 to lend money to farmers to buy small equipment and livestock. The center, a joint stock company of public agencies, is funded largely by foreign aid, including proceeds from sales of commodities, such as corn received from the West and sold at low prices to farmers. A maximum of $6,800 (180,000 lev) can be lent to farmers owning a minimum of one acre (0.4 hectares) and a maximum of $18,900 (500,000 lev) to private cooperatives. In 1993 a total of $4.7 million (124 million lev) in credit was granted. The interest rate was 7.9 percent but now floats. Collateral is 80 percent in excess of the amount borrowed. Future funding for the center is in doubt.[168]

Two other problems facing farmers are the quality of the land that is being returned to them and that fact that less land is arable than formerly:

> in the last 15 years 140,000 ha. (345,800 acres) has been taken for industrial construction, 1,300,000 ha. (3,211,000 acres) has been swamped and another 50,000 ha. (123,500 acres) superficially water-logged . . . the quality of the arable, too, has changed substantially. During recent decades basic agrotechnical laws have been disregarded

in the overwhelming drive for record yields. The rotation of crops was almost entirely abandoned and, instead, the bright prospects of continuous cropping were widely publicised. As a result of unscientific cultivation and continuous cropping, over 72% of the arable land has been eroded to various degrees. . . . The excessive application of nitrate fertilisers led to the rapid oxidation of the soil and thus to disastrous consequences for agriculture. The acidity of more than 48% of the arable is below 5.6.[169]

A final problem is how to enable and encourage assembly of enough parcels of land by those who wish to farm. According to Kopeva and Mishev, "The urgent necessity of developing land markets in Bulgaria arises from some simple facts: most of the new owners no longer or perhaps never practised agriculture and no longer live in or around the immediate locality where their new property is located. The special problem for this group . . . is that the transaction costs of transferring use rights to active farmers may exceed the available rents. Thus, much land could end up simply not cultivated."[170] Kopeva and Mishev further hypothesize that restitutees living in cities may hold on to their rural land in part as a hedge against inflation and in part because of cultural predispositions to maintain rural ties.[171]

All of these problems and predispositions led the BSP, in 1995, to propose and enact a set of amendments to the LOUAL that would have wrenched the restitution process off course. An appeal by President Zhelev to the Constitutional Court and a decision by the court finding all but one of the amendments unconstitutional seems to mean a return to the status quo ante.

Twenty amendments, proposed by the BSP and opposed by the UDF, were enacted. Some of the new provisions were:

• Any owner of agricultural land wishing to sell the land must first offer it to the state, which would have two months to decide whether to buy or not. If the state chose to buy, it would set the price; if the state chose not to buy, the owner must then offer the property to the owner(s) of adjacent property, then to farmers in the same settlement, then to the municipality, and then, only if none of these offerees chose to buy, could the owner sell on the market. The state would be required to buy if there were a shortage of land in the settlement for landless farmers or for resolution of compensation claims. "If the total land sold to the state and municipalities were really transferred to private individuals under the schemes of land settlement or compensation, this would mean that the impact of this amendment would be neutral. However, if this process did not go smoothly, the amendment . . . might reverse the flow from private back towards the public."[172]

- Small plots part of larger blocks may not be sold, and small plots must be planted with the same crop as the larger block of which they are a part.
- Newly formed cooperatives would receive the best of the land from the collective farms.
- Agricultural land not used for agriculture would be subject to a new, high tax.
- Companies in which part of the capital is foreign owned could not own agricultural land.
- Several provisions altered the restitution process, allowing land commissions to reverse their decisions in light of the amendments, and creating a category of unrestored land whose allocation would be determined by an arbiter chosen by the eligible claimants.[173]

According to the BSP, the amendments were designed to foster cooperative farming and efficient cultivation. The UDF abstained from voting on the amendments but argued that they would hinder formation of the land market and force owners to use their land in specific ways. President Zhelev vetoed the law amending the LOUAL, stating that it "touches the essence of Bulgaria's democratic reforms. The question about the land . . . cannot be a party issue."[174] Parliament overrode the veto. President Zhelev and fifty-one representatives from the UDF next filed a challenge in the Constitutional Court, arguing that the amendments violated the constitutional guarantee of private property rights. On June 19, 1995, the court, by a large majority, held that nineteen of the twenty amendments violated the constitution and reinstated the earlier nineteen provisions of the law. The amendment that was sustained ordered the dissolution of the Liquidation Councils.

In August 1995 the cabinet supported the court's decision concerning small plots: "The owners of small plots which are part of the larger blocks are allowed to trade them without state and municipal control. Owners of such plots whose land cannot be restituted in prior boundaries will receive land, not mass privatization vouchers."[175]

The struggle to change the restitution law has kindled antagonisms and has placed in sharp relief questions about the roles of the judiciary and the legislature. Prime Minister Videnov has said that President Zhelev "behaves more like a candidate for opposition leader than . . . a head of state" while the Constitutional Court "behaves like an alternative parliament."[176] President Zhelev, addressing Parliament on the fourth anniversary of adoption of the constitution, said: "No matter how the present Constitution is assessed, it is the basic political and juristic fact which the institutions and the Bulgarian citizens should comply with and observe . . . the Constitution is a guarantee that democracy will not degenerate into what Tocqueville described as the 'tyranny of the majority'. . . . The call to wage war against the Constitutional Court is a call to wage war against the Constitution."[177]

In August 1995 the court's judges and staff were ordered to surrender their offices on the grounds that they were needed for others—surely a retaliatory measure. The Bulgarian press refers to this struggle as the "war of institutions" and speculates that Videnov may try to change the constitution.[178]

**Forests**
While forest restitution has yet to begin, it is provided for in the LOUAL.[179] A proposed forest restitution law has been approved by the cabinet and will be submitted to Parliament. It would allow claims for restitution for all forests nationalized in 1947 and would return land within its former borders up to a maximum of 125 acres (50 hectares), with compensation paid for former holdings in excess of that amount. If return of the land taken is impossible, similar land nearby would be restituted or compensation paid. Only Bulgarian citizens would be entitled to own forests, and any noncitizen restitutee would be required to transfer title to a Bulgarian within three years. The state would retain forests in national parks, mineral springs areas, and areas held by the Defense Ministry.

Around 220,000 acres (90,000 hectares) of mostly forest and pasture was taken from the Bulgarian Orthodox Church. If the land was agricultural, the church was eligible to claim under the farm restitution law. If the land was forest, the church will be eligible to claim under the proposed forest restitution law. Individuals and municipalities are the other expected restitutees of forest lands.

## OWNERSHIP TRANSFORMATION THROUGH PRIVATIZATION

Of the three broad categories of real property—housing, land, and enterprises—only one, enterprises, is being transformed through privatization. Housing, as already described, essentially always has been private and, since 1990, has been freely bought and sold. Land is being or will be transformed via restitution. Some small enterprises were restituted; most had been privatized in one manner or another prior to passage of the Privatization Law. Privatization principally affects large enterprises.

This section looks at the structure and operation of privatization of enterprises, including privatization under the voucher program approved in 1995.[180]

### The Privatization Laws
Although the Bulgarian Socialist Party favored privatization over restitution, since its return to power in 1992, it has had little success in implementing its privatization schemes. "Some strata of society have power and economic benefits

that they fear losing," and so they are a brake on the political will.[181] Widespread instances of corruption, favoritism, and illegal privatization have had a chilling effect on public attitudes. A discussion of privatization under the Privatization Law must be viewed in the light of the "quiet" or "wild" and the illegal privatization that preceded enactment of the law.

Small businesses are a sector in which spontaneous privatization flourished. The directors of state or municipal enterprises contracted with their friends, often Communist Party members, to lease shops at very low rents. "The observations show, that in all former socialist countries, including Bulgaria, unofficial privatization is very rapid and means illegal or semi-legal transformation of state and public property rights into private ones . . . by a limited circle of people, mainly former 'nomenclature' and its entourage from the state companies and enterprises in an environment of full paralysis, chaos, and ineffectiveness of the old system . . . as well as ineffectiveness of the new system."[182]

The law does offer relief from illegal privatization. When a third party holds property by "misuse of power," the former owner has one year to file a claim for the property.[183]

Retail trade is now 90 percent municipal or private, leaving only 10 percent in state hands. Not all of this occurred by privatization, since many entrepreneurs launched new, small businesses. As of 1992, the number of such new businesses was estimated at 210,000.[184]

Since 1987 it has been legal for private entrepreneurs to lease state property; initially, shops and other small businesses were put up for auction and the highest bidder took over the business, often firing inefficient workers and changing the activity of the business. Anger among those laid off led to the "quiet" approach, in which businesses were taken over by their employees without color of law.

Other quiet privatization occurred in situations in which there was no public notice of auctions and when farm cooperative equipment was sold for token prices. As of 1990, the property of state enterprises could be transferred to private firms. Many of these private companies "were owned by directors and managers of state companies or their relatives and close associates. Thus, taking advantage of the legislative and economic chaos, considerable assets were transferred to private companies." Possibly 10 percent or 15 percent of the assets of Bulgarian state enterprises were transferred through these mechanisms.[185] In fact, "asset stripping has seized the entire economy like a giant octopus." Aleksandur Bozhkov, former executive director of the Privatization Agency, says "unlike the other East European countries, Bulgaria witnessed a fully legal process of asset stripping, or hidden privatization as it is popularly known. . . . Mixed partnerships involving state and private interests were instrumental in the transfer of funds from state-owned into private companies."[186]

As several ministries had been involved in privatization in different sectors, the lack of transparency resulted in allegations of abuse and corruption in the sale of land and in the sale or lease of trade and tourism units. As a consequence, in August 1990 the National Assembly imposed a moratorium on all sales of land and other state or municipal property.[187] "Particular concern is expressed about selling enterprises to the nomenklatura or to foreign investors."[188] The Bulgarian National Bank also took action in 1991 to bar insider sales; in 1993 it released a white paper on clandestine privatization in the banking sector in violation of the ban imposed in 1991.

So many small businesses were privatized prior to the sanction of the law that this aspect of privatization is almost over. Large-enterprise privatization faces major hurdles, many of a political nature. However, the Videnov government has pledged to speed up the process, which had accomplished little by 1995.

The act governing privatization—the Law on Transformation and Privatization of State-Owned and Municipal Enterprises—was not adopted until spring of 1992.[189] It applies to both small business and large enterprises. The Privatization Agency was established in the fall of 1992 and charged with responsibility for the privatization process.[190] It, too, has not been immune from charges of corruption and incompetence. "Not surprisingly, the level of corruption is high. It is difficult to say the same about the level of competence. Privatization required accountants, valuation experts, lawyers, bankers, etc. Restructuring and rising unemployment made a lot of people look for opportunities around privatization and they went to ministries and privatization agencies or specialized private firms."[191]

Privatization is initiated by one of several actors: by the ministry responsible for an enterprise, by the Privatization Agency, by the managing body of the enterprise, or by a majority vote of the employees. Who is responsible turns on the size and ownership of the enterprise. State enterprises with a value of $380,000 (10 million lev) or less are the direct responsibility of the appropriate ministry or, if there is none, of the Council of Ministers. Those enterprises with a value greater than $380,000 (10 million lev) and less than $7.5 million (200 million lev) are the responsibility of the Privatization Agency. The larger enterprises, with a value of $7.5 million (200 million lev) or more, are privatized by the Privatization Agency after the approval of the Council of Ministers.[192] Privatization of municipal enterprises is the responsibility of the municipalities.

People who have been restituted property that is part of an enterprise proposed for privatization—and 80 percent of the enterprises that existed in the late 1940s were subject to restitution claims—may file a claim with the Privatization Agency.[193]

State and municipal enterprises customarily are transformed into either joint stock or limited liability companies. The companies may be sold by auction of shares, public tender, open sale, negotiation of sale price, or a combination of these procedures. Former employees are entitled to buy up to 20 percent of the shares under preferential terms, which permit up to a 50 percent reduction in the price of the shares. Enterprises that have not been transformed must be sold at auction or by tender.[194] If 30 percent or more of the employees bid for the enterprise and win, the purchase price is reduced by up to 30 percent.[195]

The responsible agency determines what form of sale to select and follows much the same procedure as in the Czech Republic. Any auction must be advertised, and bidding may be open or closed. The auctions are with a reserve price set. There must be more than one bidder at the first auction, but one bidder, offering the minimum price, can succeed at a second auction. If a second auction fails, the price may be reduced in a successive offering by up to 30 percent, and then in successive reductions of 10 percent up to a total of 50 percent of the initial price.

The ministries were required to develop a privatization strategy and send an annual schedule for privatization to Parliament for its approval by June 30, 1993. That year ended without action by Parliament.

Appraisal of assets is a task for which a nonmarket system has had little experience. The Privatization Agency has a training program for appraisers and has licensed 2,000 of them. Some licenses are limited to specific areas of expertise, such as real estate. Appraisers bid for the opportunity to value assets of enterprises, which often include land. They must use two methods of appraisal, selecting among net present value, liquidation value, appraisal by use of comparables, and internationally recognized methods. There is now competition among licensed appraisers, and the price of appraisals has declined.

The agency responsible for privatization is required to publish in the *State Gazette* a list of sales, including the property, the buyer, the price, and the terms of payment.[196]

The law mandates the creation of a fund into which the revenues from enterprise sales must be deposited[197] and specifies how the revenues shall be allocated; of particular interest are the requirements that 20 percent of revenues be deposited in a mutual fund to be created by the state and that 10 percent of revenues be placed in a fund to assist agriculture.

Municipalities retain 50 percent of the proceeds of their sales, applying these funds to "redeem bad loans of municipal enterprises and for investment purposes. These funds may not be used for current expenses." Thirty percent of the proceeds is allocated to social funds and 20 percent to the mutual fund.[198]

When real estate is privatized, the tenants are held to have an indefinite term, which is defined to mean that one month's notice of termination is required. However, the law provides for an extension of up to six months from the date of approval of the decision to privatize.[199]

The foreign investment law of January 1992 permits 100 percent foreign ownership of enterprises and full repatriation of profits. Since foreigners may not own land, the only way a foreign purchaser may bid on realty is through investment in a Bulgarian company.[200]

Each recent government had announced its intention to create a mass privatization program but failed to do so. The current government submitted its program to the National Assembly in October 1995, and it became effective in January 1996. Vouchers are being offered for shares in 3,900 enterprises, valued at $3.1 billion (211.3 billion lev). There will be two privatization rounds with 1,227 enterprises offered in 1996 and the rest in 1997. About half of the enterprises are industries, with construction, tourism, and agriculture accounting for most of the rest. Ten percent of the shares of all enterprises will be earmarked for restitution claims. Large enterprises will remain under state control, with only 25 percent of their shares in the voucher program. Vouchers could be used to acquire 67 percent of the shares of medium-size enterprises and 90 percent of the shares of small enterprises. Each citizen over eighteen years old—around 6.7 million people—may receive voucher certificates with a face value of 25,000 lev (about $400 at current exchange rates) in return for the payment of 500 lev ($6.35) at one of 3,100 post offices. Students and pensioners pay only 100 lev, or the price of five loaves of bread, for the vouchers. The government predicted that 4 million people would buy vouchers. However, as of the mid-May closing date for voucher purchase, only 2.7 million people had bought them, with over 50 percent buying at the 100 lev price. The vouchers can be transferred to relatives but cannot be sold.[201] Half of the vouchers can be used in the first round and half in the second, either by direct purchase of shares or through investment in privatization funds. A Securities Commission has been created to license all privatization funds. As of May 1996, six funds had been licensed.

The new head of the Privatization Agency and of the Center for Mass Privatization, Kalin Mitrev, is committed to mass privatization, but cautious in his forecast: "This is very important for Bulgaria. It shows, after all the political uncertainty and the delays, that the reform process is back on track. It is one of the main criteria by which the government will be judged. It will enable the development of a Western-style securities market and greatly expand foreign investment opportunities. . . . Mass privatization is about transferring ownership, it does not solve the long-term problems of the economy."[202]

Another commentator sees vouchers as a better route to fair, rapid privatization: "In order to maximize the net present value of the future flow of value-added from such firms, privatization should be made faster! Selling through auctions or tenders, however, is not necessarily the fastest way. Voucher schemes might be helpful. Having more, better and cheaper products might be not enough if the process is considered unfair. This could happen easily if, because of the wish to privatize quickly, firms are being sold "cheaply" or few groups are perceived as the main beneficiaries. The unavoidable redistribution of wealth should be eased by wider distribution of ownership through free vouchers. . . . The recent 'Berov' proposal, based on a deferred purchase, is a creative transfer of the Czech technology."[203]

However, yet another commentator finds the Czech system of voucher privatization inappropriate for the Bulgarians:

> First, voucher privatization is affordable only in a country which has a low level of indebtedness externally and internally. Bulgaria remains one of the most indebted former East bloc countries and should therefore consider the Hungarian model of privatization where substantial hard-currency revenue from sales of domestic assets to foreigners is used to finance current account deficits and debt repayments. . . . Bulgarian enterprises are in a lot worse economic and financial shape than Czech enterprises and the general level of depression of the Bulgarian economy is much greater than in the case of the Czech Republic. Given the initial adverse starting conditions at the enterprise level, the Bulgarians are not in a shape to be able to afford to pay the price paid by the Czechs for voucher privatization.[204]

## Experience with Privatization

At this time, large-enterprise privatization is beset with obstacles and is hardly launched. In this area, Bulgaria is behind many of the Eastern and Central European countries. How the voucher system will work remains to be seen in 1996.

Bulgaria anticipates considerable nonmarket privatization in which enterprise assets are distributed for free to put them into the private sector. A majority of the large state enterprises are said to be so heavily in debt that no one will bid for them. Of the limited number of enterprises that have been offered for sale, many have failed to find buyers. On the other hand, the then director of the Privatization Agency was dismissed, in the summer of 1993, after completing two successful privatization projects that resulted in 100 percent private ownership, with foreign/domestic investment in a 80/20 ratio. The first project, completed in May 1993, was to the Belgian company Amilum and the Bulgarian Biochim Bank. The bank took 19 percent of the stock of a corn processing factory in a debt for equity swap, and Amilum acquired 81 percent of the stock, promising that 1 percent of the stock would go to the employees. The value of the purchase was $24 million (634 million lev). The then director commented: "It was the starting of privatization and the first two transactions that had gone through that led to my dismissal. The government and the forces that are behind it were quite unhappy with a type of privatization that they could not control, a type of privatization that encouraged foreign investment, a type of privatization that encouraged 100 percent private ownership of all enterprises."[205]

Privatization plans of several of the ministries and some of the early results give a sense of some of the difficulties experienced. Here we consider the ministries of industry, construction, trade, and agriculture.

The Ministry of Industry has engaged in a triage process, with the three categories being: (1) those industries meeting the criteria of the law and that are in good financial condition, with good future prospects, and some interest from investors; (2) those industries that might become marketable but that need preprivatization restructuring, often carried out by a management company under contract, including segmenting of the company and completion of partly built sites; and (3) those industries that should be liquidated. Methods for disposition include direct sale, giving shares to workers, joint ventures, and combinations of the above. The ministry anticipates privatizing from eighty to one hundred enterprises, mostly by sale to employees. Given the debt carried by the industries, the Ministry expects to realize only from $19 to $27 million (500 to 700 million lev) from the sales. The outlook is not sanguine: "Experts say the ongoing depression in production and companies' deepening cash crisis pose serious obstacles to the progress of the privatization program. Ministry figures suggest that less than 20 per cent of industrial enterprises with fixed assets valued at under 10 million lev are profit-making concerns or break even. There is almost no solvent demand on the part of Bulgarian natural and juristic persons."[206]

The ministry had received 126 proposals for joint ventures as of November 1993; the largest number—18—came from prospective investors from Russia. Twenty-five of the joint venture proposals were approved as of then.[207] One of the ministry's sales was to a Swiss chocolate manufacturer, which bought a chocolate factory, and another was to a German brewer, which bought a two-thirds interest in a Plovdiv brewery.

The Ministry of Construction has categorized the enterprises in its charge into eight groups; the percentage shows the estimate of industries by category:

**1.** Enterprises needing foreign investment funds, including the cement industry: 4 to 5 percent;
**2.** Enterprises planned for direct sale to foreign investors: 2 to 3 percent;
**3 and 4.** Enterprises whose assets are likely to be attractive to employees and local investors: 60 to 70 percent;
**5 and 6.** Enterprises needing restructuring: 10 to 15 percent;
**7.** Enterprises with cadaster and/or water supply problems: 15 percent;
**8.** Unsuccessful enterprises that need to be liquidated: 9 percent or less.

The ministry targeted twenty-seven enterprises, mostly cement factories and building construction companies. Among the latter group were six housing construction factories, operating at 30 percent of capacity. These factories had substantial debts, mostly incurred between 1988 and 1990.[208] One additional problem is that the enterprises are equipped to build Soviet style prefabricated units, while future demand is likely to be for other forms of housing.

One priority of the Ministry of Trade is to privatize the service sector, allowing a high level of employee participation. This approach is motivated in part by the concern that if the sale were to outsiders, the current employees might vandalize or steal assets.

The Ministry of Trade's privatization plan for 1993 called for disposition of fifteen enterprises and initiation of the process for an additional fifty-five enterprises. As of August 1993, the ministry had held twenty-five auctions and sold nine enterprises, raising $760,000 (20 million lev) from the sales. One sale is illustrative of the process: An auto service station was auctioned to its employees who failed to raise the purchase price, so a second auction was held and the property was sold to a Bulgarian distributor for Daewoo.[209]

The Ministry of Agriculture holds 486 enterprises that are to be privatized. Despite seventeen auctions and seven tenders, only four transactions had been completed as of November 1993. Interest in the auctions ranged from nonexistent to sparse.[210]

**General Outcomes**
Results overall, as of the close of 1995, fell far short of projections. The government had marked 318 enterprises for the initial stage of privatization, with the intent of completing the process in 218 of these enterprises by the end of 1993. The anticipated proceeds from these sales was $79 million (2,085 million lev).[211] The Privatization Agency reported that only 65 enterprises actually were privatized. In terms of money, $4.4 million (115 million lev) was realized. The then director of the Privatization Agency commented on some of the problems delaying the process: ". . . the financial insecurity of the transactions impedes privatization. No revolving fund has been established, there are no regulations for the management of the state stake in companies, and enterprises submit misleading information."[212] In 1994 only 180 enterprises out of the 3,200 state-owned enterprises were sold. In 1995 around 600 firms were marked for sale; only 243 actually were sold. In addition, some 1,200 municipal enterprises were sold.[213]

Municipalities also have adopted privatization programs. The Greater Sofia Council, through the Sofia Municipal Privatization Agency, determined that, of its 183 enterprises, 95 should be privatized in 1993, including groceries, restaurants, hotels, and two construction companies. Auctions are the principal tool, but tenders also will be used. As of autumn 1993, Sofia had held only one successful auction, the sale of a downtown textile shop. Some twenty other shops had been sold by tender. "In spite of good will and efforts, however, most of the auctions and tenders conducted so far result in a failure. Usually, nobody wishes to buy at the initial offering price and new auctions have to be organized for the same property after a reduction of the price."[214] The pace in other municipalities turns on the political will and economic status of the municipality. A number have sold half of their enterprises.

## FORMATION OF THE MARKET

At the close of 1994, markets existed for urban land, small businesses, and housing. Although farmland legally can be sold, very few restitutees held titles to their land. Forest land had not been restituted, and few large enterprises had been privatized. Information about number of sales, length of time property is on the market, and actual market price is extremely limited.

### Urban Land and Housing

Since 1990, when market price sales of housing were allowed, the market has exploded. There are now 400 realtors in Sofia and 1,500 throughout the country, although only a few do a substantial business. The twenty-five larger firms have computer listings and share some information on sellers, but not on buyers or on sales prices. One weekly newspaper is devoted solely to Sofia area housing available for purchase or rent. While there is much information about asking prices, comparable information about actual sale and rental prices is very limited. As previously noted, actual sales prices are not recorded, and such transaction data as exist are not public. The sales information that does exist for Sofia appears to indicate that there is a distance gradient which may in part reflect the fact that the unpopular prefabricated housing estates are on the outskirts of the city.

Realtors are unwilling to divulge sales prices, in part because this information is their stock in trade and in part because their 1.5 percent commissions (3 percent if they represent both buyer and seller) are based on actual market, while the presumably much lower "basic market" is the price declared at the notary and used by the realtors as the basis for calculation of their income tax.

The basic market price is set nationally by human settlement types I to VIII and by zones within each type,[215] with the price per square foot, in 1993, ranging from $0.03 to $0.49 (8 lev to 130 lev per square meter). The price is corrected by coefficients "reflecting the availability and the condition of the social and technical infrastructure, the transport access, the pollution, etc."[216]

### Asking Prices

Table 2.3 presents June of 1993 average asking prices for apartments for sale in some of the principal cities of Bulgaria.

**TABLE 2.3: AVERAGE APARTMENT ASKING PRICES, JUNE 1993**

| City | Dollars per square foot | Levs |
|---|---|---|
| Blagoevgrad | 22 | 5,891 |
| Burgas | 30 | 8,058 |
| Lovech | 15 | 4,033 |
| Pleven | 24 | 6,322 |
| Russe | 20 | 5,200 |
| Sofia | 43 | 11,397 |
| Stara Zagora | 21 | 5,406 |
| Varna | 31 | 8,262 |
| Veliko Turnovo | 21 | 5,520 |

In Sofia, asking prices were double those in six of the other cities and 50 percent higher than asking prices in the two Black Sea coastal cities, Burgas and Varna.

## Sofia Sales and Rentals

Only one source was found that compares asking prices and sales and rental prices.[217] While tables 2.4 and 2.6, prepared from these data and respectively reporting on sales and rentals, distinguish between areas of the city, they do not differentiate by apartment size for the sales units or by type of construction. It also is not clear whether houses as well as apartments are included in the sales data, nor whether the terms "housing estates" and "prestigious city" and "prestigious suburbs" together include all areas outside of center city. Table 2.5 presents sales data that are differentiated by location and type of construction. None of these sources estimates the volume of turnover in the period for which it is reporting.

**TABLE 2.4: SOFIA HOUSING, ASKING AND SALE PRICES, 1ST QUARTER 1993**

| Location | Asking Price | | Sale Price | |
|---|---|---|---|---|
| | Lev/sq.m. | $/sq.f. | Lev/sq.m. | $/sq.f. |
| Center City | 13,000-20,000 | 49-76 | 10,000-15,000 | 38-57 |
| Prestigious City | 14,000-21,000 | 53-80 | 10,000-15,000 | 38-57 |
| Prestigious Suburbs | 14,000-22,000 | 53-83 | 9,500-12,000 | 36-45 |
| Housing Estates | 7,500-9,500 | 28-36 | 7,000-9,000 | 29-34 |

There was little locational disparity in the asking price for units in center city, the prestigious city, and the prestigious suburbs. However, average asking price in the housing estates was only about half that of asking price in other locations. There was no locational disparity between sale prices for units in center city and in the prestigious areas of the city. This is somewhat surprising, since it is widely believed that center-city dwelling units are being sold for nonresidential uses at far higher prices than residential users can or will pay. Therefore, high asking prices and high sale prices for center-city locations might be expected. Both center-city and prestigious city units sell for around three-quarters of their asking prices. There is a gap of 40 percent between asking price and sale price of units in the prestigious suburbs. The asking price and the sale price for housing estate apartments show little disparity, suggesting that the units are quite uniform and that their market value is well known.

Table 2.5 presents sales data for 1992[218] for apartments, differentiated by type of construction and organized by district of the city.[219]

**TABLE 2.5: SOFIA AVERAGE APARTMENT SALE PRICES, 1992, LEV PER SQUARE METER.**

| District | 1 Room | | 2 Rooms | | 3 Rooms | | Over 100 sq.m. | |
|---|---|---|---|---|---|---|---|---|
| | Brick | Prefab | Brick | Prefab | Brick | Prefab | Brick | Prefab |
| 1 | 12,000 | — | 12,500 | — | 13,000 | — | 14,000 | — |
| 2 | 10,500 | — | 11,000 | — | 12,500 | 10,200 | 14,000 | — |
| 3 | 10,000 | 9,000 | 10,000 | 9,000 | 11,000 | 9,500 | 12,000 | 10,000 |
| 4 | 8,200 | 8,000 | 9,000 | 8,700 | 9,000 | 9,000 | — | — |
| 5 | 7,500 | 7,000 | 7,700 | 7,500 | 8,400 | 8,000 | 8,400 | 8,000 |
| 6 | 5,700 | 5,000 | 5,000 | 6,000 | 5,000 | — | — | — |

Several observations can be made about these data. Brick construction is preferred over prefabricated units, by margins that vary from $0.76 per square foot to $8.74 per square foot (200 lev per square meter to 2,300 lev per square meter) and show the least range in District 5, the location of the high-rise housing estates. Larger units bring a higher price per square foot (square meter) in all districts except the sixth, the outer suburbs. Price declines as distance from the center city increases.

In comparing the data in tables 2.4 and 2.5, Center City and District 1 are the same, Prestigious City is similar to District 2, Prestigious Suburbs are similar to District 3, and Housing Estates are the same as District 5. There is a close match of prices in all categories. In neither table is it possible to determine if housing is being sold for residential or for office occupancy.

For sales of plots of land (with no definition of size of a plot), there was a reported 50 percent disparity between asking and sale prices in the center city and a 13 percent disparity in the prestigious suburbs.[220] Land near Mount Vitosha, a scenic and desirable location, is said to sell for $3.80 to $4.90 per square foot (1,000 to 1,300 lev per square meter).

Rental data shown in Table 2.6 provide both asking price and rental price for apartments differentiated by size as of the first quarter of 1993.[221]

**TABLE 2.6: APARTMENT ASKING AND RENTAL PRICES,
IST QUARTER 1993, PER UNIT, PER MONTH**

| Size | Asking Price | | Rental Price | |
|---|---|---|---|---|
| | lev | $ | lev | $ |
| I BR, 50sq.m./500sq.f. | 1,800-2,300 | 68-87 | 1,000-1,500 | 38-57 |
| I BR, 65sq.m. | 3,000-5,000 | 114-189 | 2,000-3,000 | 76-114 |
| 2BR, 100sq.m. | 6,000-8,000 | 227-303 | 3,500-5,000 | 133-189 |

People are willing to pay about two-thirds more for a 650 square foot (65 square meter) rental apartment than for a 500 square foot (50 square meter) apartment. While they will pay 41 percent more for a 1,000 square foot (100 square meter) apartment than for a 650 square foot (65 square meter) apartment, the rent paid per square foot (square meter) is less. The disparity between rental price and asking price for apartments is between 61 and 63 percent.

The cheapest rental price shown here is $0.76 per square foot (20 lev per square meter) per month. For the very few people still renting municipal housing, the rate is between $0.038 and $0.11 per square foot (1 and 3 lev per square meter) per month. Unfortunately, the reports cited here do not provide information on the scale of sales and rentals. Given the high unemployment and low incomes, it is likely that most people, having acquired a home in prior years with the assistance of a substantial subsidy, are not now in the market, regardless of their level of satisfaction with their home.

## Agricultural Land

In 1992 the Institute of Agricultural Economics and Farm Organization suggested starting prices for agricultural land as a basis from which buyers and sellers might negotiate. The prices were based on 11 soil types and 250 subcategories that reflect production costs and crop yields. The prices range from $46 per acre (3,000 lev per hectare) to $460 per acre (30,000 lev per hectare).[222] "The experts tried to predict the influence of some market factors but make no claim to a high measure of accuracy as long as there is no real market."[223] Projected rents have been set, and information on the "ten most suitable crops for Bulgaria and other essentials for future land buyers or tenants" has been provided.[224] "The valuations are applicable when state or municipal land is sold, when landowners must be compensated for land lost to agricultural use, when land is allocated to poor or landless farmers, and as a guide for private landowners engaging in market exchange. But the main purposes for these land valuations is for future land taxation. . . . To what extent these prices approximate to those which would pertain in an fully active land market currently has to be a matter for speculation."[225]

As of May 26, 1994, there had been only 318 sales of agricultural land totaling 378 acres (153 hectares). All of this land was of poor quality for agriculture, and the new uses are to be urban—housing, small factories, and motels.[226] Since the prices were based on urban uses, they are not helpful in assessing the market for land for farming. Very limited information on farmland leases showed 320,000 acres (129,500 hectares) under lease at prices ranging from $1.90 to $23.40 per acre (200 to 2,500 lev per hectare).[227]

Two companies have listing services for those who wish to buy, sell, or lease: The Ministry of Agriculture and the Ministry of Construction participate in one along with a private company, and the other is a subsidiary of the newspaper *Bulgarian Farmer.*

## PUBLIC ROLES IN THE MARKET

The market for property, both urban and rural, will operate subject to influences emanating from the public sector. Taxes and regulations are prime examples. The government has made clear that the property tax is to be an important revenue source for the municipalities. Yet a functional, fair property tax is dependent on accurate land records. As the agricultural land restitution program vividly illustrates, a private land ownership system also is dependent on a reliable system of land records. One of the more time-consuming and expensive tasks of rural restitution and privatization in Bulgaria has been the establishment of a viable system of maps and land records. Until this system is fully in place, sales cannot be recorded properly; until sales are recorded properly, the creation of market based assessment data for land and building taxation is impossible.

State and local government land use plans and implementing regulations can be expected to affect land values as some lands are marked for rural uses and others for development.

### Land Cadasters and Records

The existence of a functional, current, publicly accessible cadaster showing all titles and boundaries is an essential foundation for the system. Bulgaria has undertaken to develop such a cadaster, with the U.S. Agency for International Development (AID) providing $10 million toward the costs of upgrading the 1939 cadaster.

Two components of a land registry system in the West are that transactions are a matter of public record and that the purchase price for property is accurately recorded. Bulgaria has not made a commitment to provide public access to records. Nor has the necessity for reporting of actual sales price been addressed.

In respect to urban land records, Bulgaria is in a more fortunate position than many other former Communist countries. Urban land records have been well maintained, although the Ministry of Construction does state that 15 percent of its properties have either cadastral and/or water supply problems. Land transactions are recorded at a city's Notary's[228] Office, with the transaction showing buyer's and seller's names, location, size, and "basic market"[229] price, or official rather than actual market price. Transactions are filed by name of owner, not by location. The Cadastral Office is separate, and, to learn of changes in land holdings, its staff must go to inspect the notary's records, a task undertaken only every several years. Records are entered by hand. Because delay in recording and lack of accurate cadastral records are problems for banks contemplating lending, several banks are considering providing the financing to update the system.[230]

Rural land presents a far more taxing problem, since most records had been destroyed and since, as a result of collectivization, few old boundaries remained. As discussed earlier, there have been substantial difficulties in establishing title to rural lands and in re-creating former boundaries. Once restitution is complete, rural land records will be available once more, and this time the records will be computerized with a geodetic survey base.

## Land and Building Taxation

Bulgaria currently has two land taxes in place: a transfer tax on sale and a tax on conversion of agricultural land. Neither tax, nor the proposed property tax, is based on market prices. A tax occasioned by land transfers is the income tax on realtors' commissions. This should be based on actual income; as reported earlier, it is not, since the realtors' practice is to report basic market as the transaction price. The value-added tax (VAT) does not apply to land transfers or land leases.

The Ministry of Finance levies the transfer tax on sale of realty at a rate of 9 percent. However, since the sale price declared to the notary is the "basic market" price, not the actual market price, the ministry is not collecting its due. While the law specifies that the seller should pay the tax, in practice it is split between buyer and seller.

The Removal from Agriculture Tax was adopted in 1973, based on a similar concept in Czechoslovakia. The tax is incurred on the conversion of agricultural land to nonagricultural uses. The tax, payable to the state, is calculated on the expected 100-year yield of the land for a given crop, one commonly grown in the area and suited to the particular soil. In 1973, of course, a state enterprise converted land to a non-agricultural use. The enterprise paid the tax to the state budget, and the funds were used to improve other agricultural lands. The tax rate is now about to be raised by somewhere between four and six times. Owners who are converting their land from agriculture rather than selling it pay only half of the tax levied in the case of sale.

The Ministry of Finance is proposing to institute a land tax, to be levied on land-owners and users, to serve as a source of revenue for municipalities. The tax would rely on basic market price, using eleven categories of land, with the tax rate linked to the category. Location, availability of infrastructure, and access to transportation all would be included as rural coefficients, and there would be a different set of coefficients for urban areas. Nonarable land, highlands, and state and municipal land (unless the latter two were rented for private use) would be exempt. Owners of restituted land would receive a five-year exemption starting from the date of issuance of title. Owners of orchards would be taxed when their trees started bearing fruit. Even if the actual market value was below this calculated market price, the tax would be levied on the basic market value.

When market prices did not exist, the role of the basic market price is apparent. As data about actual transaction prices become available, however, the taxing authorities would be well advised to levy the taxes on market prices. To achieve this, honest reporting of sales information is necessary.

## Land Use Planning as Market Regulator

Decades of living within the framework of state planning have left people loath to constrict whatever market forces for development there may be. Yet land use planning is in place and operational. During the Communist era, the state developed environmental and urban plans, as well as five-year economic plans and city master plans. These past plans, embodied in today's neighborhoods and networks, shape and constrain opportunities. In addition to the traditional role of the city architect's office in reviewing building plans, the state is now demanding more planning responsibility, particularly to protect natural resources.

### State Plans

The Country Planning Act of 1973 was the principal national plan for location of urban populations and for provision of urban housing. The plan projected the 1990 population at 9.4 million (the actual 1990 population was 9 million) and set target populations for each of five regions. "In 1970 there were great differences between the levels of urbanization in these regions, and the Act called for a more careful choice of investment projects, in order to reduce them. It is the intention that this should be achieved by 1990, when it is planned that forty percent of the working population in each region should be employed in industry and twenty-five in the tertiary sector."[231]

Another target was to provide individual dwelling units for each family by sometime in the 1980s. When the state failed to meet its own targets for housing construction, it made state enterprises responsible for building houses for their workers.

The need to protect natural resources was recognized in 1973, when seven national parks were designated, as well as numerous nature reserves and historic sites. In 1976 plans were set forth for protection of the Black Sea coast. And the eighth Five-Year Plan, for 1981 to 1985, called for creation of nature protection areas. In 1983 the state published a regional plan, which included maps of natural resources and of cultural and archeological sites. These maps are a base for current and future regional planning.

Today, no nationwide regional planning is under way, but there are projects for specific regions, of which the most prominent is that for the Black Sea coast. In 1993 rules were published governing land use near the coast.[232] The rules create two zones: One covers the beach, dunes, landmarks, and all land within 660 feet (200 meters) of the beach. Construction other than roads and waterfront development for resorts and piers is prohibited. The second zone covers farmland, recreation areas, natural landmarks, and parks as well as urban settlements within some 3 miles (5 kilometers) of the beach. The rules set procedures for development within this zone, including review for environmental impacts. The municipalities in the region are to conform their land use and land tenure plans to the state rules.

A regional plan is likely to be developed for the Danube, although some municipalities along the river want a free development zone, not plans that might limit development.

The European Bank for Reconstruction and Development funded development of a master plan for the port of Varna. The plan recommends improvements at the container terminal, including dredging for deeper draft ships and installation of modern container-handling equipment. The plan also recommends privatizing much of the port's activity, a step that requires action by the National Assembly. The plan is timely because Varna is a key port on the Danube-Main-Rhine waterway as well as a port with cargo links to Ukraine, Georgia, Russia, the Mediterranean, northwestern Europe, and the United States. Plan implementation would improve Varna's prospects of becoming a regional transportation hub.[233]

The National Land Commission became operational in 1993. Commission members include deputy ministers from appropriate ministries. In addition to its oversight of the municipal land commissions, it is charged with responsibility for evaluating whether nonagricultural or nonforest uses should be allowed on agricultural or forest lands. Its policy is to limit construction to towns and villages with infrastructure. The commission seeks municipal recommendations on conversion proposals, particularly as to the usefulness of the proposed development. About 10 to 15 percent of proposals are denied.[234] Municipalities may make their own determinations for projects under 2.5 acres (1 hectare).

## Planning in Sofia

Sofia grew rapidly and changed character under communism as industries and worker housing were built. The housing of the 1950s was mid-rise, walk-up apartment buildings with nearby parks, schools, and shops. Also in the mid-1950s a new city center was built, on the Soviet model, with the Council of Ministers, Communist Party headquarters, and the TsUM department store all located on Lenin Square.

The master plan, or GenPlan, of 1961 sought to accommodate the rapid population growth due to migration from the countryside. It was followed by the 1969 transportation and communication plans and then by the approval by the Council of Ministers, in 1971, of the revised GenPlan, which emphasized the northwest-southeast axis of the city.

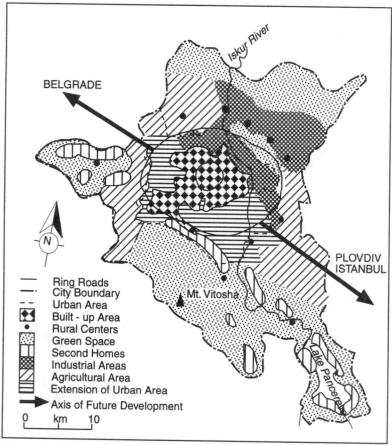

**Map 2.2 Plan for Future Development of Sofia, 1969**

By 1975 Sofia had built several housing estates for from 10,000 to 40,000 people, and the housing type had become predominantly high-rise panel construction. "Apart from relieving central-city congestion, these neighborhood units are also seen as a convenient social tool for planned urban development. The State is able to utilize official norms for size and services without class distinction, together with benefiting from mass construction. . . . One therefore sees in Sofia the application of the socialist model of spatial urban organization, whereby a series of such neighborhood units, situated around a political and cultural focus and within easy reach of some industrial plants, is able to retain the socialist planning principles of uniformity and predetermined size."[235]

Today's Sofia is a legacy of the Communist era planning and building. It also is shaped by a different legacy—its parks and tree-shaded boulevards. Including Vitosha National Park, which lies within the city's boundaries, 20 percent of Sofia is open space, making it one of the greener cities of Europe.

The Urban Planning and Building Act, often amended, applies to Sofia as to other municipalities. It is a confusing statute, and revisions are being proposed. The office of the chief architect still exercises rigid control of development within the borders of Sofia, often in the absence of clear land use regulations.[236] An architect presenting a plan to the office of the chief architect does have the opportunity to explain his concept and to seek reasonable amendment of the plan. It is not unheard of for money to change hands to obtain development permission. If a prospective building is to be three stories or less, one of the city's ten districts monitors construction.

Sofia, like other municipalities, is required to adopt a comprehensive plan after allowing opportunity for public comment; if it fails to do so, the 1973 national plan controls land use.

Sofia is authorized to plan for the forty-four villages in its metropolitan area but is reluctant to do so. Urban fringe planning lacks strong regulatory controls, and is open to scattered suburbanization.

## CONCLUSIONS

The choices that Bulgaria has made, should have made, or has yet to make concerning restitution and privatization are inextricably bound with its political, economic, and social Communist past and post-Communist present.

Bulgaria, as many other countries in Central and Eastern Europe and the former Soviet Union, is governed by a party—the Bulgarian Socialist Party— formed by erstwhile Communists. Many people in power are the same ones who held power during the Communist years. Their contacts and their experience in the workings of the old system enabled them to profit from and shape the new system. Successive BSP governments in which some of these individuals have had leading roles have blocked privatization, delaying action, diverting assets, and destroying popular confidence in the privatization process.

The current government has voiced a commitment to privatization and a strong market economy. Zhan Videnov, the prime minister, has stated that privatization is essential to economic recovery. There are expectations, in Bulgaria and abroad, that his government will deliver on its promises.

Prime Minister Videnov, President Zhelev, and the Constitutional Court have been engaged in a critical test of the division of authority among the legislative, executive, and judicial branches of government. During the Communist era the law was what the State Council and the secretary general of the party said that it was. Now, under the 1991 Constitution, there are explicit provisions defining the formation of and powers of the branches of government. The Constitutional Court was created to determine the validity of legislation in light of the provisions of the constitution.

President Zhelev had had recourse to the Constitutional Court four times as of mid-1995. In three of those cases, including one concerning amendments to the agricultural land restitution law, the court held that challenged legislation violates the constitution. Prime Minister Videnov and BSP members in the National Assembly have expressed anger that the constitutional test thus can overrule the wishes of the majority of the legislature. This is a critical time. Establishing the independence and authority of the judiciary system, including the Constitutional Court, is essential to building a strong, resilient democracy.

Regarding the provision of social services, medical treatment was free under communism. Housing was heavily subsidized, and unemployment—to the extent that it was allowed to occur—was compensated. Pensions were assured. Today much of this safety net has been withdrawn, and, where it is in place, there are insufficient funds in the national exchequer to meet obligations fully. The political success of the BSP has in large measure been due to its ability to gauge how far people are willing to risk their fragile security against a promise of a better but distant future. Past retrenchment on privatization promises may have reassured the electorate, but it has chilled the international lending climate. Choosing a course is fraught with difficulties, but vacillating is even riskier.

Under the Communists Bulgaria changed from an agricultural to an industrial economy. The efforts to industrialize agriculture, however, proved misguided, with both the land and the farmers suffering from the effects of giantism. As a satellite economy of the Soviet Union, production was geared to Moscow's demands. Now both agriculture and industry must be rebuilt. What the economic engine for this economy is to be is not yet evident. To date, only tourism and services are expanding, with many new service businesses being established. Foreign investment is very low when compared with that in other countries of Central and Eastern Europe. With the approval of the General Agreement on

Trade and Tariffs (GATT), one hope is that Western Europe will become a more accessible trading partner than at present. Yet excess agricultural production and continuing agricultural subsidies are serious problems for both West and East. Development of markets in the Middle East and restoration of former trading links with Comecon countries are under way but need strengthening. Economic indicators in 1995 are positive but fragile.

Housing is in private hands, yet the housing sector is stagnant and housing conditions are poor. A substantial portion of the existing housing stock is badly deteriorated, and new construction is at a virtual standstill. Prices are far beyond the buying power of most people, few housing subsidies exist, and mobility is limited. Yet, given the critical needs to privatize industry and to rebuild the farm structure, the government is choosing to defer investment in the housing sector.

Restitution of small businesses has been achieved successfully. Restitution of agricultural land may be a triumph for equity, but it threatens to be a serious impediment for agricultural efficiency. Bulgaria's historic pattern of small farms, reinforced by the 1921 and 1948 seizures of holdings over 50 or 75 acres (20 or 30 hectares), was fundamentally altered by the Communists' imposition of the cooperative and collective farms. Although the Communists may have been correct in believing that bigger would be better, much, much bigger proved much worse.

Now restitution is re-creating a pattern of small holdings but with many times more owners than before. With the 1.7 million claims representing some 4.6 million heirs, a majority of Bulgarians will receive a bit of land. Over 90 percent of the bits restituted so far are under 2.5 acres (1 hectare). Many of the restitutees are city dwellers, neither ready nor equipped to take up rural life. And their restituted land would be too small to support them anyway. Whether they will hold on to their land for symbolic reasons remains to be seen.

Reallotment of holdings is a first step toward more rational, efficient land management, particularly when it results in consolidated tracts. Some restitutees have insisted on restitution within former boundaries, but these are predominantly small tracts in mountainous areas. Far more land is being restituted through reallotment than through restoration of real boundaries, an encouraging outcome.

Formation of voluntary cooperatives is occurring, is compatible with farm management practices prior to communism, and is an appropriate step, in the Bulgarian context, toward restored agricultural productivity. The early move by some farmers to assemble larger holdings by leasing from those who do not wish to farm is another encouraging sign.

Progressing from gaining access to the land to the possession of title, which establishes the right to sell or transfer land, turns upon paying for a deed. If the parcel is only an acre or two and the restitutee has no intention of farming it, he or she has little motivation to pay for the deed. Because property transfer is very important, so that people who do not intend to farm can either sell or lease their land and assembly of more efficient tracts can begin, lowering the price of a deed to a nominal sum was a critical step for the government.

The BSP heralded the National Assembly's spring 1995 move to institute onerous restrictions on cultivation and disposition of land as an efficiency measure. The decision of the Constitutional Court that the new provisions of the law violated restitutees' property rights should ensure the completion of the restitution process. It cannot, of course, assure the reshaping of agriculture in the direction of efficiency.

Privatization under the Privatization Law did not start until 1993 and had made little headway by 1995. International lending agencies, in particular, have widely criticized the process and its pace. If it is true that up to 15 percent of industry was privatized either illegally or outside the intent of the law, and that the assets transferred in this way were among the stronger in the nation's economy, future privatization will present problems. Many industries face liquidation, presenting the specter of even more unemployment.

The Vidanov government has made a strong commitment to speed up privatization, relying on sales, share exchanges for bad debt bonds, and mass privatization. The voucher program may energize people to invest their very limited resources in enterprises with good prospects. Efforts to create such a program should not detract from efforts to encourage foreign investment in Bulgarian enterprises.

The large number of urban properties offered for sale is clear evidence of the emergence of an active urban market. The characteristics of this market in Sofia, so far, show a preference for more central locations and for larger units, as well as distaste for the high-rise prefabricated housing of the Communist period. More accurate portrayals of the market structure call for accurate public records, available to public scrutiny.

The rural land market is in an embryonic state, awaiting conclusion of restitution and provision of a credit structure.

Regarding land records, a modern cadastral system will be in place when the restitution process is complete. Building on that essential first step, it is vital to restructure the recording process so that land records are updated as transactions occur. Open access to land records is a high priority, as is a system that achieves honest recording of actual sales prices, not, as is current practice, the "basic market" price.

In the area of land taxes, both the existing transfer tax and the proposed annual property tax depend for their success on accurate data on market transactions. At present the transfer tax is collected by the Ministry of Finance. The municipalities need a dependable source of tax revenues, and the government's proposal to assign the revenues from the property tax to the municipalities is a logical step. Other steps would include assigning the revenues from the transfer tax to the municipalities as well and, when the structure is in place, authorizing the municipalities to collect the taxes directly.

Both national and municipal land use planning will be vital in creating a structure for future development. Institution of land use controls is important but is likely to be opposed by those who want freedom to develop what and where they wish.

The constitution, the restitution law, and the Black Sea coast law all show a laudable concern for protection of natural resources, including agricultural lands, forests, and sea coasts. It is important to enforce these laws and to secure local conformity with them.

## A Summing Up

There are many reasons for optimism about the future health of Bulgaria and, in particular, about the emergence of a stable land and housing market. Bulgaria is rich in agricultural and tourist resources and may have worthwhile reserves of offshore oil and gas. It is well situated to supply markets both east and west, and its transportation links, by water and land, are excellent. Despite decades of deprivation and upheaval, its people are positive in attitude. Restitution, for all its complexity and unwieldiness, has given some evidence of government commitment to fairness, a vital factor in building confidence.

It would be Panglossian, however, to overlook the many difficulties that Bulgaria faces. Dismantling unproductive industry and creating economically viable alternatives for the labor force is most critical. The voucher program for privatization may imbue citizens with a spirit of involvement in the economy, but it cannot save failed enterprises. Rebuilding a strong agriculture sector requires consolidation, yet this threatens to deprive more people of jobs. Finally, Bulgaria requires strong, competent leaders in government to plan and implement the transition.

## PEOPLE INTERVIEWED

**Alexander Bozhkov,** former Director, Privatization Agency, Sofia; now Deputy Leader, Union of Democratic Forces; also included here are excerpts from a tape commenting on a draft of this chapter, recorded by Mr. Bozhkov on January 7, 1994.

**Stewart Campbell,** Director, Project Management Unit, PHARE Program, Ministry of Agriculture, Sofia.

**Todor Gradev,** Center for the Study of Democracy, Sofia.

**Genovava Hadjidimitrova,** Deputy Director, State Savings Bank, Sofia.

**Michael L. Hoffman,** Advisor, U.S. AID Technical Assistance in Housing and Urban Development, Sofia.

**Dimiter Kebedjiev,** Head of Information Systems Department, National Centre for Regional Development and Housing Policy, Sofia.

**Maya Koleva,** MTK Consultants, Sofia.

**Theodor Kolarski,** Architect, Sofia.

**Diana Kopeva,** PHARE Program, Ministry of Agriculture, Sofia.

**Angel Kutsov,** mayor, and the chairman and members of the Liquidation Council, Tsveran Marincheshki, Stoyan Enchev, Dimiter Krantov, and Milyo Turgunski, village of Saedinenie.

**Gabriel Labbad, Georgi Petkov, Svoboda Tosheva,** and **Valentin Stoev,** International Bank for Investments and Development, Sofia.

**Alfred Levinson,** American University in Bulgaria, Blagoevgrad.

**Ivailo Mishev,** President, ATM Construction Company, Sofia.

**Nikolai Nikolov,** Secretary, Municipality of Hissar, and members of the Land Commission.

**Harlan Pomeroy,** Central and East European Legal Initiative, American Bar Association, Sofia.

**Villy Raykovska,** Senior Program Coordinator, Open Society Fund, Sofia.

**Lyuben Stoev,** American University of Blagoevgrad, Blagoevgrad.

**Lada Stoyanova,** Program Specialist, U.S. AID, Sofia.

**Mitio Videlov,** Head of Urban Planning Department, and **Slavtcho Yankov** and **Georgi Georgiev,** National Centre for Regional Development and Housing Policy, Sofia.

**Gerald Zarr,** Representative, U.S. AID, Sofia.

# 3

# LAND AND HOUSING PRIVATIZATION IN CZECHOSLOVAKIA/THE CZECH REPUBLIC

This chapter discusses the formation of markets and the privatization of real estate in Czechoslovakia in 1990-92 and in the Czech Republic into 1995. Restitution, or reprivatization, is virtually complete for urban property and well advanced for rural property. Privatization has been vigorously promoted and, except for state farms and forests, is also virtually complete. Yet much remains to be resolved. "Real" prices exist alongside administered prices and rent controls. New forms of ownership have been established but old ones persist. Many constraints limit the fledgling markets in real property. Some aspects of the process of market formation have been characterized as chaotic.

Reflecting on economic systems, Václav Havel, president of Czechoslovakia and now of the Czech Republic, has written: "Though my heart may be left of center, I have always known that the only economic system that works is a market economy, in which everything belongs to Someone—which means that someone is responsible for everything. . . . The attempt to unite all economic entities under the authority of a single monstrous owner, the state, and to subject all economic life to one central voice of reason that deems itself more clever than life itself, is an attempt against life itself . . . the only way to the economic salvation of this country . . . is the fastest possible renewal of a market economy."[1]

How has Czechoslovakia, then subsequently the Czech Republic in its first three years, from 1993 through 1995, and, in particular, the City of Prague, proceeded with privatization of real estate? After more than forty years during which land was considered to be a commodity without value and yet during which time much land and many buildings remained nominally private, the reestablishment of a market in land and in housing is a major undertaking.

This research is based on discussions with public officials in both the Czech and Slovak republics and in the cities of Prague and Bratislava; with research staff in private consulting groups and in academic settings; with local and foreign investors; and with American and British advisors on privatization. (At the end of this chapter we list the individuals who contributed to our inquiry and for whose help we are most grateful). We obtained data bases that reflect some of the recent changes. We reviewed available articles and laws, but must caution that much is still in transition.

## CZECHOSLOVAKIA AND THE CZECH REPUBLIC

### Government

Czechoslovakia became a nation in 1918, at the close of World War I and the fall of the Austro-Hungarian empire. Its establishment united Bohemia and Moravia (which had been under Austrian domination) with Slovakia (ruled for 1,000 years by Hungary, in turn becoming part of the Habsburg monarchy). Prague, the chief city of Bohemia and a major center in the monarchy, became the new nation's capital. Bratislava, Hungary's capital between 1526 and 1784, was designated as capital of Slovakia. The boundaries of the new state included substantial areas in west and north Bohemia and north Moravia inhabited by Germans, the Sudetenland. Portions of Slovakia were predominantly Hungarian.[2] Borders drawn in 1918 lasted only until 1938. First Nazi Germany seized the Sudetenland, with its largely German population. Shortly after, Hungary grabbed parts of southern and eastern Slovakia. Then Germany intervened again, establishing a nominally independent Slovakia under German control. A day later residual Bohemia and Moravia were occupied, and ruled, until the end of World War II as a German 'Protectorate.'

Map 3.1    Dissolution of Czechoslovakia, 1938–1939

Yalta and Potsdam clearly placed newly liberated Czechoslovakia in the Soviet sphere (with the small easternmost portion of the prewar state, Ruthenia, absorbed into the Soviet Union). The Communists exerted growing influence after 1945; the party won 1948 elections with a plurality and took full control in a coup in that year. Forty years of Communist rule under Moscow's domination began. "This era can be characterized by continual shortages, caused mainly by general weakness and ineffectiveness of the communist economy, by heavy arming, by conversion of the highly developed Czech machinery industry to war (mainly heavy) industry and last, but not least, by underwriting financial and material subsidies to the communist states or parties all over the world. The richness and western style of Prague has in this 40 years been slowly eroded, and a successive paucity of quality and image of the town—mainly because of inadequate or zero maintenance—has begun."[3]

During the brief "Prague Spring" of 1968, the late Alexandr Dubček became first secretary of the Czechoslovak Communist Party and sought to introduce "socialism with a human face": a third way that would lie between capitalism and communism. His six months of reform were crushed by the Soviet-led invasion by five Warsaw Pact countries in August. A few reforms survived invasion, including allocation to the Czech and Slovak republics (constituent units under the postwar nominally federal structure) of some powers formerly exercised centrally.

Communist rule did have some positive effects.[4] Social indicators showed upward movement. Major additions were made to the stock of housing and infrastructure, though often of low quality. Dwellings, allocated through nonmarket means, became available at very low rents. Data regarding income per capita showed that inequality was decreasing. Some caution is appropriate in assessing such information, however, without including noneconomic benefits, such as perquisites.

The government created in 1989, when the "Velvet Revolution" toppled the Communists, expanded the powers of the republics by transferring to them control over housing, the environment, agriculture, industry, culture and education, and the administration of justice. Other government functions, centralized during the forty plus years of Communist rule, were allocated to the lower levels of government and hundreds of municipalities.

By 1992 the giddy, heady optimism of the days after the Velvet Revolution was replaced with uncertainty; it peaked in mid-1992, with the resignation of President Václav Havel. The dominant concern in 1992 was the split between the Czech and Slovak republics. Petr Michalovič, a Slovak planner in Bratislava, voiced a widely held position in an interview: "It has been like a poker game among the politicians in which each player bluffed and then couldn't back down." Politicians negotiated the terms of the split, while bureaucrats at the federal level were quitting their offices and seeking new positions. Many Slovaks resented what they saw as decades of domination by the Czechs, and many Czechs felt that they had been carrying the Slovak economy. Yet a 1992 poll showed that only 25 percent of either group wished to separate.

Nevertheless, 1993 began with the creation of two independent nations, the Czech Republic and Slovakia. Havel was elected head of the new Czech Republic, which is governed by a four-party coalition, with Prime Minister Václav Klaus's Civic Democratic Party (ODS) dominant. Separate central banks and currencies were established. The full panoply of governance in each nation implements often distinct policies. For example, the Czech Republic has exhibited a greater commitment to industrial privatization The impacts of division, some of them on land policy, are still taking shape. Slovaks are in the same position as other foreigners in terms of purchase of housing and land in the Czech Republic.

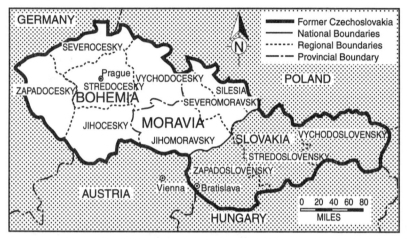

**Map 3.2    Czech Republic Political Subdivisions**

ODS favors creation of a large number of regional authorities, while its three partners seek creation of thirteen regions with a greater autonomy from the central government. At present there are eight regions and eighty-five districts in the Czech Republic. While the constitution requires regionalization, this appears to be a lower priority for the present regime.

The government of the capital city of Prague, while more complex than that of smaller cities, shares with them a common framework. The city, governed by a mayor and city council, is divided into ten districts, each with a mayor and council. The ten districts occupy all the land area of the city—193 square miles (495 square kilometers). Some districts are further subdivided into forty-seven municipalities, each also with a mayor and council.[5] The municipalities are former villages, added by annexations in 1967 and 1972, and therefore exist in the outlying districts only. These former villages retained some autonomy, although there is confusion as to its extent. Further annexation is unlikely because of resistance from the now-outlying municipalities.

Considerable overlap among the powers of the cities, the districts, and the municipalities fuels the usual conflicts over land use decisions between those who have a whole-city perspective and those with more local concerns.[6]

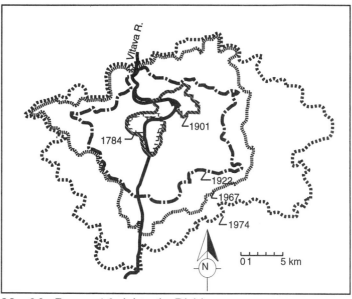

**Map 3.3    Prague: Administrative Divisions**

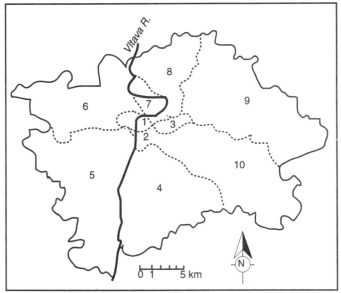

**Map 3.4    Prague: Development of Administrative Area**

## Population

Czechoslovakia in 1992 had a population of 15.6 million, two-thirds of whom lived in the Czech Republic. About 300,000 Slovaks lived in the Czech Republic; 50,000 Czechs in the Slovak Republic. In addition to Czechs and Slovaks, the population included 600,000 Hungarians in Slovakia. About two-thirds of the area's 500,000 Gypsies live in Slovakia. The Gypsies, or Rom people, effectively are the underclass, poorer in income and housing and suspect by many.[7]

How the split of Czechoslovakia into two nations will affect the population distribution is not yet clear. Over 300,000 Slovaks have applied for Czech citizenship. Czechs living in Slovakia can keep Czech citizenship; most apparently have done so. As of 1994, the population of the Czech Republic was 10.3 million.

Many people still live in rural areas and small towns; this is particularly true in Slovakia where, as of the 1991 census, half the people lived in the countryside or in towns with fewer than 10,000 residents. Almost one-third of the population lived in cities of 50,000 or more. The major cities are Prague, with 1.2 million people (1.7 million in the larger Prague region); Bratislava, with 445,000, or about 10 percent of Slovakia's population; Brno, with 393,000; and Ostrava, with 332,000.

Population growth has been and is low, although relatively few people were able to emigrate over the past half century. In 1991 the number of births was the lowest since World War II. The population is aging, and households are smaller. Consequently, the number of households is increasing, which contributes to unsatisfied housing demand, especially in large urban areas.

## Land

Czechoslovakia had four broadly defined regions, distinct in terrain and resources. Bohemia is to the west, with Prague at its heart. The dominant character is gently rolling land offering broad vistas of fields and forests; mountains edge the region to the south, west, and north. Moravia, with Brno its major city, is similarly structured. Silesia, with Ostrava as its main urban area, is to the north, and is rich in coal mines and steel mills. Slovakia is to the east. This is the most diverse region, with rich bottom land along the Danube where Bratislava, the capital, is located. North are vast fields, and farther north high mountains, the Tatra range, along the Polish border. Lower mountains cross much of central Slovakia.

Thirty-seven percent of the former Czechoslovakia was cultivated and 36 percent forested.[8] The most fertile soils are in the south, including the bottomland along the Danube River and the lowlands of South Bohemia.

## The Economy

After the Communist downfall, Czechoslovakia showed the highest economic indicators in Central and Eastern Europe, consistent with its prewar situation.

Gross national product (GNP) per capita was $2,360 in the Czech Republic and $1,840 in the Slovak Republic as of 1991 ($4,370 and $3,020 respectively in 1995).

Gross domestic product (GDP) fell immediately after the Velvet Revolution, by 14.5 percent from 1990 to 1991. From 1993 to 1994 it was up 3 percent, and up 4 percent in 1995. However, with 1989 as 100, GDP only had reached 73 by 1994. The private sector has been growing rapidly, accounting for 65 percent of GDP in 1994, up from 4 percent in 1990.[9] The average annual income (1991) was $1,920 (51,600 koruna).[10] By 1994 it was $2,880.

Foreign investment in 1991 was $1.73 billion with U.S. investors supplying 29 percent and German investors 17 percent. In 1995 it was $2.3 billion with the ratios about reversed. Over 90 percent of these funds were invested in the Czech Republic.[11] Growth rates in exports and imports have been high, and show the best record in Central and Eastern Europe.[12] In late 1992 the Czech and Slovak republics entered an agreement with Poland and Hungary to establish a free trade zone, which should be fully operational in ten years or less.[13]

Inflation, suppressed under the former regime, reached 56.6 percent in 1991. It was brought under control and was only 11.1 percent in 1992. It rose to 20 percent in the Czech Republic in 1993, largely as the result of the adoption of the VAT (value-added tax) with a rate of 23 percent. Inflation declined significantly in 1994 to 10 percent and is now under control. Wage controls were introduced in 1993. Consumer prices increased by 10 percent in 1994.[14]

Unemployment, virtually nonexistent before 1989, was 4 percent in the Czech Republic and 12 percent in the Slovak Republic in 1991. This difference, which continues, is largely due to Slovakia's prior heavy dependence on military production and exports to the Soviet Union. The Czech Republic's unemployment rate was 2.6 percent in 1992, 3.4 percent in 1993, 3.5 percent in 1994, and 2.8 percent in 1995,[15] a rate that is expected to rise as inefficient state firms are privatized and new managers cut their bloated work forces and as the bankruptcy law, enacted in 1993, comes into wider use. Counterbalances to these forces are the wage controls and the flow of jobs from the West. With wages only about 10 percent of those in Germany, for example, there has been a steady flow of jobs to the Czech Republic as well as to Poland, Hungary, and Slovakia.

By 1992 most prices were set by the market. Land and housing rents are among the major exceptions. Certain services, including health and transport, also are still controlled, as is the cost of fuel. A typical household spends 27 percent of income on household goods and clothes; 25 percent on food; 17 percent on taxes and insurance; 14 percent on rent services and repairs; 16 percent on savings and repayments of loans; and 1 percent on other expenses.[16] The 1991 census showed the following distribution nationally of conveniences among households: color television, 56 percent; car, 44 percent; automatic washing machines, 43 percent; telephone, 30 percent; and weekend house, 10 percent. In

Prague, the figures are higher: for example, 28 percent of families have weekend houses, a reflection of the population density and living conditions in the city.

Also as of 1991, the average dwelling unit had living space of about 470 square feet (47 square meters) and the average living space per person was 160 square feet (16 square meters). In the Czech Republic, the average single-family house includes four bedrooms and a kitchen with a total area of some 1,500 square feet (about 150 square meters). Typical flats cost around $8,000 (200,000 koruna) in the 1980s, but in the early 1990s they sold for $20,000 (500,000 koruna), well beyond the reach of most people. By 1994 they cost about double.

Housing vacancies vary by location, with the figure 9 percent nationally but only 3 percent in Prague. There are empty buildings in some areas. Some factories that owned apartment buildings are defunct and the apartments vacant. In portions of northern Bohemia and other regions, half of the flats are empty or occupied by squatters. Some of the housing in the countryside is too run down to rehabilitate, though it is occupied.

With a sharp reduction in government support of housing, construction fell to less than 10,000 units in 1993, down from about 70,000 in 1990. Some 15,000 units were completed in 1995, and that figure is expected to be half again as high in 1996. Most of the recent buildings, however, are bought by the affluent (often foreigners); are located in the periphery of cities, especially Prague, and thus require infrastructure investment; and intrude into agricultural land. A further consideration is the significant recent improvement to the housing stock through modernization and rehabilitation.[17]

Agriculture in the Communist period was almost totally socialized, organized either as cooperatives or as state farms. Although the state farms were substantially larger, there were fewer of them. The cooperatives were responsible for two-thirds of agricultural production on about 85 percent of the land, the state farms for one-third. Unlike other socialist economies, Czechoslovakia was self-sufficient in food, and farm workers were well paid.

The Czech Republic is an industrialized state; in 1994 agriculture made only a small contribution to GDP—five percent—and accounted for only 6.9 percent of the labor force, both as of 1993. Agriculture has problems: In 1993, losses in this sector totaled $320 million (8 billion koruna) and production has declined. Private farms are increasing; as of mid-1993, there were 38,000 of them. Of these, 8,000 are over 25 acres (10 hectares) and 735 are over 250 acres (100 hectares). The latter constitute 55 percent of the land in private farms.[18]

## LAND AND HOUSING POLICIES FROM 1918 TO 1989

Land ownership patterns have been transformed repeatedly, both prior to and during the Communist era, to match shifting ideologies and due to the effects of occupation and war. Who owned land, what the concept of ownership meant, and, for rural areas, the size of parcels have all varied markedly.

## Early Democratization

In the 1920s, Czechoslovakia under Tomáš Masaryk nationalized the land of the predominantly German and Hungarian nobility, who owned tracts in the range of 25,000 acres (10,000 hectares). This land was redistributed to the peasants and recorded in their names, thus creating a pattern of small and mid-size farm holdings. Vast holdings of the Catholic church were left intact.

## Expulsion of the Sudeten Germans

With the close of World War II, when victorious Allies redrew boundaries, Sudetenland and southern Slovakia were once more assigned to Czechoslovakia, essentially reestablishing pre-1938 borders. After the years of German occupation, the Czechs were eager to be rid of the German presence. As a result, between 1945 and 1948, some 2.5 million Czechs of German ancestry were expelled from the Sudetenland and approximately half a million Czechs of Hungarian ancestry from Slovakia, under a decree issued by President Eduard Beneš in 1945. No compensation was paid. Under the law of June 21, 1945, 122,000 Czech and Slovak peasants were given the land that had been expropriated—paralleling the situation in Poland. They did not keep it for long.

## Communist Land Policies

To the Communists, land ownership was repugnant as a concept and irrelevant in practice. What mattered was the right to use land, and this was determined by the government. Socialist property law distinguished between property rights accorded to classes of users. The state and state-owned entities had an "ownership right of operational administration" even if ownership title was not included in the bundle of property rights.[19] Lower in the hierarchy were cooperative property, as in agriculture, where all use rights were transferred to cooperative farms; personal property such as the single-family residence a person could own; and private property. The last, such as means of production and private urban real estate, was seen as an unwanted residue of capitalism. The distinction between title and use rights was and remains a central issue.

## Rural Policies

Two-thirds of the land remained nominally private throughout the Communist era, the largest part in farm cooperatives. Even though the owner retained title, and this title may have been shown on the cadaster, owners of 97 percent of farmland had no use rights. The exception, in which farmers had both title and use rights, was very small tracts in mountainous areas.

Beginning in 1945, with the Beneš decree, the government began seizing control of land and allocating small plots to peasants. As of 1948, the Catholic church owned 6 percent of the country's agricultural land and hundreds of estates, monasteries, and churches. These properties were taken and incorporated as part of state farms. The monks and nuns were imprisoned, sent to camps, or directed to work in factories.[20] Over the next forty years, farm policy shifted from encouraging use by individuals farming small plots, to forcing collectivized agriculture both in cooperative and state farms, to bowing briefly to farmer demands for household plots, and then to forced collectivization on an even vaster scale.[21]

The smaller plots created by the first postwar reforms, mainly in the Sudetenland, were soon recognized to be nonviable. Government policy thereafter reversed course and, in the 1950s, peasants were forced to place the land in cooperatives. Since the peasants had originally been attracted to the area by the right to their own land, many saw no reason to stay and returned to their native villages. Criminals and Gypsies pressured to work on the co-ops became part of a poor labor force farming poor land under a poor management system.[22]

The co-ops peaked in number in 1960, when there were over 8,000 of them, averaging 940 acres (380 hectares) each. In the 1960s, responding to pressure from the farmers, each farmer was offered 1.25 acres (0.5 hectare) for his own use. Then, in the 1970s, policies changed again, and some of this land was reabsorbed into the cooperatives as part of a scheme to make them much larger, spanning up to twelve villages. However, in areas where the land was most arable, the government faced strong opposition from the farmers, whose resistance prevented it from taking their small parcels. By 1980 only around 1,000 cooperatives were in existence but each averaged some 6,000 acres (2,460 hectares).[23]

The number of state farms, principally located in the Sudetenland, fluctuated, from 183 in 1950 to a high of 270 in 1960, dropping to 184 in 1990. Each farm grew larger, attaining an average size of over 18,000 acres (7,350 hectares) in the 1980s.[24]

One outcome of farm policies on cooperatives and state farms was that the state-dictated production targets could be met only by depleting the soil and using too much inorganic fertilizer.

> The Communist regime, guided by the ideological doctrine of parity between rural and urban areas, treated agriculture as a single giant industrial plant, and turned farmers into employees. . . . [V]illages ceased to be true villages and become more like dormitory communities for agricultural laborers. . . . Animals were moved from pastures and well-kept stables laid with clean straw into vast factory barns where they stand in stalls on metal grates, often never seeing the sun or having the run of a meadow in their entire lives. . . . The land was polluted with chemical fertilizers. Plowing under the strips and hedge

rows dividing the fields and introducing heavy machinery led to the destruction of the ecological balance, to erosion, and to the disintegration, compacting, and deadening of the soil. . . . All this must be changed. . . . First of all, our villages will once again have become villages, modern and pleasing to the eye. . . . Agriculture should once again be in the hands of the farmers. . . . In part, these will be small farmers who have been given back what was taken from them; in part, larger family farms; and in part (and a large part, at that!) modest cooperatives of owners or commercial enterprises. The gigantic cooperative enterprises are not working and should be divided and transformed.[25]

Forest management plans have been in effect since the time of Maria Theresa in the mid-eighteenth century.[26] Prior to 1948, there were many private forests, but the majority belonged to the state, municipalities, and nonprofit groups such as the Catholic church. Starting in 1948, the state seized private forests, and clear-cut and replanted them.

## Socialization of Urban Properties

The predominance of public ownership and control was a reaction to very real shortcomings and limitations associated with the *ancien regime* and the inequities of industrial capitalism. But it is now generally conceded (and was certainly known by many in the past) that the Communist system was ineffective, inefficient in allocating land and housing. It failed to raise living standards of the bulk of the population and erected many impediments to labor force mobility, which is a requisite of a growing industrial society. In part these troubling and unwanted outcomes were the result of administrative procedures that sought to replace markets with clearly spelled out standards and criteria. But the inefficiencies were also the consequence of systemic failure. In particular, as land and housing had no real prices, they came to be over- or underused. For example, older, central areas were underutilized; upkeep lagged; and industrial users kept an excess of land for their own uses.

## Housing

Ownership of housing in apartments, the predominant urban dwelling type, became subject to major shifts as socialist ideology shaped policy. Almost total socialization was achieved within the first postwar decade. Single-family houses and widely held second homes remained private. Together these constituted about one-third of the nation's stock of dwellings, particularly in small towns and rural areas. Owners of these properties, which constituted the house and its curtilege, could sell them freely. In Prague, in addition to single-family houses, which constituted 5 percent of the stock, an additional 5 percent of apartment houses stayed in private hands.

During the Communist period, the state was the principal builder of housing. The newly constructed units were placed in the hands of municipalities and enterprises. The state also acquired private units, administratively assigning households to them. Cooperatives played an important role, and individuals were able to construct single-family units.

The Communist-era housing stock additions were mass-produced apartment blocks (so-called *panelaky*), made of prefabricated concrete, and clustered on the periphery of cities and even smaller towns. During the 1960s the government began building high-density settlements of up to 100,000 people each on the urban fringe. Using heavy machinery, series of identical structures were built of standardized components which were manufactured off-site.[27] While these apartments are well equipped, with central heating, elevators, and bathrooms, they were badly built, often leaky and drafty. They constitute sterile dormitory areas with few jobs nearby and generally lack services, shops, and amenities. People do not like them and, where possible, flee on weekends to cottages in the nearby countryside. This "prefabricated housing . . . was directly based on the standard Soviet form . . . there was effectively no choice of construction system, which in turn produced rigidly uniform rectilinear blocks."[28]

By 1958 it was evident that the state was incapable of providing housing for everyone. The waiting time for a state-owned apartment could be up to ten years, unless one belonged to the nomenklatura or some other favored group. Such delays led to a black market in housing. To secure a larger apartment or one in a more desirable location, people advertised in newspapers and offered bribes of several thousand crowns per room. Households possessing more than one apartment were the source of the black market supply. For example, a married couple might obtain one apartment through the public waiting list or their employer and another by inheriting from a deceased relative.[29]

Housing cooperatives were authorized as a practical and ideologically acceptable measure to increase supply. Some cooperatives were unsubsidized, but most relied on state assistance. For the latter, funding came one-third from the state, one-third from members when they joined, and one-third from the members over time. The state gave a thirty year, 1 percent credit to cover this final one-third share. The nominal interest levied on co-op purchase together with the sizable state contribution for such units provided major support to the middle-class population. For years only the interest on the housing loans to cooperatives (and to single-family home builders) was paid back; now the principal is coming due for many owners, who generally lack the means to repay it. Members were required to put in sweat equity—3,000 hours of labor per person. Despite this inexperienced labor, these units were better built than those built by the state. During the 1970s and 1980s, these early co-ops were merged with other co-ops as a part of state pressure to hold control over all institutions in society.

The state's role in housing construction continued to be substantial until the 1980s, when it declined sharply. From 1986 through 1990, 5.11 dwelling units were built per 1,000 population. Only 24 percent was state and municipal while 42 percent was cooperative and 32 percent private. ("Other" constituted 2 percent.)

There was little maintenance and rehabilitation of the housing stock, which is consistent with the low priority given services in contrast to production in Communist countries. Rents were controlled and set at uniformly low levels for the entire Communist period.

### Enterprises

Socialization of industrial and most service establishments began immediately with the first postwar government. By the 1950s, public ownership was almost complete.

A major owner on the Prague urban fringe is the city-owned Company for Prague Construction, which forced people to sell their property to it during the 1970s and 1980s, augmenting the city's land bank. The city turned the land over to a state farm, the Company for the Farms of Prague. This company farmed the land until the city architect's office (the municipal planning body) authorized the Construction Company to build. In fact, the Communist Party decided when land would be developed or when some small parcels would be sold to a privileged few, such as party officials.

## RESTITUTION, TRANSFORMATION, AND PRIVATIZATION

Today, private ownership has again assumed significance. The right to own land is recognized as a basic right. In 1991 Czechoslovakia adopted the Council of Europe provisions, which are somewhat analogous to the U.S. Bill of Rights. Known as Law # 23-1991, it assures protection of ownership, be it state, cooperative, or private. The socialist preeminence accorded state ownership was abolished in 1992 by amendment to the 1964 Civil Code.[30] Restructuring and privatization of enterprises has been a priority of post-1989 Czechoslovakia and the successor Czech Republic, although Slovakia appears to be less ready to undo government ownership and control. Of course, privatization has significant consequences for the distribution of land and housing.[31]

The overall process of restoration of property rights in Czechoslovakia and the Czech Republic involves three partially concurrent, partially successive processes: restitution, transformation, and privatization. Restitution returns property to those with claims to assets taken by the state in the process of socialization. Governments may not retain lands otherwise subject to restitution if there is no specific enabling law. Thus, if there is a restitution claim, a city cannot retain land planned for a new metro stop or a school. Similarly, the Company for Prague

Construction holdings are now subject to restitution claims. Transformation alters the structure of cooperatives, where use but not ownership rights had been taken, to give members a direct say in their management and clearer ownership. Privatization transfers property to new owners by one of several means, including auctions, sale, and participation through vouchers. Once rights have been restored, expropriation may occur only if authorized by a specific statute.

Restitution, transformation, and privatization are complex processes, and each is linked to the other. There is as yet no government document that summarizes their outcomes; we attempt such a summary later. Transformation was completed in 1993; restitution and privatization continue into 1996.

## Restitution[32]

Restitution is the process of honoring claims of individuals and/or entities whose property was taken with no or inadequate compensation. Issues that require resolution are: From what date will claims be honored? Who may claim? To what are the claimants entitled—the property itself, or equivalent compensation? Only after restitution claims are resolved can the privatization of property still remaining in state hands occur. All types of property—housing, farms, forests, and enterprises—have been subject in one manner or another to restitution claims. By the end of 1994 the resolution of these claims was not complete for farms[33] and forests but was largely complete for other properties except where an extension of the claim period into 1995 has delayed the process.

Czechoslovakia made a commitment to restitution on moral grounds; in the words of then Deputy Prime Minister Pavel Rychetsky: "Persecutions and confiscations were more intensive here than in neighboring countries, with the exception of the Soviet Union, so there is greater moral awareness about the propriety of returning property. Seizures were carried out in violation of the law as enacted by the Communists. Some people were evicted on short notice and some were sent to hard labor for the 'crime' of belonging to the 'enemy class.'"[34]

The moral argument was paralleled by the position that restitution was a sure way to reduce the scope of government, enlarge the private sector, and assure among a large part of the population commitment to the new order.

A number of restitution acts are in effect, passed in 1990 and 1991, with some subsequent amendments. In order of passage they affect church nonagricultural lands, small businesses, many nonagricultural properties taken after 1948 (large-scale restitution), and agricultural cooperatives to the extent that title was taken from former owners, state farms, and multifamily housing. None of the acts provides for restitution of any property taken prior to 1948.

The cutoff date has enormous significance. Much property was taken for public use between 1945 and 1948 by the interim democratic regime in which Communists played a key role. German and Hungarian owners, seen as wartime perpetrators, and losers, experienced major takings of property,[35] as did capitalists and the Catholic church. These were not subject to restitution. Jewish losses under German occupation also are excluded.[36]

Some 100,000 ethnic Germans and Hungarians remained, and their land was confiscated by the Communists after they came to power in 1948. In 1991, Czechoslovakia adopted a set of provisions promulgated by the Council of Europe that, among other assurances, states that the right to own land is a basic right. In 1990 and 1991, restitution laws were passed, justified on moral grounds as well as by the desire to increase the role of the private sector. None of these laws provides for restitution of property taken prior to 1948, under the Beneš decrees, and this remains a source of conflict between Germany and the Czech Republic. The Czech Constitutional Court, in 1995 and 1996, has, however, upheld the rights to property restitution of those Czechs of German and Hungarian ancestry who lost their property after 1948. The Court, overruling lower court decisions, interpreted the restitution law as stating that such claimants, whether or not they for a time were stripped of their citizenship by the Communists, are entitled to restitution. Thus a minority that still feels discriminated against in the Czech Republic has had its rights upheld.

The courts are overloaded with restitution claims and there are not enough judges to handle the cases. With the private-sector demand for lawyers and higher pay, it is difficult to interest competent lawyers to be judges.

### Church Properties

One of the first moral claims honored was that of the Catholic church. After considerable public debate, the first restitution law was enacted in 1990, at which time properties, but not agricultural land, were offered to the church. Many holdings had deteriorated so badly that the church did not request their return. In other cases, the structures were being used as museums, or some other public or charitable facilities, which makes transfer "complicated."[37] Agricultural land, and in particular the highly valued 600,000 acres (240,000 hectares) forests which the church holds as its economic base, had not been returned as of the end of 1995. Prime Minister Klaus and his Civic Democratic Party are adamant that property taken before 1948, including some church property, will not be restituted. The issue remains unresolved into 1996.

### Small-Scale Restitution

The small-scale restitution law, passed in October of 1990, applies to about 80,000 properties taken by the state between 1948 and 1990.[38] (The major seizure of property came in the 1950s.) The properties were mostly family businesses such as rental houses, shops, and restaurants. "Everyone felt that it would be very troublesome to sell this kind of property in an auction since the former owners were often still living in the same house with his/her former shop, pub, etc. That is, continuity of ownership in these cases was usually not completely broken."[39] Prior owners (individuals and legal entities) and their heirs who were Czechoslovak citizens and Czech residents were eligible to file claims.[40] Foreigners could claim restitution if their claims had not been resolved by international treaties. Claims had to be filed prior to April 30, 1991, or by individuals, August 31, 1991. Once the claim was filed and proof of title established, the property was returned or compensation was paid.

Successful claims were established for about 30,000 properties.[41] In Prague, less than 50 percent of eligible enterprises were claimed in restitution. No figure is available on value of property returned through small restitution.

There are several situations in which the property as such was not returned. If no claimant survived, or if the claimant lived abroad and did not return, there was no eligibility. If the property had been improved since seizure, the restitutee had the choice of claiming the property and paying for the value of the improvements, or receiving indemnification. Conversely, if the property had deteriorated, the title holder was entitled to compensation in cash up to $1,200 with any remainder paid in bonds or vouchers for purchases of shares of former state enterprises. If formerly open land had been built upon, the former title holder may receive only indemnification. If the state had sold the property to a private person, the former title holder was entitled to the purchase price paid by the private person or the price under indemnification, if this was the larger sum. Implementation of these principles varied from case to case.

In the present period of transition, there remain three types of housing ownership: municipal ownership of former state housing (including buildings formerly held by state enterprises),[42] private housing, and cooperatives. As of the 1991 census, there were 5.3 million dwelling units, of which about 2 million were municipally owned, 2 million were private, and 1 million were in cooperatives. Some of the former state housing was subject to restitution claims.

Apartment houses that have been restituted present serious problems.[43] The owner has the right to claim one flat for his family but must find a comparable flat for a sitting tenant in order to require the tenant to move. This leads landlords to evict tenants by cutting utility services or refusing to repair. As of 1994,[44] apartment building owners could sell units so long as they gave the sitting tenant the right of first refusal. This provision, however, does not enable landlords to terminate leases of tenants occupying the unit under a pre-1989 lease.[45]

## Large-Scale Restitution

The law governing restitution of properties, including realty and immovables, was passed in February 1991.[46] The law applies to individual citizens, including émigrés who returned to live in Czechoslovakia prior to January 1, 1990, whose property was confiscated after February 25, 1948, and prior to January 1, 1990. Although there was some support for choosing an earlier cutoff date, the "principal motivation for using 1948 as the cut-off was to avoid the problem of the property belonging to the Sudeten Germans. . . . If the cut-off line were to fall before 1948, the German issue would have to be addressed, opening an extremely sensitive political problem."[47]

The deadline for claims was September 30, 1991. In July 1994 the Constitutional Court overturned the provision of this law limiting claimants to citizens resident in Czechoslovakia. Nonresident citizens were given until May 1, 1995, to file claims.[48] Claims under this act must have been made and resolved prior to any actions under the Large Privatization Law. More than 250.000 claims were filed not including those that may be filed under the extension for nonresident citizens, with a total value of over $2 billion (50 billion koruna).

As with the provisions for restitution under the Small Enterprise Act, claimants had a specific time in which to file proof of title. Disputes over title could be taken to the Ministry of Privatization and then appealed to the courts.

### Industrial Enterprises

Some 1,400 claims for restitution of industrial property were presented for a value of $1 billion (25.5 billion koruna), or 3.6 percent of the total value of Czech industrial property.[49] As of 1993, restitution accounted for only 1.8 percent of the value of industrial property returned to the private sector as of 1993.[50] Shares were restituted in 613 enterprises, and restitutees also were given preferential acquisition rights to shares in 129 enterprises. The government's early estimates were that 10 percent of state-held property, worth over $10 billion, would be returned under this law.[51] Actual enterprise restitution to date has come to $640 million (16 billion koruna).[52] Owners of about 60 percent of Czechoslovakia's large enterprises, including Bat'a shoes and Škoda automotive works, were not eligible for restitution because they were compensated when the factories were taken in 1945 or because nationalization took place prior to 1948.

Owners of shares in large enterprises who were entitled to restitution receive compensation. The initial 30,000 koruna ($1,200) is paid in cash and the remainder in shares initially paid from the Federal Fund of National Property and subsequently from the Czech or Slovak Funds of National Property. All of these funds are segregated from the general budget. All enterprises must deposit shares representing 3 percent of their assets in the appropriate fund.

### Farms and Forest Lands

Agriculture was heavily subsidized during the Communist period and continues to receive some subsidies. Wages have been good, and there are incentives to maintain aspects of the current system. The debate regarding restructuring of agriculture has been protracted and final disposition of state farms still is not complete.

Restructuring of agriculture takes two distinct forms. For state farm holdings, there is first restitution. Where there are no claims, as is the case with most of the state farm holdings, the farm property then is subject to privatization in the same manner as other state enterprises. For cooperative farms, the primary means has been transformation, but there also has been some restitution.

As of the end of 1994, most of the privatization in the agricultural sector has been by means of restitution.[53] The Privatization Department of the Czech Republic Agriculture Ministry sees restitution as a priority. The majority of potential claimants filed on time.

In the Czech Republic, there were about 250,000 claims, often representing many heirs, for agricultural restitution. Of these, 88,000 were for property on state farms, valued at $840 million (21 billion koruna); 11,000 were for co-op farm property, valued at $760 million (19 billion koruna); 145,000 were for forests; and a few were for other types of property.[54] Many farmers or their heirs did not file claims because it would take too much capital—which they cannot raise—to make their former farm efficient. Most claims were granted.

The Land Records officer makes restitution decisions. While few cases are rejected outright, more difficult claims are pushed back in the pipeline. Proof of title is difficult to obtain because of the incomplete records; thus an amendment to the farm restitution law states that the contract of sale may be used to show probable ownership.

There are 316 state farms and agricultural enterprises with a book value of $1.9 billion (48 billion koruna); claims to this property were 43 percent of this total book value. As of the end of September 1993, property valued at $550 million (13.7 billion koruna), or 65 percent of the value of all claims, had been restituted. As of early 1995, two-thirds of all agricultural claims were said to have been settled. If the land claimed had been urbanized, the restitutee was given either land of equal value for farming located elsewhere or compensation based on farm value. The Ministry of Agriculture is responsible for organizing reallotments where restitution leads to ownership of multiple tracts.[55] Prior to amendment, the law limited to 150 hectares (375 acres) the amount of arable land that could be returned. Now there is no limit. However, as of the end of 1994, about 80 perent of claims settled were under 12.5 acres (5 hectares).

State farm restitution continued into 1995. One complication is that some land in state farms does not belong to the state, because it was taken from cooperatives and added to state farm holdings. Sorting this out has led to delays. Another complication relates to farms in the former Sudetenland, where the Czech claimants held the land only from after 1945 to the early 1950s. Most of the large state farms were created on lands confiscated there. With the Constitutional Court's rejection of the Sudeten German claims, restitution there can proceed. Another delay resulted from the 1994 Constitutional Court decision allowing nonresident citizens to claim and giving them until May 1995 to do so.

As previously described, most farmers who were forced into the cooperatives did not lose title to their land; therefore, restitution to co-op members mostly involves compensation for chattels and particularly machinery. Nonetheless, there were over 11,000 claims, totaling $760 million (19 billion koruna), of which $500 million (12.7 billion koruna), or 67 percent of the total claimed, had been settled as of the end of September 1993.[56] Restitution claims under the law applicable to cooperatives were honored for lands and other assets seized after February 1948 and before January 1, 1990, the same period as with state farm restitution. Claims, however, did not have to be filed until March 31, 1993.[57]

Few of the perhaps 3 million people—20 percent of the population—who became landowners through restitution or otherwise are actually farming,[58] as restitutees need not promise to continue farming. New owners by way of restitution seem to be interested in selling their property. Many of the restitutees are city dwellers who have few links to the land, which they would just as soon sell as lease. Yet, who would buy? While there is not much demand, there is a large supply of land. Among other problems, many of the plots are small and noncontiguous. Thus, most of those whose lands were restituted rent the property to cooperatives or to a newly emerging group of entrepreneurs and companies. By the end of 1993, these latter farm enterprises owned about 35 percent of agricultural land, with the co-op share declining to below 50 percent.

When leases are made, land rent is decided on by theoretically free negotiated agreement, generally at about 1 percent or less of the land "price" per year. This is not the market price; it is a price officially calculated by ministerial decree. This decree, "Oceňování půdi" [pricing of land], was issued by the Ministry of Finance in 1991 and was in force until 1995. Its avowed purpose was to establish the basis for the land tax (the user pays the tax) and was applied at the scale of large cadastral units. Beginning in 1995, taxes will apply to specific plots. It is not yet clear to what extent such assessments will reflect "real value" as distinct from "market value".

In general, it is the owners of large farms who are ready to continue with farming. Ministry guidelines support this: Farms on the order of hundreds of hectares would appear to be optimal, as a result of the infrastructure needed. Some small farmers who have recently seen their lands returned do want to make a go of it but are not sure how. One possibility appears to be some form of reconstituted cooperative. The firm Terra Bohemica is ready to serve as a management consultant for such restituted property owners as well as for state farms.

### Forests

About 40 percent of the 6.5 million acres (2.6 million hectares) of forests were private before 1948 and potentially subject to restitution claims.[59] In fact, forest lands were subject to more claims—145,000—than any other type of rural property. Unlike agriculture, where little external demand for products currently exists, there is substantial demand for wood from Austrians and Germans. A Czech Forest Fund has been set up, similar to the Land Fund, to hold and distribute restituted forests. As of mid-1993, property worth $290 million (7.2 billion koruna) had been restituted. Decisions remain to be made as to how much of the rest, much formerly church-owned, will be privatized and how much will remain in state or local ownership.

**Natural Resources Land**
Land with mineral resources will not be restituted, but prior owners will receive equivalent parcels or compensation instead. In national parks, former owners can reclaim their land but must then use it in accord with park management plans.

## Transformation

The Law on Agricultural Cooperatives (the so-called Transformation Law) was adopted at the end of 1991;[60] in May 1991, the law governing restitution of cooperative lands was passed.[61] It is important to understand that cooperative members continued as de jure owners, if not de facto. Under communism, exercise of use rights on land had been blocked. Current law envisions several possible futures for the cooperatives: in particular retaining the cooperatives but, in effect, as tenants of the owners. There was much debate over the provisions of this law, with some calling for total privatization and others arguing on behalf of those who worked the farms but owned no land. Shares in the cooperatives are issued on prior holdings or work. "[M]embers of the existing cooperatives (about 400,000) who did not contribute their own property but would become hired laborers after 20 or 30 years of work in these cooperatives. At present members of cooperatives receive a share in income on the basis of their performance and their pay does not reflect whether and how much land, cattle or machinery they contributed to the cooperative."[62]

Each co-op was required to design a scheme for reorganization into one of three types of entities—a limited liability company, a joint stock company, or a cooperative—by the end of 1993. The Ministry of Agriculture was not directly involved in their transformation, although if the co-ops failed to adopt a plan, in a few cases the ministry withheld their subsidies. The co-ops themselves are responsible for changes through councils formed by each. Other than conforming to general land reform regulations, they were free to proceed as they wished.

The co-op determines its asset value and sets aside 25 percent thereof; the remainder forms the net property. In distributing shares to this net property to three categories of entitlements—co-op members who contributed labor only, co-op members who contributed land and/or chattels, and nonco-op members whose property was taken—contributed land is to be valued at 50 percent of net property, with allocation of shares based solely on size of the former holding; contributed capital, usually chattels, at 30 percent; and labor participation, measured in years of work, at 20 percent. The 25 percent withheld first was offered for sale to all people in the above categories at 1,000 koruna ($40) per share.

Any shares not subscribed in this offering could be bought by anyone. There is some concern that this system will lead to splintered ownership of the co-ops, making management difficult.

By the end of 1993, 1,205 old cooperatives were transformed into 1,658 new entities. Of these, 1,092 were new agricultural cooperatives and 181 trading cooperatives. The remainder were reestablished as other types of cooperative, joint stock companies, and limited liability companies. Only 20 co-ops failed to transform themselves; these are being liquidated. The average size of the new co-ops is about 4,400 acres (1,800 hectares).[63]

## Privatization

In 1991 ownership of small state-owned enterprises was turned over to the municipalities. Under this provision, some apartment houses were transferred to municipalities, including state-held apartment buildings where two-thirds or more of the interior space was occupied by housing and for which there were no restitution claims. They may not be sold, since there is no law providing for such sales. The law transferring assets to municipalities also removed price controls on commercial space, so that the municipality is able to lease to the highest bidder.

State properties not restituted under the programs just described and not turned over to municipalities are being sold by the state through two privatization programs, one for small enterprises and one for large enterprises. Small-enterprise privatization occurs by auctions of properties, while large privatization relies on submission of bids, with some shares of each enterprise's stock reserved for voucher sales and for distribution to employees. Small-enterprise privatization is far advanced; large-enterprise privatization also has converted many of the state firms.

Real estate has a central role to play in the privatization process,[64] as the one asset sure to be valued. Many of the factories, shops, and service establishments are burdened by antiquated or ill-suited machines and equipment, inappropriate product lines, and inventory with no demand and intangibles with no value. The space and location from which a new business can be operated which establishes the worth of the property to be privatized.[65] At the same time, the one factor in short supply for the opening of a new enterprise is an attractive and suitable venue. Given the proportionately little space devoted under communism to commercial and service activities, a shift to the market economy implies the need to change land and space use as well.

### Small-Enterprise Privatization

Consider Havel's description of small-enterprise privatization:

> In 1990, I was present at a meeting of our three governments (Czech, Slovak, and Federal) to decide on the basic outlines of a law on small-scale privatization. I supported the notion that employees in businesses that were to be auctioned off should be allowed certain advantages, in the form of either preemptive purchasing rights or loans at lower interest rates. My reasoning was based on a fear that the attractive businesses would be bought up by people who had come by their wealth in highly suspect ways (members of the former Communist nomenklatura, black-market currency dealers, and the like) and the less attractive would remain unsold, a burden on the state. . . . On the other side, many arguments were brought forward supporting a version of the law in which all interested parties would be equal, just as their money was equal, and no one would be given any advantages just for having worked in a particular business for a certain period of time. . . . A vote was finally taken, and the position I supported was defeated by a small majority. . . . The auctions have been successful. . . . Many businesses were indeed purchased by their employees. On the other hand, I often hear complaints that 'all the power is being given back to the Communists.'[66]

Small businesses that were not restituted had to be sold at auction. Nationwide in the former Czechoslovakia this constituted approximately 50,000 enterprises. The auctions were held by the 100 district Privatization Commissions in a two-round process, with the first round held early in 1991 and the second round beginning in mid-1991 and continuing through 1992. After the auctions, well over 10,000 units remained which were added to entities disposed of in large privatization.[67]

A reservation price, the Ministry of Finance book value for land and cost less a low depreciation rate for buildings, was set for each property. While principles of the process were set by the Ministry of Privatization, implementation was by the National Property Fund.

Only Czechoslovak citizens were eligible to bid in the first round. Bids were not accepted unless they were for at least 50 percent of the assessed value of the property. Successful bidders could not resell their property to foreigners for two years. Over 20,000 small businesses were sold in the first round, some 13,000 in the Czech Republic and some 7,000 in the Slovak Republic. Businesses that did not sell in the first round were offered again in the second. Eligible bidders included current or former citizens or foreigners with permanent resident status. In this round the sale price had to be at least 20 percent of assessed value.

Proceeds from the auctions were split with 70 percent going to the republic and 30 percent to the local government where the property is located.[68] While only about one-fourth of sales included real property in the first stage, by the end of 1992 half of the properties and three-fourths of the privatization receipts were from properties that included real estate.

The City of Prague is a key actor in privatization. For some enterprises the city was the founding organization; for others it acquired the asset after 1989. Such enterprises include factories, appliance repair shops, even a state farm on the city's edge. Holdings include unbuilt land that was owned by a state company. While residential real estate has been transferred to localities, more than half of nonresidential properties remained in state hands in 1993. The city will ask for transfer of such property as well.

The city did obtain at no cost industrial land (formerly owned by the steel works ČKD) in Dolní Počernice, which has given the municipality the opportunity to develop the urban fringe. Another project involved a factory in poor condition in D'áblice; the project is to build a new urban center there. There are indications that the Ministry of Privatization does have some "social" criteria, inasmuch as Prague was said to have fought hard to get these holdings. The city seems to have been advantaged because the proposals were consistent with the master plan.

By 1993, the city received privatization schemes for some 53 enterprises where it was the "founding organization" or originator; and for another 500 or so projects where it was not. Proposals that embodied some social purpose, or where the property would allow use as appropriate substitute for activity in a restituted building are said to be given an advantage. Responses to bids are not solely on the basis of price.

The market has been reborn in Prague, with auction prices varying dramatically by location.[69] In the first round in Prague, a floor of $0.80 per square foot (200 koruna per square meter) was set for the auctions. Enterprises on Charles Street near the Charles Bridge, a favorite tourist haunt in the Old City, sold for as much as $10 per square foot (2,500 koruna per square meter). Department stores, especially those that are effective monopolies in the newer, *panelaky* areas, brought very high prices at auction.

Since the auctions there have been substantial changes in character and intensity of uses in the center.[70] However, where the purchaser acquires a shop providing basic services, the city requires that at least a semblance of these services continue to be offered. "When a shop is located in a free standing building the whole property can be sold, very often including the land. This case accounts only for 11 percent of all auctions in Prague. . . . In the majority of auctions . . . only a lease is offered. . . . The reason of this is that small businesses are usually located on the ground floor of residential buildings, and the state attempts to avoid splitting of buildings among several owners. Nevertheless a five year lease is guaranteed for a new owner by law since the property was bought at an auction. Only leases were sold in the center of Prague in 1991. In this area of the city average sales price was more than twenty times higher than starting price."[71]

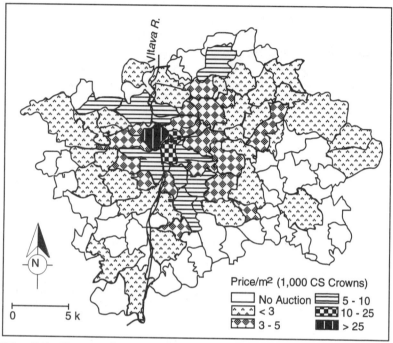

**Map 3.5 Prague: Small Privatization Auctions, 1991–1992: Average price for non-residential premises**

The fifty-to-one difference between the prices paid in the auctions for one square meter in the center and in the outskirts shows both the value of a central location and the absurdity of equal prices of land or rents under the socialist system.[72]

For Prague, where less than 50 percent of the small enterprises were claimed in restitution, the process of privatization sales is largely finished. Sales were primarily to Czech citizens, although there are reports that foreigners acquired property illegally through straw parties. The sales data are said to be inaccurate, though the differences just mentioned appear to be consistent with other information.

The city continues to own buildings and can transfer certain rights to districts. It must give approval before the district privatizes a structure. Citywide procedures exist, but districts do have considerable leeway whether they keep or sell. The motivation to sell is high, since maintaining and repairing residential property is costly, and public bodies lack funds.

Housing privatization principles that apply to the City of Prague and to its districts (as adopted by the Council) anticipate that 20 percent of the transferred housing will remain in municipal ownership, to be used for social purposes, with the remaining 80 percent privatized. The policy, stressing "preferential rights of tenants," is to offer a sequence of opportunities: first to a legal entity created by tenants occupying more than 50 percent of space; if not interested, then to a similar entity of tenants occupying less than half the space, or to a lessee of non-residential space (provided this exceeds 10 percent of space and is not used by a foreign, state, or similar enterprise); if not interested, then the housing remains the property of the city, whereupon it can be offered in public bid.

Tenants' organizations pressured the Prague mayor's office in 1993 to give tenants more rights. The municipality agreed to keep a building if a tenants' legal entity did not buy, thus precluding public bid. The tenants' organizations feared that if only one tenant offered to buy, he or she might be backed by speculators and the price offered could be less than would be generated by a public bid.

Proceeds from real property sales are distributed with 50 percent to the city, 10 percent to the district, and 40 percent to the fund for reconstruction and maintenance and environmentally friendly heating systems.

## Large-Enterprise Privatization[73]

Large-enterprise privatization is critical to the restoration of a healthy market economy. It is the focus of much external technical assistance and the activity most discussed in the international press. State farms and industries are covered under this law. However, since land ownership is a relatively minor aspect of industrial privatization, and, since the focus of this study is land and housing, our discussion of large-enterprise privatization is brief.[74]

The Large Privatization Act[75] was passed in February 1991 and took effect in April 1991. The legislation contemplates that enterprises would be privatized in two near-term bidding waves, in subsequent bidding a few years later, and by liquidation. It applies to the almost 5,000 large enterprises with annual incomes ranging from $50 million to $500 million. All such enterprises except the railroads, nuclear power plants, and telecommunications facilities are subject to the law. By mid-1993 over 4,000 of these enterprises had been privatized.[76]

The privatization process for state enterprises is as follows. The current managers prepare a plan for privatization; others interested in acquisition also may prepare a plan. These plans may draw upon the Ministry of Privatization's current data about the enterprise; this information, by law, is available to all interested parties although current managers are said to benefit from inside knowledge. The plans may propose privatization by direct sale of assets, by auction, by public tender, by transfer to municipalities, by offering to employees, and/or by voucher. To the extent that direct sale or public tender is chosen, interested parties prepare bids. Finally, the winning bidder is chosen not solely on the basis of price but also on such bases as retention of labor force and current site. While the process is under way, the assets of the enterprise are held by the National Property Fund.

Table 3.1 provides data on the status of large-scale privatization in the Czech Republic as of December 1993.[77]

**TABLE 3.1: LARGE-SCALE PRIVATIZATION IN THE CZECH REPUBLIC, DECEMBER 1993**

| Method of privatization | Percent of enterprises | Dollar value (millions) | Koruna value (billions) | Percent by value |
|---|---|---|---|---|
| Auction | 6.8 | 232 | 5.8 | 0.7 |
| Tender | 6.7 | 768 | 19.2 | 2.2 |
| Direct sales | 22.3 | 1,852 | 46.3 | 5.3 |
| Joint stock company | 23.6 | 30,172 | 754.3 | 86.5 |
| Unpaid transfers | 30.8 | 1,200 | 30.0 | 3.4 |
| Restitution | 8.1 | 260 | 6.5 | 0.7 |
| Restitution with buy-in | 1.7 | 380 | 9.5 | 1.1 |
| **TOTAL** | **100.0** | **34,864** | **871.6** | **100.0** |

Several items are of note: While the municipalities received almost one-third of the enterprises, their value was relatively low; the next largest number of enterprises were transformed into joint stock companies, which were by far the most valuable of the enterprises; and restitution played a small part both in the percent of enterprise assets and the value of the property.

An early example of successful privatization was the June 1991 sale of the Rakona Company, the nation's largest soap and detergent maker, to Procter & Gamble for $20 million. The Ministry of Privatization chose Procter & Gamble over three other bidders, in part because it agreed to invest an additional $24 million to upgrade the plant and install environmental controls.[78]

Foreign investment is governed by the new Commercial Code[79] which provides for creation of joint ventures with Czech citizens or companies through joint stock companies, limited liability companies, and partnerships, as well as several other forms of organization.[80] Foreign investors are screened for suitability by the Ministry of Privatization; expatriate experts are on staff.

Vouchers have been issued as the principal means to make shareholders of Czech citizens and to create a market based on supply and demand. "Of the three East European pioneers, Czechoslovakia has proceeded furthest down the road of using voucher privatization to distribute state property in an egalitarian manner. . . . Since voucher privatization of one sort or another is either under way or seems certain to be attempted in most of the post communist economies, the Czechoslovak experiment is potentially of great regional significance."[81]

The Czech Republic has recommended that from 20 to 30 percent of the shares of a corporation be reserved for acquisition through the voucher system, while the Slovak Republic has set a figure of 35 percent. At the end of 1993, however, 45.5 percent of the assets of joint stock companies had been allocated to vouchers.[82]

Every Czech citizen over eighteen, resident in the country, was entitled to purchase vouchers, worth 1,000 points and priced at 1,000 koruna ($40). After a slow start, 80 percent of those eligible, or 8.5 million people, bought vouchers. Most of the voucher holders participate in bidding for shares of one of 800 mutual funds that have been organized to invest in the market. Most chose to trust their points to the mutual funds; some funds offered the bonus of small loans to those who invested all of their points in them. For example, the Czech Savings Bank offered loans of $350 at 16 percent interest and attracted long lines of customers. "The funds offered to make investments for their customers. As a come-on, they pledged to buy back any shares they bought for a customer for 10 or 15 times the $35 the customer paid for his privatization coupon. It was a fair bet. They expected two million people to take part, and that would make each coupon worth roughly $5,000 in terms of the total book value of all the companies on sale. But the response to the offers was huge: 8.5 million people bought coupons, and handed 70% of them to the funds. . . . With such an abundance of coupons, the value of each one is just $1,130—not $5,000. Yet the funds are stuck with their original repurchase promise."[83]

Investment firms are limited to holding a maximum of 10 percent of the equity of a joint stock company.[84] They also may not trade more than 5 percent of their assets on the secondary market of either the Prague or Bratislava stock exchange. Other than this, in 1993, their operations were not subject to administrative supervision. "It remains to be seen whether the private investment funds and other institutional investors now appearing in Czechoslovakia can effectively control the managers of privatized firms. It is also unclear how the government will ultimately regulate the funds. So the Czechoslovak approach seems problematic both in terms of administrative viability (efficacy) and in terms of the kind of capital allocation this approach is likely to produce (efficiency).[85]

Market action progresses through a sequence of waves and rounds. Stock in all companies in a given wave is offered at the same price. The first wave began June 1991 and included 2,210 firms, including two state farms. In the first round, which ended in June 1992, 1,492 companies were available for purchase (988 in the Czech Republic). All shares offered were offered at three points. Ninety-two percent of the 8.53 billion points were bid in the first round, 5.84 billion by the mutual funds and 2.02 billion by individuals.

The success rate in buying shares was 40 percent for the funds and 32 percent for individuals. If the bids are at a price 25 percent or more higher than that set, the vouchers are returned and the company is placed in the next round at a higher price. This was the case for 421 companies in the first round. The Hotel Jalta in Prague, for instance, was priced at 300 points per share in the second round.[86] If the bids received are fewer than the number of shares offered, shares are issued to those who bid at the stated price, and the excess shares are offered in the subsequent round at a lower price. This proved true for 1,022 companies in the first round. Supply and demand, at the price set, were even for 49 companies. In the first round citizens could bid for shares in companies regardless of their location. In that round, Czechs acquired 2.6 million shares in Slovak firms and Slovaks acquired 7.5 million shares in Czech companies.[87] "While Czechs and Slovaks thrust their coupons at good-looking Czech companies, nobody is wild about Slovakia's losers, least of all their own workers. Invest in this company?' asks a man who tends machinery at a transistor plant in the town of Piestany. It's in trouble. The price is going down.' The plant has shut for a forced holiday; it hasn't made a sale in three months. When privatization is complete, all it will have is a mob of owners who got their shares for a song. It will have no capital, and no future."[88]

The second wave took place in 1994. Almost 900 companies were privatized then, including 185 not sold in the first wave.[89] The second wave did not include any state farm properties. "By August 1993, only 99 privatization projects out of a total of 1,414 proposals for these 316 state farms had been approved. . . . For all these reasons, state farms have been removed from the second wave of coupon privatization."[90]

These 99 projects represented only 33 percent of the total value of the property of the farms that remains to be privatized. As of 1994, the estimated value of state farm properties awaiting privatization was just over $1 billion (26 billion koruna). In 1995 the state still owned 10 percent of the land of the Czech Republic; of this, 500,000 hectares (1,250,000 acres), or more than half, will be offered for sale. Preference will be given to neighboring property owners and farmers with only Czechs eligible to buy. In the interim, the property was under lease, usually to its former managers.[91]

## Housing Cooperative Privatization

In the past co-op housing units could not be freely sold. (They were transferred conditionally to a new member.) But the price was in fact a negotiated one, not openly stated. Exchange was, and continues to be, premised on the notion that the co-op remains the owner.

July 31, 1992, was the deadline for co-op members to request that their flat be transferred to them as private owners. However, the person making the request must immediately repay his share of the outstanding debt of the co-op. Further, the co-op's agreement with the bank that provided the loan requires immediate repayment of the entire loan at current rates if there are ownership changes. The state, which owned the banks, formerly provided a subsidy so that the rate of interest was 1 percent. Now these subsidies are over, and the current rate is 9 percent. Since this repayment provision obviously would have effectively foreclosed transfers of co-ops, the Ministry of Finance agreed to continue the subsidy rate for co-op members not wishing to reclaim title while requiring any co-op member requesting title to repay his share of the loan at the current rate.

In some co-ops as many as 90 percent of the members are seeking title to their flats; in other co-ops the figure is around 40 percent. This is a clear reflection of people's desire to escape from the co-op structure and management and, probably more important, to be able to sell their flats at last.[92] At the moment there is no capital gains tax, so, for instance, owners who can pay off the debt on a flat for 50,000 koruna and then sell it for 150,000 koruna, have a real incentive to do so.

## Restitution, Transformation, and Privatization: An Overview and Summary

It is not possible to provide an accurate summary of the transfer of real property from the public to the private sector. Sources differ widely on data, and it is extremely difficult to find reporting for comparable times and events. Some data are for Czechoslovakia, some for the Czech Republic; some claims are for items such as cows and tractors, some for land; some tables summarize the number and value of claims, some the number and value of property actually returned. Value is usually book value, not market, although where property was offered for sale in privatization, the data could reflect market price. Much is still in progress: The municipalities have not finished implementing policies on privatization of housing; state farm and forest restitution is continuing; some additional restitution claims have yet to be processed; and enterprise privatization is not complete. What is clear is that ownership has become widely diffused through a combination of transformation steps. About 25 percent of all Czechs now own farm or forest lands, up from 2 percent before 1990.[93] Most of the remainder is farmed by restructured cooperatives.

Restitution has three components: church property, small restitution, and large restitution. For church property, almost no data have been found on the number of properties either claimed or returned, or on their value In calculating the amount and value of property restituted under both small and large restitution, it must be recognized that an unspecified amount of property was transferred by the state to the 6,000 municipalities. This property included apartment buildings; land, sewer, and water systems; and transit systems, with an estimated value of at least $14 billion (350 billion koruna), of which $1.2 billion (30 billion koruna) in value is attributed to large enterprises.[94] How much of this property then figured in either small or large restitution is not clear.

Small restitution for Czechoslovakia consisted of the return of some 70,000 apartments and 30,000 businesses; how many were in the Czech Republic and what their value was is not known.

Large restitution for the Czech Republic includes industries, rural enterprises, and natural areas. For industries, there were 1434 claims valued at $1 billion (25.5

billion koruna).[95] Rural enterprises include three subcategories of property: state farms, cooperatives, and forests. Here the data are explicit as of late 1993. For state farms, which in 1990 totaled 2.7 million acres (1.1 million hectares), there were 88,000 claims valued at $840 million (21 billion koruna). This would result in creation of farms averaging 31 acres (12.5 hectares).[96] Property valued at $550 million (13.7 billion koruna) had been restituted by the end of September 1993.[97] There are two aspects to privatization of the cooperatives: transformation, affecting most co-op property, and also restitution, with 11,000 claims for property valued at $760 million (19 billion koruna), of which $500 million (12.7 billion koruna) had been restituted as of the end of September 1993. There were 145,000 claims for forest land valued at $620 million (15.5 billion koruna); by mid-1993 property valued at $290 million (7.2 billion koruna) had been restituted.[98] No figures on the amount of natural resource lands claimed or their value are available.

The bulk of the 6.2 million acres (2.3 million hectares) of land in the cooperatives was transformed into new, voluntary co-ops averaging 3500 acres (1400 hectares) in size.[99] This land now is part of the market system; what its value may be is not known.

Privatization, like restitution, is divided into small and large, with the dividing line here roughly set at $50 million (1.25 billion koruna) in annual income. The share of real property in the total privatization process is not known.

Small privatization affected some 40,000 enterprises in Czechoslovakia, of which 22,000 in the Czech Republic were sold for about $1 billion (25 billion koruna).[100] Enterprises not sold through small privatization were transferred to the large privatization program. Large privatization concerned some 5,000 enterprises in Czechoslovakia, including the state farms; the estimated value of these enterprises was $23.9 billion (597 billion koruna).[101] As noted earlier, large privatization also included the firms that did not sell through small privatization. In the Czech Republic, as of December 1993, 30 percent of the enterprises (though these only account for 3.4 percent of the value of all enterprises) were transferred to the municipalities. Another 9.8 percent of enterprise shares were restituted; these constituted 1.8 percent of the value of the enterprises. Transformation of the enterprises into joint stock companies accounted for 86.5 percent of the value of all enterprises, and for these joint stock companies, voucher privatization covered 45.5 percent of the value. State farm privatization has lagged, awaiting completing of restitution. In 1994 the estimated value of state farm property awaiting privatization was over $1 billion (26 billion koruna).[102]

## THE NASCENT REAL ESTATE MARKET

It is difficult to describe the market for real estate in Czechoslovakia and the Czech Republic for several reasons. First, while privately held dwellings now constitute the majority of units, a large part of the land still remains in public hands. Second, a wide range of impediments (such as sitting tenants and rent control) burden most property from the perspective of present or potential owners. "The still unclarified and legislatively unsettled property rights of a considerable part of the agricultural land and the lack of sales of state land form significant obstacles to the development of a rigorous and properly functioning land market. This is further hindered by the unfavorable economic situation of the agricultural sector."[103] Third, price information is hard to come by, as market prices are but one of a set of valuations for a given property and generally are not available in the public domain.

The best information available on the evolution of real estate markets is for urban property, particularly in Prague. Therefore here we focus on how Prague has changed in the last years and how several price systems exist side by side. "The Prague area is going to explode. There already are some 137,000 second homes in the nearby countryside, many of which are of good quality and can be converted to year-round housing. At retirement, many people will migrate out to these houses or to villages. The *panelaky* will become housing for the poor and criminals, just as they already are in some western European cities."[104]

There are 500,000 housing units in Prague, mostly apartments, although 13 percent are single family houses. Housing consists of four types, located in roughly concentric rings: the core. The inner city, the outer city, and rural areas.

The core, the historical district, provides apartments for 6 percent of Prague's residents; over half of this housing predates the twentieth century and virtually all the rest was constructed prior to 1939. Population has been declining here.

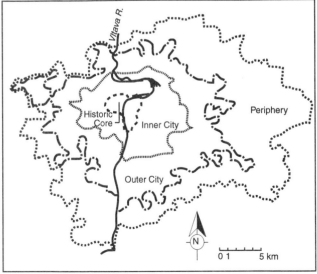

**Map 3.6    Prague: Urban Zones**

However, the demand for nonresidential space for offices and shops is intense. This is especially so in the 2,500 acres (900 hectares) that constitute the central Prague protected area, the largest historical preservation district in the world. One result of the pressure is that new functions are drawn to the area: For example, the number of offices and shops is increasing. Residential space, however, is declining. There are conflicts: while investors may seek high, quick returns, cheap renovation is at odds with historical values. And there is the social issue of whether the present residential tenants (often, but not exclusively, pensioners) are being equitably treated. "To bring a dwelling in an historic building up to the required standard costs . . . from five to ten times the cost of new suburban construction. Furthermore, renovation usually results in halving the number of dwellings provided, due to regulations on living space, sanitation, and associated conditions."[105]

The inner city, built from the mid-nineteenth to mid-twentieth centuries, is a dense mix of working-class and middle-class housing, much of it in acute need of modernization, plus shops, theaters, factories, rail yards and storage depots, and some institutions.[106] This area covers 7,500 hectares (18,750 acres), and half of the city's residents, or 600,000 people, live there.

The outer city has twice the area of the historic core and the inner city combined. It consists predominantly of *panelaky,* built in large clusters for up to 100,000 residents. Half a million people live here, but many must commute elsewhere to work.

The fourth area, beyond the ring road and the metro, is still rural in character. Its 50,000 residents live mostly in single-family housing in small communities.

There is a shortage of housing in Prague, in part because households have been becoming smaller and because there has been some total growth in the population, and in part because people who have flats in the core and inner city do not relinquish them. At death the right to a flat is inherited; if a person has no heir and shares the flat with someone serving in a caretaking position for at least three years prior to death, that subtenant then "inherits" the flat lease. Any unclaimed units escheat to the city, which is widely reputed to take bribes to sell them, usually for offices, since their price—not subject to rent controls—is higher. Another factor is that in the Communist decades, many city housing units were allowed to deteriorate—by one estimate, in numbers equal to one-half of new construction. Other units were converted to commercial and other uses.[107]

Rents in the core and inner city were set in the mid-1930s and a ceiling was established in 1938. In 1953 currency reform resulted in cutting rents by a factor of five. Even with the slight increase in 1963, the doubling in 1992, and the deferred 40 percent increase for 1995, rents would need to be increased perhaps five times to approach market price. Only then would rents justify investment in repairs and maintenance. (Services such as garbage collection, water supply and even elevators may be priced as the provider chooses and added as fees to rents.)

Management and maintenance of housing will improve as privatization advances. Already several districts in Prague have contracted with new, private firms to manage housing stocks. These private firms take the place of the former government agency charged with repairs but notorious for its failure to make them. District 7 has hired six private firms to do the work. The charges for services by these firms vary from area to area; some have a fixed fee per apartment for management and a different fee for maintenance, while some allocate a percent of rent for management and maintenance.[108]

Through 1989 the central part of Prague was characterized, by far greater residential use and associated services (retail trade) than that found in cities of Western Europe. In the past few years, there has been a rapid infusion of commercial spaces, such as offices and shops catering to much larger markets and to tourists which has led to much pressure on center-city tenants to vacate their residences. The transition to a use, density, and rent structure more characteristic of that found in capitalist nations has been rapid.[109]

With the rigid land use regulations and agricultural policies in place under the Communist regime, the limits of the urban areas (in Prague and elsewhere) were characterized by a sharp break from high-density *panlaky* settlements to active agricultural use. Given the more flexible position taken by the Ministry of Agriculture and fiscal incentives and constraints facing local jurisdictions at the fringes of urban areas, lower-density residential construction is beginning to appear. Commercial and industrial developments can be seen in certain such outlying areas too, as along major highways leading from Prague to the west.

Regarding the market in Prague, a number of distinct real estate prices exist at one and the same time. These include (1) the administered or official price, as set by the state for tax purposes (transfer, inheritance, gift, property, and so on); (2) prices for special purposes: bank loans, insurance, and the like; (3) prices set for restitution; and (4) modeled market price in part reflecting real purchases and sales as these reflect partial knowledge of actual sales and purchases, prewar information, and understanding of conditions in Western Europe.

Local appraisers make judgments based on their knowledge of the market. In Prague there are several groups are trying to create multiple listing systems,[110] but most real estate brokers are opposed and will not share their data. Brokers, of whom there are several hundred,[111] take properties for sale on one- to three-month exclusive agreements. Most deals are for leases, and the broker receives a commission of 15 to 17 percent of one year's lease value. In fact, in 1992, the Association of Real Estate Agents tried to set guidelines for commissions but was sued for monopolistic behavior.[112] Long-term leases were not desirable until the passage, in 1992, of the Commercial Code, since formerly the leases did not run with the land. As a consequence, a new purchaser could terminate an existing lease. It has been noted that much property was ambiguously held. To date there is what amounts to a gray market, with pseudo-ownership. Under conditions where leases are indefinite and there is no possibility of eviction notice, the lessee has no responsibilities or liabilities of ownership, such as tax payment and maintenance.[113] One type of real estate shows its value depressed by continuing rent control as well as laws protecting sitting tenants: there is an oversupply of restituted apartments, amounting to one source to 10,000 to 15,000 apartments.[114] A building offered at $400,000 (10 million koruna) will yield only $144 (3,600) koruna per month in rent, a sum not worth collecting.

A detached house near Prague would cost $100,000 to $130,000 (3 to 4 million koruna), with the land accounting for something like over one-third of the cost in a vaguely defined market. Recently sale prices have increased considerably but rents in apartments are low and still controlled. They would typically account for 5 percent of income whether in newly privatized dwellings or in the remaining municipal structures; to this would be added charges for utilities. Foreigners are not covered by rent control.

Real estate agents say that sales or long-term leases typically take place some three to six months after a property is put on the market.

Since only the nonresidential portion of a building is free from rent control, such space is at a premium and generates a building's value. Prices for nonresidential space are said now to approach market value.[115] ". . . [I]n the center of Prague . . . rents have increased sharply by up to fifty times their 1989 level. Not only non-effective enterprises and warehouses are pushed out but also basic service facilities as well. Highly specialized luxury shops, travel bureaus and consultancies are replacing them. The rents paid by foreign companies are set purely by market laws and amount to up to 70 DM per square meter ($4.14 per square foot) monthly."[116]

There is evidence that center-city office rents are discouraging foreign companies from leasing space. A recent news report states that over 200 U.S. companies, including Coca-Cola and McDonald's, have chosen to locate their headquarters in Vienna rather than in Prague or Budapest because rents are twice as high as in Vienna.[117] Prices are expected to drop as the supply of rentable restituted properties comes on the market. "Investors are holding off now, given the political uncertainties. Americans prefer to buy in the U.S. at the currently depressed prices. Some Germans and Austrians are investing, feeling relatively comfortable with the practices in Czechoslovakia. There are few agencies with any ability to market property, either for rent or sale. There is a huge gap between the cost of restoration of existing structures and the asking prices for them. The City of Prague is turning to foreign banks and lawyers for help in marketing property."[118]

While the value of structures is established mainly by office and commercial space, there is also a continuing gray market for illegally subletted apartments. Tenants sublet their apartments for much higher rents and live elsewhere.

The City of Prague expects to hold on to some nonresidential properties to assure provision of social and other services and also as revenue sources, with the space leased at market prices. Such prices depend on building quality plus location. They are negotiated, to as high as $40 per square foot (10,000 koruna per square meter) per year. Leases written earlier are being honored, some for as long as twenty years.

In order to build on the outer fringe of Prague, one must purchase land from the municipality. The Ministry of Finance's suggested price is 800 to 1,000 koruna per square meter ($3.20 to $4 per square foot),[119] but the actual price paid depends primarily on whether the city grants permission to develop. If restricted to open space uses, the land sells on the market for around 400 koruna per square meter ($1.60 per square foot), while if the City Council approves use for housing, the price rises to 2,500 koruna ($10). Those speculating in farmland are said to have a 50/50 chance of change in the master plan; the earlier philosophy that all agricultural land should be protected has been modified so that significant natural resources are preserved, but other land may be approved for development. The Agricultural Ministry is ready to see perhaps 3 percent of the least desirable land, the least "rentable" land, withdrawn from farming.

The city has been loath to allow foreign investors into the hotel market, since tourism is such a major income source. However, in 1992 American bankers and lawyers, working with a Prague/New York investment firm, were employed in 1992 by the city to help it auction lease rights to the Prague Hotel. The advisors estimated the revenue stream that the hotel could generate and what would constitute a reasonable return for the investor. The city then concluded an agreement with Hyatt, which became one of the few foreign hotel management companies in Prague.[120]

Several government agencies are now considering the value of land as a component influencing infrastructure investment and providing a potential source of capital for development. For instance, the city and the Czech Ministry of Economic Development have explored exploitation of the air rights over the rail yard adjacent to the main railway station. The national railway network also has many vacant yards; their development could raise money to improve a very run-down system.[121]

The Prague Transit Agency has turned to the market to increase its revenues. Its assets have a value of 33 billion koruna (about $1.3 billion), exclusive of land. Charging very low fares and using no zone system, the fare box yields only 25 percent of operating costs and probably 12 to 15 percent of total costs, including capitalization of the system holdings.[122] Advertising in the stations and on trains and trams brought in 20 million koruna ($800,000) in 1992. Shops in the stations are leased and, as leases expire, rents are raised.

Analytic studies (including gravity models) were used in planning the transit system, but they excluded land value as a component. Because the 1984 plan reflects well the directions that the planners had anticipated, the Transit Agency is able to concentrate on technical aspects of system design. With respect to land around future stations as a source of revenue, the agency is making some feasibility studies of what investors might pay, possibly as a fee, for the right to develop near the station. The agency's strategy is to use ninety-nine year leases, but as some land already has been privatized, it will be necessary to work with the private land holders in planning its future use.

Lands that were owned by the city or municipalities of Prague became state lands in 1948; they must be returned under the Act on the Capital of Prague. Lands formerly owned by Prague on behalf of the Transit Agency will be retained and leased.[123] Some may even be developed by the agency. Many sites were acquired 100 years ago and what was then outlying area is now central and valuable. There may well emerge some conflict between the city's plans and the municipalities' wishes for use of these lands.

## CONSTRAINTS ON MARKETS

Several public sector actions constrain the market for urban and rural land. For housing, rent controls are a significant factor. For both land and housing, the difficulties in obtaining credit are often an insuperable obstacle. Finally, land use planning, to the extent that it is enforced, influences where development will and will not occur. There are valid reasons for the public sector to act as it is doing nonetheless, it is important to see the linkage between the actions and the response of the market.

### The Constraints of Housing Policy

Housing policies, in place for over forty years, still impede formation of a free market in property. Some state housing is still in public ownership, although now it is in the hands of municipalities. Because rent controls are still in effect (although modified somewhat upward), they yield low rents and limit mobility. Low investment, almost as low as in the Communist era, continues in maintenance of the "nonproductive" sector, reducing the quality of the stock. Sitting tenants continue to have rights of occupancy that impede allocation of space to other uses and users.

Rent on many residential properties continues to be controlled as it has been for over fifty years. The rent generally covers heating, hot water, and the space itself. The basic price nationwide varies from $0.04 to $0.09 per square foot (1 to 25 koruna per square meter), depending on the listed category of the flat. The four categories are defined by provision of central heating, hot water, and bathroom. Category 1 has all this equipment; category 4, none. Newer flats have somewhat higher rents because they offer more facilities.

Rent has remained the same for some flats since 1936: through occupation, change in regime, currency reforms. Thus in some cases people still pay only $4 (100 koruna) per month, because the rent was set before the war. The average rent is some $12 to $24 (300 to 600 koruna) for "3 + 1" state flats (three rooms and the kitchen, 500 square foot, 50 square meters). The rent is roughly twice as much for the same size cooperative flat.[124]

Rent control will be phased out over up to seven years, with areas of low demand, such as north Bohemia, freed sooner. As of 1994, housing built after 1989 without state participation and housing occupied by foreigners was altogether removed from rent control. On controlled units, rent levels went up by 100 percent in July 1992 with a further average increase of 40 percent due in 1995 by ministerial decree (postponed from January 1994). While these increases do exceed inflation rates, they still, as noted earlier, do not generate sufficient revenue for maintenance, not to speak of modernization. Municipalities have the right to float around the fixed rents (20 percent up, 15 percent down) taking location into account. It is recognized that some provision will need to be made for those less able to pay these higher rents. "The leading idea of state flat policies [is] to accelerate introduction of the individual social grants system in the favor of socially weakest renters, especially families with children, handicapped people, pensioners, etc., but in the way that makes it impossible the grants to be used for other purposes than those originally meant, i.e., for paying the due rents."[125]

Rent control is a volatile public issue. Market advocates maintain, buttressed by research, that charging real rents would have major positive effects.[126] It would generate sufficient rent revenue from the large part of the resident population able to pay substantially more than the 5 percent of income now going into housing. Such revenues would have measurable impact on maintaining and improving housing and would stimulate mobility and open valued housing stock (especially in central cities). And it would unburden the public fisc. Sufficient surplus could be generated to provide direct aid to targeted populations (such as elderly pensioners) although it might require their move to more modest, remote residences. There are, of course, many champions of rent control who believe that the burden on those now protected would be severe.

Location as a factor in setting rents was introduced only as of 1993, when the Czech Ministry of Finance established regulations setting the highest rents that may be charged. All dwellings will be subject to limits on the maximum that may be charged. Revision of the rent structure will be a major step toward increasing mobility in housing occupancy and fostering of a private market.

While there are maximum prices for commercial properties, the law allows cities, in conjunction with their districts, to designate areas free of any limits or zones where there can be designated prices in excess of the official amount.[127] Of Prague's ten districts, two have chosen to have no limits anywhere: including Prague 1, encompassing the Old Town, and Prague 9, a bleak industrial and high-rise area. Other districts have specified some streets with no limits and some with limits at multiples of the ministry maximum: Prague 2 (inner city) for instance, limits some streets at 200 percent and some at 400 percent of the maximum. Business taxes and certain fees are based on these locational rates.

### Financing Acquisition and Development

Lack of financing for acquisition of property is one of the critical shortcomings of the effort to rebuild the market. In the housing sector, no longer are generous subsidized credit terms offered to purchasers of cooperative apartments. Co-ops have recently even turned to foreign investors for capital.[128]

The first mortgage bank came into existence in 1993; four operated in early 1996. Typically, when credit is available, it is short term (five years) and at high interest (15 percent). These mortgages are available to builders for reconstruction or new construction but not to purchasers. In mid-1992 a new bank, backed with Austrian and German capital, opened to enable individuals to save for two years and obtain a four- to six-year loan for construction of a home. In late 1995, a degree finalizing conditions for home mortgage loans was issued. Subsequently funds for subsidy of interests were allocated by the cabinet. Yet it is conceded only few mortgages will be made. These will flow largely to the affluent and will not be subject to rent controls.[129] This continued very limited availability of credit is a serious constraint on development.

In the business sector, credit also is very scarce. The Czech and Moravian Guarantee and Development Bank was established in 1992 by the Czech Ministry of Economic Policy and Development and major Czech banks to assist small and medium-size businesses. This bank is to provide loan guarantees to entrepreneurs to aid in the purchase of land, buildings, and equipment. The viability of the loans issued to this point in under question. When repayment on the loans, especially real estate ones, come due in 1995 to 1998, a financial market crash may result, some analysts fear. Furthermore, the failure rate of loans to small businesses is high: Up to one half of the shops go under. Consequently a glut of ground-floor commercial space may arise in many urban areas.[130]

Within a more restricted circle, the Golem Club, known as the "millionaires' club," tries to help its members arrange financing for acquisitions such as department stores and small factories. Since the best recommendation for membership is "50 million koruna in debt at a good bank," however, its members may well be capable of finding their own financing.[131]

Lack of farm credit is a major factor impeding restitutees from engaging in farming and voluntary co-ops from modernizing. As of 1994, a fund had been established to provide some assistance to farmers. "Long term credits have been almost impossible to obtain for farming. This is particularly difficult for farmers due to the capital required during a period of restructuring and modernization. . . . In January 1994, the Czech Support and Guarantee Fund for Agriculture and Forestry . . . was established. . . . The Fund is expected to guarantee up to 80 per cent of the value of the loan taken, with the remainder provided mainly by the farmer, but also by the commercial bank involved."[132]

## The Uncertain Role of Land Use Planning

Forty years of central state planning have left a residue of antagonism toward planning of any sort. "Planning is viewed as inconsistent with the fundamental goal of post-Communism: to build a market economy free from public sector interference. In their enthusiasm for a market economy, the current leaders are trying to dismantle all forms of government regulation and purge the bureaucracy of all traces of Communist ideology. Comprehensive urban planning is one of the casualties of the 'decommunization' process. . . . The Czech Republic is becoming a nation of private property owners who are in no mood to have their use and enjoyment of the property constrained by planners. For their part, Czech planners have no experience with how to create regulations that can guide but not hinder private market decisions."[133]

Nonetheless, land use planning is alive if not flourishing, particularly at the municipal and regional levels. The fact that controls to implement the plans are limited and unpredictable is one more impediment to the market, presenting developers with an uncertain prognosis for their proposals.

## Planning at the State and Republic Levels

Although the role of the state had already greatly diminished prior to the separation of the republics, the delegation of three land use planning functions warrants discussion here.

The Federal Ministry of Agriculture asserted a strong land use planning role with its policy of retention of agricultural land. During the Communist period self-sufficiency in food production was stressed although there also was much waste. Today there is a food surplus and a desire that farmers not continue farming poor soils. The republic ministries are now the ones empowered to prevent the conversion of farmland to urban uses.

In 1991 the federal government delegated to the republics responsibility for housing, with only a few exceptions. Rent levels were federally set, but now they are in the hands of the two republics.

Responsibility for planning and building research rests in the Czech Republic with the Research Institute of Architecture and Building. This is financed by the Ministry of the Environment but also does work for the Ministry of Economics. The institute has three branches, one in Brno concerned with physical planning, one in the "Black Belt" of north Bohemia concerned with the physical environment, and one in Prague concerned with housing and urban development.[134]

Another power of the state that affects land use is the power of eminent domain. Lower levels of government have not been able to use eminent domain without specific enabling legislation is being passed by the state. Such legislation was passed in 1992 to acquire land for public buildings, protect natural areas, and provide access to public facilities such as recreation sites.[135]

## Planning in the City and Region of Prague

In the past, Prague was a very rich city and invested in land, buying farms on the outskirts. For example, land in Dejvice (today a densely built apartment and commercial zone in the northern part of the city) was bought during the 1920s and equipped with infrastructure. It was then sold for development in accord with the city's plan, partly to the state for offices and partly to individuals. The metro system conceived early in the century is similar to that which was built starting in the 1960s and which serves the area today.

Today the Prague region consists of 380 jurisdictions. While only 10 percent of the land is built up, 85 percent of the people live in communities of 5,000 or more. The current regional population (1.7 million) is projected to rise to 2 million by 2,000. Planning for the Central Bohemian Agglomeration of Prague, as the region is named, is the responsibility of TERPLAN, formerly a public agency and now a private organization that acts as a consultant. The plan is being coordinated with the master plan.[136]

Planning, inclusive of preparation of a master plan, is the responsibility of the chief architect's office.[137] The master plan locates public infrastructure, establishes land use at the block scale, and sets overall density levels. Cooperation is said to be extensive between the major players in planning for the Prague Region, namely TERPLAN, the city's chief architect's office, and the Prague Transit Agency, which has both city and regional responsibilities.

Approval by the Ministry of Agriculture is needed where units larger than 25 acres (10 hectares) are withdrawn from farming. (Appropriate levels of regional and municipal government, must give approval for smaller withdrawals.) Today, as production is given less priority, the ministry is said to be more flexible and "tolerant" of withdrawing land from farming.

Cooperation in planning between the Prague Transit Agency and city and regional planning bodies has a long history. In 1992 the manager of the Transit Agency had been chief transportation planner for the city architect's office. Currently 70 to 80 percent of the population use mass transit, and future plans will continue to give this priority. Car ownership, however, also is very high. The metro will continue to serve high-density zones. An old, obsolete railway line heading southwest from center city will be converted to a high-speed regional rail line; much lower density housing will be built in this area. A new regional rail line is also under consideration to the northwest, to the airport, and on to the industrial city of Kladno. This would open lands in this direction to denser settlement.

Communist local authorities destroyed historic cores in many cities of Czechoslovakia, or at the very least failed to devote sufficient resources to their maintenance and preservation. The chief architect's office in Prague, however, was largely effective in protecting the heart of the city. In 1971 the government established a 2,250 acre (900 hectare) area, including Prague Castle, the Old Town, and part of the New Town, as a protected historic district. Located here are thirteen National Cultural Monuments and 1,400 historic sites and structures. Much of the preservation and rehabilitation work done over the past two decades has, however, been superficial, providing beautiful facades that often conceal interior deterioration.

The city architect's office aims is to retain the current population of 65,000 in this district so that it does not become simply a tourist enclave. Doing so poses problems, however, as the housing here, as has been noted, is in the worst shape of any in the city and yields the lowest rents. The historic buildings are woefully in need of major repairs, particularly to the roofs.[138] At the same time, with 200,000 jobs, this is the area with the greatest demand for office and other commercial space.

The former master plan for Prague was adopted in 1986, and was intended to be valid for ten years. The City Council considers changes to land use once or twice a year. Changing land that is specified as park or open space to development land is very difficult.

The 1986 plan will be succeeded by a new plan almost completed in early 1996; work on it began in 1991.[139] This covers the whole 193 square miles (500 square kilometers) of the city, with its 1.2 million population (0.5 million more live in the surrounding region). A major focus is on renewal of the inner city, to make the housing more attractive and thus to discourage sprawl in the outer fringe. "The finished plan . . . will contain a binding document setting forth detailed regulation plans. The new Master Plan must react to the changing situation of land ownership and housing stock (via the process of restitution) and to the return of the market economy in the country. Major changes can be expected in rent policy (market prices), and consequently extensive changes in distribution of tenants can be expected. It is probable that many people, mainly older, will decide to leave Prague and live in their cottages. Similarly, major changes can be expected in the historic core of the city, where today the lowest rents are found and consequently the biggest concentration of old and poor people."[140]

Whereas the Communists encouraged dense urbanization, building 250,000 new apartments in high-rise prefabricated buildings, today the city architect's office recognizes that people want garden districts built for the future. In part the villages surrounding Prague can meet these demands. These villages are eager for revenue and can obtain it by bargaining with developers for contributions such as construction of part of the local water supply system or roads. The plan shows density projections of 260 people per square mile in the center city, 130 people in the high-rise housing areas, and 40 people in single-family housing (700, 350, and 150 people per square kilometer, respectively).

Design and amendment of previous master plans were solely in the hands of the city's chief magistrate, the city architect, and the mayor. The public participated in developing the new plan. Now each of the fifty-seven district or municipality mayors has his not-in-my-backyard concerns and is ready to do battle over the plan as it affects his area. One proposal to build a ring highway has drawn particularly vocal opposition from property owners.

Problems with plan implementation, as distinct from plan creation, involve not only the city architect's office but also the districts and the municipalities. Developers, entrepreneurs, and businessmen view the architect's office with scorn and hostility, considering it to be "a 'fossil' [that] will be abolished. Obtaining building permits is a hassle; you must deal with three levels of government, each with different ambitions. The municipality has the greatest power; if it agrees with the developer's proposal, and the district concurs, the City plan will be modified to match the proposal."[141]

Obtaining the appropriate permits to build is a trying process, for as many as thirty permits may be required as circumstances dictate, such as conformity to historic district requirements. At a minimum a land use permit must be secured from the city architect's office and a construction permit from the district's department of construction. While violators of such regulations are fined, the fine for major infractions—about $200 (5,000 koruna)—is so small that it is not a deterrent. There is no "one-stop shopping" or person to expedite the permit process. Architects often try to perform this function for their clients. "The chief architect's office responsible for determining the acceptability of projects submitted for development currently has no established guidelines for approving or rejecting proposals. This means there is room for corruption, conflicting views, and mismanagement."[142]

Another source of concern is corruption and control of development by a closed cabal. This been noted in Prague[143] and in other cities. Several people interviewed characterized the process of obtaining construction permits as "horrible." Many find bribery the easiest and quickest route. A lawyer more circumspectly said: "The rules are not hard and fast. They vary from municipality to municipality. For instance, Prague 1, where many old and valuable properties are located, proceeds very carefully, with no hint of corruption, while Prague 6 is much looser. One must remember that it is still early days, and many municipal administrators have little experience with permitting. They may be reluctant to take decisions for which they might later be blamed."[144]

There is no zoning law to back up the master plan. "The absence of a zoning ordinance is a real problem. The municipalities often disagree with the city architect's office, whom they view as 'meddlers and interferers' with no responsibility for the consequences of their actions. Zeal for historic preservation often leads to arbitrary decisions."[145]

## INSTITUTIONAL INFRASTRUCTURE

The market is shaped in part by the government-created infrastructure. Reestablishing and maintaining accurate cadasters and land records, mapping the market so that current data are available, and establishing a market-based land tax system all are critical components of a market system.

### Cadasters and Land Records

Geodesia, a state agency, has maintained all land records at the district *(okres)* level. In Prague, the city's districts have Geodesia offices. The records are uniform nationally, showing owner, user, location in the cadaster, size, whether the land is built or unbuilt, and claims of other parties such as easements and liens. Significantly, no information on the price paid on transfer transactions is included. These records do not have probative value and they are not public. The parties go to a notary with a contract, which remains private. The document then is presented to the cadastral office, which registers the contract but not the sale price. Finally, the tax office receives a payment, based on rates applied to the administered price.

Other problems exist with land records. There are excellent records from 1850 to 1959; in 1960 the government abolished the existing system and thereafter recorded only some transfers. This indifference to land records was based on the Communist view that land use, not land title, was significant, and, of course, the state controlled land use. In 1964 the Act Regarding Evidence of Real Estate was passed. It is still in effect.[146] Under this law, recording is evidence but not proof of title.

A new law revising the record system took effect January 1, 1993.[147] It establishes a Land Records office with branches at the district level. The law is modeled on the system that existed under the monarchy and during the First

Republic. The records of this office will have probative value and will be public. Title transfer will be effective as of the date of record.[148]

Cooperatives pose a complex recording problem. In those cases in which people voluntarily joined and worked as co-op members, titles were transferred. In cases in which people did not join voluntarily or where there was confiscation, the people kept title but could not use the land. Today, people in both categories can ask for restitution.

While there is a privatization data base, land as a component and other real estate are not separate categories. Data are arranged by founding organization (the state enterprise that was responsible) and do include asset value.

## Steps toward Reliable Price Data

Says one expert: "Everyone wants to keep the chaotic market because collusion serves the various parties best. It's easy to convert apartments to offices illegally, it's easy to ignore regulations on shops, and it's easy to evade taxes. Real estate brokers keep their information to themselves as their stock in trade. Only the city does seem to want to understand how the market is working."[149]

The Czech and Slovak republics have set land prices in several circumstances; these official prices often are widely (or wildly) at variance with prices actually paid in a transaction. There is as yet no means of obtaining global, accurate information on prices or price gradients. Under current law, domestic purchasers of land are not required to report the actual amount paid.

Prices actually paid in a transaction need not be registered or recorded; they are not subject to regulation. In the absence of multiple listings, the private sector also does not record prices in a systematic way. The Ministry of Finance does have records of foreign purchasers; such purchasers had to be approved until 1992, and subsequently the information has continued to be recorded.

Ministries of Finance of each republic set values of land and buildings for purposes of restitution claims, taxation, and establishing a minimum for offerings at auctions.[150] These values serve as a base for taxes regardless of the actual sale price. There is at present no mechanism for using comparable sales as an input for establishing these values. Instead, a point system is used for evaluating land and buildings. In Prague, the base land price is $6.50 per square foot (1,700 koruna per square meter); in other large cities, $3.20 (800 koruna); and for the least populated places $0.80 (200 koruna). Prices of individual plots are adjusted by coefficients reflecting location relative to center; prices of buildings are adjusted by coefficients reflecting commercial space in the structure. It is widely understood that the official prices do not reflect actual transactions. "Many Czechs admit only to selling at the official price, and in Crowns, thereby cheating the Government of tax revenue and hard currency. These 'official' values should be abolished for sale/purchase purposes and lawyers bound under law to state the actual sale price and in what currency. This would create an instant source of invaluable revenue."[151] Where, as is the case in several major cities, administered values are estimated in reference to comparable properties in West European cities, overvaluation seems to result.

## Mapping the Market

Maps that will provide information on markets are beginning to be created. The Ministry of Finance has issued a decree requiring cities to develop maps of land prices, at a scale of 1:5,000, by 1996. This is the first commitment to mapping and making public information about the land market. The aim of the mapping is to show current market price and to provide an information base for the future. One firm, HP Services, was engaged to create such maps for several cities, including Prague, Karlovy Vary, and Brno. The Karlovy Vary map was completed in 1993.[152] The Ministry of Finance is expected to publish it as the official map on which to base fees and taxes such as title transfer tax, inheritance tax, and land tax. Once the mapping process is well advanced, it is anticipated there will be annual updates.

HP Services's methods include plotting land price curves based on gradients for German cities and other European urban areas. Factors include location, building quality, city size and region, size and orientation of property, zoning designation, and potential use. The firm also obtains from real estate brokers the prices paid for unbuilt land and then compares these to the prices paid for sites with structures in order to estimate the value of the land. The brokers share this information with the firm because it, in return, assists them with their feasibility studies for prospective developers. Estimates are made as to what a particular site could generate as income if developed.[153]

Firms working on maps for Prague and other cities appear to use similar methods. One consultant sought to blend four sources: (1) historical values from Prague in prewar years, which generated a profile very similar to that in German cities; (2) theoretical maps using methods employed in Germany, which are based on statistical analyses of factors such as distance from urban centers, building use and age, land use controls, and so on; (3) statistical analyses of *asking* prices of property currently on the market, inasmuch as real estate agents are very reluctant to share actual transaction data; and (4) the lease prices from small privatization.[154] Other consultants have used similar methods and for their own use have generated computer models and maps reflecting land and building values.[155]

## Taxation of Real Property

Three tax laws affecting real property took effect on January 1, 1993.[156] These laws concern taxation of land and buildings, property transfer taxes, and tax administration, and provide for tax collection by the state.

The new law governing taxation of land and buildings has two parts: The first concerns land and the second concerns buildings and the land under their footprints.

Through 1992, farmland was taxed if it was classified in the first twenty-one of forty-two classes of soil quality. One effect of this law was to penalize the holders of good soils and encourage the farming of poor soils. Before revision of the tax, about $40 million (1 billion koruna) was collected annually, while farms on the poorer soils received $200 million (5 billion koruna) in subsidies.[157] After 1989, subsidies were reduced. The new law for taxation of land, which alters the incentives of the prior law, incorporates location and type of use as well as soil quality and is based on some one hundred categories of land type. The Institutes for Agricultural and Forest Lands of the Ministry of Agriculture have coded land by quality, location, soil type, and other factors and have projected annual income from these data. These categories will be used to establish a basis for farm and forest land taxation under a 1991 decree entitled Oceňování půdi.

A number of land uses are exempted: some forests; some water bodies; defense sites; state and municipal lands, including state-supported organizations such as universities; Land Fund holdings; diplomatic properties; church-related land; land held by political parties; land surrounding hospitals, museums, and cultural sites; land to protect environmental resources such as reservoirs; nature sites; and land used for power lines, pipelines, and transportation routes. In addition, there are some short-term exemptions; for example, restituted agricultural land up to 10 hectares (25 acres) and restituted forest land are exempt for five years.

Agricultural land assessments will be based on the area multiplied by the price of land per square meter. Prices of farmland, forests, water bodies, and other lands were established under a decree issued by the Ministry of Finance in 1992. These base figures are modified by two coefficients: use of the land and class of municipality. For instance, buildable lands are considered to be the base. Vineyards, hop yards, and orchards are assessed at 0.75 of base; forests, fish ponds, and feedlots are assessed at 0.25 of base; and other open lands are assessed at 0.10 of base.

There are nine classes of municipality by population size, and the assessment coefficient varies from 4.5 for Prague down to 0.03 for municipalities of less than 300 people.

The system of exemptions for buildings and their underlying land is similar. In addition, residential buildings that have been restituted are exempt for fifteen years so long as they are not sold. The base is determined by the area of the building footprint and the character of the use. For instance, the base price for apartments, residential outbuildings, and buildings for agricultural production is 1 koruna per square meter; for summer houses, 3 koruna per square meter;

for garages, 4 koruna per square meter; for industrial buildings, 5 koruna per square meter; and for other buildings, 10 koruna per square meter.

There is a height coefficient of 0.075 koruna per square meter for each story larger than two-thirds of the footprint. The same set of coefficients as for land applies for size of municipality.

The new transfer tax creates a tax on sales, gifts, exchange, and inheritance of real property. The transferor will pay, although the buyer/donee/heir is obligated to pay if the transferor does not. However, if the sale is the result of a court order, as in bankruptcy, the buyer pays. The base price, established by the Ministry of Finance,[158] depends on the category of transferee: It is 1 to 5 percent for spouses or relatives in a direct line; 3 to 10 percent for relatives not in a direct line or persons who have been part of a common household for at least one year; and 4 to 20 percent for others.

## CONCLUSIONS, RECOMMENDATIONS, AND PREDICTIONS

Markets are in formation, price levels are being established, and new ownership patterns are beginning to be diffused. Yet these processes and environments are only partially in place. Markets are not fully operational, and a large portion of the housing stock and land reserve remain under full or partial state control. Equilibrium prices (and ones that sharply differentiate property distinct in location or quality) do not yet exist. Ownership of real estate is assured, yet the rights associated with this ownership often are circumscribed and cannot be fully exercised.

Those interviewed often described the present situation as chaotic. While this may be somewhat of an exaggeration, certain ambiguities, indeterminacies, and uncertainties are central to the housing and land situation. Not all rules are in place, and there are different expectations on the part of buyers and sellers, state and private entities, and landlord and tenants. Information is sorely lacking on the prices paid in the course of a given property exchange, for example. There are widely divergent expectations as to the way the system works, can work, and will work. One of the several consequences is that many participants are deferring decisions, while others enter the "market" precipitously.

The use of the word "market" at this juncture may be premature. Some of the housing and land indeed is in private hands and subject to relatively unfettered exchange, but much real estate remains under state control, especially in the case of state farms. Monopoly and oligopoly will continue for some time. The state also continues to intervene in ways other than as a mere property owner: Examples include rent control, maximum sale and lease prices, and restrictions on entry by foreign purchasers.

In brief, most property on the market consists of urban buildings (some apartments, some apartment houses, small commercial properties), and some urban lots. Only a very small part of agricultural land or forests is in an active market at this time. What there is on the market largely originates as a restituted asset, and has been put to lease.

Currently there appear to be segmented markets and specified rules for distinct groups of participants in the real estate domain. Citizen/residents are accorded rights and access to assets denied (often more affluent) foreigners. Those with restitution claims had advantages that those without lack. At least so far, sitting tenants have rights which significantly exceed the rights of others. Such differentiation adds to the complexity if not outright chaos of the environment.

Perhaps the most important of the numerous unanswered policy questions is how to determine an appropriate range, form, and style for government intervention and the exercise of public policy in a setting where there is, on one level, an intense commitment (and expectations both from within and from outside) to private enterprise and free markets, and where there are, on the other level, residual aspects of major state participation and ownership as well as traditions exercising a strong pull in an opposite direction. It is by no means clear what the future holds for such forms of intervention as local planning, land-use directed environmental management, or the shaping of settlement patterns by means of directed infrastructure investment. It is also not clear how far the present (not to speak of future) administrations will go in housing policies that target help or a safety net to vulnerable parts of the population, such as pensioners or young families in the first stages of household formation.

A second basic question still unanswered revolves around the intense search for devices that build up commitments to the new postsocialist system. Will widespread (though far from universal) home ownership, together with stock ownership of enterprises by means of vouchers, be effective? It would appear so. But will the more elusive concept of a market, with significant changes from extant price levels and rents, further serve to build support for the new system? This would appear to be less certain. An important facet of this issue is who indeed are the new owners: under restitution, under auction, and as subsequent purchasers. There are some indications that "black" money has gone into home and business purchase; at the same time, many hold that money has "no color." In some instances local purchasers are no more than fences for foreign interests; the policy implications here are also ambiguous. Establishment of new credit institutions should expand ownership opportunities.

In the past forty years tenants received high levels of subsidies; this must be reassessed under the new conditions. Undoubtedly many instances (related to life-cycle patterns) of housing overconsumption and locationally inappropriate consumption exist. It is difficult to separate the pricing policy for housing from the entire pricing systems under socialism. It is easy, however, to observe that allocation of resources led to undermaintenance. It is also true that the concept of equity in shelter access and use was often perverted and misapplied under the former regime. It has been argued that higher rents would generate sufficient surplus to assist those truly in need (and that institutional means would be found to channel such surplus to assist them).[159] But this would be conditional on greater household mobility than has existed to this point.

The first tentative findings of price levels generated by commercial space auctions in Prague are intriguing.[160] Together with rapidly changing land use (especially in retail shops), these findings suggest that the "Western" urban model, with its rent gradient declining from the center, is being reintroduced into the city rather quickly. The form, use, and price distortions of half a century apparently were far less rigid and cemented in place than it might have been reasonable to suspect. It is not clear how these changes will impact the large number of units, both residential and supporting trade and services, of the suburban postwar housing districts, with their residential density at variance with the U.S. pattern (but perhaps not so distinct from that found, for example, in the environs of Paris).

Finally, although we have only limited understanding of the environment and the political context in which decisions must be made, we wish to offer some observations and tentative suggestions regarding planning, land, and housing in the Czech Republic.[161]

The absence of zoning mechanisms and the relatively heavy handed use of master planning creates problems. We strongly urge that steps be taken to put in place land use, density, and related zoning controls. We also strongly urge that related forms of land use and environmental controls be adopted, including height and bulk regulations for planned urban districts, regulations governing use of air rights, and billboard and sign controls for both urban and rural areas.

It will require much sensitivity and adaptation in the course of the significant forthcoming rent rise to ensure that populations at risk—the elderly, the disabled, and what are sure to be a growing number of unemployed—be assured minimal housing. Prompt attention must determine whether this is to be achieved by housing allowance, access to state housing, or other means.

The issue of second homes, leisure and recreation districts, and village development also requires attention. We are convinced that, at present, there is the risk of scattered housing (with many and large social costs) in the outskirts of major cities, in desirable mountain and other settings, and along major highways. Local jurisdictions, co-ops, and state farms have short-term incentives to allow such construction. However, this construction can generate costly infrastructure requirements and destroy the very environments which urban populations are seeking.

## PEOPLE INTERVIEWED

**Václav Bašek,** Department of Economy of Agriculture, Czechoslovak Ministry of Economy.

**James Bednar,** U.S. AID, Prague.

**Tomáš Bettelheim,** Lowell White Durrant, Prague.

**Jiří Blažek,** Department of Geography and Regional Development, Charles University, Prague.

**Vavřinec Bodenlos,** Czech Ministry for Economic Policy and Development.

**Tomáš Böhm,** Terra Bohemica, Prague.

**Anthony Chip Caine,** Office of the Chief Architect, Prague.

**Petr Čermák,** Czechoslovak Ministry of Privatization, Prague.

**Anna Červenková,** *EKONOM,* Prague.

**Ivan C. Chadima,** Euroinvest CSFR Inc., Prague and New York.

**Annet deKlerk,** Department of Social Geography and Regional Development, Charles University, Prague.

**Alexander Drier,** Central European University, Prague.

**Pavel Dvorský,** DATAREAL and APRES, Prague.

**James Guidi,** Apple Computer IMC, Prague.

**Antonin Götz,** Institute of Geography, Academy of Sciences, Prague.

**Petr Halouzka,** Research Institute for Building and Architecture, Prague.

**Milan Hašek,** Prague Public Transport.

**Jiří Hrůza,** TERPLAN (Czechoslovak Institute for Regional Planing), Prague.

**Stanislav Jelen,** Department of Restitution, Czech Republic Ministry of Agriculture, Prague.

**Charles Jelínek,** Czechoslovak Ministry of Privatization, Prague.

**Stiubhard Kerr-Liddel,** Velkostatek Hořín, Mělník.

**Nicholas M. Kirke,** Agentura Kirke, Prague.

**Jaroslav Kohout,** Research Institute of Architecture and Building, Prague.

**Jiří Kokoška,** KOPPREA, Prague.

**Eva Kunová,** Office of Privatization, Mayor's Office, Prague.

**Jaroslav Macháček,** Center for Architecture and Urbanism, Academy of Sciences, Prague

**Petr Michalovič,** Research on the Human Factor, Institute of Building, Economics, and Organization, Bratislava.

**Jan Mládek,** Czechoslovak Ministry of Economy, Prague.

**Vojtěch Panik,** Slovak Ministry of Regional Development, Bratislava.

**Ivan Plicka,** Chief Architect's Office, Prague.

**Hana Prchalová,** Department of Housing Policy, Mayor's Office, Prague.

**Tomáš Procházka,** Secretary, The Golem Club, Prague.

Ferdinand Radouch, Czech Office for Surveying, Mapping and Cadaster, Prague.

Simon Renton, Partner, McKenna & Co. Solicitors, Prague and London.

Monika Rutland, White & Case, Prague.

Samin, Real Estate, Prague.

Zdeněk Škopek, Department of Strategy, Czech Republic Ministry of Agriculture, Prague.

Antonín Skružný, Investis, Prague.

Irena Smekalová, Department of Housing Policy, Czech Republic Ministry for Economic Policy and Development, Prague.

Christopher Smith, Lovell White Durrant Solicitors, Prague.

Jiří Stehlik, Department of Privatization, Ministry of Agriculture, Prague.

Jaromír Stejskal, Scientific Information Department, Research Institute for Architecture and Building, Town Planning Department, Brno.

Miroslav Svatoš, Department of Agricultural Economics, University of Agriculture, Prague.

Milan Svoboda, Department of Strategy, Czech Republic Ministry of Agriculture, Prague

Luděk Sýkora, Department of Geography and Regional Development, Charles University, Prague

Petr Tajcman, U.S. AID, Prague.

Joel Turkewitz, Central European University/Privatization Project, Prague

Jan Urban, *EKONOM,* Prague.

Luděk Urban, Institute of Economic Sciences, Charles University, Prague.

Anna Vitová, Czech Republic, Ministry of Privatization, Prague

Pavel Vorlíček, Prague.

Václav Zajíček, Chief Architect's Office, Prague.

Marcela Zaveralová, ALFA, Prague.

Ivan Žikeš, ARK, Prague, and RECOM, Karlovy Vary.

# 4

# POLAND:
# LAND AND HOUSING IN TRANSITION[1]

In the eyes of the world economic community, Poland has been an outstanding performer among the countries of Central and Eastern Europe. The shock therapy has worked. The private sector is now dominant, accounting in 1995 for more than half of the gross domestic product (GDP). Growth has been the highest in Europe (save East Germany): 3 percent in 1992, 4 percent in 1993, a robust 5 percent in 1994, and more than 6 percent in 1995. During the years from 1991 to 1995, personal consumption grew at annual rates of from 4 to 7 percent. Since 1988 the number of passenger cars surged by half and that of telephone lines by a third. In 1995 every second Polish family possessed a car and a telephone. Between 1988 and 1995, the average size of dwellings increased from 59.1 to 63.9 square meters, or 9.2 percent. During this period standards of dwellings improved significantly. Household amenities in urban areas, including indoor plumbing, bathrooms, central heating, and washing machines, increased by several percentage points, while in rural areas they increased 10 to 20 percent. In 1994, on average, every Pole made one trip abroad (compared to every second Pole in 1989). The number of foreigners arriving in Poland during this period exceeded 74 million (as opposed to 8 million in 1989). Since 1989 the number of college students doubled while water and air pollution was cut by half. In 1994 and 1995 industrial output and exports grew at double-digit annual rates, while unemployment, inflation, and the budget deficit were shrinking. In December 1995, Poland's foreign exchange reserves reached $15 billion (compared to $6 billion in December 1994). Western confidence in the Polish economy has been on the rise. During 1995, $2.4 billion arrived as foreign direct investment (FDI). Hungary and Poland have been the most successful among the Central and Eastern European countries in attracting foreign investors. Between 1990 and 1995 these two countries received more FDI than all other countries of the region together, excluding Germany.

Yet not all the news is good. In FDI, per capita Poland still lags behind several smaller countries, such as Hungary, the Czech Republic, Slovenia, and Estonia. In addition, unemployment and inflation rates remain high, having reached 15 and 22 percent, respectively, in December 1995. Housing construction plummeted; the number of dwelling units completed was down from

150,000 in 1989 to around 60,000 in 1995. In 1995, the total number of households exceeded that of dwellings by 1.58 million, up from 1.25 million in 1988. Crime surged. The speed of reform is hampered by increasing income inequality and pervasive fatigue from transition. Endless fights among dozens of parties, coalitions, political factions, labor unions, and other groups is a significant destabilizing factor. The old pre-1989 Communist constitution has been amended several times but, unlike in other Central European countries, it was not entirely replaced by a new democratic constitution. No restitution law was agreed upon. Fiscal and monetary policies suffer from inconsistencies and lack of stability. Open and hidden subsidies to selected industries and enterprises in the form of idiosyncratic tariffs, ad hoc tax exemptions, and debt forgiveness, remain common. Privatization of large enterprises is moving too slowly.

Interviews with 1,004 Poles in the summer of 1994 reflect these transition pains.[2] Compared to five years ago, 55 percent considered themselves worse off. Only 18 percent found themselves better off. Looking to the country's economic future in the next few years, 34 percent thought that there would be gradual improvement while 26 percent expected economic deterioration.[3] As to their own prospects, 36 percent were optimistic, and 22 percent were pessimistic.[4] Asked whether individual freedom or equality with minimal class differences is more important, 43 percent of Poles chose equality and 36 percent chose individual freedom.[5] The return to power, in September 1993, of the former Communists, and, in particular, the election of their leader, Aleksander Kwaśniewski, as the President of Poland, in December 1995, is further evidence of popular fear of conditions under a free market system. Hanna Suchocka, a former prime minister, is one of many people critical of the West for offering encouragement and support but then, seeing progress toward recovery, closing borders to Polish goods.[6]

In the land and the housing sectors, the urban real estate market has expanded, hampered, however, by continuation of rent controls on a third of the housing stock, high prices of dwelling units offered in the open market, inadequate mortgage financing, and uncertainties over title. Privatization of enterprises appears to have been delayed intentionally, especially since the fall of 1993 when the post-Communist government of Prime Minister Waldemar Pawlak was installed. The rural market is stagnant. As urban jobs were eliminated, the farm overcrowding worsened. Farmers' real incomes slumped by 50 percent. State farms struggled with high indebtedness and negative profitability. The state assistance from a farmer-friendly Pawlak government was not enough to overcome the numerous obstacles, such as severe droughts during the summers of 1992 and 1994, increasing foreign competition, and shifts in domestic demand. As a result, the state is finding few buyers as it seeks to privatize its farms.

The absence of a restitution law, except for church properties, is a continuing impediment to both the urban and rural markets. Given the very large losses in human lives during World War II under both the Germans and the Soviets, the major shifts in territory after the war, and the consequent population redistribution, the difficulties posed by restitution are more profound than elsewhere. Also, there is a smaller constituency demanding it than in other countries. Most housing never was taken, although owners in urban areas were required to accept state-selected tenants who paid low rents that remained below the maintenance cost. Most farms stayed private. Those whose property was taken included all or almost all of the large land owners; churches and religious orders; owners and shareholders of large industrial firms; Warsaw real estate owners; former and current residents of prewar Eastern Poland; as well as all those Poles, Jews, Germans, Ukrainians, and others who, during or after the war, were killed and left no heirs or who moved or stayed outside of postwar Poland (escaped, fled, were evacuated or deported, or remained in the former Eastern Poland).

This chapter discusses the state of the Polish economy under communism and today; then describes the issues surrounding the question of restitution and the actions in place to date; discusses the process of privatization, in particular the status of state farm privatization; documents the evolution of real estate markets; and briefly surveys the institutional structure—cadasters, tax, credit, and planning—that affects land and housing.

## POLAND UNDER COMMUNISM: POLAND TODAY

A recent poll surveyed people as to conditions that are better today than in 1989 and those that are worse. A majority of those polled feel that today there is more crime, more corruption, a greater gap between rich and poor, more hostility between people, and a weakened safety net. However, on the positive side, a majority note more political freedom, opportunities for individual initiative, and independence from foreign powers.[7] Many Poles are uneasy and unsure about trading of economic and social protection for the freedom to compete and to succeed or fail. In this century Poles have suffered a great deal of fear, loss, and insecurity. Their hope for a middle way (a "social market") is doubtless reflected in their political support for the post-Communists.

### Geography

What constitutes Polish territory has changed radically over time. Poland is the second largest Central European country, after Germany. Its area and population, for comparison, are roughly equal to those of New Jersey, New York, and the New England states combined.

During the nineteenth century Poland was obliterated as an independent nation, divided among Russia, Prussia, and Austria. At the conclusion of World War I, Poland again became an independent nation, though this independence was soon threatened by the Polish-Soviet War of 1919-20. The tides of battle shifted several times, but ultimately the Poles won.

In 1939, at the outset of World War II, Poland covered 150,000 square miles (388,000 square kilometers). Only 54.4 percent of this territory remained part of Poland after the war. During the war Poland was occupied by the Germans and the Soviets. In accordance with a plan of Stalin's, approved by Churchill and Roosevelt at Yalta and finalized at Potsdam, Poland was made to cede its prewar eastern territories, constituting 69,000 square miles (177,000 square kilometers), to the Soviet Union. At the same time Poland was granted 39,000 square miles (101,000 square kilometers) that had previously belonged to Germany, bringing its total area to 121,000 square miles (313,000 square kilometers). Thus, postwar Poland is only 80 percent as large as prewar Poland. Only 67.6 percent of today's Poland was Poland before the war. In general, Poland's newly acquired territories were better developed economically than those transferred to the Soviet Union. Yet, in 1945, the post-German territories were almost depopulated and heavily destroyed by the war operations and the actions of the victorious Soviet army.

The land of Poland consists of rolling hills in the north, near the Baltic coast. Central Poland is predominantly flat. In the south, the Carpathian and Sudety mountains form the border with Slovakia and the Czech Republic. The principal river, the Vistula, rises in the mountains and drains north, forming an S as it winds through Cracow and Warsaw before emptying into the Baltic at the Gdańsk estuary. The Odra (Oder) River also rises in the mountains and flows northwesterly until it is joined by the Nysa (Neisse) River, forming part of the border with Germany. On the northeast and east, Poland is bordered by Russia, Lithuania, Belarus, and Ukraine.

In 1994 (figures for 1990 in parentheses), 59.77 percent (60.07 percent) of the land was in agricultural use, 28.58 percent (28.41 percent) in forests, 3.19 percent (3.16 percent) in transportation and communication systems, 3.18 percent (3.04 percent) in housing, and 2.65 percent (2.64 percent) was water. Of the land in agriculture, 76.68 percent (76.86 percent) is arable and cultivated, 13.00 percent (13.22 percent) is in meadows, and 8.74 percent (8.47 percent) in pastures. The quality of agricultural land varies by location, with the best soils in the southeast, except for the mountains, and the poorest in central and northeast Poland.

Warsaw became the capital in 1596, when Poland's Swedish-born king decided to move the capital from Cracow. Today Warsaw occupies an area three times that of the 1939 city, with the newly developed districts consisting of high-rise concrete panel construction apartments similar to those in the other Soviet-style cities of Eastern Europe. The other major cities of Poland, in addition to Cracow, are Gdańsk, Poznań, Lódź, and Wrocław.

## Population

The 1931 census offers detailed information about employment, ethnicity, religion, and urban versus rural residence. The population of Poland then was 31.9 million. Of this, 68.9 percent declared Polish to be their mother tongue, 13.9 percent Ukrainian or Ruthenian, 8.6 percent Yiddish or Hebrew, 3.1 percent Belarussian, 2.3 percent German, 0.4 percent Russian, and 2.8 percent either indicated some other tongue or unknown. The largest proportion of urban residents—77.8 percent—was for the people whose mother tongue was Yiddish or Hebrew, while the largest proportion of rural residents, 96.7 percent, was for those whose mother tongue was Belarussian. By religion, 64.8 percent were Roman Catholic, almost all of them Polish; 10.5 percent were Greek Orthodox, almost all of them Ukrainian and Ruthenian; 11.8 percent were Orthodox; 9.8 percent were Jewish; and 3.3 percent were other or unknown. The Orthodox were primarily in farming—88.1 percent of the Greek Orthodox and 92.4 percent of other Orthodox. As to the Jews, 42.2 percent were in manufacturing and 36.6 percent in trade. For those who were employers or self-employed, 60.2 percent of those in agriculture were Roman Catholics, 70.6 percent of those in trade were Jewish, and 62.5 percent of those in education and culture were Jewish.

By 1939 the total population had risen to 35 million, of whom 11.5 million lived in areas of Poland that became part of the Soviet Union at the end of the war.

During the war 6 million Poles were killed, many of them in German concentration camps and Soviet gulags, and many in the resistance movement activities against the Germans. By 1946 the population had shrunk to 23.9 million. With the annihilation of the Jews and the transfer of Eastern Poland to the Soviet Union, the population remaining in Poland was 85.8 percent Polish, 9.6 percent German, and 4.6 percent other or unknown. As of 1995, Poland was almost exclusively Polish; of the 38.7 million people, 98 percent were Polish and 2 percent other (Ukrainian, Belarussian, Lithuanian, German, or Jewish).[8]

Warsaw underwent a particularly dramatic decline and recovery. In 1939, at the time of the German invasion, there were 1.3 million inhabitants; by 1945, after Hitler's destruction of the city, the population had dropped to 160,000. Some 700,000 people had been killed, including more than 300,000 Jews and the 200,000 participants in the 1944 uprising.[9] By 1993 the population had well surpassed the 1939 figure, reaching 1.64 million.

Almost two-fifths of the people still live in rural areas: 41.3 percent in 1980, 38.3 percent in 1992, and 38.1 percent in 1994. Overpopulation has been and remains a rural problem, particularly acute in southeastern Poland. Birth rates in the countryside always have been much higher than in urban areas: above 30 per 1,000 from 1918 to 1939, compared to around 15 in large cities; 21 per 1,000 in 1980, compared to 18.4 in urban areas; and 15.0 per 1,000 in 1994, compared to 10.9 in urban areas. Natural increase has slowed noticeably during recent years.

The rate per 1,000 rural population was 10.3 in 1980, 6.0 in 1990, and 4.0 in 1994. The corresponding rates for the urban population were: 9.2, 3.0, and 1.5. Due to slow industrial growth before 1939 and a weak service sector from 1945 to 1989, the cities could not easily absorb the excess rural population, although there was considerable migration from farms to the cities.

According to a popular image, peasants are poorly educated and live apart from the rest of the modern world. This image finds some support in a comparison of rural and urban conditions as of 1988. The proportion of adults with at least high school diplomas was 15 percent in rural areas and 41.2 percent in the cities. This proportion for those with college education was 1.8 percent in rural areas and 9.4 percent in urban areas. Almost three-fifths of all rural dwellings were classified as substandard, as compared to one-fifth of urban dwellings.[10] On the other hand since then progress in the countryside has been significant.

Poland is overwhelmingly a Catholic country. Along with Ireland, it tops the world in proportion of people—98 percent—who declare themselves to be believers in God. As of 1993, 90.36 percent of the population described themselves as Roman Catholic; 1.41 percent as Christian Orthodox; and 0.22 percent as Protestants. Only 1,330 people declared themselves Jewish.[11]

## Government

Under communism government was unitary, with the state exercising all powers. Today there are three tiers of government, each with powers and responsibilities: the state; the *voivodships,* or regions; and the *gminas,* or municipalities. In 1990 local government was reenfranchised as a legal entity, forty years after its right to own and manage property had been abolished. Taxing and spending powers are specified in the Act on Local Autonomy. Currently there are 1,622 rural *gminas,* 535 mixed (urban-rural) *gminas,* and 308 urban *gminas.*

In 1945, after World War II, the country was divided into 17 *voivodships;* 330 *poviats,* or counties; 704 towns; and 2,993 *gminas.* In 1955 the *gminas* were replaced by 8,790 *gromadas,* or rural districts. In the mid-1970s the country was realigned into 49 *voivodships* and 2,465 *gminas.*

On average, *voivodships* cover 2,500 square miles (6,400 square kilometers) and have a population of 800,000, while, on average, *gminas* cover 50 square miles (130 square kilometers) and have a population of 16,000.

Under the Communists, central control was, of course, in the hands of the Communist Party whose leaders, closely watched by Moscow, included Bolesław Bierut, Władysław Gomułka, Edward Gierek, and Wojciech Jaruzelski. In 1980 the struggle of the Solidarity Union, under the leadership of Lech Wałęsa, began at the Gdańsk shipyard. This movement led to independence for the trade unions and laid the ground work for the Communists' fall from power in 1989.

The first Solidarity-led government, which took office in September 1989, was that of Tadeusz Mazowiecki. In a decision from which many bitterly dissented, this government chose to look to the future rather than seek to punish those who had ruled for forty-five years. Mazowiecki drew a "thick line" to separate the Communist past from the democratic Third Republic of Poland. One outcome was that the Communist nomenklatura, armed with wealth and political know-how, was soon able to reenter the fight for power.

Segmentation of political organizations is very high—twenty-nine different political parties had representatives in the first freely elected Sejm (the lower house) in October 1991. Between summer 1989 and spring 1996, Poland was run by eight governments, all of them formed by fragile coalitions.

In the September 1993 elections the former Communists benefited from the newly revised election law. Although the law set minima of 5 percent and 8 percent of the vote for parties and coalitions, respectively, thus reducing the number of parties in Parliament, it also provided for bonus seats for the big vote winners. The result of this was to award the two leading post-Communist organizations, the Democratic Left Alliance and the Polish Peasants' Party, 66 percent of the seats in the Sejm on the basis of a mere 36 percent of the vote. Several factors led to the post-Communists' success. Although the West hails Poland as a success for its administration of shock therapy, those affected have a different perspective. The pensioners fear for the future of their pensions, the factory workers found redundant also are fearful, and many are not ready for the plunge into the uncertain waters of capitalism. "The ex-Communists had the advantages conveyed (at least over the short term) by a cynicism that masked itself as pragmatism. While the parties of the old Solidarity coalition were splintering over interesting, but often esoteric, points of political philosophy, the ex-Communists presented themselves as experienced and practical managers who had learned from the errors of the past and whose heads were not stuck in the clouds of theory."[12]

Poland has a unified court system with three tiers: the district courts, each covering several municipalities and having general jurisdiction as courts of first instance as specified by law; the *voivodship* courts, also courts of first instance but for larger claims and for special areas; and the appellate courts, including the Supreme Court, the Supreme Administrative Court, the Constitutional Tribunal, and the Tribunal of State.

The Supreme Court, which is divided into several divisions, has about one hundred judges who serve five-year terms. Cases on appeal are heard by three-judge panels. The Constitutional Tribunal, unlike similar courts in Bulgaria and the Czech Republic, cannot invalidate a law on constitutional grounds. It can only advise the Parliament on such questions. In March 1996 President Kwaśniewski asked Parliament to amend the "little constitution" so that the holdings of the Constitutional Court would be binding on Parliament.

## The Economy

In Communist Poland, the availability and prices of food and housing were two social issues of grave political importance well understood by successive party leaders. Their political survival, to a great extent, was a function of the success of their policies on food and housing shortages. Yet despite intense efforts, they failed, one after the other, to find satisfactory solutions. Today, in the transition to a market economy, the agricultural sector continues to suffer. It remains the least efficient sector of the Polish economy. Housing also presents problems. Most Polish families cannot afford new dwellings. Some of them still have to share dwellings with strangers. Also, the distribution and quality of old dwellings remain problems.

The Polish economy can be divided into two broad sectors of economic activities: "official" activities, which include the state, municipal, private, and mixed sectors, and "unofficial" activities, or the so-called second economy.

### Official Economic Activities

State economic activity is a sector of the economy legally owned by the State Treasury and directly or indirectly managed by the state. The State Treasury owns property of this sector.

Municipal economic activity was introduced by the March 1990 Law on Local Self-Government that granted the *gminas* the status of a legal person. The *gmina* has become subject to civil law. It can engage in economic activity, both nonprofit (public utilities) and for-profit business; it can own assets and liabilities, including real estate.

Private economic activity has been actively encouraged since 1989. Before 1989, as a result of intense state regulations, there existed a wide gap between the right to own and the right to dispose of property. The state closely controlled the basic microeconomic decisions concerning production input sources, quantities produced, product allocation, and prices and wages.

Other forms of official economic activity constitute a mixture of units that do not fully qualify as either private or public, such as: social and political organizations; mixed companies with the participation of the state, municipalities, and private capital; cooperatives; and others. In the past, some of these organizations, such as labor unions and political parties were practically state organs in themselves. The cooperatives were a peculiar form of ownership. Despite their "private" status, their autonomy was marginal and, before 1990, they did not differ in a substantial way from regular state enterprises.

### Unofficial Economic Activities

Unofficial economic activities, also referred to as the "black," "second," or "underground" economy, works within or at the margin of the official one. It includes all illegal and semilegal economic activities that have not been officially registered, and that, in general, are not accounted for by the state statistics. Before 1990 this sector was tacitly tolerated by the Communist authorities. It fulfilled many important functions. For example, it served as a security valve, providing households and businesses with various goods and services, both necessities and luxuries, that could not be obtained from the inefficient and inflexible official sector—whatever the state was unwilling or unable to deliver, the unofficial economy provided. It also was an important way for the authorities to penetrate activities outside of the direct state controls—the black marketeers were heavily infiltrated by the state security apparatus. In addition, it was a significant source of income to corrupt nomenklatura members, state police, and other officials.

The flourishing second economy was a product of Soviet-style economic rigors combined with Polish-style social freedoms, disobedience, and disorder. While the rigors produced the need for a second economy, the freedoms made its functioning possible. The main pillars for this activity were Poland's relatively liberal foreign travel regulations combined with a highly overvalued dollar. The businesses run by the Polish amateur merchants were highly lucrative, especially because of the significant absolute and relative price differentials between West European and East European countries, as well as the internal price differentials among the Soviet bloc countries.

Despite the changes in the political and economic system after 1989, the second economy not only did not contract but expanded greatly. Many factors explain why this has been so, including:

- the fiscal system: Private employers stay underground to evade taxation and other payments such as health care and social security.
- the liberal work security system combined with high unemployment: Workers are motivated to collect their unemployment benefits and work illegally in the unofficial sector.
- the weak banking system: Bank loans are barely available to small private businesses which are forced to use different non-bank money sources.[13]
- the weak law and order system: This system was weakened, in part, purposely by the new authorities to make Poland compatible with a Western-style democracy; in part, it became less effective because of the dismantling of the old security forces. Poland turned into a link in a new international mob network that deals in car thefts, narcotics, and prostitution.
- the liberal foreign travel system: Combined with significant price and wage differentials between Poland and its neighbors, the travel system enables and motivates cross-border shopping trips and other profitable activities, including illegal work, by tourist-businesspeople. While not all of these activities are illegal, tariff and tax evasion is pervasive.[14]

In Poland under communism, the private sector's share in the national economy was significantly higher than in other Communist countries. For example, before 1989 in Bulgaria and Czechoslovakia, the contribution from the private sector to national income remained below 1 percent.[15] By contrast, the Polish private sector was much larger, accounting for a quarter of GDP during the 1960s. Its share decreased to a sixth between 1975 and 1980, declining as a result of the intense etatization policy of the Gierek regime during the 1970s and an overall decrease of the importance of agriculture, which had served as a bulwark of private economic activity. Between 1980 and 1988 the proportion of GDP produced by the official private sector remained in the vicinity of one-fifth. In 1989 it jumped to one-third,[16] and reached more than two-fifths in 1991.

In 1994 the private sector's share of GDP was 52 percent. This share for labor was 61 percent[17]; for fixed assets, 39 percent; for capital investment, 44 percent; for exports, 51 percent; and for imports, 66 percent. For the nonfarm activities the corresponding numbers were: GDP, 49 percent; labor, 47 percent; and assets, 33 percent. Only in five categories of production did the private sector account for more than half of their labor force: 96 percent in agriculture, 95 percent in trade,[18] 79 percent in construction, 74 percent in hotels and restaurants, and 62 percent in real estate and business services.

These numbers do not include the second economy, which is estimated to produce an additional 20 to 30 percent of GDP. It is estimated that about one-half of those registered as unemployed (or about 15 percent of the labor force in 1995) are engaged in different kinds of unofficial activities. Also family members who help the owners of the 4 million individually owned farms and small non-farm firms are not fully accounted for by the official statistics. Other individuals not covered by the official statistics are the owners and employees, often part-timers, of unregistered firms. If all of these are included, then the Polish economy of 1995 emerges as a predominantly private one in which the public sector accounts for only about 25 percent of labor force activities, including 20 percent in the state sector (which is increasingly "commercialized") and 5 percent in the municipal sector. The increase in the importance of the private sector has been especially significant in foreign trade, which until 1989 remained an official state monopoly; no private firm was allowed to export or import without a state permit. The private sector's share grew, between 1990 and 1994, from 5 to 51 percent in total exports and from 14 to 66 percent in total imports. Again, these numbers do not include several billion dollars of small scale "over-the-border" trade with the neighboring countries.

Warsaw now has an active stock exchange that operates under the 1991 Law of Public Trading and Trust Fund, modeled after the Lyons, France, Bourse. The Exchange, symbolically, is located in the building of the former Central Committee of the Polish Communist Party. Operations began in April 1991, with the trading of shares of five privatized companies. After a modest start, the Exchange boomed in 1993 but has been relatively sluggish thereafter.[19]

The banking system includes 9 state commercial banks, the state agricultural bank, 80 private banks, and 1,600 agricultural co-op banks. Two of the commercial banks have been privatized, while the others have been recapitalized and required to adopt plans for dealing with bad debts. The state agricultural bank is $890 million in debt and is likely to receive an infusion of funds. Around 25 percent of the private banks are insolvent, and some of them are being merged into state banks. "The government now says it wants to consolidate banks before privatizing them, on the grounds that regional banks need to be replaced by stronger national groupings. But this process is fraught with difficulties, not least the question of how to price a newly merged bank. More ominous is the possibility that the Polish government is no longer keen to privatize the banks at all. There have been worrying signs of greater government interference—members of the supervisory boards of banks have been sacked, for instance, and replaced by political appointees."[20]

## Manufacturing

Poland was traditionally an agricultural country. Its very name derives from an old Slavic word, *Pole,* meaning "arable field." Throughout a thousand plus years of Poland's history, manufacturing, trade, and other city-type industries were held in low regard. Some of them were considered morally dubious (especially trade and banking). A deeply rooted model of a "good" Pole was either a simpleminded modest villager, God-fearing and hardworking, or a romantic nobleman-knight, loving the fatherland, courageous and trustworthy during war, caring master of his estates during peacetime, enjoying an idyllic life insulated from worldly business by the fields, forests, and rivers of his lands.

This antimercantile/antibourgeois Polish philosophy of life was reinforced by a more recent history. Since the mid-1600s frequent wars have destroyed Polish towns and cities. The partition of Poland by foreign powers, 1795-1918, stimulated patriotic and altruistic feelings. During the last two centuries, in Poland, a popular capitalist/American life model—from bootblack to millionaire—was pushed aside by another one—the model of an impoverished nobleman who sacrificed his estates (and eventually his life) in the struggle for freedom of his country. Selfish founding of new businesses, acquiring property, and getting richer was not fashionable.

These antibusiness altruistic attitudes were quite compatible with both the traditional teaching of the Catholic church and the progressive socialist ideology that dominated country's political scene since the late 1800s. Also, the occupiers (Bismarck's Germany as well as Stalin's Soviet Union) viewed Polish industrialists as their enemies. More often than not the occupying powers treated Polish lands as their colony; Poland was to provide food for the German army, not tanks.

After consecutive bloody uprisings, even those few Poles who possessed a business lost it. They were killed, or imprisoned, or had to leave the country, while their property was destroyed during combat, taken away by the authorities, or both. After World War I Poland remained a predominantly agricultural country. In 1921 less than 10 percent of the labor force was employed in industry. (See Table 4.1.) Industry's relatively high contribution to GDP reflected the high relative prices of industrial products, or the so-called widely opened scissors between industrial and agricultural products, the latter being relatively much cheaper than the former.

**TABLE 4.1: SHARE OF MANUFACTURING AND CONSTRUCTION IN POLAND'S ECONOMY, 1921–1995, PERCENT**

| Labor | | GDP | |
|---|---|---|---|
| Year | Percent | Year | Percent |
| 1921 | 9.5 | — | — |
| 1931 | 12.3 | 1935 | 45.0 |
| 1950 | 25.7 | 1947 | 39.0 |
| 1977 | 39.8 | 1978 | 64.4 |
| 1985 | 35.9 | 1985 | 59.9 |
| 1990 | 35.4 | 1990 | 54.2 |
| 1993 | 31.6 | 1993 | 40.0 |
| 1994 | 30.0 | 1994 | 42.9 |
| — | — | 1995 | 44.2 |

As concerns ethnicity, according to the 1931 census, which categorized people as Polish, Jewish, German, and other, about 52 percent of owners of industrial enterprises (employers and self-employed) were Polish and about 40 percent were Jewish, 2 percent were Germans, and 6 percent all others. Among the white-collar employees in industry, 70 percent were Polish, 21 percent Jewish, 6 percent Germans, and 3 percent all others. Almost all Jewish and many Polish owners and white collar workers perished during the war.

After 1945 Poland experienced a period of the Soviet-type rapid "socialist industrialization" and was transformed into an industrial country. By 1950 a quarter of Poland's labor force was employed in industry. That proportion increased by about one-half percentage point annually to reach its apogee in 1977-78, when two-fifths of the Polish labor force were working in industry, accounting for almost two-thirds of GDP. At that time, according to official statistics, Poland was classified as the tenth biggest industrial producer of the world. During the 1980s the proportion of the labor force employed in industry stabilized at 35 to 38 percent. Since 1988 it has fallen by a percentage point every year. In 1994 industry accounted for 30 percent of the labor force. Each of its main subgroups, fuel and energy (including mining), machinery, food, and construction, accounts for about 20 percent of total industrial output.

In Communist Poland as in all other Soviet bloc countries, industrialization was to play a crucial role in the program of economic growth and social change. A main political mission of the industrialization was to create a large and power-ful industrial working class whose effective leadership/dictatorship, according to Karl Marx, was necessary for all socialist transformations. The economic and social missions of industrialization were to create material foundations for a modern soci-ety, provide jobs, secure decent living standards for millions, and generate means for housing, education, and health care. These means were managed partly cen-trally and partly by the enterprises themselves, which became involved in expen-sive social programs that provided hefty subsidies to housing, municipal facilities, trade and distribution, education, culture, entertainment, and health care.

All large industrial enterprises were state owned. Due to the Communist prin-ciple of ownership indivisibility, all real estate and other property was owned by the state, not the firms. Until 1981 the financial autonomy of state enterprises was quite limited, with the state absorbing most of their net revenues. The well-known soft budget constraint system was widely practiced.[21]

The (Lenin) Nowa Huta steel mill in Cracow served as a symbol of new socialist Poland in the 1950s. The Płock refinery, constructed to process Soviet oil pumped to Poland through a newly built Friendship pipeline, was a major investment of the 1960s. During the 1970s two major Gierek undertakings were the Huta Katowice (supposedly the largest steel mill in the world) and the small-car Fiat factory in Bielsko-Biała, the latter of which embodied the consumer socialism that Gierek preached. It brought to Poland modern Western technol-ogy and was to provide people with a popular car, affordable and economical.

In the late 1980s Poland was dominated by giant state enterprises, such as coal mines in Silesia and in central Poland, copper mines in western Poland, oil refiner-ies in Płock and Gdańsk, steel mills in Warsaw, Cracow, and Katowice, the Cegielski machinery factory in Poznań, the Gdańsk and Szczecin shipyards, the Bielsko-Biała car factory (Polski Fiat), and the Ursus tractor factory near Warsaw.

All of the large factories erected by the Communists turned into powerful political centers that, during the 1980s, became home for the Solidarity labor union. The workers' organizations in these factories played a crucial role in bring-ing the workers' state to an end.

Heavy industry was blamed for many Communist-era evils: fast urbaniza-tion that uproots traditional values, discrimination against the villagers, over-crowded industrial giants, environmental devastation, low usefulness and bad quality of industrial production.

The Communist authorities did not allow for any large-scale private industrial companies. Those few Poles who successfully managed to run small industrial shops had to operate at the margin of legality and to make suspicious deals with the Communist nomenklatura.

The 1990-92 recession struck manufacturing harder than other branches of the economy. If 1989 is considered as 100 percent, by 1992 Poland's GDP totaled only 82.9 percent, with manufacturing reaching only 66.4 percent; transportation, 68.8 percent; agriculture, 93.3 percent; construction, 94.6 percent; trade, 108.6 percent; and housing, 133.5 percent.

Market-oriented manufacturing reforms have been difficult and painful, involving major structural transformations away from coal, steel, and machinery toward consumer-oriented products. Due to an obsolete technology and the lack of market experience, many enterprises could not compete successfully in a more open and more liberal economy after 1989. Yet after a few years of rapid decline, the situation in industry turned around and a strong recovery began. Manufacturing's gross output grew by 6.2 percent in 1993, by 11.9 percent in 1994, and by about 11 percent in 1995.

Privatization in manufacturing has been sluggish. In 1994 only 44 percent of the manufacturing labor force worked in the private sector, as compared to 60 percent for the whole economy. This slow rate can be explained partly by the power of industrial state enterprises and also by their recent economic successes. Privatizing an enterprise that provides jobs to thousands of people is a complex procedure, both in terms of its logistics as well as inherent political risks. In a country run by weak minority governments and divided legislatures, decisions concerning large plants are difficult to reach. Paradoxically, the relatively good performance of state enterprises during the last two to three years has weakened the motivation for their privatization.[22]

### Agriculture

Polish agriculture is full of spectacular contrasts. On the one hand, it was and continues to be an activity of great importance. Under communism it enjoyed more freedom than any other industry or social group. Under democracy it constitutes a bastion for always powerful peasant parties. At the same time, agriculture has been the least productive industry, stagnant and backward.

A major handicap of Polish agriculture has been its unfortunate spatial structure. At the beginning of the twentieth century there existed, on the one hand, a small number of large landed estates of mostly capitalist character in the West and semifeudal character in the East, and, on the other hand, a very large number of small subsistence peasant holdings. In 1921 only a third of all farms were classified as self-sufficient (an area above 12 acres [5 hectares]). Larger farms—those of 25 acres (10 hectares) or more—accounted for 68.7 percent of farmland.[23] Estates—farms above 125 acres (50 hectares) constituted only 0.9 percent of all farms, but their owners held almost half of the land.[24]

In 1993 the situation was not much better. Only about 40 percent of farms were more than 12 acres (5 hectares). Of the 44 million acres (18.7 million hectares) of farmland, as of 1993, 78.3 percent of this land was in individual farms (76.2 percent in 1989), 13.9 percent was in state farms (18.7 percent in 1989), and 3.3 percent was in cooperative farms (4.1 percent in 1989).

Also as of 1994, 95.4 percent of farm workers are in the private sector.[25] The farm economy is not robust; hidden unemployment is high, estimated at a few million farmers.

Table 4.2 presents the share of the private sector in agriculture from 1960 until 1993. Note that, in this table, cooperatives are not included in the private sector. In this period, the status of individual farms in Polish agriculture can be best depicted by a U curve. As a result of policies in general unfriendly to individual farming during the 1960s and 1970s, the private sector shrank. However, at the end of this period, the private sector began recapturing its share.

**TABLE 4.2: PRIVATE-SECTOR AGRICULTURE AS A SHARE OF ALL AGRICULTURE**

| Private Sector Share | 1960 | 1980 | 1989 | 1993 |
|---|---|---|---|---|
| Labor | 90.8 | 77.9 | 79.1 | 95.4 |
| Land | 72.6 | 69.3 | 71.1 | 78.3 |
| Cattle | 88.5 | 72.8 | 82.1 | 89.0 |
| Gross output | 88.8 | 78.6 | 79.6 | 86.0 |

Although the numbers presented in Table 4.2 are notable for a Communist state, it is important to emphasize that the effective degree of "privateness" of Polish farmers was not as high as is usually the case in countries with market economies. A peculiar combination of monopolistic and monopsonistic practices existed in agriculture. Agricultural supplies and procurement were largely state controlled. At the same time, a sizable private segment has existed. Some rural services remained in private hands; for example, farmers were able to sell a part of their produce at farmers' markets where prices were not directly controlled.

One of the most challenging dilemmas for the Polish post-1989 reform leaders is the economic weakness of many small private farms. Most of them are subsistence farms, doomed to extinction under a competitive market economy. Many of the farmers are old and emotionally attached to their land. They will resist any policy that, while aiming at economic efficiency, would lead to major shifts in land ownership. If agricultural labor is to become as productive as labor in other industries, about three-quarters of the people currently employed in agriculture would have to be shifted to other economic activities. The social pain and its political costs of such an operation make it hardly feasible. Yet, a continuous process of countryside marketization can be expected: more hired labor, more mechanization, and increasing average farm size.[26] Socially it will result in greater polarization—more large (and expanding), modern, highly productive farms in contrast to many small, poor (and contracting), subsistence farms.

*Agriculture in the Past: 1918 to 1989*

To give a fair picture of Polish agriculture under communism, it is necessary to look back to the conditions that prevailed after World War I and under the Nazi and Soviet occupations. Food is an especially strategic resource during difficult times—the wars, social upheavals, and economic breakdowns that were quite frequent in the eventful history of Poland during this century. Access to food defined political, economic, and military powers. Both foreign occupants during wars and Communist dictators imposed stiff controls over agricultural production and food distribution. The Nazis punished those who traded food illegally with the death penalty.

Polish agriculture was heavily damaged by World War I and then by the Polish-Soviet war in 1919-20. About 75 percent of farm buildings were destroyed and much land lay fallow.[27] After a quite successful recovery in the 1920s, Polish agriculture was hit by the Great Depression. Then, after another recovery, the German and Russian occupations began. Under both, terror, land confiscation, and mass deportations were the rule.

A major obstacle to agricultural growth was the so-called widely open price scissors—relative price differentials between urban and rural products. Before World War II, the relative underdevelopment of industry made industrial goods scarce and expensive, while the prices of food remained low. This was especially dramatic during the Great Depression when food prices were so low that small (and inefficient) food producers could barely survive. Between 1928 and 1935 the prices of agricultural output declined twice as fast as those of agricultural input. Consequently, the scissors, already wide open in 1928, opened even wider.[28] During World War II food, due to its scarcity, gained significantly in value.[29] After the war in Poland, as in Soviet Russia in the 1930s, socialist industrialization was accomplished by underpricing agricultural products and pumping the funds up from villages to the cities. By making machinery expensive and food inexpensive, the artificially wide-open price scissors kept farmers' revenue often below the level of their full production cost.[30] The fact that relative prices of two major production factors in agriculture—labor and land— tended to decrease over time indicates the low attraction of agriculture. Low profitability and low wages stimulated a negative selection: Weak and low-skilled labor, mainly women and elderly, stayed, and the strong and high-skilled labor, mainly men and youth, left. Nominal wages in agriculture between 1960 and 1990 grew about 30 percent more slowly than average wage growth.

Polish farmers, by their sheer number (people and territory) and "class solidarity," have always been a difficult social group to control. Successful preservation of the private sector in agriculture after 1944 was both a major cause and effect of the "mildness" of the Polish Communist dictatorship, which had to, or chose to, allow for more personal freedom and more anti-Communist resistance than did regimes in other Communist countries. While the Communist authorities were too weak to cause private agriculture to wither away, they were strong enough to thwart its expansion. This stalemate had a negative effect on the performance and growth of private agriculture.

Even though the country was under a totalitarian dictatorship, one that officially preached a Marxian dogma of the need for public ownership of all means of production, over two-thirds of all farmland—over half of Communist Poland territory—remained, at least formally, privately owned. About 80 percent of the crucial strategic commodity—food—was produced by private individuals who often applied condemned bourgeois practices: They exploited hired labor, invested capital, and sought to maximize profit.

In Poland, Communist institutions coexisted with a grass-roots opposition movement. The former were "legal" but suffered from lack of legitimacy; the latter was illegal (most of the time) but enjoyed support from millions of Poles. The individual farmers coexisting with state bureaucrats and apparatchiks personified a uniquely eclectic and chaotic version of market socialism. They were the only large-scale private individual owners in the Soviet bloc countries. Poland had more private activities, more market, and more individual initiative than any other Communist country.

After 1945, on the land that remained Polish, agriculture offered many opportunities: many small producers, private ownership of the land, relatively high homogeneity of agricultural products. All these features created good conditions for the establishment of a competitive dynamic market. Yet the Polish Communist regime never permitted this market to operate freely and used a variety of measures to control tightly the individual farmers. These measures included forced expropriations, restrictions on selling and buying land, administrative price regulations, constraints on trade, quota deliveries in kind, and, later on, tie-in transactions —farmers were forced to sell to state agencies specific quantities of their products in order to be eligible for such crucial supplies as coal, fertilizers, and animal feed that were barely available outside of state-controlled distribution.

In 1952, when the system of forced deliveries was at its peak, it accounted for more than 90 percent of all grain sold by farmers. (This time was also a peak of Stalinist terror in Poland.) The discrimination against larger, more productive farms was especially severe, particularly in the case of farmer-capitalists (those who hired paid manpower). The authorities were sensitive to any symptoms of capitalism, such as good condition of the buildings, a clean yard, and competent work organization. In 1952-53, an average tax burden for smallholders was about 10 percent of their estimated income, while owners of larger farms paid 40 percent.

After 1956 the economic policy toward agriculture became more liberal. Obligatory deliveries were reduced and, in the 1970s, abolished completely. While fiscal burden was diminished, many bureaucratic regulations continued to stymie economic activities and pushed peasants into a black market.[31]

The struggle of Polish peasants provided them with strength and endurance but had a negative impact on their economic well-being. Often farmers found it difficult to obtain supplies of many necessary industrial products and had to learn to be self-sufficient.

In Communist Poland, agriculture was not favored, as were manufacturing and other industries, and its position in the economy dwindled. While, according to official statistics, industrial production between 1938 and 1989 increased thirty-three times, agricultural production less than doubled. During this time, cattle herds increased by 1 percent; pigs by 151 percent,and sheep by 29 percent,while the population increased by 9 percent.

*Agriculture Post-1989*

Since 1989 agriculture, together with the rest of the Polish economy, has undergone major changes. The changes in agriculture, however, were not as traumatic in Poland as those in other Central and Eastern European countries. Less privatization was implemented, since over 70 percent of agriculture was already in private hands. For many years Poland has had "white," "gray," and "black" markets of hired manpower, land, buildings, machinery, livestock, and agricultural products, so the marketization of Polish agriculture produced less spectacular effects than elsewhere.

The situation of forestry is different. Forests constitute 28 percent of Poland's territory. As of 1994, 16.7 percent were owned by individuals (17.0 percent in 1990) and 82.4 percent were owned by the state treasury (82.5 percent in 1990). There are no provisions either for restitution or sale of the state forests.

In 1989 almost two-fifths of the population lived in the countryside. Agriculture accounted for one-fourth of Poland's total labor force and one-fifth of total fixed capital. Factor productivity in agriculture was the lowest among all industries and, in relative terms, underwent a very steep decline. In 1938, while accounting for about 55 percent of labor and 15 percent of capital stock it produced 33 percent of GDP; in 1989, the corresponding numbers were: 26 percent of labor, 22 percent of capital stock, and 12 percent of GDP. Shock therapy severely affected farmers. Between 1989 and 1993 agriculture's contribution to GDP (in current prices) decreased from 12 to 7 percent.[32] The share of agricultural investment in total investment decreased from 14 to 6 percent. The size of livestock herds decreased dramatically: cattle by 32 percent, pigs by 7 percent, and sheep by about 50 percent. At the same time the agricultural share of labor, capital, and land remained almost unchanged.

Despite its very low GDP share, Polish agriculture continues to play a crucial role in the economy. More than two-fifths of household expenditures are directed toward food (including 13 to 18 percent on meat) in Poland, compared to one-sixth in the U.S. Polish households spend two to three times more on food than on housing, while the converse is true in the U.S. This fact, of course, reflects the heavy subsidies housing in Poland has received.

The major events in agriculture after 1989 have been relative price changes, structural shifts, and efforts to sell state farmlands; the first two are discussed here, while sales are discussed later.

In July 1989 the last Communist government, shortly before its dissolution, decided to free all food prices. This move created chaos in the market and led to skyrocketing inflation. While farmers' revenues increased significantly, this prosperity was short-lived. After the Balcerowicz shock therapy was introduced in January 1990, a farm depression began.[33]

While between 1988 and 1993 the average real wage in nonfarm industries decreased by 20 percent, the real income of farmers declined by 60 percent,[34] and real investment in private agriculture declined by 80 percent.

As the financial situation of farmers deteriorated, their demands for state intervention increased. Among other things, farmers demanded the introduction of minimum prices for agricultural products, often at a level not only above the current domestic market prices but also above world prices. The government granted several concessions under pressure from an active peasant lobby tacitly supported by the church. It founded a number of institutions to deal with the crisis in agriculture, including the Fund for Debt Reduction and Restructuring of Agriculture (Fundusz Oddłużenia i Restrukturalizacji Rolnictwa) and the Agricultural Market Agency (Agencja Rynku Rolnego). The former was to design a financial policy, the latter was to set up appropriate measures to stabilize agricultural prices ("to keep the prices in domestic market within an acceptable range of fluctuations around the world prices"). Import tariffs were significantly increased; since August 1991 most agricultural imports have been charged a duty of 20 to 40 percent. Also, other barriers were introduced, including licenses and strict regulations concerning veterinary and phytosanitary conditions. An obvious result of this policy was further upward pressures on prices and wages. Also, food exports became less competitive on the world market, while, despite tariffs, foreign competition remained strong.

Between 1989 and 1990 the profitability of state farms declined by half, and in 1991 they ended up deep in the red. The average rate of loss (negative profit) in the years 1991-92 came to 22 percent. In those years the performance of state agriculture was worse than that of any other major industry, including such traditional nonprofits as housing and municipal facilities.[35] Stripped of most subsidies, the state farms borrowed heavily from the state to buy machinery and feed, paying from 30 to 60 percent interest. In spring of 1993, almost 750,000 acres (300,000 hectares) remained fallow, because the farms were denied further credit.

Since 1990 the share of cooperatives and state farms in agricultural activities has declined. Between 1990 and 1993 the number of cooperatives decreased from 2,270 to 2,170, their land share declined from 4 to 3.3 percent, their labor share dropped from 3.7 to 2.2 percent, and their output share fell from 7.9 to 3.6 percent. A greater downsizing occurred in the state farm sector, where labor share declined from 9.4 to 4.6 percent, while its land share declined from 20.0 to 16.4 percent.

In addition to weak demand, another factor that has reduced agricultural income per capita is the absorption of idle workers released from manufacturing. Paradoxically, the backwardness of Polish agriculture now plays a positive role providing a cushion for reforms in other economic sectors. Polish agriculture can absorb more labor than agriculture in a more advanced economy.[36]

The prospects for the outflow of excess labor force from the countryside are not good. A high unemployment rate makes it unlikely that manufacturing and services can absorb excess farm workers. Thus, labor productivity in agriculture will remain low for a longer period of time; as will the competitiveness of Polish food products, unless agricultural wages remain low and the structure of output evolves toward labor-intensive products.

Farmers carry little debt, in part because few sources of farm credit exist. As of 1991, only 10 percent of the 2.1 million farms were pledged for any debt, and only 1 percent of farmers had defaulted on their loans. Land taxes are low, and farmers also are subsidized by state payment of over 90 percent of the contributions to the Farmers' Social Security Fund.

### Housing

Poles are not happy with their housing, which has been a crazy quilt of private and public ownership with a complex set of controls on occupancy and disposition. Many families waited for a decade and longer on lists for co-op housing after having made a down payment. Some of them still do not have an apartment. Many owners are forced to accommodate unwanted tenants at rents that do not cover maintenance. Some families still live doubled up with parents or others. Some can not move, even if they no longer have a job, because there is no housing in a location where jobs exist. The situation in housing has been helped by lower birth rates and emigration. Quality, distribution, price, and access remain serious obstacles to the decent housing for all that so many successive leaders have promised.

The government has attempted some improvement, so a new law has given the *gminas* power, within limits, to set rent levels and the state provides housing allowances for the poor. However, a dwelling allocation system (the "public management of dwellings") persists and covers a large proportion of apartments and houses, with rents controlled until 2005.

*Housing Under Communism*

Paradoxically, in Communist Poland, shelter status defined an important stratification by dividing people into Haves and Have Nots—those who possessed an apartment (an official apartment allocation) and those who did not. The housing industry was an external manifestation of the centrally planned economy at its worst. By partly observing and partly violating property rights in real estate, Communist authorities created many legal and social problems, and a thriving black market. Almost no family in Poland has not been affected by the housing chaos. Even today a large number of Poles live in one place but are formally registered in another place—the name labels on apartment doors and the names listed in telephone directories may be quite misleading. There are still homeless owners of houses and those who own no dwelling but live in comfortable apartments paying a relatively low rent. Some people lost and purchased back the same unit more than once.

More often than not, the Communist authorities chose to ignore, rather than to take over, legal property rights to residential buildings. The separation of the right to own from the right to use became pervasive. Little attention was paid to ownership title. In many cases, when an effective transfer of the ownership title took place, the formalities were not pursued and were considered unimportant.[37]

After World War II all residences were subordinated to a system of public management of dwellings, within which the main role was played by the so-called *kwaterunek,* run by the municipal authorities. Almost all of the existing urban housing stock was organized by number of dwelling units, and each family had to apply for an official allocation of a unit. An owner of a larger apartment building could apply for assignment of one of its apartments for his or her family. *Kwaterunek* authorities turned down many of these applications, often because of the applicant's unwelcome social roots, or simply because all the apartments had already been allocated to other tenants. In general, one family was allowed to use no more than one unit. Many apartments were shared by two and more families. Special regulations governed who could occupy what size and kind of apartment and how much the rent should be. Rents, calculated on the size of apartments and their technical standards, were collected by the apartment owners, socialized and private, and were supposed to cover the cost of maintenance without allowing for any profit to property owners.[38] Most of the time, however, they remained below this cost, which resulted in forced owner's subsidies, gradual financial decapitalization (the cost of maintenance was charged to equity), and gradual physical decapitalization (devastation of the buildings). The prewar housing stock, in particular, was not properly maintained and today has the lowest standard.

After World War II, the dictator of Stalinist Poland, Bolesław Bierut, initiated a large-scale effort to rebuild the country. He waged a passionate propaganda campaign aimed at the construction of new modern apartment buildings
of brick, cement, glass, and marble, bright and spacious, "beautified" by soc-
realistic ornaments, to be contrasted against old, dense, dark, and dirty capitalist housing. Each of the new buildings was to be a symbol, a monument of a new
superior social order introduced under the leadership of the Soviet Union and
the Polish United Worker's Party (Polska Zjednoczona Partia Robotnicza, or
PZPR). Housing enjoyed strong support from the highest political authorities.
The propaganda around reconstruction of old and construction of new houses
was intense. The bricklayer erecting houses in Warsaw and other cities was
declared a national hero (called maliciously by some a "Communist saint"). The
artists creating in the officially sponsored, or imposed, style of soc-realism
praised the bricklayer's effort in poems, songs, paintings, sculptures, and
movies. Out of the darkness and poverty of capitalism, out of fascist destruction, a new country emerges: "We are building our new home, to welcome our
days and you, Warsaw. . . ."

After 1956 Władysław Gomułka introduced major changes to his predecessor's housing policy. The romantic era of joyful construction ended. The comfortable "home of our dreams" was scaled down to a crowded flat in a drab
concrete-and-steel building, more often than not located in the middle of the mud
and clay of "faraway suburbs." To speed up the procedure, tenants had to move
into unfinished apartments. Gomułka vowed that, by the 1970s, each Polish
family would have its own apartment. In order to fulfill his promise, he opted for
quantity at the expense of quality. The so-called Gomulkian housing norms lowered living standards to a bare minimum. For example, each person was entitled
to only 50 to 70 square feet (5 to 7 square meters) of living (bedroom) space. A
typical 1960s Polish urban family, composed of two parents and three children,
was entitled to a modest flat (no more marble stairs and crystal lights) of two small
rooms, small kitchen, and a tiny bath totaling about 350 to 500 square feet (35
to 50 square meters). Gomułka's housing restrictions were a response to the growing housing shortage, a direct consequence of the growth of urban population from
the demand side and, from the supply side, insufficient construction of new
housing in the 1950s. Urban population increased due to several factors, including a high rate of natural population growth caused by the baby boom of the 1950s,
combined with prolonged life spans and the movement of millions from the
countryside to cities as a result of the progress in socialist industrialization.[39]

Over time, the *kwaterunek* rules tilted more to the owners, gradually increasing their rights. In the 1960s the authorities began issuing exemptions for owners
whereby entire smaller houses and parts of larger houses were removed from the
*kwaterunek* system. The apartments taken off this system were no longer controlled

by various rigid rules and regulations, such as those concerning numbers of square meters per person and persons per room. The owners became free to sell or rent their property. In the case of apartments already occupied by tenants, however, the owner's authority remained quite limited. In principle, in order to remove a tenant, the owner had to provide a replacement dwelling. Doing so was quite a difficult and expensive task. The eviction procedure was costly and complicated, often taking many years. Evicting tenants was always easier for the authorities than for private owners. The Communist authorities did it quite frequently in the late 1940s and early 1950s. Eviction proceedings were much more difficult for individuals without the appropriate connections. After 1956 evictions of any types by anybody became very difficult unless the tenant agreed to cooperate. Even the removal of an illegal or so-called wild tenant (the person without a *kwaterunek* allocation) was lengthy and expensive. Apartment "invasions" were not infrequent with homeless, or *kwaterunekless,* families breaking into vacant apartments and taking over.

Despite Gomułka's efforts and solemn promises, the overall housing situation during his tenure did not improve much. Between 1960 and 1970, the number of apartments per 1,000 population increased by less than 5 percent. In 1970, when Gomułka was ousted from office, many families remained without independent apartments, the average size of new apartments was small, and the average waiting time was longer than before.

The new Communist leader, Edward Gierek, offered to the nation an attractive and ambitious vision, distinct from that of his predecessor. Apartments, according to Gierek, must be large and comfortable. All families should get them without having to wait for long. Large apartment buildings should predominate, but individual family houses were also approved. All of the housing changes were to be accomplished by the construction of a "Second Poland," one of the buzz phrases of Gierek's propaganda campaign. "We will help!" "The Pole can make it!" "Let Poland grow in strength and people live comfortably!" were some of the new slogans welcomed by the oppressed and impoverished nation, which were to bring self-confidence and hope. The new administration demonstrated the goodwill, dynamism, and competence necessary to fix the First Poland and, in addition, to build a Second one. In the early 1970s incomes increased significantly and many higher-quality imported consumer goods appeared on store shelves. It was believed that satisfied populace would become more productive. Technological progress, in turn, was to be accomplished by loans from Western countries, which would enable the purchase of modern machinery and technology.

Yet when Gierek was removed in 1980, the waiting time in housing cooperatives was even longer than in 1970. Although the size and quality of new co-op units constructed in the 1970s improved and the number of new apartments increased (the indicator of apartments per 1,000 people between 1970 and 1980 was raised by 10.7 percent), housing supply still remained much too small to satisfy the constantly growing demand created by the baby boomers' getting married and setting up new families.

Gierek was brought to power by worker riots in Gdańsk and fell from power in the wake of another wave of workers' unrest in this city and elsewhere, unrest that led to the emergence of the Solidarity labor union. In the agreements between Communist authorities and the union, the government promised to shorten the waiting period for an apartment to no more than five years. During the 1980s, however, the number of apartments constructed systematically decreased. The waiting time often was twenty years or more; in many locations the waiting lists became unrealistically long and new applications were not accepted.

The following is a list of the most typical owner/tenant arrangements for dwelling units in the 1980s in Poland:

1. Unit owned and occupied by the owner.
2. Unit owned by a cooperative, in which the tenant possessed a so-called owner-type membership, which had to be purchased. It could be sold or inherited, but permission from the cooperative was necessary. Certain restrictions applied. For example, a married couple could not possess more than one co-op apartment, and the apartment could not be sold to a person who was not a permanent resident in Poland.
3. Unit owned by a cooperative, in which the tenant possessed a nonowner-type membership. In this case the apartment was not transferable. Tenancy could, however, be inherited, under certain conditions, by family members who lived with the co-op member.
4. Unit owned by the state, which was usually administered by a municipality or a state enterprise. During the preceding twenty years many of these apartments were sold to their occupants at a fraction of market price (the price that occupants would have had to pay if they purchased the same apartment from a private owner).
5. Unit owned by an individual occupied by somebody else with a valid formal allocation, with rent paid to the owner.
6. Unit occupied by a person without a *kwaterunek* allocation based on a private sublet contract between the owner and the tenant.
7. Unit occupied illegally by wild tenants.

The owner of the dwelling unit or a co-op member could dispose of the unit, by sale, gift, or will, only in cases (1), (2), and (6), and in the last case only if the actual tenant cooperated. In the remaining cases the existing *kwaterunek* allocation, or simply effective occupation, reduced the owner's control practically to zero.

The land on which a dwelling was located normally belonged to the owner of the dwelling. Warsaw was an exception: The land was municipal property usually rented under a ninety-nine-year lease to the building owner.

In the mid-1980s a typical Polish urban family living in a large or medium-size city, would have consisted of a husband, wife, and two children. Their total monthly income would have amounted to $20 to $100 at the "black" or free market exchange rate. If they were registered as official tenants of a dwelling they occupied, they would have spent about $2 to $7 a month for rent and other housing expenses for "old" housing stock (mostly municipal housing) and $5 to $25 for new housing stock (mostly co-op apartments built during the 1970s and the early 1980s). These rents, on average, covered 20 to 40 percent of maintenance costs. During the 1980s the rents and prices of co-op apartments surged in both nominal and real terms.

Those who were not officially registered as users of a dwelling and, at the same time, happened not to be very wealthy, became a socialist underclass. They had to rent dwellings in the "free" market and pay prices that in large cities often exceeded 50 to 60 percent of household incomes, especially in the case of young couples who decided to move out from a crowded parents' dwelling and become officially "homeless". In Warsaw the monthly cost of renting a modest studio was about $30 to $50; subletting a room cost about $20; renting a basement or a modest attic room cost $5 to $10. Prices were slightly lower in other large cities and much lower in small towns.

During the 1980s there were several alternative ways to acquire an apartment. Listed in the order from more expensive to less expensive, these were to: (1) buy an apartment through the regular real estate market; (2) build a new house by oneself; (3) join a housing cooperative; (4) "organize" an apartment by different kinds of illegal and semi-legal devices; (5) apply for an apartment at the husband's or wife's place of work; (6) apply for an apartment from the municipal stock; and (7) be given an apartment by rich in-laws or inherit on the death of a relative.

Obviously, alternative (7) did not happen very often. Alternative (6) was available only to low-income families and involved an undefined waiting time. As only a few enterprises provided their employees with apartments, alternative (5) was not available to most families. Alternatives (1) and (2) were viable for only a small group of rich and/or industrious families. The cost of a house or apartment purchased via the so-called free market in large cities was very high. In the mid-1980s, for example, a two-bedroom apartment of 600 square feet (60 square meters) would have cost $15,000 to $20,000, or the equivalent of 400 average monthly salaries. Since no mortgage loans were available, a buyer would have had to pay the total amount in cash.[40] A less expensive way was to "organize" an apartment (alternative 4), but this was available only to the shrewdest people.

Connections with nomenklatura and state administration bureaucrats were often a necessary but not sufficient condition for success. This alternative would involve various illegal activities, such as: breaking into a vacant apartment and convincing the authorities to legalize this new status quo; renting an apartment from a private person and, at the end of the rental period, refusing to move out; registering as a household member in a municipal apartment and transferring the *kwaterunek* allocation from the current tenant, especially by taking care of an elderly person who would agree to this transfer; and/or simply bribing the authorities to get a *kwaterunek* allocation for a municipal apartment.

For the vast majority of families in Warsaw or Gdańsk, the only way to acquire an apartment was to join a housing cooperative (alternative 3). To become eligible for a co-op apartment, a family had to deposit a sizable amount of money—equivalent to several hundred dollars—in a special housing savings account in a bank. Next, the family had to wait for from five to twenty years, and eventually it would be allocated a modest three- to five-room apartment of 500 to 900 square feet (50 to 90 square meters). Monthly payments would be about $20. They were supposed cover the maintenance costs and rent (for nonowner-type members) or a repayment of a housing loan, i.e., construction costs (for "owner" type members). Utilities were extra.

Doubling up was a frequent choice for those who could not obtain an apartment of their own. In 1988, 15.7 percent of households were officially living in two-household apartments and 3.8 percent in apartments containing three households and more. In one-third of all dwellings the density exceeded two persons per room, and in 11 percent it exceeded three persons per room.

Housing has been composed of four sectors: public sectors—municipal, state enterprises, and cooperatives—and the individual (private) sector. The municipal sector was most important during the 1950s; cooperatives and enterprises steadily gained importance as providers of housing during the 1960s and 1970s. From 1972 on, the municipal sector has offered apartments for sale to their tenants at low prices, mainly in order to relieve the state of increasing maintenance costs. Moreover, it was intended to help reduce the so-called overhang, or large cash savings possessed by a population for whom there were not enough consumer goods and services on the market. From 1972 to 1989, 144,300 municipal dwellings were sold to tenants.

The most recent year for which detailed housing data exist is 1988, the year of the last housing census. In that year, 30.5 percent of the stock had been built prior to 1945, 14 percent between 1945 and 1960, 17.8 percent between 1961 and 1970, 19 percent between 1971 and 1978, and the remaining 18.7 percent between 1979 and 1988. There were a total of 10.7 million units for a population of 37.9 million. Ownership was split as follows: municipal, 19.4 percent; cooperatives, 24.3 percent; enterprises, 12.7 percent; and private 43.5 percent.

Maldistribution of housing has played a role similar to that of feudal serf-dom. People were turned into medieval *glebae adscripti.* Moving from one location to another, especially from a village or smaller town to a larger city, became increasingly difficult. Most often, the only way a new factory could attract workers was to construct apartments on its own. Many persons worked in jobs only because housing was provided. In pre-1989 Poland housing short-ages slowed down the rural-urban migrations necessary for rapid industrialization and hence slowed down growth.[41]

The 1989 "Round Table" pact between the Communist authorities and the opposition leaders set the minimum level of resources devoted to housing con-struction, at the request of the Solidarity-led opposition, at 7 percent of the national income; in 1989 it was actually 4.1 percent.

*Housing Post-1989*

During the first four years of shock therapy (1990-93), the Sejm (the lower house of Polish Parliament) introduced a large number of laws, amendments, and regulations, but none of these directly addressed major housing problems. In 1990 and 1991, during the tenure of the Solidarity-installed government, the share of national income allocated to housing grew to about 5.6 percent, not the 7 percent of the 1989 pact. Prime Minister Hanna Suchocka, in her most important presentation to the Sejm devoted to the foundations of her govern-ment's socioeconomic policies, skipped the housing question altogether. According to Gorczyca,[42] this reflected a quite pragmatic and brutally honest approach to housing, free from the wishful declarations and false promises given by past Communist leaders. The situation improved somewhat, as a result of comprehensive housing reforms introduced in 1994-95 (already by the post-Communist authorities).

As of the early 1990s, the general housing situation in Poland remained dif-ficult. Significant improvements occurred in housing during the last thirty years of Communist rule, but they were below popular expectations. The number of apartments per 1,000 inhabitants increased between 1960 and 1988 by 21 per-cent, from 236 to 286. The same indicator for the number of rooms per 1,000 inhabitants increased by 67 percent, from 580 in 1960 to 970 in 1988. From 1988 to 1994 housing stock statistics have continued to improve: for number of apart-ments per 1,000 inhabitants by 3.5 percent to 296, and by number of rooms per 1,000 inhabitants by 5.1 percent to 1,019. Statistically, in 1991 each Pole could, for the first time, enjoy his or her own room.[43] Newly constructed apartments have been getting larger. Between 1950 and 1970, the average size of a newly constructed apartment was around 500 square feet (50 square meters). It grew to 600 square feet in the late 1970s, 700 square feet in 1985, 770 square feet in 1989, 840 square feet in 1993, and 916 square feet in the first half of 1995.[44] An average apartment in the 1950s had 2.6 rooms, while in 1980 it had 3.8 rooms, in 1989, 4.2 rooms, in 1994, 4.6 rooms.

The progress during the last few years was helped by the steep decline of natural population increase—from 11.2 per 1,000 in 1982 to 1.7 per 1,000 in the first half of 1995, and also by emigration. Between 1981 and 1990 the official annual average of persons emigrating from Poland was 26,700, while only 1,730 immigrated. Between 1991 and 1993 these numbers were 20,160 and 5,830. In reality, all of these numbers are likely to be several times larger. If so, then the actual housing situation should be better than that presented by the official statistics.

Since the mid-1970s residential construction has declined consistently. The number of new dwellings per 1,000 population declined from 7.3 in 1975 to 5.1 in 1985 and to 1.9 in 1994. Before 1989 the "bottleneck" remained on the supply side. After 1989 it turned into a predominantly demand-side phenomenon. Prohibitive prices prevented many people from buying new apartments. Also, many construction projects remain unfinished for lack of funds.[45]

Cooperative housing is mostly located in large and medium-size cities. The dominant form of housing construction in the 1970s and 1980s, it always was heavily subsidized. Now it is gradually loosing this privileged position. The new conditions are intended to offer equal opportunity for all housing investors. When the subsidies are substantially reduced, the cooperatives are expected to be less successful in competing in the market. A major problem of housing co-ops are long waiting lists of people who paid the required basic down payment and still did not receive an apartment. In 1992 there were 2.4 million persons— 0.9 million of full-fledged co-op members and 1.5 million co-op candidates— waiting for their apartments.[46] Among the co-op members, 0.5 million have been waiting for ten years or longer. In 1992-93 in Poland there was about 4.5 million housing saving books with a total of about $250 million on deposit.[47]

In 1992 there were 4,954 housing cooperatives, though only 2,091 owned housing stock (1,031 had 200 dwellings and less, 607 had more than 1,000 dwellings). The remaining 2,863 cooperatives were just beginning or planning the construction of dwellings.

The potentially great opportunities reflect equally great difficulties for the construction industry. Weak demand is a major cause of the low number of new housing starts. Unfinished projects, bankruptcies, and failures of many developers are not infrequent, in part due to unclear titles to land, red tape, and punishing tax regulations. Banks and other lending institutions still are reluctant to finance projects that are not 100 percent presold.[48] After 1990 the relative prices of construction services and materials decreased, making construction less profitable. This was a result of increased supplies of construction materials including imports as well as an inflow of cheap, often illegal, foreign labor from the former Soviet Union.

As mentioned, many Polish cities neglected modernization and renovation, and few firms are able to do such work. Low rents failed to provide funds necessary for building maintenance. An additional obstacle has been an overcentralization of the housing industry and burdensome bureaucratic procedures. However, since 1990 the decline in residential housing construction has been accompanied by an increase in reconstruction and modernization. While, in the public sector in 1990, only 15,000 dwelling units were renovated and modernized, in 1993 that number increased to 200,000, and more was expected for 1994.[49]

A new law was passed by the Sejm in the summer of 1994 and signed by President Wałęsa in September 1994 that effectively transferred from the state to the *gminas* the power to set rents. Affected is the 25 percent of the popula-tion that lives in the 3.5 million dwelling units subject to rent control. Maximum rents are pegged to construction costs in the *voivodship,* and the annual rent may not exceed 3 percent of average, current construction cost. Due to this law, rent increased from the national maximum of $0.012 per month per square foot (ZL 2,600 per month per square meter) to $0.098 per month per square foot (ZL 22,000 per month per square meter). The rents will remain regulated until 2005, being based on location and condition of the units. The housing allowances for the poor are paid by the *gminas* which are partially subsidized by the state. These allowances range from $20 to $30 per month (about ZL 0.5 million). Table 4.3 illustrates how the allowances are determined.[50]

### TABLE 4.3: HOUSING ALLOWANCE FORMULA, 1994 LAW

| Persons per household | Maximum income per person | Maximum area of dwelling unit, square feet | Minimum fraction of income spent for rent, percent |
|---|---|---|---|
| 1 | 150 percent of lowest pension ($140) | 350 | 15 |
| 2 | 100 percent of lowest pension ($95) | 400 | 12 |
| 3 | same | 450 | 12 |
| 4 | same | 550 | 12 |
| 5 | same | 650 | 10 |
| 6 | same | 700 | 10 |

As specified in Table 4.3, a family is eligible for the housing allowance if its total income per person is equal to or less than the lowest pension, or one and one-half of the lowest pension in one-person households (this pension in spring 1994 amounted to $95 [ZL 2 million] per month); if the area of the dwelling unit that the family occupies is not larger than that specified in the table (dwellings up to 30 percent larger than the maximum do not disqualify the applicant, but the amount of the allowance must be reduced in an inverse ratio to dwelling size);

and if the allowance covers the amount of rent in excess of 10 to 15 percent of family income, as specified in column 4.

The allowance is an entitlement which must be paid to all eligible families in the form of a cash transfer to an account of the building administration. For example, a four-member family of a Warsaw University professor whose monthly income is $300 (ZL 7 million), living in a three-room municipal apartment of 520 square feet (52 square meters) for which the monthly rent is $50 (ZL 1.1 million) would pay $36 in rent (12 percent of $300). The remaining $14 per month must be covered by an allowance from the city. Prior to October 1994, this family would have paid a monthly rent of about $6 (ZL 130,000) plus utilities.

Eligible families include tenants of municipal, co-op, and enterprise apartments. Also eligible are owners of apartments and single-family houses. Not eligible are people who rent their housing in the open market (without a formal allocation of the dwelling), people who run a business in their dwelling, and people—all farmers—who pay the agricultural tax.

The municipalities include the following factors in setting rents: building location; apartment location within a building, including floor and sun exposure; amenities of the unit; and condition of the building and apartment. Any owner intending to increase the rent must provide the tenant with three months' written notice specifying the grounds for the increase. The tenant may appeal this increase to a local court.

With little new housing being built, a draft law proposes that corporations termed Social Construction Societies be formed to build apartments for rent. A new governmental Housing Fund Agency[51] will cover 50 percent of their construction costs by providing preferential loans; 40 percent will be covered by the *gminas* and other shareholders; and 10 percent by the future tenants. The state and employers would subsidize interest. Preference would be given to low- and medium-income tenants, particularly to those who had waited longest for municipal or co-op housing and those whose families are living in the worst conditions. Rent would cover all maintenance costs and depreciation.

Many apartments still are owned by state enterprises.[52] Most of these apartments are located in large industrialized areas such as Upper Silesia. The cost of their construction and maintenance was included in the production costs of the enterprises. This "social achievement" of the Communist system has turned into a major burden which hampers the competitiveness of privatized companies. Another proposal that divided the Sejm provided for a transfer of the enterprises' dwelling stock to the *gminas*. Not surprisingly, the *gminas* resist this transfer, arguing that such a burden could lead to their bankruptcy.[53] The *gminas* already own one-third of all housing. The amount they receive as rent, including the housing subsidies, does not cover the full maintenance cost.

*Housing and the National Economy*

Those who studied Polish housing from a narrow "micro" perspective, namely that of the housing market, kept emphasizing an apparent underinvestment, excess demand, and shortage. Yet a broader "macro" approach—from the perspective of the whole national economy—could lead to different observations. The excess demand was produced by underpricing, which was made possible by huge subsidies. The artificially low prices stimulated demand and discouraged supply.

On the demand side, there was a dynamically growing population with its increasing expectations for better living, strengthened by the official propaganda. In a workers' state, the working class was told of its inalienable rights, as owners of their country free of parasite capitalists. Their numerous rights included a job with dignity, education, health care, culture, recreation, and, of course, decent housing. A paternalistic state was to take good care of people, secure jobs, fill store shelves with merchandise, and build hospitals, schools, and residences.[54] The individual would support the socialist transformations, work obediently in a socialized establishment, wait patiently as these goods and services were eventually delivered, and behave in a politically approved fashion. Regarding their dwellings, the citizens should apply to appropriate socialized institutions such as their municipality, state enterprise, or cooperative and wait until their time comes. While working actively to get a house or apartment on one's own, by purchasing it on the market or by building a new one, was always a viable option, it never enjoyed the official support reserved for the socialized forms of housing.

The Communist authorities opted for a centrally controlled allocation of dwellings, which was turned into a major divide-and-conquer instrument to reward the obedient and punish the dissident. Moreover, the acquisition of property, such as a private house, involved significant risks. Those few owners of new houses, usually located in wealthy suburbs, were subject to popular scorn. They were labeled capitalists, nouveau riche, or simply thieves; most of the time these accusations were not groundless. In Communist Poland, one could acquire enough money to build or buy a privately owned house, especially in a large city, by joining the corrupted nomenklatura; running a private business that, in most cases, would operate in the gray or black market; or taking advantage of the overpriced dollar by selling hard currency earned or obtained from abroad at the black market rate. Few legal ways to become rich existed.

While, on the demand side, the policies of Communist authorities inflated the demand for socialized housing, on the supply side the policies produced scarcity. Because each square meter of socialized housing had to be supported by state funds, there were obvious budget limits to how much could be built. Other sectors also had strong claims on government funds.

Very significant inefficiency and waste existed in the construction sector. For a long time, its performance was measured by gross output rather than by final product. Since gross output was expressed by construction costs, the larger the costs (the more material and labor used), the larger the gross output and better performance evaluation of a socialist construction enterprise. As a result, Polish construction became costly and material intensive. There were no strong incentives to introduce better technologies, to modernize and save.

Because the effective housing shortage was severe, users were willing to accept new apartments regardless of their condition. What really counted was the number of new dwelling units. These were delivered unfinished in buildings often erected in far suburbs of large cities, without roads and sidewalks, or food stores and schools. The lucky tenants of those few apartments that were delivered had to begin their tenancy repairing what was bungled, finishing what was unfinished, and then waiting years before the landscape around their homes was transformed into a livable space.

As in other Soviet bloc countries, the reduction of housing subsidies has transformed the housing shortage into a slack (excess supply). Given the relatively low standards of living, the residential stock in these countries is not as bad as it may seem to be. Around 1990, the average number of persons per dwelling was 3.3 in Poland and Slovakia; 3.0 in Russia and Slovenia; 2.7 in Belgium, Canada, and Latvia; 2.6 in Austria, Bulgaria, and Hungary; 2.5 in the Netherlands and the Czech Republic; and 2.4 in Britain, Estonia, Norway, and the United States. Although these statistics do not reflect the size and standard of apartments, nor account for different size families, they suggest that the housing shortage in Eastern Europe is not as great as the lengths of the lines of people waiting for apartments would suggest.

Compared to countries with similar levels of economic development and standards of living (with a GDP per capita of about $5,000 as is the case of many Latin American countries), the housing stock in Eastern Europe does not look bad at all.[55] In Poland and other Eastern European countries, housing prices were significantly distorted. They reflected neither construction and maintenance costs nor existing demand. They showed a wide spread for similar units, ranging from nothing or symbolic prices charged for apartments allocated or sold by the municipalities and state enterprises to very high prices occurring in the free market. The level of official prices mainly depended on when the housing was constructed. People who acquired their apartments in the 1950s got them almost free, and rents paid were symbolic. Those who got their apartments in the 1960s and 1970s often had to pay a sizable down payment, equivalent to several monthly salaries, and their monthly payments were higher. Finally, those who received their apartments in the 1980s had to pay an even larger down payment, and their monthly payments (housing loan repayment) could amount to the equivalent of a monthly wage or more. This last group is composed of many low-income young couples with children who pay rent much higher than that paid by those in the first group. A large proportion of the latter are middle-aged and elderly families, often the so-called emptynesters, or single widows and widowers. Many of them are former Communist nomenklatura members who occupy large apartments at low rents and are not motivated to trade them for smaller units. It is expected that the mentioned above 1994 housing law will improve this situation.

Housing policy has had significant spillovers to other segments of the economy, such as the consumer goods market and the labor market. Before 1989 housing shortages were strongly related to shortages of other consumer goods. Housing underspending resulted in relative overconsumption of food and food shortages. The recent reduction in housing subsidies resulted in major shifts in consumption. The changes that occurred in the housing industry after 1989 well illustrate the workings of the fundamental Marshallian supply and demand laws. As the price of housing increased, the quantity demanded declined. Construction of new units was reduced because simply people could not afford them.

In the early 1990s politicians and economists argued that housing has all the features of a key industry, a nationwide propulsive activity (the "locomotive"). For example, Zbigniew Brzezinski suggested that Poland undertake large-scale housing construction projects, reminiscent of American public works introduced by Roosevelt during the Great Depression. Brzezinski's proposal sought to fight unemployment, improve the overall housing situation in Poland, and, at the same time, lift the economy out of the recession that accompanied the nation's shock therapy. Obviously, for the housing industry to be successful in this "mission," ample investment funds are necessary. Such funds have not been available. As a result, from 1990 to 1994, when the housing industry could have been a major driving force for economic reforms, it ended up as a constraint to these reforms and lagged behind almost all other sectors. Housing has constrained growth many times in the past. The population's unhappiness with housing negatively affected their labor productivity and their support for the Communist regime. By the same token, after 1989, persons living under difficult housing conditions could hardly support the reforms of a government that, in their opinion, did not improve their living standards and even failed to give them hope for improvement in the foreseeable future.

Lack of housing in some locations has been a grave obstacle to the successful restructuring of the national economy. New jobs appear mostly in consumer goods industries and services in large cities. Large-scale layoffs often take place in small towns. As workers of a factory producing machinery or military equipment are laid off, a whole town loses its economic base. In some locations unemployment is low, and expansion is hampered by a labor shortage. In other locations the unemployment rate exceeds 50 percent. The absence of housing vacancies in large cities makes stabilizing the labor market difficult.[56]

There are many reasons why housing is less amenable to market reforms than other industries:

1. Price distortions have been more severe in housing than in other branches of the economy.

2. Basic housing is a necessity good; it is indispensable so demand for it has little elasticity and flexibility.

3. Housing, by its nature, must be subject to various regulations; market allocations are not as effective as in many other industries.

4. Privatization and restitution cannot produce quick results, since many homes are occupied by tenants who cannot be easily removed for social and political reasons.

5. Construction of new homes is capital intensive. It can hardly expand in a country with no large domestic savings. Transition-related hardships cause many households to spend rather than invest. Poland's foreign debt remains above $1,000 per capita and cannot/ought not grow much more. During the last six years, foreign direct investment amounted to about $6 billion, or $2 per capita per month. This is not enough to increase Poland's investments meaningfully.

Some form of governmental controls probably will remain a feature of the Polish housing market for many years. Although many of the central government's controls may be gradually removed, they are likely to be replaced by different local regulations. The de-etatization of the housing sector will not necessary lead to a its full marketization.

## RESTITUTION[57]

No general restitution law has been enacted since 1989, although several proposals have been drafted and debated. The absence of a decision by any of the consecutive parliaments leaves unresolved the moral dilemmas posed by the actions of former authorities. Difficult questions have arisen about the marketability of titles to property. Investment[58] has been hampered and the speed of ownership transformations and economic reforms has been slowed down.

One illustration of the roadblocks remaining in the path of transition and attraction of foreign investment is the case of Huta Warszawa, now Huta Luccini. Huta Warszawa was a huge, outmoded, polluting steel mill in the Warsaw suburbs, located there by the Communists to strengthen the working class in a city dominated by intelligentsia. In 1991 the enterprise was bankrupt. The State Treasury acquired it, after creditors forgave $22 million (ZL 240 billion) in interest, transforming the principal into shares valued at $4.2 million (ZL 45 billion). In 1992 an Italian steel company, Luccini, bought 51 percent of the enterprise, including the land, for $30 million, in return for certain guarantees. Solidarity agreed to a reduction in the labor force from 4,900 to 3,300. Warsaw agreed to transfer title to 775 acres (314 hectares) of land. Luccini promised to invest $250 million to transform the plant into the most modern steel mill in Poland. The modernization did not occur, however, and, in mid-1994, the remaining 3,500 workers struck, demanding a 30 percent wage increase and modernization. Luccini argued that, over two years, it had been able to obtain title to only around 400 acres (165 hectares) and that the title dispute was tied up in court. The government had provided the court with a December 1918 decree signed by Józef Piłsudski, regarding a takeover of the post-Russian property by the Polish state, and with a decree nationalizing the land after World War II. Also placed in evidence was documentation showing that some of the land belonged to a regiment of czarist Russian artillery that had been stationed on the land in the mid-nineteenth century.[59] The court did not render a verdict concerning ownership. The whole dispute resulted in a dramatic and the longest-lasting labor dispute in post-1989 Poland and put the Solidarity-led government to a difficult test in a serious confrontation between the workers of a large plant and a foreign owner. After several weeks the dispute ended with an uneasy compromise.

Another highly publicized case involves PepsiCo, which purchased from the Polish state a renowned chocolate factory and was sued by Emil Wedel, an heir of the factory's prewar owners. Among other things, a court ruling forbade PepsiCo to use the name Wedel. The case has not been decided as of 1995.

The restitution problem, by its very nature, has been a complex issue in all post-Communist countries. In Poland, however, it seems especially complex. Perhaps this is why Poland is the only country in Central Europe where no general restitution law has been enacted.

Restitution has not been a major issue in the former Soviet Union, except its western territories. Almost all real estate there has been state property since the 1920s, and few people have any records and claims. However, as the main expropriations in Central Europe were implemented in the 1940s and early 1950s, and a significant number of former owners are still alive, restitution there is the subject of hot political debates.

While similar restitution dilemmas can be found in all Central European countries, some of Poland's restitution intricacies are unique. The scope of Poland's restitution issues makes it intractable in many ways. For example, its historical dimensions go far back in time, and its spatial dimensions reach far beyond the current Poland's borders. Its social and political dimensions cut across different social classes, different nationalities and religions, different political organizations and interest groups. Restitution's moral dilemmas embrace many definitions and concepts of "justice," "fairness," social and economic "equality," "lawfulness," "right" and "wrong." Legally it involves a plethora of laws and regulations, issued by different authorities, many of them of questionable legality; it also deals with violations of these laws and a number of past consecutive "waves" of expropriations and restitutions. Restitution's pragmatic considerations cover such issues as political and economic feasibility and the calculation of political and economic opportunity costs, both short run and long run, behind each of the restitution variants. Technical issues to be addressed include problems with: eligibility, documents that disappeared during the wars and foreign occupations,[60] valuation of confiscated property and assessment of harm due to expropriation, accounting for the passage of time (value discounting techniques), institutional framework for claim processing and restitution procedures (courts versus central administration versus local administration), sources for financing of these procedures, fiscal issues, credit availability to owners who repossessed their property, and many others.

## Historical Background

During the eighteenth century many expropriations occurred as a consequence of Poland's partition among three foreign powers.[61] During the nineteenth century many Poles lost their land and other property as punishment for participation in military resistance against the occupants. A wave of nationalizations and restitutions swept Poland after it regained independence in the wake of World War I. Based on a Piłsudski decree mentioned earlier, a large amount of the property that was termed as abandoned, mostly post-Russian, but also post-German and post-Austrian, was taken and placed under the administration of the Polish authorities.[62] Different restitution cases continued in Polish courts through 1939. In and after 1944 the Communist authorities used the Piłsudski decree frequently as a precedent for taking over the property that was classified as abandoned—left behind without an owner. These included real estate previously owned by people who were exterminated during World War II as well as by those deported or killed after the war.

While most nationalizations were quick and relatively simple in other Communist countries, in Poland they involved many stages and twists. The property was taken, returned to the owner, and taken again. From 1944 to 1962 more than thirty major laws and regulations were issued regarding nationalization of different types of property.

Paradoxically, only thirteen of these laws are covered by a June 1995 draft[63] submitted by the Communist-led Oleksy government to the Communist-dominated Sejm. This draft is confined to *selected major* violations, by the former Communist authorities, of the *selected major* expropriation laws imposed by the former Communist party. These violations were inflicted upon the citizens of the former Communist state. Instead of declaring their illegality, this draft makes them binding and final, despite the fact that they often were mutually contradictory and that some of them violated a Polish constitution that, at the time, was formally recognized by the Communist authorities.

## Changes in the Territory after World War II

No other country was subjected to equally dramatic shifts of territory. Millions of former inhabitants of Poland and Germany lost their property. The postwar migrations of nations and "ethnic cleansing" involved about 3 million ethnic Poles, repatriates and re-emigrants, most of whom arrived from the former Eastern Poland. At the same time, half a million Ukrainians, Belarussians, and others were reallocated eastward to the postwar Soviet Union, and 8 million Germans fled, were evacuated by the withdrawing German army, or were deported by the Soviet and Polish Communist authorities to the west, behind the Odra-Nysa (Oder-Neisse) new border line. Also, millions of people moved or were reallocated within postwar Poland, Germany, and the Soviet Union. Obviously, almost all who lost their property because they fled or were deported were innocent civilians—victims of the war.

## Social Dimensions

Many social, national, and religious groups of prewar and postwar Poland have a stake in restitution. Most important of them are the gentry and city intelligentsia: the Jews, Germans, Russians, and Ukrainians; the farmers and other "new" owners; and the "nonowners."

Many former owners emphasize *the historical context* of mass expropriations in the 1940s. In 1945 Poland reemerged as one of the "official" victors of World War II. Poles claim that except for the three allied superpowers no other nation contributed as much militarily to the defeat of the Nazis. During the German occupation, Poland had the largest and the mightiest underground military forces: 500,000 active servicemen. The losses it suffered during the war (in people, territory, buildings, and wealth) were greater than those of any other anti-Nazi alliance member.[64] Polish military leaders often were people who owned or administered real property—city intelligentsia (Christian and Jewish), landed gentry, and clergy. During the war, they were persecuted by both Hitler's Germany and Stalin's Russia, and predestined for annihilation. After the war, instead of being rewarded for their war sacrifices, they were targeted by the Communist regime as "class enemies," persecuted, expropriated, and often doomed to live in poverty. Many of them were jailed and sentenced to death by the Communist authorities.[65] In this context, the issue of "historical" justice often is raised.

The issue of *social justice* remains a problem as well. Before 1939 a large number of medium-size and large land estates belonged to the Polish gentry.

Many of them were killed or emigrated during or after the war. Today a large number of them or their heirs live abroad and often are better off than impoverished inhabitants of Poland. Also the size of their former estates is an issue. While, for example, returning land to previous owners involved little egalitarian concerns in Bulgaria and the Czech Republic (where most restituted farms were not large), in Poland many of the estates were very large.

Pre–World War II Poland had the largest Jewish population in the world. More than 90 percent of them (about 3 million) were annihilated by the Nazis. The Jews played an important role in the anti-German resistance in Poland. As in the case of other former owners, the few Jewish war survivors lost their property after the war. Today most of them and their heirs live in the United States and in Israel. The specificities of the Jewish restitution issue draw broad attention in international politics and the mass media. The question is whether, by whom, and how the Jews should be reimbursed for their property losses incurred during and after the war. Many Poles argue that Poland, itself a victim, destroyed by the war and impoverished by forty-five years of Soviet domination, is not in a position to reimburse war victims, either Christians or Jews, especially those who reside abroad. For Jewish war victims, the problem is complicated by the fact that some already have accepted compensation from Germany.

Old ethnic animosities and prejudices that still exist do not help the situation. Some Jews blame the Poles for not helping enough during the war and in certain cases even collaborating with the Germans. Some Poles blame the Jews for their active participation in the Communist organizations before the war, for their collaboration with the Soviet occupiers, and for their role in the postwar Stalinist internal security apparatus, which claimed thousands of lives. A wave of anti-Semitism, sponsored by the Communist authorities, resulted in a large Jewish emigration in 1968-69, creating related property problems. Some of these emigrants left behind houses, apartments, and other real estate that, according to the deed books, they still own although tenants currently occupy them.[66]

The majority of Poles would have great problems in restituting former German and Russian property because of the suffering and atrocities inflicted by these nations upon Poland's inhabitants in the past. Another argument against such restitution is that neither Germany nor the Soviet Union (Russia) paid reparations for the war's destructions, military occupations, political dominations, and economic exploitations. Who should apologize to whom and how remains an issue.

In the aftermath of a civil war between the Communist authorities and Ukrainian anti-Communist independence fighters, 150,000 inhabitants of southeast Poland, predominantly Ukrainians, were deported to Poland's newly acquired western territories. Many of them still live in Poland. All the complexities and intricacies of historical rights and wrongs remain unsolved. So is the problem of the restitution of Ukrainian property.

As a result of the 1944 agrarian reform, 820,000 new private farms were created and 250,000 private farms were enlarged. As mentioned Poland was the only Soviet-bloc country in which most of the land continuously remained in private hands until the end of Communist rule in 1989. Most land confiscated from previous landlords has been used by its new owners and their families for half a century. Would it be just to deprive them of this property now?

Obviously the problem is broader and includes many new owners who, in different ways, in different periods of time, and under different conditions, acquired property and who currently possess the title, despite the fact that this property was, is, or could be claimed by its previous owners. These new owners include: the Embassy of United States in Warsaw, the Jaruzelski family, some schools and other public institutions, owners of newly built large hotels such as Warsaw's Holiday Inn, and office skyscrapers in downtown Warsaw.

Many Poles question the fairness and justice of any form of restitution of real estate property and other wealth. People who worked for the Communist state for many years and who never owned real estate assert that compensating former property owners and not themselves is unfair, because they, too, were exploited by the state.[67] Most Poles were poor before the war and remain poor today. The return of property to those who were rich or remain rich (especially the current residents of Western countries) does not find a lot of public appeal. Of course, the passage of time is a problem as well. Grzegorz Kołodko, the deputy prime minister in the post-Communist coalition government, a "nonowner," is quoted as having asked the following question: "Why should my children be paying, for many years, additional taxes to reimburse somebody who suffered from injustice a long time before they were born?"

## Property Seized by the Communists and Restitution Eligibility

In 1944 Polish real estate fell into one of several categories, distinguished by its location, ownership, and treatment. For the purpose of this analysis, we distinguish among four categories of real property, by location: real estate in Warsaw; nonfarm businesses and urban real estate except for prewar Warsaw; rural real estate; and real estate in prewar Eastern Poland, incorporated into the Soviet Union at the end of the war. In general, Poland was predominantly rural before and immediately after World War II; therefore, the largest number of property owners were owners of rural land.

### Real Estate in Warsaw

The authorities expropriated all land and buildings within the borders of 1939 Warsaw based on an October 1945 decree.[68] Former owners were offered a six-month period during which they could apply for perpetual leasehold at low rent. In fact, almost all of the applications were denied. The decree provided for compensation that never was paid, except for some limited reimbursement granted by the laws of March 1958 and April 1985 for agricultural land and parcels for residential construction.[69] The 1985 law governs the right to file compensation claims.

Former owners of Warsaw's real estate have filed several thousand claims. Many of them are tenants in the houses and apartments they or their parents used to own. A frequent problem is the degree of destruction of the building during the war. War reparations is one issue, as is the confiscation of property and its physical shape at the moment of this confiscation; the cost of reconstruction and upgrading incurred by the state after the confiscation is another problem. Since, during the war, 80 percent of Warsaw was destroyed, many former owners were expropriated of land and ruins of a residential building rather than an actual house or apartment. An additional issue is the prewar status of mortgage indebtedness of the confiscated real property.

Among those seeking recompense are survivors or their heirs and the heirs of other inhabitants of the Warsaw Ghetto. Twenty-three percent of prewar Warsaw was owned by Polish Jews; these holdings were completely destroyed by the Germans during and after the Warsaw Ghetto uprising in April 1943. Most of the claimants have no proof of ownership, and many are requesting only some form of moral recognition.[70]

**Nonfarm Businesses and Urban Real Estate Except for Prewar Warsaw**
The January 1946 act on the nationalization of main branches of the economy resulted in a transfer to the state of all post-German industrial property, companies producing military equipment and considered important for the national defense, and other companies that had a capacity to employ more than fifty workers in one shift. The expropriation decisions were made by the central administration (ministries), not the courts, and, according to a January 1950 interpretation, included whole companies "in the broadest sense", with all their assets and inventories. No exclusions were permitted. Several other laws and decrees complemented the January 1946 law in nationalizing industrial property, including banks (October 1948), pharmacies (January 1951), property of all foundations (April 1952), and all mining companies (May 1953). Altogether, between 1945 and 1959, the state took 20,740 enterprises.[71] Most prewar owners, Poles and Germans, Christians and Jews, were dead or were living outside Poland after 1944. A few survivors and their heirs did or could file claims.

Private urban housing other than in prewar Warsaw was not nationalized, but it was placed under public management. Under the *kwaterunek* system, owners were forced to provide dwellings to renters selected by the authorities, and rents were set at levels that were below the cost of housing maintenance and repairs. Since, most of the time, title was never taken, there is no issue of ownership restitution for this property. However, there is great resentment over the inability either to terminate tenancy or to set market rents.[72]

**Rural Real Estate**

The main categories of rural land taken are large land estates taken under the land reform laws and partitioned among new individual owners, farmland incorporated into cooperatives, state farms, rural residencies, forests, former German property, and former Ukrainian property. Each presents a different set of circumstances, suggesting different outcomes in terms of restitution.

During this century, two large agrarian reforms were implemented in Poland. They are contrasted here from the perspective of restitution entitlement. The first treated owners fairly, while the second did not. The first reform was carried out under the Land Reform Act of 1925 passed by the Sejm. The second was introduced by a September 1944 decree issued by the Communist authorities at the end of World War II.[73] The aim of the first reform was social equity at the minimum sacrifice of economic efficiency. The aim of the second was as much social—taking land from the richest and delivering it to the poorest—as political—liquidation of the estate owning class.

The first reform was voluntary. Only if the predefined annual quota was not reached could the authorities use certain compulsory measures. Only land above the stated size—holdings in excess of 445 acres (180 hectares) of cropland, or, in eastern Poland, in excess of 445 to 1,730 acres (180 to 700 hectares), depending on local conditions—was taken. The owner kept the remainder of the property, including buildings. Land redistribution proceeded gradually—the effective average annual rate between 1926 and 1938 was about 350,000 acres (140,000 hectares). Owners received a compensation at market prices. As a result of this reform 160,000 farms were newly created and 500,000 were enlarged, with ownership changes of a total of 6.6 million acres (2.6 million hectares).

By contrast, the September 1944 reform was complete (all relevant property, including residential houses, was taken), compulsory, unconditional, and immediate with no compensation[74] to the owners. It covered farms with more than 125 acres (50 hectares) of arable land in postwar eastern Poland, farms with more than 250 acres (100 hectares) of total area in western Poland, and the property that belonged to Germans and their collaborators.[75] As a result of the expropriations from 1944 to 1950, a total of 24.5 million acres (9.8 million hectares) was taken. Of this, 62 percent was redistributed to peasants, while the remaining 38 percent was put into cooperatives or state farms. A total of 810,000 new farms (13.9 million acres) were created and 260,000 farms (1.3 million acres) were enlarged. As of 1950, 25 percent of Polish farms were new, established under the land reform.[76]

A major task of the 1925 reform was to enlarge and strengthen the already existing farms. The reform removed land from a tiny fraction of farms, less than

1 percent. The land affected constituted 10.2 percent of what was then agricultural land.[77] All these changes improved the agrarian structure without destroying larger farms that were more technologically advanced and produced most food supplies for the urban population and export. The objective of the September 1944 reform was to give land to as many people as possible, including nonfarmers. Its outcomes included social conflicts and violence. In the territory that was in Poland before the war, the land taken amounted to one half of all land in agriculture in 1944. The old, large farms, frequently run by people with agricultural vocational or college education and roots in agriculture for many generations, were confiscated,[78] with new, small farms often going to people with no education and no agricultural experience. Similar to the Soviet collectivization, the managerial and technical professionals, landed gentry, and kulaks (owners of large peasant farms) were replaced by incompetent new smallholders and the Communist nominated bureaucrats.

The eligibility for restitution of the former land estate owners hinges on a court decision concerning the legality of the September 1944 Land Reform Act. Should this legality be confirmed, the pool of eligible owners will be reduced to only those who claim violations of this act in the expropriations procedures.

The September 1944 reform was followed by consecutive, dramatic shifts in agrarian policy. In the fall of 1948, the Communist government initiated a program of "agricultural reconstruction" whose official aim was to improve the agrarian structure by merging small farms into larger *kolhoz* type cooperatives.[79] This collectivization was supposed to be voluntary but, after 1949, an increasing number of cooperatives were created by force. The land that had been given to people a few years before under the Land Reform was taken from them. The pressure on farmers gradually increased, as did their resistance. The number of co-ops grew from 2,000 in 1950 to more than 9,000 in 1955; the amount of farmland in the co-ops grew from 0.8 percent in 1950 to 9.2 percent in 1955. At about that time, however, major political changes took place: the Stalinist leadership was ousted, and the Polish "thaw" began under Władysław Gomułka. By the end of 1956, only 1,539 cooperatives had survived. The Polish communists lacked the power and conviction necessary to carry out an unpopular policy and the peasants won this confrontation.[80]

Title to the farmers' land most of the time did not pass to the co-ops, although the farmers' power to determine use of the land was usurped. Therefore, whenever they are granted the right to withdraw from the co-ops, there should not be any problem of retransfer of title.

Regarding state farms, by 1947 there were already 4,800, occupying 3.7 million acres (1.5 million hectares), or 10 percent of arable land. Of this total, 1,300 of the farms, occupying 0.8 million acres (0.3 million hectares) were on land that had been Polish before World War II, while the majority of the farms—3,500, occupying 2.9 million acres (1.2 million hectares)—were located on land that had been German. By the end of the 1960s the number of state farms increased to 7,700, accounting for 17.7 percent of total farmland.

In 1970 Edward Gierek came to power, after Gomułka's food price hike had proved his undoing. Gierek wanted to modernize agriculture through investment in strong, large, highly industrialized state farms. Support for co-ops and other forms of socialized nonstate farms diminished. The state farms were recognized as a "constitutionally" superior form of agricultural production and provided with massive funds.[81] As in Bulgaria, Czechoslovakia, and other Communist countries, farms were consolidated, and large state farms became even larger. In 1980, at the close of Gierek's tenure, the 2,500 state farms in existence exceeded 18.5 percent of total farmland.

Over a long period of time, land gradually was added to the state farm system as peasants relinquished their small holdings in return for state pensions. In the late 1980s this amounted to approximately 0.5 percent of all private farmland each year. None of these retirees would have a claim, since they received a quid pro quo. Only in the cases of illegal (forced) expropriations could claims be filed. Former owners of land estates that were incorporated into the state farms could file claims. As in the case individual farmers, the "legal" eligibility of estate owners hinges on the constitutionality of the September 1944 Land Act and/or its violations. Their "political" eligibility is stronger because their former property belongs to no natural person. Under certain favorable conditions they can be made eligible to acquire their former property from the state or at least to be granted the right of the first refusal.

A separate issue is the restitution of former residences, including mansions and palaces, which in most cases are state property. Some former owners limit their claims to residential housing and are willing to give up property rights for farmland.

Forests constituted 23 percent of Poland's territory in 1947, 25 percent in 1960, and 28.5 percent in the 1990s. Today of a total of 22 million acres (8.9 million hectares) of forest, 83 percent are held by the state. In 1937, 39 percent of forests were state owned. Most nationalizations carried out were based on the September and December 1944 decrees. Former owners of forests constitute another group of those who may claim that they are entitled to restitution.

Of great concern are the former farms of people of non-Polish nationalities, such as German and Ukrainian, living abroad. While the chances of the return of this property to its former owners are almost null, the possibility that some of them (especially the Germans) may purchase their former farms and estates is a serious Polish problem. Currently, foreigners are required to have a permit from two ministries to purchase a piece of land. In order to join the EU, Poland will have to change this law and make its real estate available to all EU citizens, including Germans who, being many times wealthier than the Poles, could out-bid them. What if former German owners, or their heirs, arrive by the thousands and start buying Polish land? This fear may turn to be the major obstacle for Poland to join the EU.[82]

**Prewar Eastern Poland**

Those who owned property in prewar Eastern Poland were a diverse group, including those Christians and Jews who owned houses, businesses, and land parcels in the urban areas; Jews and others who had small businesses in the rural areas; predominantly Polish owners of large land estates; and Poles, Ukrainians, Belarussians, Germans, and Lithuanians who owned small and larger peasant farms. The only groups that were granted some reimbursement were peasants and some owners of small urban houses, predominantly Polish repatriates brought to the post-German territories. Other owners, often due to their unwelcome class roots, were not reimbursed,[83] they form the largest group of claimants for restitution.

## Restitution Provisions in the Past

From the perspective of international law, the former German land awarded to Poland was treated as the equivalent of the land Poland lost to the Soviet Union. The Potsdam agreement ruled that full compensation should be given to all persons who arrived from the former Eastern Poland, regardless of the value of their property left on the former Polish territory. Also, after the war, Poland signed agreements with Soviet Ukraine, Belarus, and Lithuania in which it promised to reimburse those Poles who lost their property in the East. Limited compensation for farm owners was provided for by a law of March 1958, after which date no agrarian land claims could be filed.

Between 1948 and 1971 Poland reached agreements with many Western countries concerning claims of foreign nationals under which the country of their citizenship paid compensation.[84] No agreement ever was reached with Germany. Laws of March 1958 and April 1985 allowed for some compensation for owners of agrarian land and housing construction lots who lost their property as a result of the nationalization of Warsaw real estate.

The April 1985 Law on Land Management and Real Estate Expropriations granted the former Eastern Polish a right to restitution in the form of real estate, managed by local authorities within today's Polish borders, and to other forms of property. Among other things, this law provided for a possibility of restitution of comparable property or compensation to the owners of buildings that housed no more than four apartments. The deadline for filing claims was the end of 1988. Some 90,000 people filed claims, but as yet no awards have been made. This law limited eligibility to those who met, among other things, two conditions: They had to possess the documents issued after the war by the (Communist-run) State Repatriation Office, and they had to prove that they lived on the territory of the former Eastern Poland after August 1944. Many persons were not covered by this law, including those deported by the NKVD (Soviet internal security), after the September 1939 Soviet invasion of Poland, who had not returned to the former Eastern Poland; those who fled to Western Europe;[85] and those who were simply afraid to use the Repatriation Office.[86] In April 1991, a ruling by the Supreme Court changed this specification, granting eligibility to those who were Polish citizens, resided in the former Eastern Poland, and left after September 1, 1939.

## Recent Restitution Provisions and Cases

Except for church properties, the prospects of restitution for those who lost their property during or at the end of the war or subsequently, depends, in the absence of restitution legislation, on application of the law that governed the seizure at the time when it occurred. Limited possibilities are in place for restitution now, and there are provisions for filing claims for future restitution. Claims have been filed and heard under the September 1944 Land Reform Law and other Communist expropriation acts for actions illegal at the time of expropriation. Claims also have been filed under a 1990 act that authorized their filing, even though there was no provision for compensation.

Under an administrative ruling of the Ministry of Ownership Transformations, foreigners whose property was nationalized may apply to the courts for its return unless there is a bilateral agreement between Poland and the country of their citizenship;[87] and the claimant was a citizen of a country that belonged to the Axis. Thus all Poles and others who lived in the part of Poland that was German before the end of World War II and who were German citizens are excluded from restitution.[88]

Many lawyers contend that the entire Land Reform Act of September 1944 was unconstitutional, violating provisions of the 1921 Constitution in force at that time. This is also the position of the Restitution Council, an independent group with diverse political and social representation set up as an advisory body to the Minister of Ownership Transformation. The Polish courts have not accepted this view.

Enterprises that have been privatized have been required to set aside 5 percent of their stock for possible future purchase by voucher holders, should a voucher system be enacted as a means of restitution.

By April 1993, although it was still not clear who might claim or what kind of property could be claimed, about 140,000 claims for restitution had been submitted, either to local governments or to the Ministry of Ownership Transformation. This number included claims filed under the April 1985 act by about 90,000 people for lost property in prewar Eastern Poland and 4,500 claims for property in Warsaw. The claims were for "estates, forests, farms, lakes, enterprises large and small, mills, brick yards, service and production workshops."[89] The largest number of claims, 65 percent, were for some 5 million acres (2 million hectares) of farm and forest land, virtually all in prewar Eastern Poland. Other claims included 17 percent for urban real estate, 5 percent for businesses in the service sector, and 2 percent for manufacturing firms. The value of these claims amounted to $30 billion. By December 1994 more than 200,000 claims had been filed, half of which involved pre-war Eastern Poland; 30,000 of them concerned industrial businesses. One estimate of the total number of claims to be expected is 500,000.[90]

Although the laws provide for restitution where a claimant can prove that the taking was illegal under the governing law, the courts have provided little satisfaction under this procedure. Between January 1, 1990, and June 30, 1993, 8,585 former owners or their heirs filed claims to courts. Compensation, in the total amount of $150,000 (ZL 2.6 billion), was awarded in only three cases.[91] Only the churches enjoyed some tangible successes.

## Church Restitution

During the last few weeks of the tenure of the last Communist Sejm, in May 1989, a law was passed that provided for a comprehensive restitution of Roman Catholic church's properties. This law created a structure for filing and hearing of claims. Similar laws now apply to the Greek Catholic church and to several Orthodox and Protestant churches. So far there is no provision for the Union of Jewish Communes and some other religions although such legislation is under discussion.[92] Many former property owners resent the fact that churches have been enabled to recover their property while they have not.

During the period of nationalization, the Roman Catholic church had somewhere between 330,000 acres (130,000 hectares) and 680,000 acres (270,000 hectares) seized, as well as many buildings—17,000 in Warsaw alone. Income from the seized agricultural properties was to be placed in a church fund, but under the Communists this never occurred. Now, since 1990, the state has been making payments into the fund, starting with $2.1 million (ZL 20 billion) in 1990 and rising to $4.9 million (ZL 110 billion) in 1994. Fund revenues are allocated to social security and medical care premiums and restoration of churches.

The May 1989 law created an Estate Commission of fourteen members, half from government, half from the church, to rule on claims, which had to be filed by the end of 1992. The church was restituted farms of less than 125 acres (50 hectares) for its units that run charitable activities. Only 3,000 claims were filed,[93] although some 6,000 had been anticipated. As of November 1994, the Estate Commission had made decisions on 950 claims. Of these, 780 were settled and 160 were rejected, usually on procedural grounds.

Some of the decisions of the Estate Commission illustrate the problems faced and the compromises made. In Frombork, a hospital and a Copernicus museum had been established in a Salesian cloister. The hospital was allowed to remain for fifteen years and the museum for twenty five years. In Zamość, a large structure was returned to the church, but with provisos that a movie theater could continue to operate until 1994 and a state school until 2003. In Supraśl, the same buildings were claimed by Greek Catholics, Orthodox, and Roman Catholics. Three times already the property has been awarded to the Orthodox church. Each time the other two churches have appealed to the courts.[94]

In a conflict that ignited in Piotrków Trybunalski, a town of 80,000 in central Poland, the local authorities refused to return to the Orthodox church a large old parish house that currently is used by local police. Local councilmen argued that the town had only eighty members of the Russian Orthodox church, and they do not need a large building; the Russians were occupants and oppressors of Poland—for many people "orthodox" means "Russian czarist"; and Russia does not return much property to the Catholic church.

The building was constructed in 1872 by the Orthodox church and was taken over in 1919 by the Polish administration as a post-Russian property. In 1939, shortly before the war, the Sejm passed a law that gave the Polish State all the former Russian Orthodox church property, which remained under the administration of the Polish authorities. The Piotrków councilmen now use this law.

## Residential Property in Prewar Warsaw

A good example of a restitution nightmare was a claim put together by a New York attorney, Zdzisław Openchowski, for his client, Jan Przedpełski, a resident of New York. It concerned a house in Warsaw (5, Ikara Street) that was occupied by General Wojciech Jaruzelski and his family. According to a notarial act presented by Przedpełski, the property was purchased on September 3, 1938, by his mother, Lidia. In 1945 the building was confiscated, based on the October 1945 decree. In 1976 the military took over possession and removed the building's inhabitants. Three years later the Jaruzelskis purchased it from the State Treasury (apparently for a symbolic price).[95] Openchowski argued that the ownership title should still belong to his client because the October 1945 decree was illegal. At the time of its issue, a prewar Polish constitution was still in place. According to this constitution, to be valid an expropriation must be passed by the Sejm and could be introduced only for important "social needs." In this case the taking was introduced by a governmental decree and was not "socially" justified. Also, both the constitution and the October 1945 decree provided for a reimbursement for the confiscated property that was never granted.

The attorneys for General Jaruzelski argued that the October 1945 decree was valid and that the estate's mortgage in 1938 was charged with a high debt.

They refused an out-of-court settlement proposed by Openchowski, who maintained that the debt was not the reason for the 1945 expropriation. The initial ruling of the Warsaw court did not grant the title to Przedpełski, who was not willing to continue the procedure due to high litigation cost and uncertain outcome.

Przedpełski was indeed likely to lose. The Polish courts, especially after the installation of the so-called post-Communist government in fall 1993, have tended to rule against the former owners for several reasons. First, many judges belong to the former Communist nomenklatura that was abolished after 1989. General Jaruzelski is still a popular figure. The old Communist elites remain influential while Przedpełski is an outsider with no links to the past and current establishment. In addition, the judges are so-called budget employees and, after 1989, fell victims of measures to balance the state budget. Their salaries are low, as is their eagerness to cooperate with the reformist governments. The courts in post-1989 Poland enjoy a constitutional independence from the administrative authorities anyway. Finally, a positive ruling for Przedpełski would create a precedent and, due to the lack of a more general regulation, could lead to thousands of civil suits, which is the last thing that the overworked and understaffed courts would wish for.[96]

In another restitution case, a well known Polish aristocratic family named Czetwertyński has been considering filing a claim against the U.S. Embassy. Before World War II they owned a nineteenth-century mansion in Warsaw, designed by the famous architect Marconi, in the style of the Viennese Secession. Located on Ujazdowskie Avenue in the most elegant part of the city, it was well known for the spectacular caryatids on its facade. During the war most family members died in Auschwitz and other German concentration camps. Two persons survived: Róża, the mother, and her son, Stanisław, who spent several years in Buchenwald concentration camp. In 1945, after they managed to renovate the mansion, it was confiscated as part of the nationalization of Warsaw property. Stanisław was arrested by the Communist authorities and sentenced to several years in prison.

According to the October 1945 decree, the owners were eligible to apply to hold their property on a ninety-nine-year lease. Apparently there was never an official reply to the Czetwertyński's application and they lost their mansion. As in most of other Warsaw real property cases, the transfer of the title was never processed, and no reimbursement was paid.

In 1957 the U.S. Embassy purchased the mansion from the Communist authorities for the equivalent of $160,000. The property title was not checked at the time.[97] In 1960, despite protests by Warsaw residents, the United States decided to demolish the mansion, classified as a historic monument, and build a larger modern building.

The Czetwertyńskis' attorneys are arguing that, according to U.S. law, the purchase of property from a person who was not the owner could not confer title. The value of this property, as of 1993, was estimated at several million dollars.[98]

## Rural Property

The Rosalin mansion, near Warsaw, was built in the mid-1800s, also designed by Marconi, as a classicist hunters' residence. The estate, owned by the Krysowski family, included a 25 acre (10 hectare) park, five ponds, and about 150 acres (60 hectares) of land. The property was nationalized and confiscated in summer 1945. As a result of an appeal—several members of the Krysowski family were lawyers—the expropriation decision was voided in September 1945 by the Warsaw Voivodship Land Office, on the grounds that the estate included only 109 acres (44 hectares) of agricultural land, not more than the 125 acres (50 hectares) that made an estate subject to nationalization. In November 1948 the estate again was nationalized under a July 1948 regulation that changed the method of land classification specifying what was and what was not agricultural land. In 1949 the family was forced out of their newly remodeled house and located in a temporary, primitive bungalow. After 1950 the mansion was used as, among other things, a vacation house for Józef Cyrankiewicz, long-time prime minister in the Communist government; a site for summer camps of the Communist youth organizations; and, later on, headquarters for the Polish People's University, an educational organization. The family appealed their eviction several times to no avail.

In 1990 they started a complicated legal procedure that involved several ministries and the Supreme Administrative Court. Although the whole procedure ended successfully and the 1949 expropriation was ruled illegal, the current tenants of the mansion, a foster home for children, refused to leave. The Krysowski family made several unsuccessful attempts to repossess their mansion. Finally they decided to hire a group of gunmen, who took over their property. Most local public opinion supported the building's tenants.[99] The Rosalin case is an illustration of failure of state and local government to enforce court decisions returning property.

Another illustration concerns a spa, Rymanów-Zdrój, that was a major philanthropic undertaking of Count Jan Potocki. At the turn of the century he purchased land and built a number of sanatoria for children. In 1945 the Communist authorities took over the Rymanów Spa as an abandoned property. In fact, at that time the aristocratic Potocki family were fleeing for their lives from the Red Army. Now the son of the spa's founder has filed a claim.[100]

On occasion other people have seized property that they believe was taken illegally. For example, in the village of Beczkowo, near Kielce, farmers clearcut a 20 acre (8 hectare) pine forest. Under a nineteenth century czarist decree,

200 peasant families had been granted joint ownership of the forest. Since World War II the land has been under state control. Most of the trees were planted by the inhabitants of Beczkowo who, in the late 1940s, were "volunteered" by the authorities to afforest vacant land. Today there are about 800 heirs. In 1993, 465 claims were filed for restitution of this land. Obtaining no relief, the farmers entered the woods and, within a week, had cut it to the ground, even though the trees were forty-five years from maturity.[101]

## Restitution Proposals

At the outset of Polish economic reforms, restitution was supposed to be a prelude to fast ownership changes. The main idea was to grant justice while charging the state budget as little as possible. Several "cheap" proposals of a restitution law were considered,[102] and, by the summer of 1995, a total of thirteen drafts, each in several variants, had been submitted to the Sejm, but none has been enacted. President Lech Wałęsa repeatedly promised that restitution would occur before his term ended in 1995, but it did not.

In the late 1980s there were several proposals to reimburse the former Eastern Poles with state-owned farmland and with "unwanted" property: industrial buildings, machinery, and vacant land. No law incorporating these proposals has ever been introduced.

In spring 1991 the government of Jan Bielecki presented the Sejm with a draft restitution law. Sejm commissions worked on this draft for several months, but it was never presented in its final form before the House. The controversial draft, which became void with the parliamentary elections in December 1991, was unacceptable to those who demanded full restitution of all property seized by Communist authorities. It confined eligibility for restitution to those former owners who were Polish citizens at the time of the taking, who (or whose heirs) are currently residents of Poland and who lost their property in a way that was illegal when the loss occurred. The former eastern Poles would have been eligible for an unspecified reimbursement. The restitution, however, would not have covered the property located in today's territory of Poland that was taken over as a result of the nationalization laws. Those eligible would have been entitled to reprivatization vouchers that might have been used to purchase the stocks of privatized state firms. The authors of this proposal argued that giving away vouchers would stimulate the process of privatization, while returning physical property to its original owners would hamper it. Restitution in this form would have covered property with a total estimated value of $15 to $23 billion.[103]

In the spring of 1992 the government of Jan Olszewski elaborated another proposal that never managed to leave the government and reach the Sejm. It provided for the return of all physical property to the former owners, whenever possible, with its amount reduced by the value of new capital investments that had taken place after nationalization. Farmers who had received their land as a result of the agrarian reforms would not have to return it and people who did not live permanently in Poland would have been eligible. The draft also recognized the validity of claims by those who had lost their property in prewar Eastern Poland but did not specify how these claims should be satisfied. This last omission seriously reduced the practical value of the proposal, because this category of claims made up two-thirds of all filed claims.

The Hanna Suchocka government was installed in July 1992 and decided to revive the Bielecki proposal, which was amplified by new forms of reimbursements. In addition to vouchers (valid for five years), it now provided for physical property, either the claimed property or, if this was not possible, replacement property. Certain objects of great cultural or historic value were not to be returned. The restitution claims were to be processed by the local administration; courts were to be used only in the case of conflicts. The claimants would have to decide which form of compensation to choose. The property in the former Eastern Poland could also be claimed. Only Polish citizens who currently lived permanently in Poland would be eligible. This new draft was presented in December 1992, a few months before the dissolution of the Sejm by President Wałęsa. The restitution bill had to await the new Parliament that was elected in September 1993.

A new coalition government, this time a so-called post-Communist one, was headed by Waldemar Pawlak who, as a leader of the Polish Peasant Party, was not an eager supporter of the idea of awarding property to former owners. From the very beginning, his electorate (peasants, pensioners, some clergy) distrusted all restitution efforts providing for returning the riches to the rich. Farmers would not gain much from a restitution enactment. They are the only large social group that already owns private real property and has almost no claims. They are afraid of any change in the status quo. In particular, they fear the attempts of prewar landowners and their heirs to reclaim their former property. They do not want to lose land that they were granted under the September 1944 agrarian reform. The other member of the coalition, the Democratic Left Alliance, is the direct heir to the Communist Party (PZPR). It sought only a token restitution, reduced to a necessary minimum.

A new official governmental draft, shaped largely by the Democratic Left Alliance, provided for reprivatization vouchers for current Polish citizens and only for violations of former laws. The vouchers would be awarded under the following framework: claimants for $50,000 or less would receive vouchers equal to 100 percent of the claim; claimants for $50,000 to $150,000 would receive vouchers for $50,000 and 75 percent of the remainder; claimants for $150,000 to $500,000 would receive vouchers for $125,000 and 25 percent of the remainder; and claimants for $500,000 or more would receive vouchers for $212,500 and 10 percent of the remainder.[104]

The vouchers, valid for ten years, would increase in value by 10 percent per year and could be used to purchase land or other property sold by the state or municipalities. In addition, 5 percent of the shares of each company listed on the Warsaw stock exchange would be set aside for reprivatization voucher purchase.[105] Former owners reacted negatively to this bill.[106]

In spite of, or because of, this new proposal, Pawlak began speculating about a possibility for an unspecified "alternative" restitution scheme that would provide for gifts of vouchers to pensioners, perhaps also farmers, and others hurt by the transition. In an apparent attempt to slow down, or even kill, the restitution law, in May 1994 his Polish Peasant Party introduced a draft bill that would require a national referendum on restitution.

As mentioned above, in May 1995 a modified variant of this proposal was presented by the government of Józef Oleksy. A former Communist Party official, Oleksy replaced Pawlak as prime minister in March 1995. According to his draft, compensation would be limited to privatization vouchers for the property taken illegally between 1944 and 1962.[107] No reimbursement in kind was provided for. The vouchers could be used to buy state and municipal property at public auctions and to purchase the shares in privatized state enterprises. Municipalities would have the right to refuse these vouchers. The claims covered by this scheme were estimated at $7.5 billion (NZL 18 billion), but the value of the actual compensation would amount to only $2.5 to $3 billion. The savings would be accomplished by the introduction of high inheritance fees. Former owners who are still alive—accounting for about 28 percent of all eligible claims—would receive 100 percent reimbursement. If the owner had passed away, his or her heirs would receive the vouchers of a value reduced by special fees. Group I heirs—the closest family including spouses, siblings, children, grandchildren, and parents—would pay lower fees than group II heirs (all others). In the case of reimbursement of $4,000 or less, group I heirs would pay a 40 percent fee, while group II heirs would pay 50 percent. For reimbursements of $4,001 to $40,000, group I heirs would pay 60 percent, while group II heirs would pay 70 percent. And for reimbursements of more than $40,000, group I heirs would pay 80 percent, and group II heirs would pay 90 percent.

None of the drafts provided specifically for restitution of property seized from Jews. Only the Olszewski proposal, by allowing reimbursements for persons who lived abroad, effectively would make the Jewish real estate owners eligible (since almost all of Jewish war survivors or their heirs, still living, live abroad). The proposals did not cover former Jewish religious properties such as synagogues, cemeteries, and schools, status of which would be settled by a concord between Polish state and Jewish religious organizations, similar to the agreements made with the Catholic and several other churches.[108]

All parties involved in the restitution controversy seem to agree that a full reimbursement for property that was taken, destroyed, or left behind is not feasible. Fortunately, many former owners seek only a symbolic "moral" restitution. How good the chances are even for such a restitution remains unclear.

## Issues to Be Faced

Some say that there never will be a significant restitution law, that the problem is too complex both socially and politically. The government has authorized the filing of claims and has received 200,000 of them. Presumably more would be filed if people were confident that filing was not a vain act. Can these claims be ignored? More practically how vexing is the cloud on title represented by the unresolved claims? Many types of specific questions must be answered if a law is to be enacted.

### Political Feasibility

Many answers exist to the question of what is "just." While returning property to large landowners raises issues of social equality, not returning the property raises issues of lawfulness and international credibility of the new authorities. The feasibility of restitution remains a serious issue. Today's Poland is a country of almost 39 million. The total number of all potential claimants, including former owners and their heirs (siblings, children, grandchildren, etc.) who live in Poland would not exceed a few million.[109] Obviously, in a democratic country the concept of justice must reflect the views of a majority of its voting inhabitants, no matter how "subjective" these views are.

### Economic Feasibility

According to different published estimates, the total value of the existing and future claims would amount to from $20 billion to $40 billion.[110] It is not clear, however, whether these estimates include large land estates in the postwar Poland and all the property left behind (including large land estates) in the prewar Eastern Poland. On one hand, opponents of restitution maintain that Poland has a large foreign debt, and suffers from significant budget deficit, and simply cannot afford a large-scale restitution. On the other hand, many supporters argue that the net cost of restitution does not have to be high and that the advantages from restitution may outweigh its costs.

Apparently, there is plenty of state property that is mismanaged, subsidized by the state, and often unwanted. This property may be used for restitution. Large numbers of state-owned enterprises exist, untouched by privatization, and of low, null, or negative profitability. Also, there is a large amount of real property whose ownership and control was transferred from the state to municipalities, which cannot administer and properly maintain it. The State Treasury Agency for Agricultural Property is struggling with millions of acres of farmland, as well as houses, including historical rural mansions that are falling apart, devastated parks, and other buildings. The agency cannot find interested buyers and is making big efforts to administer this property. Some of the large vacant lots, abandoned farms, and devastated land left behind by the Soviet army have been put to useful work, but many have not.

Many preprivatization and privatization procedures have involved leasing state or municipal property at preferential rates, selling dwellings and productive assets at low prices, or simply giving property away. The recipients include former nomenklatura, company managers and workers, current tenants, or persons with "connections". As the restitution supporters believe, its "affordability" is of political rather than of economic nature.

In some municipalities the local authorities viewed restitution as an important beneficial activity that could bring former owners back to economically depressed localities, sometimes even from abroad, and could create more economic activity, investment funds, and tourism.[111]

### Eligibility
Numerous questions must be answered about who and what is eligible for restitution. What period is to be covered? From the end of the war until the fall of the Communist government in 1989? Must claimants be Polish citizens? Polish residents? What about those Poles who before the war were not Polish citizens? Some of them, for example, lived in what was Germany. What about those who escaped Communist persecution after the war and are not Polish citizens today? What about more recent waves of emigrants, Poles and Germans, Christians and Jews, who left Poland during the last thirty years and who still "partly" live in Poland. What degree of consanguinity must be established between the expropriated owner and the claimant?

### Legality and Public Policy Issues
In addition to the issue of constitutionality and mutual inconsistencies of the Communist expropriation acts, an important issue is their frequent violations by the Communist authorities. In particular, many expropriations were done "by brute force" despite the fact that the properties were not covered by the relevant nationalization laws; the administrative procedures specified by these laws often were not followed; even if the law provided for state assistance to people from whom the property was taken, such assistance was not granted; and the reimbursement specified by the law was not paid.

A different catalog of issues that could shape resolution includes such questions as: whether the property is currently in state or municipal hands, whether it is used by a public institution, such as a school or a library, and whether the property is a historic monument. A separate issue are those privately owned dwellings that formally were never taken, yet their owners still are denied free disposition of them despite the current constitution's guarantees and protections provided to private ownership. A serious problem is the rights to property of those individuals who either were granted a piece of real estate by the previous authorities or purchased a property that is now claimed by a former owner. (Among others, this is the case of the U.S. Embassy in Warsaw, described earlier).[112]

### The Value of Property at the Moment of Taking

Obviously there are many problems to contend with in assessing the value of property: its net market value before the war, assessment of war damages, changes since the time of expropriation, transformations, and improvements and deteriorations, not to mention the loss of imputed rent income, discounted over time. Apparently, much of the nationalized urban and industrial property carried significant debts from the prewar period. Many Warsaw houses and apartments had high mortgage debt, and firms carried substantial indebtedness, often from the Great Depression. According to some estimates, most businesses had a debt in the state treasury that exceeded their market value.

### Previous Compensation and Post-1989 Restitution

The question of previous reimbursements is an issue. A number of repatriates from the former Eastern Poland have accepted some form of reimbursement—often a house and a piece of land in the former German territory. Also, as mentioned earlier, some Jews have received compensation from Germany. Based on the laws of March 1958, July 1961, and April 1985, and other laws, some reimbursement was awarded to a small group of previous owners whose expropriations were ruled illegal. If these reimbursements were only partial, do their grantees still have a claim?

The idiosyncrasies of the post-1989 restitutions have produced an additional complication. The lack of a general law and of a consistent legal framework does not prevent restitution procedures. It only limits their scope and slows down the entire process by creating confusion and promoting arbitrariness. While binding court rulings exist in a number of cases restituting ownership titles to previous owners, their executability often remains a problem. The Catholic church and some other churches received a large chunk of their former property. In some cases the property was returned, or at least protected, even despite the lack of a legal basis. Apparently, the State Agency of Agricultural Property, which is in charge of state-owned farmlands, leases and sells property to former owners under preferential conditions. Some restitutions were made possible by administrative decisions of local authorities who, for whatever reason, happened to be friendly toward former owners. In July 1995 *Gmina* Warsaw-Center (Warszawa Śródmieście) selected fourteen residential buildings for returning to their former owners.

**Implementation and Its Costs**

Numerous other technical and procedural issues exist concerning the implementation and cost of the whole operation.[113] There is a concern that the restitution law will provide new opportunities for corruption on the part of the bureaucracy. A serious practical problem is also the availability of various forms of credit. The cost of a start-up on a restituted property often can be quite significant. Many former owners do not have the savings necessary to get started and cover the cost of maintenance of a piece of real estate.[114]

While restitution may be expensive, continuing to debate and not acting may be even more expensive.

## OWNERSHIP TRANSFORMATIONS

As there are major differences among what was private, semiprivate, and socialized (state-owned) under communism in Poland, Bulgaria, and the Czech Republic, consequently each country's approach toward privatization has been different. Privatization in Poland, unlike that in Bulgaria and the Czech Republic, has no base in prior resolution of the restitution question. Nonetheless, the process goes forward, although haltingly. Some state-owned enterprises undergo different procedures of "preprivatization" by which, for instance, they first are transferred to the municipalities, which are supposed to privatize them. Others are "commercialized" (corporatized) and privatized directly by state action. State farm privatization remains a state function, under the direct management of the Treasury Agency for Agricultural Property. Housing and urban real estate privatization now is mostly a municipal responsibility.

In 1990 there existed 8,500 state enterprises. By May 1995 about 5,000 of them had initiated different forms of (pre-)privatization procedures. Most of these are still in the privatization pipeline, but almost 1,500 have completed the process. Prior to 1989, the private sector played only a modest role in nonfarm economic activities, unlike in housing and agriculture. Only in transportation did the gross output share of private sector exceed 10 percent.

Since 1992, privatization of the state farms by the Treasury Agency for Agricultural Property has yielded little. The poor condition of the farms, the deep recession in agriculture, and the unresolved question of restitution cause buyers to be exceedingly scarce. Some sales of farm housing to tenants from the vast stock of half a million units have taken place.

The municipalities are offering some of their stock of land for sale or long-term lease and are selling apartments to tenants. Both of these activities are small scale, on a lot-by-lot or apartment-by-apartment basis.

Although, between 1990 and 1995, the progress in privatization was substantial, its speed was well below intentions formulated in the 1989 Balcerowicz plan of economic reforms and remained below the expectations of economic reformers. Political instability was the main factor that slowed down legislative activity concerning privatization. The economic decline during the first two years of reform was worse than expected and foreign capital investment in Poland was less than anticipated.

In addition, gradual changes in the sympathies of the electorate have made privatization increasingly difficult. The emergence of a small but visible group of "capitalists," often operating in the gray sector of the economy, generated growing anticapitalism, antimarket, and antiprivatization feelings among many Poles. The gap between rich and poor increased significantly.

The disenchanted consist of many social groups. Fearful for their jobs, (relatively) high wages, and other privileges, many Communist nomenklatura members opposed the reforms. So did workers of large heavy industry plants and employees of other "high priority" enterprises, such as miners, steelworkers, railroad workers, and army officers. They were supported (openly or tacitly) by many lower-level bureaucrats and administrators whose positions also have been threatened. The end of a "shortage" economy[115] resulted in the abolishment of the so-called seller's market (dominated by the producer) and the introduction of a buyer's market (ruled by the consumer). This sudden shift stripped a large number of various sellers of their previous privileged social and economic positions and related benefits. Providers of spare parts for Polski Fiat, owners of newspaper kiosks, and salespersons in the meat stores all suffered from an abrupt loss of market powers they enjoyed for many years in the shortage-driven Communist Poland. Obviously those who lost their jobs (especially former workers of the state farms) and those who worked in state enterprises doomed for closure viewed privatization and market reforms as a cause of their misfortune. Another large group of dissatisfied people included those who were directly affected by the government's efforts to reduce the budget deficit and curtail inflation—the employees of the so-called budget sector (public administration, health, education, and other) and millions of pensioners. Housing co-op members suffered from increased costs due to reduced state subsidies. Those who lived in houses that belonged to someone else feared rent hikes or evictions. Owners of small private businesses found it difficult to succeed under new market conditions of higher rents, higher taxes, and more competition. The usually conservative peasants also became concerned. Too much competition may prove ruinous for them as their farms are predominantly small, labor intensive, and inefficient. The threat of restitution, which might lead to the return of land to its prewar owners, made many peasants look at the progress of privatization with suspicion.

As a result, since 1991 the so-called post-Communist organizations have enjoyed growing popularity. The mainstream Solidarity Labor Union became dominated by more radical leaders and underwent a process of proletarization aimed against rapid market reforms and against a "westernization" of Poland. Other labor unions, as a rule, did not actively support any variant of large-scale privatization. On the left of the political spectrum, politicians who preached populist socialism, including the (post-Solidarity) Labor Party, have become increasingly popular. On the right, an active group of nationalistically oriented parties were unhappy about privatization which they viewed as "selling out" Polish national property to former nomenklatura, black marketeers, and foreign corporations.

Despite all these obstacles, the idea of privatization has enjoyed consistent support from the dominant political parties, especially the leaders of the centrist Democratic Union (the party of Tadeusz Mazowiecki, Hanna Suchocka, and Jacek Kuroń), of the Liberal Economic Congress (the party of Jan Bielecki),[116] and even from many post-Communist politicians. The pro-privatization attitudes of former Communist activists may reflect their pragmatic commonsense approach to the economy; or may be related to their post-1989 involvement in economic activity by buying state property, in which many former officials took advantage of their savings and of the business connections that had they developed while in office. Many politicians strongly condemned "nomenklatura privatization," and some of the buyouts were stopped. But blocking nomenklatura privatization slowed down the privatization process in general.

The Pawlak government's commitment to privatization was unclear. "Given that the finance ministry sees receipts from privatization as essential to its hopes of reducing the budget deficit and reining in double-digit inflation, you might expect this agency to be strongly supported by the government. . . . You would be wrong. . . . High officials refuse to discuss the issue. . . . Meanwhile the prime minister—who is dithering about which firms to include in a mass privatization program aimed at selling off $4 billion in state assets—this week called rumours that privatization was being curtailed 'an outright falsehood.'"[117]

The record of the Oleksy government was mixed. While the mass privatization procedures began moving again and in fall 1995 first vouchers were allocated, the whole operation was scaled down. Moreover, in the spring of 1995, a new law was passed that may slow down the privatization procedures by creating additional bureaucratic obstacles. This law has reinforced the role of the central government and the Sejm in the privatization process while limiting the influence of the Privatization Ministry and that of the workers of the privatized enterprises.

All these factors provide an at least partial explanation why, in Poland a dominant form of privatization has been the formation of new businesses rather than the transfer into private hands of state-owned enterprises. At the same time, there has been substantial reduction of state control of enterprises and a significant shift in ownership of enterprises from the state to the municipalities. The municipalities have not, however, proven eager to take the next step to privatize these enterprises.

The official objectives of large-scale privatization included de-etatization or liberation of the economy from excessive state control; reinforcement of market and related institutions; reduction of the size of the public sector and its burden on the budget; increase of economic efficiency and growth; generation of greater revenue for the state budget by sale of enterprises and by taxes on private enterprises; and setting up conditions for the development of a strong middle class.

Privatization is a process of transfer by sale or gift of state property. It must involve both the transfer of ownership and, most important, the transfer of the effective control over the property. In Poland, the process of privatization began in the late 1980s, under the last Communist government. After 1989 it was continued by the Solidarity-led administration. Full-fledged privatization was made possible by the July 1990 Privatization Law and the creation of the Ownership Transformation Ministry (Ministerstwo Przekształceń Własnościowych, or MPW). The process of privatization is complex, involving a number of laws; state legislative, administrative, and judiciary authorities; local governments; political parties; social organizations (labor unions and organizations of employers); managers and workers of enterprises; domestic and foreign buyers; and restitution claimants.

Not only does the Polish population at large not understand the process well; native and foreign "experts" do not either due to the diverse forms privatization may take, from highly centralized and bureaucratized Initial Public Offerings to unregulated spontaneous sales of individual state assets. It is increasingly difficult to figure out where each step of the privatization procedures begins and where it ends. The distinction between formal and real control is often blurred.

In many post-Communist countries, including Poland, an important part of the first stage of the privatization process and a main source of its apparent "success" was a mere bookkeeping manipulation of reclassifying all cooperative activities as private rather than public. As a result, the private sector increased significantly. In some cases this reclassification reflected a true privatization, or de-etatization, of cooperatives. In other cases no significant changes occurred. By the same token, a legal transfer of ownership title from the state to state-owned investment funds and/or millions of new owners hardly could be viewed as an effective privatization.[118] Such a procedure should be considered as nothing more than a "step in the right direction" and should be classified as a preprivatization procedure rather than a proper privatization. The lack of experience causes confusion. Such rapid and widespread privatization has occurred nowhere else in the world. Another confusing issue is terminology; many terms used are inaccurate and misleading.

Seven essential dichotomies define the structural makeup of Polish privatization:

1. "Straight" privatization versus restitution. Restitution is presented earlier; the following discussion concerns straight privatization only.
2. Preprivatization activities versus privatization proper, which consists of effective property transfers.
3. Privatization by starting new private firms versus ownership transfer of public property.
4. Privatization of state property versus privatization of municipal property.
5. Individual privatization dealing with single enterprises versus collective or "mass privatization" under which large numbers of enterprises are privatized.
6. Privatization of a whole company versus privatization piecemeal of divisions or plants.
7. Privatization by liquidation, when the state enterprise formally ceases to exist, versus privatization by capitalization, when the enterprise continues to exist under partly or completely new ownership.

Privatization in Poland has been quite decentralized.[119] The MPW has representatives in the *voivodships,* and a large part of privatization has been processed either through these representatives or through municipal authorities. In general, privatization has been proceeding faster in the more developed western *voivodships* than in Eastern Poland.

The privatization process occurs in three stages: de-etatization, preprivatization, and proper privatization—the effective and "complete" transfer of property (and control). Of course, this classification is quite arbitrary. De-etatization is a fundamental transformation of the entire social, political, and economic system, while preprivatization consists of various procedures and intermediate stages that precede privatization proper. In fact, almost all the ownership transformations that have occurred in Poland since 1989 are still in the preprivatization stage. Only a small fraction of public property has been transferred effectively and completely to private owners. In most cases, the process is not finished, and often the final stage, privatization, will not occur soon or will not happen at all. The fate of the many privatization projects under way will depend on the direction of political evolution in Poland and in particular localities. Even where the ownership title was transferred from state or *gmina* to a new owner, frequently this transfer still remains conditional, subject to installments payments that are spread over a long period of time and subject to other clauses included in the sale (transfer) agreement, such as special commitments of the new owner regarding labor employment, capital investment, and reimbursement payments to current tenants.

## De-etatization

De-etatization, or denationalization, is the process of releasing of property from direct state control and reducing the involvement of the state in running economic activities, in particular in the microeconomic decision making (on production, consumption, prices, input procurement, and output distribution). De-etatization has taken several forms: restructuring of state enterprises, handing over of enterprises to the *gmina,* and creating a legal system within which private enterprise can function.

After World War II, Poland was subject to forced etatization or "totalitarization," consisting of imposing pervasive state controls over virtually all aspects of social life and economic activities. This process of etatization was abruptly halted by the 1980 workers' rebellion and the creation of the Independent Labor Union Solidarity. The inclusion of the word "independent" in the union's name was very important. In a totalitarian state the very existence of a large organization that was officially independent from the Communist authorities was a breakthrough in the world history of state communism. In August 1980 the effective control of the state's and the Communist Party's bureaucracies began to decline. The Law on State Enterprises and the Law on Self-Management of State Owned Enterprises, introduced in 1981, significantly constrained the state's direct controls and transferred a large chunk of decision making down to the enterprises, especially to the now powerful workers' councils. The role of Solidarity and other labor unions in running the enterprises increased greatly, while that of Communist Party organizations dwindled to their lowest level since the 1940s. In the wake of the December 1981 coup by General Wojciech Jaruzelski, supervisory positions were temporarily allocated to army-appointed military commissaries. The role of the party apparatus at all levels (state, local, enterprise) further diminished.

Overall, during the 1980s, most control was effectively transferred from the state central planning bureaucracy to managers and workers' councils in state enterprises as well as to individual businesses outside the state sector. This gradual process of decentralization, deconcentration, and demonopolization was aimed at replacing a small number of giant Communist enterprises with a large number of small firms competing in the market.

Altogether in Poland by 1990, there were 3.3 million businesses, including 2.1 million private farms. By the end of May 1995, the number of businesses had increased to 4.1 million. The total number of nonfarm firms increased from 1.2 million to 2.0 million, while the total number of persons working in these firms decreased from 12.4 million to 11.0 million. Thus, the average number of workers per firm declined almost by half, from 10.3 to 5.4. De-etatization was at work in all spheres of the economy. For example, agricultural services, which previously were almost entirely under state control, underwent a dynamic process of demonopolization and privatization. The number of agricultural service private firms increased from 130 in 1989 to 5,503 in 1994 and is expected to keep growing.

Table 4.4 summarizes the changes in status of Polish economic establishments from December 1990 to June 1995.

### TABLE 4.4: ESTABLISHMENTS BY OWNERSHIP STATUS, 1990-95

| Establishments | Dec. 90 | Dec. 93 | June 95 | June 95 Dec. 90=100 |
|---|---|---|---|---|
| PUBLIC | 8,733 | 7,529 | 6,099 | 69.8 |
| State Enterprises | 8,453 | 5,924 | 4,630 | 54.8 |
| State Treasury Partnerships | 248 | 958 | 951 | 383.5 |
| Municipal Enterprises | 32 | 647 | 518 | 1,618.8 |
| PRIVATE | 3,326,451 | 4,028,856 | 4,049,045 | 121.7 |
| Cooperatives | 18,575 | 19,746 | 19,834 | 106.8 |
| Domestic Partnerships | 33,239 | 66,457 | 77,478 | 233.1 |
| Individually Owned | 3,272,992 | 3,927,600 | 3,929,817 | 120.1 |
| Nonfarm Firms | 1,135,492 | 1,783,900 | 1,900,000 | 167.3 |
| Farms | 2,137,500 | 2,143,700 | 2,029,817 | 95.0 |
| Foreign Partnerships | 1,645 | 15,053 | 21,916 | 1,332.3 |
| **TOTAL** | **3,335,184** | **4,036,385** | **4,055,144** | **121.6** |

### State Enterprises

The state enterprise (*przedsiębiorstwo państwowe*) is regulated by the 1981 Law on State Enterprises and the 1981 Law on Self-Management of State-Owned Enterprises, as amended. It has the status of a legal person and is defined as an independent, self-governing, and self-financing economic unit. The law distinguishes between two kinds of enterprises: ordinary (for profit) and public utilities (nonprofit).[120]

All enterprises must be created by their "founding organs," such as state ministries and other agencies of state and local administration or the national bank. In the case of ordinary enterprises, the role of founding organs is limited to defining the initial scope of activities, providing initial assets, and codeciding with the employee council about enterprise liquidation. All day-to-day business decisions are in the hands of a director and an employee council. However, if the enterprise fails to pay a "dividend" (a tax on the assets owned by the state), the self-management of the enterprise is curtailed and the powers are transferred to a "curative commission" in which employees representatives are a minority. Public utilities remain under direct control of their founding organs, which, in the case of losses, are obliged to subsidize those enterprises that are ruled necessary for public purposes.

The real estate and other assets provided to the enterprise remain the property of the state; however, the enterprise has an exclusive right to manage them.

These assets cannot be taken away from the enterprise. Under certain conditions, the enterprise may even sell some of its assets at public auctions and keep the proceeds. Since 1990 state enterprises have been eligible to become the owners of the buildings they use (which previously belonged to the State Treasury) and acquire land on a perpetual leasehold.

Over the last few years, the number of state enterprises has shrunk from 8,453 in December 1990 to 4,630 in June 1995, and they are doomed for complete extinction. According to the June 1995 Law on Privatization and Commercialization of State Enterprises, all of them are to be turned into one-person partnerships of the State Treasury. The state enterprise, which has been a fundamental unit of the socialist economic activity since the January 1946 Law on the Nationalization of the Basic Branches of the National Economy, will soon become history.

**State Treasury Partnerships**

State Treasury Partnerships are created in the process of corporatization,[121] or transformation of a state enterprise into a one-person joint stock company owned by the State Treasury. The owner remains the same, but the company begins to operate under the prewar Commercial Code, updated, rather than under the 1981 State Enterprise Law. Moreover, a new corporation-type management and new supervisory system is established.

The joint stock companies were originally designed as stop-gap measures. The aim of this enterprise-to-company transformation was to separate the company from its owner—the state—by creating an autonomous business that operates like a "normal" commercial for-profit firm and to prepare the enterprise for its eventual privatization.

**Municipal Enterprises**

Another important component of the process of de-etatization was the municipalization of public property, which began with the re-establishment of local governments in May 1990. The September 1990 Land Use and Expropriation Act authorized state and local governments to sell land, removing the stricture that had limited disposition of public land to leasehold. The transfer of properties—land and housing as well as small firms servicing local markets—from the state to the municipalities began promptly but is moving slowly. In some cases land must be surveyed and recorded. Until boundaries are correct and title is in the hands of the municipalities, they cannot sell property. Thus, short-term lease is prevalent.[122] Municipal enterprises are subject to the same laws as state enterprises. The municipal enterprise has a legal status separate from the *gmina* with neither responsible for the others' liabilities. As with the state enterprises, there are ordinary, for-profit enterprises; and nonprofit enterprises, largely municipal utilities. The *gmina* may not subsidize the ordinary enterprises; if they are unprofitable, they should be liquidated.

In December 1990 only 32 municipal enterprises existed. Their number increased to 647 at the end of 1993 and decreased to 518 in June 1995. Unlike the ordinary state enterprises, they were established as transitional, ephemeral organizations. Eventually they should be either privatized or transformed into internal units of the *gminas*.

## Cooperatives

While earlier cooperatives had been under the thumb of the state, under the 1982 Cooperative Law and the 1990 Law on Changes in the Organization and Activities of Cooperatives, they are now much more independent and flexible.

According to the provisions of the 1982 law, each cooperative member had an equal vote, regardless of his or her capital contribution. Foreigners were eligible for cooperative membership only as legal persons (joint ventures); no foreign natural person was allowed to join.

The 1990 law freed the cooperatives from bureaucratic controls and demonopolized them. Among other things, it abolished the cooperative unions into which the individual cooperatives were organized. Before 1990 many of these unions served as a means for state control of the activities of the cooperatives. They also were used as cover-up organizations for illegal economic activities and as the source of additional, often significant, income for the Communist nomenklatura. Under the 1990 law, the union's assets were transferred to individual cooperatives, usually with no payment or at a fraction of their value, or sold to third parties. The law also mandated new elections and a breaking up of the co-ops, if the members so desired.

Co-ops have remained a significant force in the Polish economy, especially in agriculture, housing, trade, and services. The position of cooperatives traditionally has been strong in trade, where Communist authorities used them as a substitute for private business. Since the cooperatives were somewhat less centralized and more flexible than the large state enterprises, they enjoyed support from the authorities in consumer-oriented activities, such as restaurants, small services, and light industry, such as food processing and apparel.

Housing, especially in urban areas, is the only industry that, over the last quarter century, has seen a dramatic expansion of the number of cooperatives. In 1960, 10 percent of newly constructed apartments were co-op owned. By 1970 this share had reached 50 percent, a level that has been maintained. Overall, in all sectors, between 1956 and 1980, there were around 10,000 co-ops, and membership reached 15.2 million. At the end of 1990, 18,600 were in existence; and by June 1995, this number had reached almost 20,000, a third of which were in the housing sector.

## Individually Owned Firms and Private Companies

Before 1980 the private sector officially existed, but its activities were subject to oppressive regulations and intimidation. There were some 2 million individually owned farms and a few hundred thousand small private nonfarm businesses, such as small factories and repair shops, construction firms, retail stores, taxis, and trucks. In most cases, a private activity required a license from the authorities, its production inputs (raw materials, fuels, merchandise) were rationed, and the sale of its output was also partly controlled by the authorities. The formal start of free private nonfarm entrepreneurship began in Poland shortly before the fall of communism. The 1988 Law on Economic Activity, which took effect in 1989, granted all individuals the right to conduct independent commercial activity without any permit (except for specified activities, such as production of arms, alcohol, and tobacco, for which a license was required). Individuals and commercial companies are permitted to hire an unlimited number of workers. By the end of 1990 there were 2.14 million individually owned farms and 1.14 million nonfarm individual firms. In June 1995 these numbers were 2.03 million and 1.90 million, respectively. In addition, the number of larger commercial law companies owned by the Poles more than doubled from 33,200 in 1990 to 77,500 in mid-1995.

## Foreign-Owned Companies

Poland effectively opened to foreign business in January 1989, when the first joint venture companies (JVCs) began their operations. At that time the Communist authorities viewed the JVCs as a means to open the country to desperately needed foreign capital, technologies, and management. The first JVCs were regulated by the 1934 Commercial Code and the 1988 Joint Ventures Act. To create a JVC, one had to obtain permission from the Agency for Foreign Investment. The JVCs had to have founding capital of at least $50,000, their production had to be oriented toward export or so-called deficit merchandise, and they had to meet various environmental requirements. During the first three years the new companies were granted a tax holiday. Before the Agency for Foreign Investment was liquidated in October 1991, and the 1991 Joint Ventures Act was introduced, the agency granted a total of 4,920 permits for the creation of new JVCs. Not all of these firms, however, started a business. Total foreign capital invested in these ventures amounted to $694 million, and total Polish capital reached $50 million. Foreign capital came from sixty countries: In the vanguard were Germany, investing $161 million in 1,516 ventures; and the US, investing $76 million in 436 ventures.[123]

The more liberal 1991 law eliminated many bureaucratic obstacles for foreign investors. According to this law, foreigners can operate two forms of businesses in Poland: limited liability company and joint stock company. In general, in order to start a joint venture, foreigners must follow the same procedures as Polish nationals. No permit is necessary except for a few explicitly specified cases, such as management of airports and seaports, real estate agencies, and activities related to national defense. The joint ventures are treated like other commercial law firms. No permit is required for transfers of business profits to foreign countries, and unlimited transfers of foreign currency are allowed. A tax holiday is subject to a number of conditions, including investments above $2.2 million and location in regions of high unemployment. The largest number of joint ventures occur in wholesale and retail trade. Most are located in the Warsaw region. Few joint ventures exist in agriculture, forestry, and housing, reflecting the special restrictions imposed on foreigners regarding ownership of real estate in Poland.

**The Non-Profits**

Before 1980 practically all nonbusiness organizations were closely controlled by the state. A possible exception was the Catholic church, which enjoyed limited autonomy. Solidarity was the first nonprofit organization independent of the state that ran various economic activities, such as the small-scale manufacturing and printing of newspapers.[124] During the 1980s the legislature introduced more liberal Western-style regulations for the nonprofits and enabled them to operate legally in Poland. There are two institutional forms of nonprofits: foundations and associations. Foundations are regulated by a law enacted in 1984. To be established they must adopt by-laws and register their existence in a court and with a list of business organizations. They are allowed to run businesses to support their nonprofit activities.[125] and their income is not taxable. Foreign foundations are allowed to operate in Poland. Associations are similar to foundations. They are regulated by the 1989 Law on Associations and can be established only by individuals.

**Preprivatization Reforms**

Preprivatization reforms consist of various activities that are a prelude to eventual transfer of property from the state to third parties. Their major forms have been liquidation, corporatization (commercialization), mass privatization (PPP= the Program of Public Privatization), and small privatization.

Liquidation occurs when a company formally ceases to exist. A new company may be founded in its stead that is not, in legal terms, considered a continuation of the old one. Two forms of liquidation are practiced: insolvency liquidation, or bankruptcy, which is regulated under the 1981 Law on State Enterprises; and liquidation of a viable enterprise, which is regulated under the Privatization Law and results in transfer of assets to a new company. Liquidation may involve lease, contribution in kind, or sale of assets; only the last form is a proper privatization.

Polish law authorizes three forms of lease of the assets of a liquidated enterprise, all of which should end up with an eventual transfer of the state property to third persons. Under the most popular form, "lease and sale", the lessee makes yearly payments of principal and interest, and ownership title is transferred at the end of the contract, after all the payments are made.

In the case of contribution in kind, the assets are contributed to a new company, usually a corporation, founded by the State Treasury together with a domestic or foreign participant. The new company does not necessarily take over the preexisting obligations of the liquidated firm. Since the old firm has been liquidated rather than corporatized, its employees are not entitled to preferential share purchase (which is the case in other privatization procedures). The whole procedure is implemented by the founding organ, which negotiates on behalf of the state with other parties.

Asset sale through liquidation requires several steps. First, the state enterprise is transformed into an enterprise in the process of liquidation, under the 1981 Law on State Enterprises, the 1990 Privatization Law, or the 1991 Law on Treasury Owned Agricultural Property. Nonagricultural enterprises are transformed by the State Treasury into one-person joint stock corporations with a supervisory board and subsequently sold to third persons. Liquidation of state farms is discussed later.

As described, corporatization consists of a transformation of the state enterprise into a one-person partnership of the State Treasury. Essentially the company continues its operations, but within a new institutional framework and under different conditions. Its activities are regulated by the commercial law. It is supposed to operate in the market under a "hard budget constraint,"[126] produce and compete, expand or contract or go bankrupt, as any other privately owned "profit maximizer"; the only difference is that its owner happens to be the State Treasury. Originally all corporatized state-owned companies were created as interim firms destined to be privatized. According to a new controversial law, which was designed by the Pawlak and Oleksy governments and passed by the Sejm in June 1995, these companies become a mere replacement for the old "soft-budget-constraint" state enterprises. Privatization does not necessarily have to follow corporatization. At least some of treasury companies are to remain permanently in the hands of the government.

The mass privatization program, passed by the Sejm in spring 1993, provides for the privatization of several hundred large enterprises.[127] The decision to participate in the program by particular enterprises must have been made by consensus among all interested parties: management, workers, the founding organ, and the MPW. In certain cases it would also involve the Anti-Monopoly Office. To participate in this program, enterprises had to be transformed into one-person joint stock companies of the treasury. Most of their shares (60 percent) are distributed to specially created financial intermediaries—National Investment Funds (the NIFs)—that become the legal owners of the shares. Each of the NIFs holds a majority of the shares in about thirty companies and holds minority shares of the equity in all other privatized companies (400 or so). The remaining 40 percent is divided between the companies' employees (15 percent) and the state budget (25 percent).

After numerous postponements and delays, by the end of March 1995, fifteen NIFs were established as closed-end joint stock companies (which are not allowed to issue new shares). They are managed mostly by foreign firms, but members of their supervisory boards are mostly Polish. In July 1995 the allocation of the shares among the NIFs took off. The task of the NIFs is to monitor the performance of the companies in their portfolios. The shares in the funds themselves have been offered to Polish citizens since the fall 1995. All citizens, eighteen years or older (about 27 million people) are eligible to purchase these shares at a cost of $20 per person, or 7 percent of the average monthly wage.[128] The shares of the funds will be traded on the Warsaw Stock Exchange.[129]

The preprivatization procedures just described do not apply to small firms that have been handed over by the state to the *gminas*. The Municipal Commercial Activity Law regulates the local shops and other small commercial units now owned by the *gminas*. In most cases the *gminas* have rented or leased these businesses to individuals. The whole process was quite idiosyncratic. For example, out of over 10,000 shops owned by the *gminas* that were rented in the first half of 1990, only 9.3 percent were allocated by an auction; the auction prices were often thirty to forty times higher than bureaucratically set rents. Even when auctions were conducted, bidding was often limited to insiders, or the insiders were given preferential treatment in the form of rental "give-backs." Insider pressure was strong. Labor unions used unemployment and inflation threats to push for low rents.

## Transfer of Ownership

Through 1995, the main forms of the transfer of state property to third parties were: (1) "spontaneous" privatization, practiced mostly in the late 1980s; (2) sales of assets of liquidated state enterprises and municipal property; (3) "quick" privatization, the sale of whole enterprises without prior corporatization; and (4) capital privatization, the sale of corporatized companies.

Spontaneous or nomenklatura privatization was an early form of privatization, mostly before the installation of the first Solidarity-led government in fall 1989. It consisted of unregulated and uncontrolled conversion of state property into private ownership by the members of the Communist elite. In most cases it was not clearly illegal but did involve abuses of political power and taking advantage of gaps in the emerging banking and commercial laws. An example of spontaneous privatization would be liquidation of a healthy but nominally bankrupt state enterprise and its purchase at unrealistically low prices. Nomenklatura members created private companies (often joint ventures) that entered into sweetheart deals with state enterprises and siphoned off their resources, exporting at subsidized prices or leasing equipment at artificially low prices. The actual extent of spontaneous privatization is not known, but likely its scope was relatively small. Nevertheless, it resulted in an outcry of public opinion and shaped the whole Polish privatization program, especially in the use of significant central government control

So far, liquidation has been the main privatization method due to its low cost and legal simplicity. It also offers significant advantages to insiders (employees) who are able to manipulate the whole process. It can be described as a better-controlled form of spontaneous privatization. The sale decision is made by the founding organ together with the MPW and after consultation with the director and workers' council. Insiders are usually the initiators of this procedure and prime bidders for the assets. The sale must be public, advertised in the local and national press. The winning bid, however, does not have to be the highest in monetary terms. Important issues taken into consideration by the founding organ include the overall credibility of the buyer and bids from the employees. The most frequent terms are a 40 percent down payment followed by sixteen quarterly installments. Through June 1995, 2,366 nonfarm enterprises, along with 1,651 state farms, had started their liquidation procedures. However, in most cases only the procedures under the 1990 Privatization Law (those affecting economically healthy nonagricultural enterprises) resulted in effective privatization (977 out of 1,044 enterprises privatized in this way completed the property transfer). In the remaining cases the process has been slow. Only 26 percent of the insolvency cases had completed the privatization procedures.

Quick privatization is a special subcategory of privatization through liquidation. It was launched by the MPW in July 1991. Quick privatization begins by an invitation issued by the founding organ of a state enterprise to potential investors (legal and physical persons, including employees) to enter into negotiations. If successful, they lead to the liquidation and sale of the company. Originally this method was designed for small and medium-size firms. Later it was extended to large companies and large foreign investors such as FIAT, General Motors, and International Paper Co.

Capital privatization consists of selling the shares of previously corporatized state enterprises through public offerings, trade sales, management and employee buyouts, or a combination of these methods. The initial public offering (IPO) of the securities of a corporatized state enterprise is the most complex and time-consuming privatization method. It is applied only to a small number of companies with good reputations. A major difficulty with this method is setting initial prices. None of the companies has a solid record of performance in a market economy. Their book values are calculated according to a Communist system, often based on artificial administrative prices. The valuers need help from insiders, who tend to suggest low prices. Trade sales are sales of large blocks of shares outside the financial markets, usually through a public invitation to tender, a public auction, or a negotiated private placement. In trade sales, investors often are foreign companies that acquire the majority of shares and take over company management. Management and employee buyouts occur primarily in the cases of small and medium-size companies. In these leveraged buyouts, the state serves as the creditor, and the loan is raised on the security of the company assets and is supposed to be paid off from the profits. Through June 1995, 140 firms had been privatized by capital privatization. Only 25 of them went public (via an IPO).

## State Farm Privatization

An early task of the Solidarity-led government was the designation of an agency to hold title to the state farms and to have the authority to restructure them and to dispose of their assets. In 1989 the Civil Code was amended to specify that the treasury henceforth was the owner of state property, including the state farms.[130] The Treasury Agency for Agricultural Property (AWRSP) was created in October 1991 and began its operations in 1992. This agency is responsible for state farm property, specifically "for rational use of the state's agricultural resources, job creation, and restructuring and privatization of these assets."[131] It holds all rights and obligations that inured to the Treasury as owner of the state farms. It oversees the farm managers and is authorized to donate land to the *gminas,* donate land for state forests, lease land to farmers, and issue bonds and sell land, buildings, and equipment. Land may be sold for second home development if this is in accord with the local plan. If there is no demand for the land for any of these purposes, the agency must manage it.[132]

The AWRSP is managed by a president, chosen by the prime minister in consultation with the ministers of agriculture and privatization, and a board of nine, chosen by the ministers of agriculture, privatization, finance, and labor and social policy in consultation with appropriate committees of Parliament. The AWRSP has sixteen divisions, fifteen are geographically determined and one is responsible nationwide for experimental farms and research units.

The State Treasury is not the only source of AWRSP holdings. Farmers, on retirement, may turn in land to the State Land Fund in return for a pension. Fallow land also may be contributed.

The following map shows the distribution of state farmland, emphasizing its concentration in the north and west, and also shows the amount of land held by the AWRSP in each of its divisions as of the end of 1993. The total amount is about the same throughout northwest Poland and around Warsaw. However, only in the far northwest does state land exceed 50 percent of all farmland. Most farms agency managed are located in this territory, which before World War II belonged to Germany. This part of the country is less densely populated, with poor sandy soils.

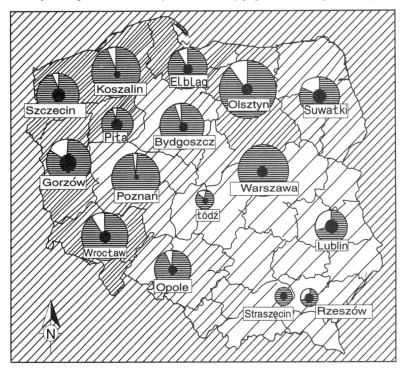

Area of AWRSP Agricultural Land, Thousands of Hectares

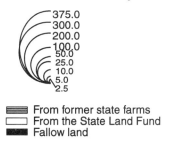

375.0
300.0
200.0
100.0
50.0
25.0
10.0
5.0
2.5

▤ From former state farms
☐ From the State Land Fund
■ Fallow land

The share of state owned land as a % of total agricultural land

5   10  20  30  40  50    %

**Map 4.1   Land in AWRSP Possession, December 31, 1993**

The Agency, before attempting to sell land, must develop plans for restructuring the farms, determining what lands should remain in farming and what lands have development or recreation potential, what lands should be sold or leased, and what lands should be kept. These plans are developed in consultation with the farm managers, considering how to make the farms efficient and how to assure continued employment. A joint task force of the World Bank and the European Union[133] recommended that, in the interest of efficiency, the state farms not be dismantled and sold piecemeal. They further recommended that the state retain title and lease the land and buildings. Though the evidence is not clear, the Agency may have heeded this advice; so far it has offered rather limited amounts of land for sale.

Property worth less than 50 tons of rye may be auctioned. All more valuable property must be advertised in the press and bids solicited. Bidders have the right to review farm production data and must specify how they would use the current labor force; this is a consideration in selecting the winning bid.

Early results have shown a buyer's market prevailing. During 1992 only 123,000 acres (49,000 hectares) were leased, generally for eight to ten years with the possibility of renewal for up to thirty years. Rent was set in relation to yield and location and ranged from 120 to 450 pounds per acre (150 to 500 kilograms per hectare) of wheat. Some 95 percent of the land was in temporary management, 73,000 acres (29,000 hectares) awaited a management agreement, while 38,000 acres (15,000 hectares) lay fallow. Out of 128,680 dwellings then in the agency's portfolio, only 3,316 had been sold. Total sales revenue was $6 million (ZL 80,300 million), or a third of total estimated value.[134]

By the end of March 1993, more than 200 public auctions had been organized at which 0.7 million acres (0.3 million hectares) were offered for sale. There is no minimum amount of land that must be purchased. Only 0.059 million acres (0.024 million hectares) found buyers; the remainder is retained as "treasury farms" and leased to individuals or employee-owned companies. During the next few months another 0.7 million acres (0.3 million hectares) were offered at auction, but only a small proportion was sold or leased.[135] Prices paid ranged from nominal—$0.005 per square foot (ZL 8 per square meter) in northeastern Poland—to from $2 to $6 per square foot (ZL 340,000 to ZL 1 million per square meter) near large cities for land ripe for development.[136] A number of factors can explain this very low level of interest in purchasing agricultural land; these include:

- The poor financial and agronomic condition of state farms
- The lack of a restitution law and unclear legal status of some properties
- Bureaucratic procedures—foreigners are required to obtain a permit from the Ministry of Internal Affairs

- The deep recession in agriculture—decrease of farm profitability
- The location of state farms mostly in northern and western regions, while the surplus agricultural population is mostly in central and southern regions
- Limited financial capacity of farmers—lack of private savings and virtual nonavailability of farm credit for the purchase of land
- Monetary instability, high inflation, and high (nominal) interest rates

Foreigners have not expressed much interest in the land. As of March 1993, only forty-two permits had been requested, of which four were granted and thirty-eight were denied.[137] Altogether, foreigners have purchased about 790 acres (320 hectares), or 0.001 percent of Polish territory, mostly as a result of the purchase of privatized enterprises, not state farms. Based on these figures, the claim, made by some, about selling out Polish land to foreigners was hardly substantiated. While the authorities have not actively supported purchase of land by foreigners, its lease for terms of five to thirty years was encouraged.

The following map shows the amount of land under AWRSP management as of the end of 1993, by district, and by current disposition. The agency had found buyers for 1.77 percent of its holdings nationwide, or 145,000 acres (58,600 hectares), had donated 0.25 percent of the land, or 20,000 acres (8,000 hectares), had leased 2.2 million acres (899,000 hectares), and had 5 million acres (2 million hectares) under its own management.

Although houses and apartments on the farms may be sold, the tenants have a first right of refusal at a favorable price. The houses on state farms are offered to tenants who have been tenants for at least the past three years, are retired or disabled, or have been laid off due to restructuring of the farm. For these tenants, the housing is priced at market value less a deduction for labor on the farm, calculated at 3 percent per year up to 80 percent of the market value. Market value varies by location, type of dwelling, and condition, with a range of $4 to $25 per square foot ($40 to $250 per square meter). Housing sold to others is subject to the right of tenants to remain indefinitely. Rent may be set at a sum to cover "the utilization of the said houses and apartments."[138] As there are almost half a million homes, inhabited by 2 million people on the state farms, these are not insignificant provisions.

Most housing on the state farms remains with the tenants, either farm workers or pensioners, as lessees. A few districts, mostly in the northwest, have made considerable progress in selling or transferring units, but as can be seen on the next map, it is not clear whether these are sales to tenants or to others or gifts.

Through May 1995 the agency had taken over almost all state farms and other agricultural state enterprises (1,651 firms), 10.8 million acres of land, 0.33 million dwelling units, and 0.2 million workers (see table 4.5.) It had managed to

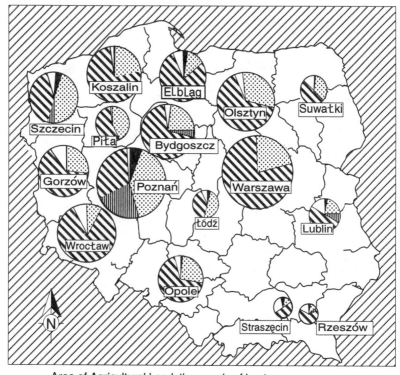

Area of Agricultural Land, thousands of hectares

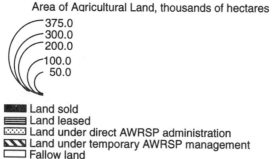

- 375.0
- 300.0
- 200.0
- 100.0
- 50.0

■ Land sold
≡ Land leased
⋯ Land under direct AWRSP administration
⤫ Land under temporary AWRSP management
□ Fallow land

**Map 4.2    Land in AWRSP Management, December 31, 1993**

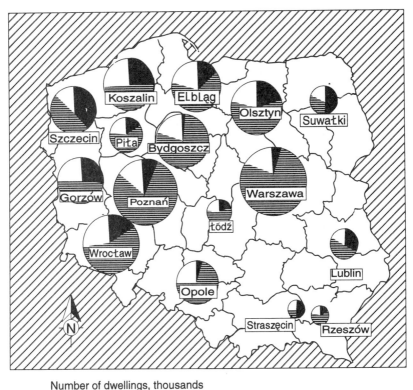

Number of dwellings, thousands

40.0
30.0
20.0
10.0
5.0
2.5

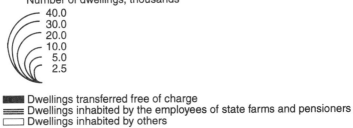

Dwellings transferred free of charge
Dwellings inhabited by the employees of state farms and pensioners
Dwellings inhabited by others

**Map 4.3    Apartments under AWRSP Management, December 31, 1993**

sell only 3.7 percent of all land it took over. Also, it gave 0.7 percent of its land free of charge to other owners. The remaining land was leased (53.9 percent) or entrusted for temporary management (22.9 percent), or other (18.8 percent).

**TABLE 4.5: RESOURCES MANAGED BY THE AWRSP**

| | 1992 | 1993 | 1994 | May 1995 |
|---|---|---|---|---|
| | | End of period (cumulative) | | |
| **Taken over by the agency:** | | | | |
| Number of state agricult. enterprises | 723 | 1,340 | 1,647 | 1,651 |
| Land, thousand acres | 3,587 | 8,250 | 10,583 | 10,795 |
| Dwelling units, thousands | 129 | 276 | 326 | 327 |
| Workers, thousands | 90 | 175 | 193 | 193 |
| **Allocated by the agency:** | | | | |
| State Treasury farms created | 0 | 1,557 | 1,770 | 1,802 |
| State Treasury farms liquidated | 0 | 253 | 636 | 862 |
| Land transferred to other owners, | | | | |
| thousand acres | 27 | 174 | 379 | 497 |
| Sold | 24 | 147 | 310 | 403 |
| Transferred free of charge | 3 | 24 | 53 | 76 |
| Other | 0 | 3 | 16 | 18 |
| **Owned by the agency:** | | | | |
| Land, thousand acres | 3,554 | 8,078 | 10,203 | 10,299 |
| Leased | 122 | 2,297 | 4,953 | 5,816 |
| Transferred for temporary management | 3,323 | 5,065 | 3,512 | 2,469 |

## Urban Housing Privatization

The *gminas* are actively promoting sale of their housing, primarily to tenants.[139] These sales have been as controversial as everything else in the housing industry. Strong arguments against the sales were based on social justice: The stock was built from public funds and was allocated to a few households that, over the years, have enjoyed a privileged status with low rents. The access to preferential sales is not fair. Furthermore, despite the municipal sector's large future financial needs, it stands to lose its assets when discounted prices are applied in the sales.

Municipal officials argue that the only feasible way of quickly stopping expensive subsidies to public housing is to sell the housing to current residents. This argument is bolstered by data on rents for municipal housing in Warsaw. Through 1994, the gap between public and private rents was very large: $0.012 per square foot (ZL 3,000 per square meter) per month for public apartments, compared to $0.40 to $0.80 per square foot (ZL 90,000 to ZL 180,000 per square meter) for private apartments. The municipal rents covered only a third of maintenance costs. As described, while public housing rents increased by several times in fall 1994, they still remain a few times below the market clearing level.

## Municipalization

The process of municipalization belongs to all four types of transformations: restitution, de-etatization, preprivatization, and proper privatization. Three examples
are used to illustrate this process: Wola, a district of Warsaw; Sztynort, a
depressed agricultural region in northeastern Poland; and Jastarnia, a recreation
and tourism locality on the Baltic sea shore.

In 1990, in the Warsaw district of Wola, 3,000 pieces of real estate were
selected for title transfer from the state to the *gmina*. By the end of 1993 the district was granted 2,450 decisions by which it took over 85 million square feet
(8.5 million square meters) worth $300 million (ZL 5,500 billion). Major stum-
bling blocks in the ownership transfer included frequent lack of necessary documents and inconsistent records, including differences between the Warsaw deed
records and local land records. Another problem was mixed property. For
example, some buildings awarded to the *gmina* were located on privately owned
land. Long lines in the public notary offices was another delaying factor. The
transfer has not ended and will continue through at least 1997.

The Sztynort palace complex is located on a peninsula between two large
lakes in northeastern Poland, on former German territory. The palace was built
in the fifteenth and sixteenth centuries by the Lehndorffs, a German aristocratic
family. In 1945 it was nationalized by the Polish state and used to house, among
other things, state farm offices, a kindergarten, a water sports complex, stables,
and a hotel. After 1989 it was taken over by the municipality, which could not
afford the maintenance costs, not to mention its reconstruction and renovation.
In 1991 an auction was announced in the press. During the next three years there
were twenty-five bids for purchase or lease (by nonprofits, businesses, and private persons). In December 1994 the *gmina's* council decided to sell this property to a Pole who lives permanently in Austria. The "true" buyer was her
husband, an Austrian businessman, Dietrich Traitler. (The fact that she is Polish
and he is not German but Austrian was of great importance.) The Traitlers
offered to pay the *gmina* $150,000 (ZL 3.5 billion) and promised to spend
another $500,000 (ZL 11 billion) over a two-year period to cover the cost of con-
struction of substitute dwellings for and reallocation of thirty-eight families
who lived in the palace complex. They promised to develop a modern high-quality
recreational center with 250 sleeping places, restaurant, swimming pools, new
yacht port, horse stables, a 45 acre (18 hectare) park, golf courses and other attrac-
tions. The total cost of this project is estimated at $30 million (ZL 650 billion).
Most of Sztynort's inhabitants support this sale, even though this would be the
first case in Poland in many years of relocation of a whole village. Many people
in the area have been unemployed for three years or more. While they are counting on employment opportunities in constructing the recreation center and later
in the center itself, yet it is not clear how suited the former state farm workers

are for this kind of business. Interviewed villagers recall with nostalgia the time, before 1989, when there was a state farm, on which they all were employed. Every few weeks they were transported to a nearby theater. There was a feeling of relative prosperity and comfortable security. Some (few) villagers oppose this sale, mostly for nationalistic reasons.[140]

The Jastarnia *gmina* is located on a narrow peninsula that separates the Gdańsk Bay from the (open) Baltic sea. After 1989 the *gmina* was given a number of hotels and luxury vacation houses that had been used by prominent Communists. The municipality was not able to afford the maintenance costs and decided to sell several of the hotels and vacation houses at auction. Hotel Bryza was sold to Zbigniew Kulczycki for $600,000 (ZL 11 billion). Hotel Neptun was sold for $1.7 million (ZL 30 billion) to a Polish bank (PKO) to be used as a training and recreation center for its employees. Also, many other hotels and services were upgraded. A small airport was built to be used by new Polish capitalists-millionaires, such as Adam Smorawiński, Aleksander Gawronik, and Zygmunt Solorz, who became frequent guests of these hotels.

In Communist Poland the inhabitants of this region disliked tourists, believing that they were eating up modest local resources. While at that time local authorities made efforts to discourage tourists, today all the efforts go in the opposite direction. Currently 4,500 permanent residents in the *gmina* have registered more than 1,200 businesses. Jastarnia has become an area with one of the highest concentrations of capitalism in Poland. Official unemployment is at 17 percent but in reality there is no idle labor available. Among other things, to attract tourists the *gmina* built a sewage treatment plant. The quality of water in the nearby bay has improved greatly. To attract businesses, the *gmina* lowered port entry fees charged to fishing ships. As a result, 300 new small fish processing and smoking firms moved in. The *gmina* decided to collect and process restitution claims quickly. The former owners, whose property was illegally nationalized after the war, received their estates back, whenever possible. In other cases they were awarded other post-Communist vacation houses. This quick restitution is believed to have been very successful.[141] It was instrumental in attracting former owners and their heirs along with their money and entrepreneurship.

## MARKETS: PRICES AND LOCATIONAL DISPARITIES

### Urban Real Estate, Except Residential

Until now the scale of industrial real estate transactions has been limited. The most frequent seller has been the treasury in the course of disposing of state enterprises and their assets.[142]

There is also a market for land that has been approved for industrial use. Such land may be in private hands and relatively simple to acquire. The price paid for this land varies from $0.20 to $5 per square foot (NZL 5 to 120 per square meter) in Warsaw and from $0.10 to $4 per square foot (NZL 2.50 to 100 per square meter) in and around the other large cities.

The market for land with industrial buildings is more complex and relatively slow. The standards of most existing buildings are low. It was estimated that the average cost of upgrading these buildings and bringing them to the level of Western standards would amount to about $30 per square foot.[143]

There are few sales of office buildings, but a growing market for office rentals is strongly linked to whether the offices meet Western standards. If they do, foreign companies will pay a price ranging from $1.50 to $5 per square foot (NZL 35 to 120 per square meter) per month depending on location.[144]

According to Healy & Baker, an international marketing firm, the demand for new office space in Warsaw will grow annually by 0.5 to 1 million square feet, while that for new commercial retail space will grow by 25,000 to 50,000 square feet. More than 10,000 acres (4,000 hectares), or about 8.5 percent of land, in the City of Warsaw is available for commercial development.[145]

According to the State Agency for Foreign Investment, promoting foreign investment calls for simplifying the laws concerning acquisition of real estate and reduction of bureaucratic obstacles.[146]

## Urban Residential Land and Housing

While the private sector accounts mostly for single-family homes, the public sectors—municipal, state enterprises, and cooperatives—account predominantly for multifamily buildings. The municipal buildings tend to be older than those belonging to the other sectors. The four sectors are mutually intertwined, there are privately owned apartments in publicly owned buildings and publicly administered apartments in private buildings. In the former case, the individuals usually have property right to the apartment, whereas the land is on perpetual lease.

There is no official monitoring of the sale of housing, so the price data presented here are limited. The prices in co-op housing were always much closer to market prices than the prices in the municipal sector and the enterprise sector. The average purchase price of new co-op apartments in the second quarter of 1993 in Warsaw was $44 per square foot (ZL 8 million per square meter); in the third quarter of 1995 it was $60 per square foot (NZL 1,450 per square meter).[147] The major advantage of cooperatives over private sector housing was not the price but the financing conditions. Currently the cooperatives are still a major player on the market, but the role of the private sector gradually is increasing.

While the housing market in many countries suffered from recession since around 1989, Poland was not affected until 1992. In Warsaw during 1991, private-sector housing dollar prices increased by about one-third. Prices of land also increased significantly—in certain suburban locations by several times. Prices stabilized at the end of 1991 and began to fall in 1992. This was an unexpected blow to Polish investors, because for many years operations in the Polish real estate market were sure to produce substantial profits and were considered an investor's haven. At the end of 1991, a continuing solid "surplus of demand over supply" in the Polish real estate market was predicted that supposedly would keep pushing the prices up for several years ahead. This phenomenon was said to occur "for a very simple reason—there is no chance of supply satisfying demand until at least the mid-1990s. This creates an important reason for investing in Polish real estate."[148] Michał Chydzik, one of the authorities in the Polish real estate market, argued in the summer of 1991 that housing prices must keep rising in 1992 and later because of the supply shortage. According to published estimates, the apparent housing shortage amounted to about 6 million units.[149]

As we have argued earlier, given the level of actual economic development and productivity in Poland, there was no evidence for a "true" shortage. In the absence of heavy subsidies, it is unreasonable to expect that Poles could afford much more housing. Therefore, the decline in demand for nonsubsidized housing should not be surprising. Of course, many other factors also affect the housing market, but without radical progress in economic growth and households' income, no large increase in effective demand for residential housing can be expected. For example, in a U.S.-like mortgage system a standard loan would usually involve a 10 to 20 percent down payment and a thirty-year loan at a 7 to 10 percent interest. Often an additional requirement is specified that total mortgage payments (capital and interest) together with real estate taxes and house insurance payments not exceed 26 to 28 percent of gross household income. Under such a system, very few families in Poland could qualify.[150] Only an active housing policy supported by hefty subsidies could substantially increase the effective demand for new housing.

Between 1988 and 1992 precious metals and hard currency savings lost a great deal of their purchasing power. Real interest rates on long-term zloty saving accounts were positive in 1990 and 1991 but turned negative in 1992. According to the advice provided by *Home&Market,* only parcels well selected for future development continued to be a potentially good investment, although the risk remained substantial. After 1993 the average (relative) price of parcels decreased as well.

A major shift in forms of individual investment took place. Before 1993 households could purchase foreign cars and real estate or put their savings into bank accounts. In 1993, however, a large chunk of savings was located in the shares of privatized banks, state enterprises and other securities—a fact that explains the fabulous achievements of the Warsaw stock exchange in 1993.

In that year the housing market stabilized at a relatively low level. It remained unexpectedly calm despite such potentially destabilizing events as a successful no-confidence vote against the Suchocka government in May, the introduction of the value-added tax (VAT) in July, early elections resulting in a victory by former Communists in September, unstable and high inflation, and growing unemployment. Also, despite a decrease in construction of new apartments, there was a substantial increase in their supply in the open market. As a result of a change in the financing regulations, a large part of new co-op apartments became too expensive for eligible co-op members and were offered for sale in the open market. A novel form of housing supply was "raw" apartments or preconstruction contracts offered by the construction firms.

Between fall 1991 and spring 1993, the dollar prices of Warsaw apartments decreased from 10 to 30 percent,[151] with the largest decline occurring in the prices of medium-size apartments (2 to 3 bedrooms).[152] The median price of an apartment in Warsaw decreased from about $60 per square foot (ZL 7 million per square meter) in 1991 to about $50 per square foot (ZL 8 million per square meter) in 1993.[153] At that time, a Warsaw resident, with his or her monthly wage of about $250, could afford five square feet a month. For comparison, in the United States, a square foot costs about $100. With an U.S. average monthly wage of about $2,000 one could acquire twenty square feet.

In 1993 in Warsaw, in terms of cost per unit area, the most expensive were large apartments, then houses, then small apartments. The cheapest apartments were small studios of less than 300 square feet (30 square meters) and standard two-bedroom units of around 500 square feet (50 square meters). Many of these apartments were built in the 1950s through 1970s, and quite a few were available. Higher prices were asked for apartments in good locations, and in buildings not exceeding four floors. The greatest demand was for large one-bedroom studios, 300 to 400 square feet (30 to 40 square meters), as well as for larger three- to five-bedroom 750 to 1,000 square foot (75 to 100 square meter) apartments in the most expensive districts of Warsaw, such as Żolibórz and Wilanow. Single-family houses were priced from $30,000 to $200,000. Telephones were an especially desirable feature. In terms of the number of phones per 1,000 inhabitants, Poland ranked at the bottom of Europe's list.[154] Brick construction was preferred over the concrete panel construction of the Communist era. Access to green open space also was a selling point.

In 1993, the geography of the Warsaw residential real estate market was as follows: The cheapest apartments were available in eastern Warsaw, in predominantly working-class neighborhoods in the district of Praga North, at $30 per square foot (ZL 5 million per square meter). The flats in the new high-rise buildings, often of relatively good quality, built during Gierek's housing boom period but located far from the center of Warsaw (e.g., Ursynów and Natolin in southern Warsaw), were $50 per square foot (ZL 8 million per square meter). In higher-income, good residential neighborhoods, with many prewar buildings with large rooms with high ceilings, in the district of Żoliborz (northern part of the city) and uptown Mokotów (southern Warsaw), prices were $70 per square foot (ZL 11 million per square meter). The most expensive buildings were in Historic Warsaw—Old Market, New Market, and in the diplomatic district along the Ujazdowskie Avenue. These mostly old (rebuilt after the war) buildings cost about $90 per square foot (ZL 14 million per square meter).

In terms of transaction size, between 1992 and 1993, 2 percent of all residential estate transactions in Warsaw exceeded $500,000, 20 percent cost between $100,000 and $150,000, and 18 percent cost between $75,000 and $100,000. The easiest to sell were the most expensive apartments.

Two types of rental properties have existed in Warsaw: large apartments and houses, where tenants were almost exclusively foreigners, and small apartments and rooms, where the tenants were predominantly Poles.[155] The rent range for three- and four-bedroom luxury apartments is $1,000 to $3,500 per month.[156] In 1993 the number of high standard dwellings available for rent was much larger than in the previous years. While previously the demand was directed toward old houses, in 1993 it shifted toward modern high-quality apartment houses. Many luxury dwellings were in the district of Mokotów, where schools for foreign children also were located. The average asking monthly rent for this type of dwellings amounted there to $1,700 for an apartment and $3,900 for a house.[157]

Smaller dwellings, while still very costly, were more affordable for Poles. A two-bedroom apartment of 500 square feet (50 square meters) rented for about $300 a month, or an average monthly salary. According to the Drągowski Real Estate Agency, in August 1993, in Warsaw, the lowest available rents were $0.17 per square foot (ZL 30,000 per square meter) per month. The cheapest studio rented for $110 (ZL 2 million) per month and the cheapest-three bedroom apartment rented for $220 (ZL 4 million) per month.[158]

Land prices in the outskirts of Warsaw ranged from $2 to $10 per square foot (ZL 0.3 million to ZL 1.8 million per square meter), with the cheaper land not served by any infrastructure. There was considerable variation in price paid for similarly situated, similarly serviced land, depending on the pressure on the seller to unload the property. The down payment was customarily 10 percent.[159] The spatial distribution of prices of real estate parcels well reflected the geography of dwelling prices. As shown in Map 4.4, the most expensive parcels were located on a stretch along the Vistula River extending from Łomianki and Młociny in the northwest to Józefów and Konstancin in the southeast. Most of this territory lies on the west bank of the Vistula.[160] Łomianki was a dynamically growing center of small private businesses (manufacturing, trade, services). Konstancin was famous for its good climatic conditions, with pine trees growing on light sandy soils. It had been long inhabited by Communist dignitaries; many party leaders lived there, especially since the Gierek period. The territory in the southwest around Podkowa Leśna was less expensive. This has been home for many intellectuals, including well-known dissidents and anti-Communist opposition leaders. A large number of more expensive parcels on the east bank were located in Praga Południe (Praga-South)—a part of Warsaw traditionally used as a residential area for diplomats and foreign businessmen. Within the borders of .Warsaw City, the parcel with the highest average prices occurred in Śródmieście (Downtown Warsaw) and Wilanów.

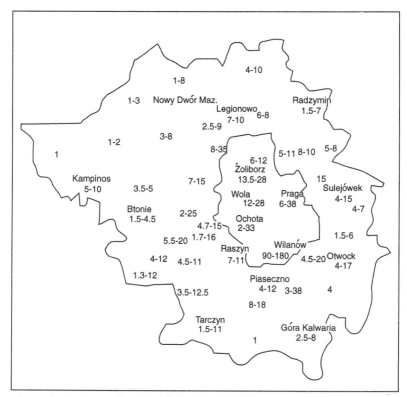

**Map 4.4    Warsaw Parcel Prices**

The customary practice for a would-be seller or renter was to list the property with a number of real estate agents. Since there was no multiple-listing service, this was thought to be the best way to increase the chances of finding a buyer or lessee. A prospective buyer/lessee calls the agent and makes an offer, which the agent then transmits to the seller/lessor. If an agreement is reached, the real estate agent's commission may be 3.5 percent, or it may be another rate set by the individual agent.

Data on Cracow real estate were developed by Kałkowski (1992-93), who collected a large number of commercial advertisements from Cracow newspapers between January 1991 and December 1992. Real estate ads made up about 10 percent of all advertisements. The average number of properties advertised in the papers included in the survey was 723 a month in 1991 and 526 a month in 1992.[161] Cracow was a purchaser's market, according to Kałkowski. A much larger number of sale offers were recorded than purchase offers. The gap between the two, however, shrank substantially in 1992. The total number of dwellings offered for sale amounted to about 50 percent of the number of new apartments built during the same time.

In 1992 a sharp decline of about two-thirds occurred in the number of persons willing to exchange apartments. This was said to be due mostly to high transaction costs (fees and taxes) which seems to work against the "normalization" of the housing structure. Pre-1990 rents were highly subsidized and did not necessarily reflect the size and standard of apartments. An obvious objective of housing policy has been gradually to remove the existing misallocations by deregulating rents. Most of the exchange ads sought to swap larger apartments for smaller ones, which, given the existing shortage in Cracow, should be considered positive.

Rent offers was the category with the highest growth rate, a phenomenon that can be explained by a decline in the number of new apartments and by price increases. Young families in particular who could not afford to buy were forced to look for apartments for rent. On the supply side, the declining real incomes of many households pushed them to rent. Apartments make up most of the real estate market in Cracow: 55 percent in 1991 and 68 percent in 1992. Single-family houses and parcels play less important roles. Between 1991 and 1992 the number of houses offered for sale decreased by almost one-half (from 116 to 64 a month), and the number of parcels decreased by more than two-thirds (from 176 to 55 a month). At the same time the number of house purchase offers remained almost unchanged, at about ten a month, while that of parcel purchase offers almost doubled, from eleven to twenty one a month. As a result the ratio of sale offers to purchase offers in both cases shrank dramatically: from 11 to 6.7 for houses and from 15.6 to 2.6 for parcels. This reflected the belief that real estate was a good capital investment.[162]

Map 4.5 is a map of the prices of Cracow's parcels. The isocost lines (expressed in zlotys) identify the main concentrations of high-price lands: in the west in the old part of the city around the Wawel royal castle, the central part of Cracow (Śródmieście), and Nowa Huta in the east, where a large new city was erected during the 1950s along with the huge Soviet-style steel mill.

Prices in other large cities were usually lower than in Warsaw and Cracow. In 1992-93, in small and medium-size cities of 50,000 to 200,000 inhabitants, average asking prices remained below $22 per square foot (ZL 4 million per square meter). Because of market sluggishness, the actual transaction prices were estimated to be 10 to 30 percent below the asking prices.[163] According to data collected in 1993 by Poland's Main Statistical Office, concerning actual dwelling prices on the open market, by *voivodship,* the highest prices occurred in the Warsaw *voivodship,* and the lowest in the Legnica *voivodship* in south-western Poland. An average price of 1 square meter (10 square feet) of a standard two-bedroom apartment, equipped with all basic amenities, including telephone, in April 1993 was $39 per square foot (ZL 6.5 million) in the Warsaw *voivodship* and $18 per square foot (ZL 3 million per square meter) in the Legnica *voivodship.* The most expensive *voivodship*s, after Warsaw, were the following, at $30 to $31 per square foot: Cracow; Ciechanów (a small *voivodship* close to Warsaw); two mountainous *voivodship*s in south-east Poland with many attractive recreation areas and especially strong links to the USA, Nowy Sącz and Rzeszów;[164] and northern *voivodship*s with large ports on the Baltic sea, Szczecin and Gdańsk. The average price for Poland was overall $26 per square foot (ZL 4.3 million per square meter).

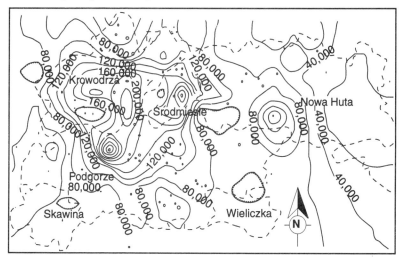

**Map 4.5    Parcel Prices in the City of Cracow, Spring 1993, Thousands of Zlotys / Square Meter**

Residential prices for rural areas, except the most attractive recreation areas, were much lower. For example, a brick farmhouse with 32.5 acres (13 hectares) of land, an orchard, and farm buildings was sold in 1992 for about $10,000.[165]

In 1994-95 zloty prices of dwellings tended to grow at a rate below inflation. The consumer price index in Poland was about 30 percent in 1994 and in the first few months of 1995 and then decreased to about 20 percent at the end of 1995. During this period the exchange rate of zloty to dollar grew at a lower rate. It was 1.59 in January 1993, 1.80 in July 1993,[166] 2.16 in January 1994, 2.26 in July 1994, 2.43 in January 1995, 2.37 in July 1995, and 2.52 in January 1996. Thus, during 1994-95, both the nominal zloty prices and the nominal dollar prices grew; in real terms, however, dwellings were becoming cheaper in zlotys and more expensive in dollars. Price changes varied for different dwelling categories. In general, market prices of dwellings remained beyond the reach of most Polish families, although their long-run affordability increased during the 1990s. In Warsaw, for an average monthly wage one could purchase 2.8 square feet of dwelling space in 1990, 4.7 square feet in 1993, and 5.0 square feet in 1995.[167]

The following is the information provided by Piotr Kowalski from the Strzelczyk Corporation, one of the larger real estate agencies in Warsaw.[168] In spring 1994 the Warsaw Stock Exchange suffered a crash. As a result, in summer 1994 the Warsaw real estate market became more active, especially in its demand for smaller 1-3 bedroom apartments. Nevertheless, large apartments in old houses remained the most expensive per square meter. In September 1994 the price of a small 3-bedroom apartment in a building constructed during the last thirty years or so was $43 per square foot (ZL 10 million per square meter), while the price of a large 5-bedroom apartment (more than 100 square meters) in a pre-war building would amount to $61 per square foot (ZL 14 million per square meter). Availability of a telephone line no longer affect the price, since the waiting time for a line had diminished to a few days or a few months; before 1989 it had been many years. The average price of apartments in Warszawa-Śródmieście (Downtown Warsaw) was $70 per square foot (ZL 16 million per square meter). In Praga-Północ (Praga-North) it was $43 per square foot (ZL 10 million per square meter). Also, demand for cheaper single family houses increased significantly. The most wanted were houses priced at $40,000-$60,000 (ZL 1 to 1.4 billion). Unlike in 1992-93, the market for more expensive houses $120,000 (ZL 3 billion) and more was sluggish. A good profit still could be made acquiring agricultural land close to Warsaw. For example, it was still possible to buy such parcels in Konstancin for $0.3 per square foot. After the "reclassification" of these parcels into residential construction parcels, one could sell them for about $0.8 per square foot.

According to the information provided by another major Warsaw real estate agency, the Drągowski Agency,[169] in 1995, the fastest growing prices were for standard two-bedroom apartments which, a few years ago, had been the least in demand. Apparently, an increasing number of young families, who before could afford no more than a studio or a one-bedroom apartment, in 1995 were able to upgrade their living conditions.[170] An growing number of people purchased apartments as an investment rather than for their living needs. During 1995 the rent was growing at a lower rate than inflation. In Warsaw, the rent for a 500

square foot (50 square meter) apartment was $250-$750 (NZL 600-1800), or
$0.50-$1.50 per square foot (NZL 12-36 per square meter) per month. A major
shift was a decrease in demand for large apartments in old houses. Formerly they
often were rented as office space. Since modern high-standard office space in
newly constructed buildings increased in 1994-95, the zloty prices for these apartments grew at 6 to 15 percent, solidly below the inflation rate. In other cities,
where the demand for office space has been much smaller, the prices for these
apartments (per square meter) have been the lowest of various housing types for
several years. The main problem has been high maintenance costs. In general,
together with the construction of different kinds of commercial buildings, the
interest in renting or buying apartments for nonresidential purposes has been
decreasing and is expected to continue to decline. This process should push down
dwelling prices.

## Agricultural Land

Before 1989, where a market for private agricultural land and buildings existed
it was sluggish most of the time, because of agriculture's poor economic performance. In the early 1990s private land sales continue, as they did during the
Communist years, but are hampered by title questions, problems with mortgage
loans, overall low (or negative) profitability of the agricultural sector, and uncertainties about the future market for agricultural goods.

As seen in Table 4.6, agricultural land prices have not kept pace with the
prices of consumer goods. The land prices have fluctuated dependent on political stability, status of private land ownership, and the situation in the food market. Prices were influenced negatively by the forced collectivization around
1950, by the Western embargo in the early 1980s after imposition of martial law
in Poland, and with the transfer of power from the Communists to Solidarity in
1989-90.

### TABLE 4.6: MARKET PRICES OF AGRICULTURAL LAND, 1948–1992

| Price Indicators | 1948 | 1960 | 1980 | 1990 | 1992 |
|---|---|---|---|---|---|
| I hectare in hundreds of kg rye | 46 | 102 | 38 | 68 | 120 |
| Land price index [lpi]; 1960=100 | | 100 | 100 | 15,643 | 43,422 |
| Consumer price index [cpi]; 1960=100 | | 100 | 178 | 39,915 | 96,796 |
| Ratio, cpi/lpi | | 1.00 | 1.78 | 2.56 | 2.23 |

Between 1960 and 1985 the price of agricultural land grew more slowly than
that of agricultural products: The price of a hectare of land expressed in kilograms of rye decreased by 21 percent and expressed in kilograms of pork
decreased by 38 percent. Between 1985 and 1992, agricultural land gained

value compared to agricultural products: Its price increased by 50 percent with respect to rye and by 5 percent with respect to pork. Yet when compared to an overall consumer price index, land prices tended to decrease over time.

In 1992 the Treasury Agency for State Property organized 406 agricultural land auctions, at which it managed to sell 35,000 acres (14,000 hectares) and to lease 184,000 acres (74,500 hectares). Sale prices ranged from a high of $300 per acre (ZL 1.7 million per hectare) in the Poznań region to a low of $80 per acre (ZL 0.5 million per hectare) in Gorzów Wielkopolski in western Poland. Most parcels did not find a buyer. The average price for those that sold was $170 per acre (ZL 1 million per hectare). Leases tended to be eight to ten years long, with the possibility of renewing them for thirty years. Lease price was based on anticipated yield in wheat and varied from 150 to 500 kilograms of wheat per hectare.[171]

Poland has received a grant of 25 million ECUs to foster the agricultural land market, in part by restructuring the state farms, encouraging rural cooperatives, and stimulating the establishment of businesses providing farm services.

## CREDIT SYSTEMS FOR PROPERTY ACQUISITION

A major problem of post-1989 Poland's real estate market is not loan availability but loan affordability. Few families and firms can afford to take large loans for housing construction and purchase, business development, and farm acquisition and modernization. Before 1989, in many cases, the affordability of housing was related to a person's standing in the Communist hierarchy. Although almost everyone had to wait in line for an apartment, the lines for Communist nomenklatura members and their relatives and friends tended to be shorter than those without nomenklatura connections. Except for the state support for those acquiring apartments and houses through a cooperative, bank loans for construction of houses were limited. The loans for dwelling acquisition were almost nonexistent. Since 1989 efforts have been made to introduce a Western-type mortgage system. However, the costs of borrowing remain high and substantial impediments still exist.

Until 1989, the housing finance system consisted of four major forms: low-rent municipal housing, heavily subsidized co-op housing, housing financed by state enterprises, and highly speculative private housing.

The state totally financed municipal housing for the *gminas*. Tenants' monthly payments were well below the cost of maintenance.

The financing system of co-op dwellings was designed for all families, except the poorest, who needed a dwelling. The procedure began with an application filed at a housing cooperative. After formal approval, the applicant became a co-op candidate. He or she then had to save a down payment through deposits in a special housing savings book that was established at a branch of the PKO (Polish Saving Bank) and registered with the housing cooperative.[172] The saving procedure was similar to that of the retirement or college saving systems practiced in many Western countries. The saver would make monthly deposits of certain amounts of money over a long period of time (many years), which made him or her eligible for a substantial subsidy from the state or the employer. Another option was to deposit the total down payment at once (in order to shorten the waiting time), but in this case no financial assistance from the state was available. The amount of down payment differed from period to period and from cooperative to cooperative. It depended on the cost of construction. The amount increased with the size of the city and the size of the dwelling. The maximum dwelling size was strictly regulated. It depended on the number of family members included in the co-op application. For example, a couple with one child would be eligible for a so-called M3 apartment (a unit for three persons)—two (bed) rooms of about 400 square feet or 40 square meters in the 1960s or three (bed) rooms of about 600 square feet or 60 square meters in the 1970s). If the couple was young enough (in reproductive age), it was qualified as "expandable" and hence eligible for an M4 unit, which was 10 to 20 square meters larger. To become a full co-op member, one had to be at least eighteen years old and possess a full down payment on his or her housing account. If these conditions were satisfied, a person was given a spot on the official waiting list and the "proper" waiting time began. After from three to twenty years a co-op apartment was allocated.[173]

After moving in, the co-op members had to make monthly payments to cover construction costs and interest (both heavily subsidized), rent, other costs and utilities. The payments depended on whether the co-op membership was of the so-called owner type or non-owner (tenant) type. All apartments remained the property of the cooperative, but after the entire principal and interest were paid off, member-owners acquired the right to sell their membership (to sell the right to use their apartment) to a third party, subject to a co-op approval.[174] Among other things, to be eligible for a co-op apartment a family had to give up all ownership and use rights to any other dwelling unit (summer houses were not covered by this requirement), be permanent residents of Poland, and, in many large cities, possess a special residence permit.[175]

The housing loan payment system was essentially similar to many social programs in the West that are in different ways supported, heavily regulated, and subsidized—directly or indirectly—by the government. If a family decided to pay in small installments over a long period of time, usually 30 to 60 years, they were eligible for state cofinancing. The interest on co-op housing loans was low. For many years it was not adjusted for inflation, so the real rates were highly negative.[176]

Eligibility for enterprise dwellings was reserved only for the employees of a given enterprise. Usually apartment houses were constructed by large state enterprises, often by the so-called green-field plants—large factories or mines located in a new location, where no residential housing existed or was available. Some enterprises acquired dwellings through local housing co-ops. Financing of the enterprise dwellings differed from enterprise to enterprise. In some cases it operated in a similar way to the municipal housing; in other cases it was arranged along the lines of co-op dwellings. The enterprise housing was subsidized from special social (housing) funds that a company was allowed to set aside for this purpose. In some cases these dwellings were almost free to tenants. The waiting time for an enterprise dwelling was often much shorter than that for a municipal dwelling or a co-op dwelling. In some cases, these apartments were available immediately upon the arrival of new workers.

Market transactions, carried out in cash, occurred for both privately owned real estate and co-op owner-type memberships. A typical transaction proceeded as follows. After all the negotiations were finished, carried out with or without the help of a real estate agent or a professional attorney, on a mutually agreed settlement day, the buyer and the seller would meet in the dwelling being sold. The buyer handed over a large quantity of cash, in zlotys or hard currency (usually U.S. dollars and German marks), or both, in exchange for the keys to the empty apartment. The formalities followed: The two sides signed a purchase-sale agreement, with the recorded price usually much lower than the true transaction price. The parties recorded an ownership title transfer in the case of a real estate transaction or the co-op membership transfer in the case of a purchase of a co-op apartment. Sometimes these transactions consisted of a swap, apartment for apartment, and one side paid only the difference, if any, in cash. The sales tax was a substantial percentage of the price, but the regulations about how to calculate the tax base kept changing. Thus, the effective tax rate varied, depending on time and circumstances, from a very low rate to a very high rate of 20 percent of the true price or more. Usually no loans were available for these private transactions, not even short-term bank loans.

After 1989 major changes to the housing finance system were introduced gradually. The rents in municipal and other forms of housing using a similar system of payments (enterprise dwellings and other dwellings which remained under the public management) increased faster than inflation. As mentioned earlier, a new system introduced in 1994 brought about substantial rent increases along with subsidies for low-income families. The whole system is administered by the *gminas.*

Major changes were introduced into the housing loans system. As a result of banking corporatization, the banks were separated from the state budget and granted autonomy. Interest rates began being determined by the market, influenced by the central bank's refinancing rate. Until the end of 1989, interest rates on long-term co-op housing loans were between 3 and 6 percent; in January 1990 they were 115 percent; they then decreased together with the inflation rate. Housing subsidies were substantially reduced and their forms have kept changing. For example, in 1991, the subsidy for an old co-op housing loan was set at 32 percent of total interest payments. The debtor had to pay 8 percent, and the remaining 60 percent was capitalized by the state bank. In 1992 the government began buying out the capitalized interest in cases for the amount of the loan payment in excess of 25 percent of a family's income. This operation consisted of swapping subsidies for debt which, according to Herbst and Muzioł-Węcławowicz (1993), was harmful to the housing market. It curtailed access to bank credits on which the effective demand for housing relied heavily. New housing low interest loans were rarely available. Due to the lack of credit records, unstable economy, and low trustworthiness of most borrowers,[177] banks favored high-interest, short-term loans over the medium and long-term loans used in housing. The PKO remained the only bank obliged by law to provide housing loans.

Regarding new housing loans, a distinction was introduced between the eligibility of housing builders and dwelling purchasers. The former were eligible for medium-term construction loans at a market-level interest rate. Home buyers could apply for mortgages at a quarterly adjustable interest rate by means of the so-called dual index mortgage method, which took into account both the changes in the officially published average wage and the changes in the interest rate set by the Central Bank. In 1992 the conditions for housing loan eligibility were defined as follows: Down payment of 20 percent of total cost, 48 percent initial interest rate adjusted quarterly by the dual index mortgage method, the total amount of the loan no more than thirty six monthly family incomes, and total monthly payment no more than 25 percent of monthly family income. This payment was updated quarterly, based on an official index of nominal wage changes. If this index increased while a particular family's income did not, the payments could exceed the 25 percent of the income. Nonpayment could lead to eviction.[178] These conditions were very rigid, and only the richest families qualified.

As of June 1992, a calculation of loan eligibility could look as follows: the average price of a new co-op apartment was about $42 per square foot (ZL 5.7 million per square meter); an apartment of 600 square feet (60 square meters), with three rooms plus kitchen plus bath, cost about $25,000. The mortgage loan to cover 80 percent of this amount would require a $560 monthly income (36 x $560 = $20,160). Since the median monthly salary was below $200, the majority of two-earner families could not qualify.

From April 1992 to April 1993, the PKO bank made only 8,300 mortgage loans, including 5,800 loans for the purchase of co-op apartments. The average loan amounted to $10,000 (ZL 160 million). The nominal interest rate was roughly at the level of the consumer price index, so the real interest rate remained close to zero.

In June 1993 a new regulation was introduced, setting the effective level of monthly payment at 25 percent of actual monthly income, updated based on the changes in specific family income rather than the statistical index of the overall wage changes. The ceiling was defined at forty-seven monthly household incomes at an interest rate of 42 percent,[179] which made PKO mortgages and equity loans more accessible. The bank could require, however, cosignatures from two to a dozen and more people. Penalties for late payments were introduced at a level of up to 100 percent. If a family fails to pay even one monthly payment, the bank can evict it from the dwelling without providing another apartment and can auction the unit.[180]

In 1992, under the auspices of the World Bank, a mortgage fund was established with an initial capitalization of $400 million, $200 million from the World Bank and $200 million from the state budget. The first construction and purchase loans were granted in 1993. The eligibility conditions were relatively strict, with the World Bank formulating detailed technical requirements concerning the house to be built. Only landowners or tenants on a ninety-nine-year lease are eligible to borrow. The borrower may be a private company, a co-op, or an individual wishing to build a single-family house or buy a new unit as a primary residence. A developer-borrower must have presold 60 percent of the units and put up an equity share of 25 percent. Because of required high monthly payments, loans are available only to high income individuals.[181]

The Polish-American Mortgage Bank began its activity in December 1992, with founding capital set at $16 million. Its objective has been to stimulate the real estate market in Poland, especially the purchase of single-family houses. The bank has been operating according to the American mortgage system and has used its American experience. For developers, it has provided short-term loans (expressed in US dollars), for up to one year, at a 14 percent interest rate, up to 60 percent of the value of the building. Home buyers are eligible for loans under the following terms: The cost of a house must be less than $80,000, 25 percent of this cost must be paid as preconstruction down payment, and another 25 percent at settlement. The remaining 50 percent is provided as a fifteen-year loan at a fixed dollar annual rate of 12 percent, adjusted for the zloty-to-dollar exchange rate.

The Cracow Industrial Commercial Bank (ICB) also makes housing loans. ICB will lend up to 70 percent of construction cost, with a cost maximum set by an indicator of the Ministry of Physical Planning and Construction. ICB also offers mortgages for ten years with adjustable interest rates which was 40 percent at the end of 1993.[182]

All mortgage loans still operate on a relatively small scale. In general, the Western-style mortgage system has not arrived yet in Poland. In 1992-93 many new co-op construction projects began without any bank loans, using only cash funds collected from co-op members' down payments. Loans are used in the second stage of construction. As a result, a larger number of families could afford the investment; this practice brings down the interest cost to only 10 to 12 percent of the total construction cost. Previously, the interest payments made up about 50 percent of this cost.[183]

The general trend in housing finance has been moving in the right direction. Today apartment prices better reflect construction costs than ever before. Since 1992, the relative prices of privately owned apartments and those of old co-op owner-type memberships decreased, while the relative prices of new co-op apartments increased. The subsidies were either completely abolished, or substantially curtailed, or replaced by a bank loan. In the case of default, the loans were capitalized by the bank. The real interest rates are adjusted with changes in the overall price index. Gradually the enterprises and municipalities are getting rid of apartments by selling them to their occupants at prices that better reflect the current market situation. Yet despite all these positive trends, the major problems in housing finance remain.

## Farm Credit

Two funds provide assistance to farmers. The European Fund for the Development of Rural Poland, established in 1990, has revenues from sales of food given to Poland by West European countries. Between 1990 and 1992, $90 million (ZL 990 billion) was lent to 4,700 farmers at an interest rate 25 percent lower than the discount rate.[184] The Agency for Restructuring and Modernizing of Agriculture, a government agency, subsidizes commercial loans to farmers with a maximum term of eight years. The interest may not exceed 20 percent; as a benchmark, the consumer price index for 1993 was 35 percent.

## THE INSTITUTIONAL INFRASTRUCTURE: LAND RECORDS AND PROPERTY TAXATION

A great strength of a market system is the ability to rely on transfer prices as evidence of relative value of properties and to use this information to create policy and adjust tax systems. However, this strength is vitiated if transfer prices are either not recorded or heavily distorted.

Poland has two advantages: Its land records are more current and more accurate than those in countries in which most property was socialized, and it has maintained a system of property taxation. Today all land transfers are recorded, and the records are public. In addition, Poland differs from other

Central and Eastern European countries in that it is moving to accurate reporting of transfer prices, a major step toward fair and accurate property taxation.
Delays in the recording process form the stumbling block.

## Land Records

Land records for property that remained private during the Communist years are
in reasonable shape. The records for property that became part of the state holdings were not systematically updated by the Communists and are being reconstituted slowly as property is privatized. A national cadaster and land
information system is being created and will serve as the base for property taxation; as of 1995, it had not been completed.[185]

Prior to World War II, land records were maintained at the local level.
Poland operated under three different systems—Austrian, Prussian, and
Russian—which led to a certain degree of confusion.[186] Registry under the
Austrian and Prussian systems included recording of transactions in books,
including information about boundaries, size, and names of seller and buyer. Price
was not included. A cadaster was operational. Under the Russian system, the local
registry office simply collected relevant documents, and there was no cadaster.

Under the German occupation during World War II, recording of transactions continued as before. However, about 20 percent of the land records were
lost, particularly in Warsaw.

During the Communist era, the local government was an arm of the state and
remained the site of land registries until 1964. There were two laws calling for
the completion of a national, standardized cadaster, but they were not fully
implemented.[187]

Sales of private property were supposed to be recorded, although sometimes
they were not.[188] There were many reasons why private parties to a sale did not
wish to publicize it by observing the recording requirements, including desires
to avoid taxation and to circumvent restrictions on property transfers. A permit
was required for transfer of several types of farm land: farms established under
the 1944 land reform, farms on land that had been formerly German, and farms
above 12 acres (5 hectares) with soils of moderate to good quality. In 1957 the
law on farm real estate ownership was amended to raise the size of property subject to permitting to 37 acres (15 hectares), including both the previous holding
and the acquisition, or 50 acres (20 hectares) for farmers raising livestock.[189] The
aim of these laws was to prevent the acquisition of land that would result in recreation of "kulak"-type large private farms. If too much land was held by one
owner, it could be expropriated.

For years cooperative apartment buildings were recorded as an entity. Not
until 1991 was each unit—dwelling or shop—listed in the land records separately.
This change was a necessary precursor to mortgage financing.

Since the state operated under the principle of indivisibility of its assets, ownership was not lodged in a particular enterprise or municipality, and transfer of use rights from one unit of the state to another did not constitute transfer of ownership. State enterprises and municipalities used property and managed it from day to day. Sometimes they had the right to lease property; since they did not own it, in principle they could not sell it. Within this system, registry often was neglected. In the land records, title may still be listed as being with the pre-Communist owner. Consequently, as state farms are privatized, the question of title must be clarified. Also the right of local governments to dispose of property transferred to them is open to challenge because title is lacking. The State Treasury and the Treasury Agency for Agricultural Property are responsible for reestablishing ownership title and rights to public property.

Today, seller and buyer take their property transfer agreement to a notary, now a private entrepreneur rather than a state employee.[190] There are now 1,000 notaries in Poland; they earn from five to ten times as much as judges and are in the highest-income category in the country.[191]

The notary and clients agree upon a fee, but it may not be higher than 3 percent of the declared price of the transaction. Under regulations of the minister of justice, a declining maximum fee schedule is in effect for large transactions.[192]

It is the notary's responsibility to report the transaction to three public agencies: Information about boundaries, nature of the estate being transferred, names of transferor and transferee, deed restrictions, and mortgage(s) is sent to the local court, where the official land records have been kept since 1991.[193] Information for incorporation in the cadaster is sent to the geodetic office of the local government, the keeper of the cadaster.[194] And price information is sent to the treasury for tax purposes.

The land records are available for public scrutiny. At present, recording property transfers is a slow process. In Warsaw, the average time for the courts to process a transaction is ten months, but it may take as long as two years.[195] One serious impact of this is that the new owner has no right to sell the property until the transaction is entered in the land records, thus the real estate market has been inhibited.

## Property Taxation

There are several types of taxes on property: agricultural tax, forest tax, tax on environmental damage, and municipal property tax. In addition, inheritance and sales taxes apply to property as well as to other assets.[196]

The agricultural tax is levied on farms of 2.5 acres (1 hectare) or larger.[197] It applies to arable land, meadows and pastures, orchards, and ponds. Exempt from the tax are land under lakes and flowing streams, vacant land, forest and park land, land in non-agricultural use, individual plots owned by pensioners or invalids of production cooperatives, and land owned by farmers who have made major investments to modernize their farm production.

The assessment is based on "accounting hectares," or projected productivity, in turn specified by soil type (of which there are six categories), type of land use, and four categories of location. The tax is the number of accounting hectares multiplied by the official price of 250 kilograms of rye, calculated by the Main Statistical Office.[198] The tax is payable quarterly, in cash.[199] Some specialty crops are taxed according to actual income. The maximum that may be imposed in tax is 40 percent of actual farm income. Deductions are allowed for 25 percent of the expenditures made for land improvements and environmental protection.[200]

The forest tax is a product of the total land in forest times the quality factor for the stand of trees times the market price per 0.15 cubic meters of coniferous lumber.[201]

Charges are levied for conversion of agricultural land to nonagricultural uses, based on the type of agricultural use and the quality of the soil and are payable annually for twenty years. There is a similar charge for conversion of forest land, and there are charges for water and air pollution and for dumping of wastes.[202]

The municipal property tax is based on the type of land use and the type of buildings.[203] Tax rates are higher on commercial buildings than on residential ones. Municipalities levy the tax but are constrained by the national government in the rates that they may set. The maximum rates are: $0.15 per square foot (NZL 3.6 per square meter) for commercial buildings; $0.004 per square foot (NZL 0.09 per square meter) for apartments, or, if the apartment building must carry insurance, 0.05 percent of the insured value; $0.006 per square foot (NZL 0.15 per square meter) for other buildings; and $0.0005 per square foot (NZL 0.012 per square meter) for other nonagricultural realty. Municipalities may reduce the taxes and grant exemptions to specified categories of taxpayers.

Stamp duties are 1 percent of the value of property acquired by foreigners when permission is approved, 2 percent on loans excluding loans by financial institutions, and up to 2 percent on company contracts, depending on the value of initial capital, 2 percent on movable property, 5 percent on immovable property, and 2 percent on such other property rights as cooperative apartments.[204]

Using the same basis for assessment as for the property tax, the rate for a mandatory social security premium is determined. The social security benefits are unrelated to the premium paid.

The inheritance tax on apartments runs around $35 to $40 per square foot (NZL 850 to NZL 1,000 per square meter).

There is a capital gain tax on sale of housing, with the tax based on the difference between acquisition and sale prices. The gain is included with ordinary income and taxed at the same rate—21 to 45 percent for individuals and 40 percent for corporations. The individual's tax is reduced if the buyer reinvests in other housing. There is also a 10 percent transfer tax on the sale of realty.

## LAND USE PLANNING AS MARKET REGULATOR

As in other former Communist countries, planning has a bad name in Poland. However, land use planning was more neglected than pursued during the Communist era, during which more decisions on allocation of sites were made in response to political pressure than to reasoned judgments about growth and location. One unfortunate holdover from the Communist period is the ability to obtain permission to build by paying bribes.

The government acknowledged the need for municipalities to update master plans and to have the capacity to finance land acquisition and infrastructure construction with the passage, in 1991, of the Act on Special Conditions for Realization of Housing Construction in Years 1991-95.[205] New building codes and zoning ordinances are needed. Whether the tight limitations on conversion of agricultural land to urban uses should be relaxed or revised needs to be considered. In direct opposition to these limits on removing land from agricultural use, many municipalities are using planning power, reinstituted at the municipal level, in urban fringe areas to encourage strip development, second home development, and scattered subdivision rather than to retain farmland.

Land use plans are developed at both the municipal and *voivodship* levels, but it is not yet clear which takes precedence if differences between them cannot be resolved.

### Warsaw

Who plans and what they intend has a particularly terrible history in Warsaw. The Nazis' plan for the city, entitled "Warsaw—Demolition of the Polish City, Construction of the German City, Eviction of the Jews," called for almost total destruction of the existing city and building of a new city for 100,000 Germans as well as a camp for 800,000 Poles. Starting in 1939, with the conquest of the city and destruction of 10 percent of the buildings, the Germans then proceeded to raze the northern part of center city following the 1943 Jewish Ghetto Uprising and to demolish and burn the whole of the left bank of the city following the Warsaw Home Army uprising of 1944. All told, the Germans destroyed 80 percent of the built up-area of Warsaw, including almost all of the city's historic buildings.[206]

After the war, Communist Poland undertook an extraordinary reconstruction of the Old Town so that it is an almost exact replica of what the Germans had turned to rubble. Between 1945 and 1960, the Old Town, the New Town, and the Royal Road all were reconstructed.

The government tripled the city's land area, taking land for a vast urban land bank to build high-rise apartment buildings and also for public buildings, such as schools and hospitals, and for enterprises. Since land had no value, the use to which it was put often was opportunistic rather than planned. There was a plan for green wedges and a policy of separating major types of land use. Although the quality of environment produced by forty years of Communist planning was damaged, it is incontrovertible that, from the rubble of the Nazis, a largely new city for over 1 million people was built in twenty years.

Now the city has an exceptional opportunity. It still holds a large land reserve that could be used to assure the implementation of a land use plan designed to create environmentally healthy, attractive new neighborhoods and to correct some of the deficiencies in services and facilities in the rather bleak Communist-era developments. The land could be offered on ninety-nine-year leases with strict requirements for plan compliance and with provisions for municipal collection of betterment should land use changes be allowed in the future. At the moment, however, the city appears more concerned about gaining revenues from sales or leases than about the unusual planning opportunities that it has.

## CONCLUSIONS

Economists agree that the worst is over and that the Polish economy is on a strong, upward path. Poland is outperforming other Central and Eastern European countries in its recovery. Annual growth of 4 to 7 percent in the next several years is predicted. By agreement with creditor nations, Poland's foreign debt has been reduced, and foreign investment is increasing. The private sector has surpassed the public sector in share of output and labor force. There is a flourishing second economy, not counted in the official statistics. High urban unemployment remains a problem. Several times as many farm workers as needed, two-digit inflation, and increasing income inequality contribute to the sense of doubt and pessimism expressed by many Poles.

Concerns over the economy led to rejection of the Solidarity-led reformist government and the return to power of former Communists. Although the current government states its commitment to proceed with privatization, recent actions do not seem to be fully consistent with this commitment. Over 4,000 firms remain state owned, including almost all of the 500 largest companies. The program of mass privatization was slowed and scaled down. Many blame this situation on members of the former nomenklatura who are protecting their positions and their rewards from those positions. The Polish Peasant Party, the party of the former prime minister Waldemar Pawlak, does not support privatization in general and of the food processing industry in particular.

Much state property, particularly small businesses and apartment buildings, have been transferred to the municipalities as the first step toward privatization. Now it appears that many municipalities share the state reluctance to proceed.

The Treasury Agency for Agricultural Property, with its holdings of 7.4 million acres (3 million hectares) of land and half a million houses, has the responsibility of planning the future use and ownership of this part of the farm property. Much of the housing will be sold, at very modest prices, to the tenants, while other tenants will continue to rent. The auctions that have been held for farmland have evoked little interest, largely because the agricultural sector is in the doldrums.

There is no action yet on privatization of state forests.

Thus, for different reasons privatization in large industrial enterprises and in agriculture is not moving as anticipated at the beginning of the market reforms.

Restitution is the most complicated issue among the panoply of issues that need resolution before the market for land and housing can become fully functional. So far, only the Catholic church and a few other churches have achieved passage of a restitution law. The failure of successive parliaments to agree on any of the proposed restitution laws is evidence of the divisiveness of this issue. The fact that there is a smaller direct constituency for restitution than in the other countries of Central Europe is doubtless one reason for inaction. Another reason is that so much territory was shifted from Poland to the Soviet Union and from Germany to Poland following World War II that restitution of former rural holdings is largely impossible, leaving the choices of alternative property or compensation.

The properties most affected by the failure to make a decision on restitution are land and buildings in Warsaw, the over 20,000 enterprises taken in the January 1946 Nationalization act, and estate farmland and forests taken in the September 1944 agrarian reform. The largest group of potential restitutees, however, are the survivors of those who lost urban and rural property in prewar Eastern Poland. Failure to settle this issue leaves a cloud on title to many properties.

The 1994 housing law improves conditions for landlords while still providing protection to needy tenants. The municipalities, now owners of over one-third of the housing stock, will have power to set rents for all units rented under the *kwaterunek* system and other units covered by the public management of dwellings. The state will provide housing allowances to low-income families. The new rents' regulations will last until at least 2005.

Over 2 million people still wait for cooperative apartments, having made the requisite savings but never having been offered an apartment. Their prospects remain bleak. Housing construction subsidies have been reduced, leading to a sharp decline in construction. Housing loans for construction and for home buyers are available, for affluent people. These are first steps in meeting the need for a system of housing finance affordable by a much larger share of the market.

As most housing and most farmland was private throughout the Communist period, there always has been a market for housing and land. However, the market was severely constrained by regulations. Today the urban market is more active, subject to the affordability of credit. The market operates much as in Western countries, with extensive advertising of properties and their asking prices and an active group of real estate agents handling transactions. In Warsaw, Cracow, and many other cities, it is possible to chart locational differences in housing prices.

Private sales of farmland are subject to the same poor market conditions as sales of state farmlands.

Good progress is being made to re-create land records where they were lost or not maintained during the Communist years. Accurate sales prices seem to be recorded, a step to be encouraged. Marketability of property remains impeded by slowness in recording and, for some properties, by title questions.

Urban and rural property is subject to taxation by systems that impute value to the property or its yield. Once real market data become more widespread, it will be desirable to convert to a system of assessment based on market value.

## PEOPLE INTERVIEWED

*(all persons were from Warsaw, unless specified otherwise)*

**Wiesław Antoniak,** Director, State Land Fund, Agency for Agricultural Property

**Władysław Brzeski,** Director, Real Estate Institute, Cracow

**Henryk Jędrzejewski,** Director, Department of Town Planning and Municipal Engineering, Ministry of Physical Planning and Construction

**Piotr Jaworski,** Spatial Organization Division, District of Mokotów

**Edward P. Kozłowski,** Housing Specialist, World Bank Housing Project

**Wladyslaw Łukasik,** Deputy Director, Warsaw Division, Agency for Agricultural Property

**Stefania Markowicz,** Head, Department of Land Management, City of Warsaw

**Hanna Matraś,** Ministry of Construction

**Alina Potrykowska** and **Marek Potrykowski,** Research Professors, Institute of Geography and Spatial Organization, Polish Academy of Sciences

**Józef Pyrgies,** Director, Resources Management Department, Agency for Agricultural Property

**Witold Śnieć,** Center for Privatization, International Foundation for Capital Market Development and Ownership Changes

**Andrzej Stasiak,** Professor, Institute of Geography and Spatial Organization, Polish Academy of Sciences

**Danuta Strembicka,** Deputy Director, Department of Town Planning and Municipal Engineering, Ministry of Physical Planning

**Jacek Szyrmer,** Department of Geography, University of Liege, Liege, Belgium

# 5

# CONCLUSIONS

In this chapter we compare the steps taken since 1989 in each of the three countries to restructure ownership of land, housing, and other property in the context of the countries' policies concerning property rights. We describe particular difficulties faced and responses to them. Finally, we suggest what the portents may be for the future of the privatization process in each of the countries and what impacts these outcomes are likely to have on their economic and social structures.

We wish to emphasize that tremendous, profound changes have occurred since 1989 and that these societies have embarked on new courses that alter the relative strengths of the state and private sectors in decisions affecting real property, despite the uncertainties and even the perils of change. Each country has its own unresolved privatization problems. For example, in Bulgaria, the legislature attempted to restructure the farm restitution program, leading to a conflict between it and the judiciary; in Bulgaria and Poland, there has been inadequate commitment to large-enterprise privatization, resulting in a very slow pace of change; in the Czech Republic, industry, private as well as public, remains bloated, and the wide dispersal of shareholding may enable managers to retain control and avoid restructuring large enterprises; and in Poland, there still has been no decision on restitution except for Catholic and other churches' properties.

All three countries feel the continuing heavy hand of the nomenklatura, alienating the public as they cherry-pick the best assets and exact tribute in return for permission to build. Nonetheless, overall the achievements are many, and some forms of an independent, private property market are flourishing. While realistic property valuation is in its infancy, the structure to make it possible is being created.

## SETTINGS FOR THE TRANSITION

Bulgaria, Czechoslovakia, and Poland shared some common characteristics when the transition began, the most obvious being the forty-five or so years of Communist rule with its categorical assertion that the state was in charge of property. There were, however, notable differences among the countries, differences that have exerted a strong influence on the sequence of events in these nations.

## Political Orientation

The political orientation and earlier alliances of each country contributed to its level of acceptance of communism and of Soviet dominance.

When Bulgaria achieved independence in 1878, it owed a debt to the Russians for helping it break free from centuries of Turkish dominion. Yet its Hapsburg monarchs allied it with the Germans in both world wars, switching sides late in World War II only after a Soviet invasion. Thereafter, Bulgaria was closely tied to the Soviet Union and had a strong Communist party. Compared to Poland, Bulgaria suffered less loss of life and less physical destruction during the war and its territory was altered very little.

Czechoslovakia became an independent, democratic country after World War I, merging Bohemia and Moravia with Slovakia. Although Germans occupied the country during War II, and most of its Jewish population was exterminated in concentration camps, physical damage was not great. Only minor border changes occurred as an outcome of the war. There was limited resistance to the Communist takeover, and the Communist Party remained strong into the 1980s. The Prague Spring of 1968 was but a brief flowering of resistance to Soviet control.

At the end of the eighteenth century, Poland was erased from the map, divided among Russia, Prussia and its successor, Germany, and Austria. Then, like Czechoslovakia, it became an independent republic in 1918. In September 1939 Poland was invaded by the Germans and the Soviets. During World War II Poland suffered heavy loss of life and physical destruction, especially of Warsaw, and extensive revision of territorial boundaries. Soviet control was challenged openly in the late 1970s by members of the anti-Communist resistance, and, in 1980, the Solidarity Union, with more than 10 million members, took the first steps toward overthrowing the Communists.

## Religion and Ethnicity

Among the three countries, only in Poland was there a powerful religious force to counter the Communist ideology.

Bulgaria is predominantly Christian Orthodox in religion. The church was suppressed throughout the Communist period, so that, while many Bulgarians are nominally Christian Orthodox, today many profess no religion. Turks have been the only substantial minority population; most emigrated to Turkey when, in the 1980s, the Communists required them to take Bulgarian names and then closed the mosques. Subsequently, many have returned, and their rights are protected.

In Czechoslovakia, which was more Catholic than Protestant, the Communists closed most churches, which were not powerful opponents. Ethnically, the population was diverse: Czechs dominant, then Slovaks, Hungarians, and Gypsies in descending proportion of the population. A substantial German minority of three million people, most of them Czech citizens, was expelled after World War II.

This treatment of the Sudeten Germans is an issue that still roils relations between the Czech Republic and Germany.

Poland became a homogenous country following World War II after the annihilation of the Jews and the redrawing of borders so that only a few Belarussians and Ukrainians still inhabit the country. The Catholic church always has been a dominant force in Polish life, with 94 percent of the population baptized as Catholics. During the Communist era, the church, especially in the face of adversity, strengthened its spiritual influence.

## Economic Structure

Investment and migration policies in all three countries under communism were designed to promote rapid industrialization and urbanization.

Bulgaria changed the most but, in 1989, still lagged considerably behind Czechoslovakia and Poland. Czechoslovakia began and ended the forty-five years of Communist rule as the most developed and the wealthiest of the three nations. Poland retained a much higher level of private production, with the private sector accounting for 19 percent of national income in 1988, compared to minuscule shares in Czechoslovakia and Bulgaria, where enterprises were nationalized.[1] Average annual growth in gross domestic product from 1981-1985 was 3.7 percent for Bulgaria, 1.8 percent for Czechoslovakia, and minus 0.8 percent for Poland.

Table 5.1, which shows the relative positions of the countries in 1988 in purchasing power for food (with West Germany set at 1), demonstrates Bulgaria's lag.

### TABLE 5.1: PURCHASING POWER FOR FOOD, 1988

| | Relative Food Costs | | |
| --- | --- | --- | --- |
| | Bulgaria | Czechoslovakia | Poland |
| Pork | 4.1 | 3.4 | 2.0 |
| Beef | 5.9 | 3.7 | 1.7 |
| Bread | 0.9 | 0.5 | 0.5 |
| Coffee | 18.2 | 10.4 | 17.8 |
| Milk | 2.7 | 2.0 | 0.7 |

In 1985 employment in agriculture as a percent of all employment was 23 percent in Bulgaria, 12 percent in Czechoslovakia, and 27 percent in Poland, reflecting both Czechoslovakia's early move to an industrial economy and Poland's continued and extensive private farming throughout the Communist years.

## Land Policies

Due to many factors, including the Russian revolution, all three countries had carried out some land reforms starting in the early 1920s to redistribute holdings from larger landholders to those with little or no land. These reforms were repeated in the late 1940s when the Communists came to power, resulting in widespread ownership but small and very inefficient parcels.

Then, in Bulgaria and Czechoslovakia, in a reversal conforming with Communist ideology, private farms and the extensive church holdings were incorporated into state-controlled cooperatives or into state farms and forests, affecting, respectively, 99 percent and 97 percent of rural land. Title to land in cooperatives remained private but use rights were lost. Title to land taken for state farms and forests was lost, and compensation rarely was paid. Old boundaries were obliterated, land recording systems often were ignored, and industrialized agriculture was introduced. Production was pushed at the expense of soil erosion and degradation and water pollution.

Only in Poland did farmers manage to resist state ownership or control, keeping most farmland in private hands. The lands of the Catholic church, however, were taken. Most of the state farms in Poland were formed on the former German territory assigned to Poland at the end of World War II. As of 1988, 76 percent of Polish farmland was private, and 39 percent of the population lived in rural areas. Forests, however, were taken by the state, and, again as of 1988, only 16 percent were private.

As industrialization and urbanization were fostered, land was needed for urban expansion. The Soviet model prevailed in all three countries. Industries often were allocated much more state-owned land than they required. Vast housing estates were developed on city outskirts, frequently with few services or amenities and with poor transportation links to jobs. Newcomers to city life were housed in these estates.

## Housing Ownership and Subsidies

Housing policies differed considerably among the three countries, although all provided heavy subsidies for housing construction and acquisition and protection for tenants. All generated expectations for housing acquisition that they did not meet, and this gap between expectations and results became a prime source of discontent with the regimes.

When the Communists came to power, Bulgaria did not nationalize existing housing, except that of people owning multiple units. Later, as new housing was built, most of it was sold. As early as the 1970s, the cooperatives and private builders accounted for half of new construction. By 1985, 85 percent of all housing was in private ownership while 15 percent was public rental housing. There were regulations on sale, with the state controlling prices. While there was a market, official prices bore little relation to covert, actual prices.

Czechoslovakia allowed rural and village residences, including second homes, and most single-family urban homes to remain private. New construction, mainly apartment houses, was heavily subsidized, but few funds were allocated for maintenance of existing structures. With rents controlled, this assured deterioration. It also assured immobility of residents, since people in older, convenient, inner-city apartments had no incentive to leave them. As of 1988, 34 percent of housing was public-sector rental units, 19 percent was cooperative, and 47 percent was private. The urban areas had a much larger share of state housing than the rural areas. As in Bulgaria, there was a market for housing but no record of actual transaction prices.

In Poland, the state for the most part did not take existing private housing. However, it instituted a system under which families were allocated space in apartment buildings with the rent set by the state. The owner could neither choose tenants nor evict them and, due to very low rents, could not afford to maintain the building. Every successive Communist leader promised to provide more and/or better new housing, but none satisfied expectations. The bulk of production shifted, in the 1970s and 1980s, from the state to cooperatives, but cooperatives benefited from large state subsidies. As of 1990, 29 percent of housing was owned by the state or by state enterprises, 14 percent by cooperatives, and 57 percent was privately owned (including co-op units of members with property rights).

## THE TRANSITION, 1989–1995

In each of the three countries, the transition has had many similar characteristics. Each country has seen a proliferation of new political parties, with consequent shifting coalitions as each seeks to bargain with larger parties to gain some of its goals. This multiplicity of parties has presented the question of threshold levels for representation in the legislatures.

Most of the former Communists are now called social democrats, acting within a democratic structure, but some—a minority—argue for a return to communism. The Catholic church in Poland is so concerned about the post-Communists' role in government that it issued a warning from all pulpits that parishioners should not vote in the November 1995 presidential elections for anyone who held a responsible position in the former totalitarian government.

The former Communist managers and officials, commonly referred to as the nomenklatura, have continued to wield considerable influence not only in the political arena but also in the economic sphere, often behind the scenes and in transactions of questionable legality. As a result of the "quiet" or nomenklatura privatization, by which the people have transferred assets to themselves, the idea of privatization has been somewhat tainted.

The role of the judiciary is being hammered out. Legislators accustomed to a system in which their laws were paramount find it chafing to have courts examine these laws in the light of newly adopted constitutions and, in Bulgaria and the Czech Republic, overturn the laws if they violate constitutional guarantees. In both countries, property rights guaranteed by their respective constitutions have been cited as the basis for overturning legislation. In Poland, while the court can indicate to Parliament in what manner the Constitution has been violated, it lacks power to overturn laws.

There have been conceptual as well as political problems with privatization of large enterprises, focusing on who will have management control and how this control will be exercised. As a result, decisions about the extensive real property holdings of many enterprises have not been made and, therefore, the properties are not on the market.

The real property markets that already existed in a two-tier structure—the official market and the under-the-table market—have shifted substantially in their relative significance, with the official market for urban properties growing at a great rate. Looking at the impacts of changing property rights on the economy, and in particular at the level of activity of the real estate market, it is quite apparent that there are already winners and losers in the transition.

Large cities are bustling with new commercial activity, particularly in the downtowns. Cars jam the streets. Most people find work, although not infrequently in the gray economy. In Prague and Warsaw there is even a labor shortage. Some construction of low-density suburban housing is beginning, although not so much in Bulgaria. Little high-rise construction is occurring. Tourist areas are being spruced up.

The disparity between conditions in urban and rural areas is marked in each country. Villages and rural areas are stagnant. Some apartments are vacant, and deteriorated buildings are not being renovated. Many people are idle or underemployed, and some farmland lies fallow.

## Politics and Transition

Changed economic circumstances shape people's attitudes toward government as protector or government as enabler, and wide disparities in attitudes are reflected at the polls. Not surprisingly, urban residents have much more confidence in the transition and in their own future than rural residents. These constituencies have a direct effect on who governs and on the choices that government makes.

In Bulgaria, the Union of Democratic Forces has its base in Sofia and the other large cities, while the Bulgarian Socialist Party is strong in smaller cities and rural areas. Polish farmers are conservative, against trade liberalization and against more privatization that might threaten them. Successors of the former nomenklatura have had enough backing to enable them to establish government control in both Bulgaria and Poland. This return of the nomenklatura has been achieved at the ballot box, in free and open elections with many candidates representing many parties. The proliferation of parties, the diffusion of power, and the necessity for multiparty coalitions are early outcomes of the new laws in these two countries. The post-Communist leaders have promised to make haste slowly, retaining safety net benefits and protecting agriculture, which is particularly threatened as these countries press to join the European Union. As part of this go-slow approach, privatization of large enterprises has been slow.

As of January 1, 1993, Czechoslovakia, already a federated state, became two nations, the Czech Republic and Slovakia, in what was called the Velvet Divorce. In the Czech Republic, where fewer people have ties to the land and where the industrial and service sectors are stronger than in Bulgaria, Poland, and Slovakia, the benefits of privatization are readily apparent. Politicians have had less opportunity to feed on rural discontent and fear. Support for privatization in all of its forms is strong. With popular and political backing, privatization across the board—small and large enterprises, farms, and urban housing—is completed or far advanced. Today, the Czech Republic is the only country of Central and Eastern Europe in which the post-Communists are not in power. It is also the only country to have achieved substantial mass privatization; whether the shift in ownership has been accompanied by changed management is open to question.

All three countries have made the transition to democratic rule, with constitutions and laws establishing the new structures of governance. All have allocated power to courts to speak as to the constitutionality of legislative actions. In a property-related case in the Czech Republic this has raised the issue of whether a constitutional court decision must be unanimous—a surprising question from the perspective of Western democracies.

All three countries have reestablished a significant, independent role for local government and have recognized the need to earmark tax revenues for local support. Ownership of urban structures with shops and apartments and of urban lands has devolved from the state to the municipalities, leaving privatization choices to the municipalities. Some municipalities, newly faced with responsibility for infrastructure and maintenance, are choosing to sell assets to generate revenues and realize profits. Others have been able to take a longer-range perspective, retaining land and buildings for planned future development or redevelopment and to secure future revenue streams. The need to provide inexpensive housing for lower-income residents has been another motive leading municipalities to keep some of their stock of apartments. Larger municipalities have granted some governance role to districts, and district versus city political conflicts over land use choices arise. NIMBY (not in my backyard) is alive and well.

## Housing and Housing Markets

As of 1989 in each of the three countries much housing was privately owned and there were active housing markets. Since that time, even more housing has been privatized, through auction sales in Bulgaria and the Czech Republic, through restitution in the Czech Republic, and through municipal sales to tenants at below-market prices in all three countries. The level of private ownership varies, with Bulgaria at the top with 95 percent as of 1993; the Czech Republic at 60 percent in 1991; and Poland at 61 percent in 1994.

Controls on rights to acquire and dispose of housing and on pricing of housing have been removed or relaxed so that they are no longer as severe an impediment to the market. Rent controls in the Czech Republic are being eased but still offer protection to sitting tenants and thus reduce the attractiveness of properties for sale. In Poland housing regulations are a greater hindrance to marketability. One-third of the housing stock is still subject to rent controls, although recent legislation has given the municipalities more power to set rent levels. The *kwaterunek,* or quartering, system is still in force. Those fortunate enough to live in centrally located, rent-controlled apartments have no incentive to move and every incentive to sublet all or part of their apartments. As each of the countries lifts more restrictions on market rents, the question of how to provide protection for the pensioners and others who are less well off will need to be faced.

One continuing obstacle to an active market, and to labor mobility as well, is the very low rate of new housing construction. Job opportunities are greater in the urban areas, but often housing vacancies do not exist. The days of heavy state subsidization of state and cooperative construction are over, and the decline in construction has been precipitous, as shown in Table 5.2. This table does not reflect the recent turn around in the Czech Republic; however, much of what is being built or rehabilitated there is new suburban housing or luxury flats for the wealthy, including foreigners.

**TABLE 5.2: NUMBER OF DWELLINGS COMPLETED, IN THOUSANDS[2]**

|                | 1980  | 1985  | 1990  | 1991  | 1992  | 1993 | 1994 |
|----------------|-------|-------|-------|-------|-------|------|------|
| Bulgaria       | 74.3  | 64.9  | 26.0  | 19.4  | 18.0  | 10.9 | 8.7  |
| Czechoslovakia | 134.2 | 112.4 | 73.9  | 63.9  | 53.4  |      |      |
| Czech Republic | 80.7  | 66.7  | 44.6  | 41.7  | 36.4  | 31.5 | 18.2 |
| Poland         | 217.1 | 189.6 | 134.2 | 136.8 | 133.0 | 94.4 | 71.6 |

The shortage or absence of credit for builders or buyers of housing has been a major factor in the decline in production. Short-term credit for construction is more likely to be available than mortgage money for home buyers. Only the more well off can afford the terms offered for mortgages, assuming that mortgage funds are available. With the diminution of state housing subsidies, renters and owners pay a larger share of their income for housing, although less than in the West. In Bulgaria in 1993 urban residents paid 4.2 percent of their income for housing, while rural residents paid 5.8 percent. In Poland the cost of housing is more substantial, rising from 13.3 percent of income in 1988 to 19.7 percent in 1993. Surveys of households' budgets disclose growing shares of expenditures for housing. In 1995 these shares were 21.5 percent in Poland and 10.7 percent in the Czech Republic.

Whether housing shortages exist at the national level is subject to considerable debate and turns upon what standards of space and quality and what vacancy rates are accepted as appropriate for a given country. In Bulgaria, the Czech Republic, and Poland, each has fewer vacancies in urban than in rural areas and has seen urban housing shortages impede labor mobility. As market reforms have been adopted, inefficient industries have been forced to close or downsize; in small and medium-size towns this frequently has meant that over one-third of the workers have lost their jobs. New businesses have been established, but usually in larger cities. Pre-1989 state regulations that restricted people from moving have been abolished. Now the shortage of affordable housing in urban locations keeps some people in their old homes far from new job opportunities, exacerbating unemployment. For example, in June 1995 the unemployment rate in the Warsaw region was 5.4 percent; in Poznan, 7.7 percent; and in Cracow, 7.9 percent; most of those listed as unemployed worked in the gray economy, while unemployment was over 25 percent in northeastern Poland where no gray-economy jobs existed. The limited supply and high price of Warsaw and Cracow apartments deterred people from moving. Many who do move are forced to double up with other families. Big-city housing shortages have grown as the market for centrally located offices and shops has exploded, with new domestic and foreign entrepreneurs outbidding housing renters or buyers for space.

One advantage of conversion of housing to offices or shops is that the new occupants are far more likely to be able to afford repairs and modernization. Renovation of old structures remains a high priority. As mentioned, where old buildings are under rent control, the owners, whether municipal or private, cannot raise sufficient funds from housing tenants. High rents on commercial space enable some upkeep and improvement to occur.

With all of these qualifications, it still can be said that the real estate market for urban housing is very active. Professions new to Eastern Europe flourish—brokers, appraisers, real estate lawyers, private notaries, and bankers are key players on the real estate scene. Asking prices are quoted in the housing advertisements that fill newspaper pages and computer listings. These and anecdotal evidence from brokers demonstrate that prices are three to five times higher in major cities than in medium-size ones. In Sofia and Warsaw median sales prices in 1993 were $44 per square foot and $50 per square foot respectively. City rent curves are taking shape, with substantially higher prices paid for central locations and for higher-quality space. The losers in the markets in all three countries are those attempting to sell apartments in the concrete prefabricated high-rise buildings of the Communist era.

## The Stagnant Rural Scene

Whether rural land is public or private, purchasers are few, the market is primarily for lease. The reasons for this are excess agricultural capacity, better wages in urban areas—12 percent higher in Bulgaria—and the difficulty or impossibility of obtaining farm credit. In Poland in 1993, wages in agriculture were 14 percent lower than the national average.

Agricultural production dropped in all three countries after 1989 and the consequent reduction of subsidies. Bulgaria's production plummeted 40.3 percent from 1989 to 1993, finally rising by 5 percent from 1993 to 1994. Czechoslovakia saw a drop of 24.8 percent during the same period, with 1994 remaining at the 1993 low. The low point for Poland was 1994, with a drop of 19 percent from 1989.

Questions of tariffs and subsidies in the European Union as well as in Bulgaria, the Czech Republic, and Poland must be resolved before the future of agriculture and forestry can be foreseen. As of 1991, despite drops in production and tariff walls, the amount of land in farming and forestry had seen little change, as shown in table 5.3. Since then, however, considerable amounts of farmland have become fallow. How much this has been due to lack of demand for farm produce, how much to delays in restitution and privatization, and how much to lack of credit is difficult to say.

### TABLE 5.3: PERCENT OF LAND IN AGRICULTURE AND FORESTRY[3]

|  | 1980 | | 1991 | | 1994 | |
|---|---|---|---|---|---|---|
|  | Farms | Forests | Farms | Forests | Farms | Forests |
| Bulgaria | 55.7 | 34.7 | 55.5 | 34.9 |  |  |
| Czechoslovakia | 53.6 | 35.8 | 52.7 | 36.1 | 54.3* | 33.3* |
| Poland | 60.6 | 27.8 | 59.7 | 28.1 | 59.6 | 28.1 |

*Czech Republic

The difficulties faced by the agricultural sector must not obscure the extraordinary achievements of Bulgaria and the Czech Republic in restituting rural land, in dissolving state cooperatives, in fostering reallotments of parcels, and in encouraging the formation of voluntary farm cooperatives. As of the end of 1993, 30 percent of Bulgarian farmland and 35 percent of Czech farmland was being privately farmed.[4] These percentages are rising rapidly, and the privatization process should be concluded in the Czech Republic and Bulgaria in 1996. Given that only 1 percent of rural land in Bulgaria and 3 percent in the Czech Republic were privately farmed in 1989, this was a rapid conversion.

The decision to restitute was partly ethical and partly political. It has turned out to be astute as well. Both nations had had a large class of small landowners; the Czech Republic had had some large estate owners as well. All of these people either were forced into cooperatives or saw their property seized for state farms. Fairness dictated that they should be compensated for their loss. They might have received compensation as shares in enterprises instead of property, but most hungered for land, and preferably the land that had been theirs or their families'. The restitution process has been scrupulous in weighing entitlements and in allotting land of similar nature and comparable value to that taken if not the actual former holdings. Those who labored on the cooperatives or state farms over the years but did not contribute land also have been granted land. As a result the entire stock of rural land, after reservations for public purposes, is being converted to private ownership. Market forces then can act to assemble land into efficient holdings. The spring 1995 action by the Bulgarian National Assembly to wrench the restitution process from its course and the overruling of this action by the Constitutional Court suggest that the process will be completed in the form in which it was initiated.

As a result of farm restitution in Bulgaria, over 50 percent of the population has or will become land owners; when forest restitution occurs this percentage will rise. Eighty-five percent of the restituted farmland is under reallotment plans, meaning that the inefficiencies of pre-Communist tiny holdings are being reduced somewhat. However, with 91 percent of restituted parcels under 2.5 acres (1 hectare), land assembly by private entrepreneurs or through voluntary cooperatives is essential to the future of agriculture.

The process in the Czech Republic has been similar, though some state farms have been privatized by restructuring proposals. Around 30 percent of the population, many of whom now live in cities, are now or will be owners of rural land after reconstitution of the cooperatives and restitution of state farms and forests. In 1993, 52 percent of the private farmers were farming less than 2.5 acres (1 hectare) and 81 percent less than 25 acres (10 hectares). However, unlike the situation in Bulgaria, the remaining 19 percent of farmers now hold an average of 193 acres (77 hectares), and they are the most successful.

Establishing boundaries, updating and re-creating cadasters and land records, determining validity of claims, and preparing reallotment plans have been monumental tasks in both countries that are now largely complete. Resolution of title claims, sometimes through court litigation, is causing some delays. Once title is settled, the new owners can sell or lease or attempt to build an independent farm. The early results show that most of these new owners currently are urban residents. Many are leasing their land, at least in the short term. As mentioned, some are joining the private cooperatives as active farmers. Few can finance acquisition of equipment and stock to operate a small, independent farm.

Poland's situation is very different, because there still is no restitution law, except for church property, despite a long succession of bills introduced in the Sejm. This situation is due in part to the fact that the people who might be entitled to rural land restitution, namely the former large estate owners and the refugees displaced from prewar Eastern Poland, lack sufficient political power to secure passage of a law. Also, existing private farmers are not eager for new competition and to give back land; already too many people farm too little land—over half of the private farms are less than 12 acres (5 hectares). Less than one-quarter of its agricultural lands is in state ownership. Poland has developed restructuring plans for this state land and its stock of one-half million houses in which privatization of the land is but one facet, with greater emphasis on leasing. Hundreds of auctions have been held, but so far the Treasury Agency for Agricultural Property has found buyers for only 1.8 percent of its holdings of state farmlands, and those buyers have paid nominal prices, except for developable urban sites. Public forests are a different question; they still are 84 percent publicly owned. How and to what extent they will be privatized has yet to be decided. Had Bulgaria and the Czech Republic followed the Polish approach of privatizing state farms by auction, the likely result also would have been few buyers but an outraged public.

## Private Enterprise and the Economy

The increasing share of the private sector in economic activity—40 percent of gross domestic product (GDP) in Bulgaria in 1994, 65 percent in the Czech Republic, and 55 percent in Poland[5]—is one indicator of the overall commitment to privatization. By this measure, the Czech Republic is the clear leader. By this and other measures, Bulgaria has achieved the greatest degree of change.

The extent of privatization between 1989 and 1994, and the climate concerning further privatization today, varies among the countries but not in parallel with their relative economic strength. As tables 5.4, 5.5, and 5.6 show, Poland is the economic leader in almost all respects, with the Czech Republic slowly recovering and Bulgaria still experiencing serious difficulties.

### TABLE 5.4: BULGARIA: ANNUAL PERCENT CHANGE IN ECONOMIC INDICATORS.[6]

|                      | 1990  | 1991   | 1992  | 1993  | 1994  | 1995* |
|----------------------|-------|--------|-------|-------|-------|-------|
| GDP                  | -11.8 | -22.9  | -8.2  | -6.0  | 1.7   |       |
| Industrial output    | -17.6 | -22.2  | -15.9 | -6.93 | 4.5   | 4.0   |
| Agricultural output  | -6.0  | -6.4   | -12.9 | -15.0 |       |       |
| Real wages           | 5.3   | -3.94  | 19.2  | -9.8  | -10.1 |       |
| Consumer Price Index | 23.8  | 338.5  | 79.4  | 56.1  | 87.1  | 121   |

*First quarter

### TABLE 5.5. THE CZECH REPUBLIC:
### ANNUAL PERCENT CHANGE IN ECONOMIC INDICATORS.[7]

|  | 1990 | 1991 | 1992 | 1993 | 1994 | 1995* |
|---|---|---|---|---|---|---|
| GDP | -1.2 | -14.2 | -7.1 | -0.5 | 2.0 | 3.9 |
| Industrial output | -3.3 | -21.6 | -7.9 | -5.3 | 2.1 | 6.0 |
| Agricultural output | -3.9 | -8.4 | -11.5 | -1.0 | 0.0 | |
| Real wages | -5.4 | -23.7 | 10.4 | 4.0 | 3.7 | |
| Consumer Price Index | 9.7 | 56.7 | 11.1 | 20.8 | 10.0 | 10.2 |

*First quarter

### TABLE 5.6. POLAND:
### ANNUAL PERCENT CHANGE IN ECONOMIC INDICATORS.[8]

|  | 1990 | 1991 | 1992 | 1993 | 1994 | 1995* |
|---|---|---|---|---|---|---|
| GDP | -11.6 | -7.0 | 1.9 | 4.0 | 5.0 | 7.0 |
| Industrial output | -24.2 | -11.9 | 3.9 | 7.4 | 11.9 | 13.7 |
| Agricultural output | -2.6 | -1.6 | -12.7 | 6.8 | -9.3 | 10.0 |
| Real wages | 24.2 | -0.3 | -2.8 | -2.9 | 1.1 | 0.2 |
| Consumer Price Index | 685.7 | 70.3 | 43.0 | 35.3 | 32.2 | 33.0 |

*First quarter

It was predicted that the small positive change in Bulgaria's gross domestic product in 1994 would rise to 4 percent in 1995. The declines in industrial and agricultural output over the period from 1989 to 1994—a drop of 74.8 percent for industry and of 35.3 percent for agriculture—have been the most severe of the three countries, although agriculture finally became positive in 1994 relative to 1993. The gap between real wages and the consumer price index continues to be substantial. Three-quarters of the population live below what Bulgaria defines as the subsistence level. Average monthly income in 1994 was only $85, compared with $250 in both the Czech Republic and Poland.

The Czech Republic occupies the middle position from these perspectives. Gross domestic product rose for the first time in 1994, at a healthy rate of 2 percent over 1993. Industrial and agricultural output, down 43.6 percent and 24.8 percent respectively from 1989 to 1994, declined no further in 1994. There is some disparity between percent increases in real wages and in the consumer price index.

Poland has enjoyed growth in gross domestic product since 1992, with the 5 percent growth between 1993 and 1994 very robust. While industrial output declined—36.1 percent from 1989 through 1991, there has been continuing growth since 1992. Agricultural output dropped 16.1 percent from 1989 through 1992 and has fluctuated since then. Real wages continue to lag behind increases in the consumer price index.

Enterprise privatization began early and unofficially. Considerable privatization in each country resulted from illegal or "quiet" acquisition of state assets by insiders, often with ties to the old regime; while widespread, the exact extent of this is unknown. In the last few years, each country has enacted laws setting forth the structure for privatizing small and large state enterprises.

Today in all three countries small business essentially is private; much of it is new business, with the remainder state businesses that were sold directly to employees or at auction, or, in Bulgaria and Czechoslovakia, state businesses that were claimed in restitution. Real property figured significantly in the proceeds from small-enterprise privatization sales. Sales of structures and leases of space for shops, restaurants, offices, gas stations, and other small businesses are part of the active urban real estate market. The service sector, intentionally neglected under communism, is experiencing rapid expansion. Particularly in the Czech Republic and Poland, which received in 1994 over 101 million and 74 million tourists respectively,[9] these new enterprises are a vital part of the economy.

Large-enterprise privatization will have some impact on the future shape of property markets. Some old, obsolete plants will be modernized; more will be abandoned, with no buyers. Efficient plants will compete on the world market for investors. Whether obsolete or efficient, the value of the sites and structures of these plants is part of the restructuring calculation. Desirable locations will attract new, higher-return uses. Conversely, marginal locations, as in heavily polluted areas, are likely to remain idle. The form of privatization also is significant. If it invites and draws investment from a broad spectrum of citizens, they will have chosen to put their assets in enterprise shares rather than in real estate, weakening the demand for land and housing.

Bulgaria experienced much large-enterprise illegal or semilegal privatization by the nomenklatura prior to 1991. It has made little headway with legal privatization under its 1992 law. Key politicians and heads of the various ministries charged with implementing the law have been reluctant to proceed in part because they profit by retaining control and in part because privatization poses the specter of even more unemployment. With unemployment in 1994 at 13 percent, the temptation to avoid further belt-tightening was strong. Only a few hundred of the 3,200 state enterprises have been targeted for privatization, and very few actually have been sold. The jingoistic promises of some politicians that they would prevent foreign takeovers of land and businesses have been easy to keep, for there has been little clamor from foreigners to invest. The voucher system, endorsed in principle for several years, was finally put in place in late 1995, as part of Prime Minister Vidnanov government's oft-stated commitment to move ahead on privatization.

Large-enterprise privatization is far advanced in the Czech Republic, reflecting Prime Minister Klaus's commitment to privatization prior to decentralization. He is a staunch believer that the early reform of property rights is critical to successful transition to a market economy.

By mid-1993, 4,000 of the 5,000 large enterprises designated for privatization had completed the process. The usual form was transformation to a joint stock company, followed by sale by bid to domestic or foreign investors of a majority of company shares and reserve of the remaining shares for bidding under the voucher system. Eighty percent of eligible Czechs chose to buy vouchers and are now shareholders in Czech corporations, usually through investment in mutual funds. The Czech Republic's success with voucher privatization has led to emulation elsewhere, including the new program for Bulgaria.

Poland, like Bulgaria, has announced its intention to employ voucher privatization but has yet to proceed. Poland's agenda, in sequence, has been stabilization—bringing inflation under control, reducing the deficit, and stimulating foreign trade; price liberalization; and then privatization.[10] Progress has been made in transforming and transferring state enterprises. Preprivatization in the form of liquidation, corporatization, or mass privatization is under way. Of the 8,500 state enterprises that existed in 1990, 2,600 were in the process of privatization by 1993, with ownership transfer completed for almost 900. The assets of these enterprises had been transferred from the State Treasury to employees of the enterprise or sold to domestic and foreign investors. Other enterprise assets had been transferred to municipalities. Some 600 enterprises have been marked for mass privatization following transformation into joint stock companies. Sixty percent of the corporate shares are to be distributed to National Investment Funds and made available to Polish citizens through vouchers. Enterprise employees will hold 15 percent of shares, and the state will retain the remaining 25 percent. There is concern that, despite Poland's robust economic performance, politicians are cooling to large-enterprise privatization and to foreign investment.

## Public Institutions in Transition

The state has not withered away, but, since the return of democratic decision making, it has voluntarily relinquished much of its ownership of and many of its controls over real property. Further, with the encouragement of new, private enterprises, many activities formerly the dominion of the state are increasingly private. Another significant part of this de-etatization has been the transfer of ownership of housing and other properties to municipalities, which now have the right to decide the future ownership and use of such properties.

Accompanying these shifts in responsibility has been the definition of new or reconstituted roles for state and local governments in the management of property. Cadasters and land records are being re-created or updated to international standards of accuracy. The state now operates in conjunction with local government to maintain these systems and specifies how recording of property transfers shall take place. Property value maps are being prepared for all large cities in the Czech Republic. Soon it will be possible for buyers, sellers, mortgage companies, bankers, and taxing authorities to have ready access to such data. Poland has begun recording accurate sales information rather than an agreed-upon artificial price. This information is essential in order for credit systems to function.

Accurate property records will be the base for new systems of property taxation. In the past it has been necessary to rely on imputed income or sales in assessing property for tax purposes. Now, with actual open-market transactions in which the market price is recorded, it will become possible to use the prices from these transactions as the base for various taxes that may be levied, including transfer taxes, capital gains taxes, inheritance taxes, and annual taxes on land and/or buildings. To date, none of the countries appears to have considered whether a property tax on land alone would be easier to assess and more effective in stimulating property maintenance and development. Authority to levy property taxes remains the domain of the state, but their collection and allocation may be a state or a local responsibility.

Due to its use during the days of socialist plans, the term "planning" remains in some disrepute. However, land use planning continues at the local level and, in some areas such as Bulgaria's Black Sea coast, at the regional level. National land use planning is primarily for designation of key features such as historic and natural resource sites. While the commitment to creation of plans remains in place, government strength in implementing them is in some doubt. Land use controls such as zoning often are lacking, and the ability to alter planning designations through use of political influence reportedly is widespread.

## OUTCOMES AND PORTENTS

The prospect of membership in the European Union (EU) for countries in Central and Eastern Europe finally is moving from an amorphous hope to concrete steps. The current twelve members of the European Union began discussions in 1995 on membership for the six East European nations that now have association agreements with it. Bulgaria, the Czech Republic, and Poland, along with Hungary, Romania, and Slovakia, are the nations marked for this first expansion to the east. The three Baltic states and Slovenia also are on the list of those preparing for membership. How long it will take for actual membership to be offered is unclear, but estimates are that it will take five or more years. In the interim, the EU is expected to provide billions of dollars in financial aid to these countries to revise their laws and practices to conform to EU norms. The EU will specify what portions of its *acquis communautaire,* or set of laws and regulations, must be enacted and adhered to. One area of particular concern is state support of industry.

Judged just by budgetary spending, East European support for industry is modest; no one can afford high subsidies. But support seeps in through the back door. In Poland, for example, the struggling steel giants are not paying part of their tax bill. This constitutes a kind of involuntary government support for steel. In the Czech Republic the financial ties between the state and some industrial behemoths are opaque, at best. Greater openness over covert subsidies will be needed before the EU is persuaded that state support is under control.[11] Social assistance for workers and environmental cleanup are two areas that will require negotiation. Farm policy and farm subsidies are issues for both the member nations and the prospective members.

The future of agriculture and its place in the economy is particularly pressing for Bulgaria and Poland. Too many farm workers and too-small farm holdings prevent efficient production. On the other hand, the despoliation caused by the agro-industrial complexes of the Communist era is not a model for the future. A structure is needed, and partly in place, that encourages privately owned and managed cooperatives for those who wish to continue in farming and moderate-size farms for entrepreneurs who will lease or purchase land from those who no longer wish to farm. Institution of farm credit is an essential part of this structure.

One concomitant of the reduction in the agricultural workforce is that jobs must be created elsewhere, principally in the service sector. Given the assumption that many of these jobs will be in urban areas, housing questions arise. Here, as in agriculture, credit is vital. Developers need it to acquire land, builders to construct housing, and purchasers to finance their acquisition. Several questions related to continuing housing subsidies that affect housing stock and its turnover have not been fully answered. Poland's new rent subsidies to those at the lower end of the income scale should make it possible to phase out rent controls and the *kwaterunek* system, thus encouraging market transactions. The Czech Republic is committed to removal of rent controls, but only the first steps have been taken. Bulgaria, with such a minute stock of public rental units, will need to consider a rent subsidy law similar to the new Polish law. The Vidanov government has announced its intention to provide such subsidies. In all three countries social stratification is likely to increase as housing choices are market driven. The Communist period high-rise apartment blocks, as the least desired housing, will more and more become home to those with no other choice, as is true of similar housing in Amsterdam, Milan, Paris, and other Western European cities. As in the West, the unwanted outcasts of a given society will all too readily be relegated to these projects, where discontent then festers. A very different prospect is that of rapid suburbanization; here, too, local governments would do well to learn from the costly and wasteful errors of such development in the West.

The Czech Republic has moved faster and further than any other country of Central and Eastern Europe to free land and housing from public ownership and to reduce public controls on its use. It and Bulgaria are the only countries to have adopted legislation specifically to restitute communal Jewish property. Bulgaria has gone far toward achieving a fair, open restitution of agricultural land in a setting of great complexity. Poland's failure to resolve the restitution question impinges on efforts to sell state farmland and urban properties. More important, although the number of potential restitutees is much smaller than in Bulgaria or the Czech Republic, many people are angry that the successive governments offered restitution only to the churches to compensate for property losses at the hands of the Communists. The role of the constitutional courts in all three countries in governance is being shaped; their decisions in Bulgaria and the Czech Republic are affecting restitution outcomes.

As we reflect on the privatization process—its successes and limitations, its achievements and further promises—the question arises as to what role there is for the public sector. Our conclusion is that there are three clear justifications for such participation: institutional infrastructure, physical infrastructure, and safety net.

Provision of an institutional, legal, and organizational base for the private sector is of paramount importance as far as land and housing are concerned. We have noted, for example, that disruption to land records and titles impedes market formation. So too does the failure to register actual sale price. The absence of zoning is an impediment to development. Without such an infrastructure, housing and other forms of construction, the land market, and the real estate sector as a whole would be limited.

Provision of physical infrastructure for housing, retail space, and industry is clearly a matter for government. While some facilities might well be provided by private or quasi-public entities (e.g. telecommunications), urban and regional development continue to hinge on an efficient and funded public sector, acknowledged to have such a role to play in the society. Issues still to be addressed include: the sources of financing (which might include bonds issued to the private sector as well as taxes on property), the level of government (national, provincial, or municipal) responsible for implementation, and the extent of public participation in the process (particularly difficult to decide where "NIMBY" issues surface). It is not, however, conceivable to create a functioning real estate sector without publicly planned, constructed, maintained, and controlled infrastructure.

The third justification is perhaps more controversial. We maintain that particularly in the housing area a safety net for vulnerable populations is essential. With both tenant and purchaser costs rising, a looming specter of unemployment, changing demographics, and shifts in regional distribution of population, support is justified—for example, as highly targeted rent control and mortgage subsidies. We look at such forms of intervention as the infrastructure to assure stability as well as social justice necessary for economic development.

Privatization in each of the three countries has vastly increased the number of stockholders in these societies. It is evident already that some of those newly endowed with property will succeed in the changed, competitive economic climate while others will not, failing to judge the market correctly, failing to obtain credit to upgrade shops, apartments, or farms, or failing to repay borrowed funds. Fear of such failures accounts in large measure for the restoration to power of some members of the nomenklatura in all but the Czech Republic. But there is also a concern that total privatization will result in the abandonment of a safety net for the less privileged of society. Where the line between state domination and private market forces will be drawn remains an open question.

# APPENDIX

## POPULATION BY AGE GROUPS, PERCENT

|  | YEAR | 0-19 | 20-64 | 65+ |
|---|---|---|---|---|
| Bulgaria | 1991 | 27.3 | 59.2 | 13.5 |
| Czechoslovakia | 1988 | 31.0 | 57.4 | 11.6 |
| Czech Republic | 1991 | 29.2 | 58.0 | 12.8 |
| Poland | 1992 | 32.1 | 57.4 | 10.5 |

## NATURAL INCREASE, PER 1,000

|  | 1980 | 1990 | 1994 |
|---|---|---|---|
| Bulgaria | 3.4 | -0.4 | -3.0[a] |
| Czechoslovakia | 4.1 | 1.7 | NA |
| Czech Republic | 1.8 | 0.1 | -1.1 |
| Poland | 9.6 | 4.1 | 2.5 |

a=1993.

## DIVORCES, PER 1,000

|  | 1980 | 1990 | 1994 |
|---|---|---|---|
| Bulgaria | 1.48 | 1.26 | 1.23[a] |
| Czechoslovakia | 2.87 | 3.11 | NA |
| Czech Republic | 3.47 | 3.52 | 3.86[b] |
| Poland | 1.12 | 1.11 | 0.80 |

a=1991.
b=1992.

## INFANT MORTALITY, PER 1,000

|  | 1980 | 1990 | 1994 |
|---|---|---|---|
| Bulgaria | 20.2 | 14.8 | 14[a] |
| Czechoslovakia | 18.4 | 11.3 | NA |
| Czech Republic | 16.9 | 10.8 | 7.1 |
| Poland | 21.3 | 15.9 | 15.1 |

a=1993.

**LIFE EXPECTANCY AT BIRTH, YEARS**

|                | Year | Males | Females |
|----------------|------|-------|---------|
| Bulgaria       | 1991 | 68.3  | 74.7    |
| Czechoslovakia | 1992 | 67.7  | 75.5    |
| Czech Republic | 1993 | 69.3  | 76.4    |
| Poland         | 1993 | 67.4  | 76      |

**STOCK OF PASSENGER CARS, END OF YEAR, PERSONS PER CAR**

|                | 1980 | 1989 | 1991 | 1993 |
|----------------|------|------|------|------|
| Bulgaria       | NA   | 7.1  | 6.6  | NA   |
| Czechoslovakia | 7.2  | 5.0  | 4.7  | NA   |
| Czech Republic | NA   | NA   | 4.2  | 3.8  |
| Poland         | 15.0 | 7.9  | 6.3  | 5.7  |

**FOREIGNERS ARRIVING IN THE COUNTRY, MILLIONS**

|                | 1980 | 1989 | 1991 | 1994  |
|----------------|------|------|------|-------|
| Bulgaria       | 5.5  | 8.2  | 6.8  | NA    |
| Czechoslovakia | 5.1  | 29.7 | 64.6 | NA    |
| Czech Republic | NA   | NA   | NA   | 101.1 |
| Poland         | 7.1  | 8.2  | 36.8 | 74.3  |

**GDP IN 1989; 1980=100**

|                | Total | Agriculture | Manufacturing | Construction |
|----------------|-------|-------------|---------------|--------------|
| Bulgaria       | 143   | 81          | 156           | 144          |
| Czechoslovakia | 115   | 100         | 124           | 109          |
| Czech Republic | 112   | NA          | NA            | NA           |
| Poland         | 110   | 121         | 105           | 93           |

**ANNUAL GROWTH RATES (REAL), PERCENT: GDP**

|                | 1990  | 1991  | 1992 | 1993 | 1994 |
|----------------|-------|-------|------|------|------|
| Bulgaria       | -9.1  | -11.7 | -6.3 | -2.4 | 1.4  |
| Czechoslovakia | NA    | NA    | NA   | NA   | NA   |
| Czech Republic | -1.2  | -14.2 | -6.4 | -0.9 | 2.6  |
| Poland         | -11.6 | -7    | 2.6  | 3.8  | 5    |

**ANNUAL GROWTH RATES, PERCENT: PERSONAL CONSUMPTION**

|                | 1990  | 1991  | 1992 | 1993 | 1994 |
|----------------|-------|-------|------|------|------|
| Bulgaria       | 0.3   | -8.4  | -2.3 | 0.0  | -0.2 |
| Czechoslovakia | NA    | NA    | NA   | NA   | NA   |
| Czech Republic | 6.7   | -28.5 | 15.1 | 2.9  | 5.3  |
| Poland         | -11.7 | 7.5   | 3.5  | 5.1  | 3.0  |

## ANNUAL GROWTH RATES, PERCENT: GROSS FIXED CAPITAL INVESTMENT

|  | 1990 | 1991 | 1992 | 1993 | 1994 |
|---|---|---|---|---|---|
| Bulgaria | -18.5 | -19.9 | 13.7 | -24.5 | -11.9 |
| Czechoslovakia | NA | NA | NA | NA | NA |
| Czech Republic | 6.5 | -26.8 | 16.6 | 4.2 | 4.1 |
| Poland | -10.1 | -4.1 | 0.7 | 1.9 | 6.0 |

## ANNUAL GROWTH RATES, PERCENT: GROSS INDUSTRIAL OUTPUT

|  | 1990 | 1991 | 1992 | 1993 | 1994 |
|---|---|---|---|---|---|
| Bulgaria | -14.2 | -20.7 | -16.2 | -7.7 | 4.5 |
| Czechoslovakia | NA | NA | NA | NA | NA |
| Czech Republic | -3.3 | -22.3 | -10.6 | -5.3 | 2.1 |
| Poland | -24.2 | -11.9 | 3.9 | 6.2 | 11.9 |

## ANNUAL GROWTH RATES, PERCENT: GROSS AGRICULTURAL OUTPUT

|  | 1990 | 1991 | 1992 | 1993 | 1994 |
|---|---|---|---|---|---|
| Bulgaria | -6.6 | 4.5 | -12.9 | -15.1 | 1.3 |
| Czechoslovakia | NA | NA | NA | NA | NA |
| Czech Republic | -2.3 | -8.9 | -12.1 | -2.3 | -5.6 |
| Poland | -2.2 | -1.6 | -12.8 | 1.1 | -8.0 |

## GDP PER CAPITA (NOMINAL), AT MARKET EXCHANGE RATE, DOLLARS

|  | 1990 | 1991 | 1992 | 1993 | 1994 |
|---|---|---|---|---|---|
| Bulgaria | 1,939 | 846 | 958 | 1,140 | 1,113 |
| Czechoslovakia | NA | NA | NA | NA | NA |
| Czech Republic | 3,050 | 2,358 | 2,790 | 2,710 | 3,488 |
| Poland | 1,545 | 1,996 | 2,196 | 2,260 | 2,402 |

## CONSUMER PRICE INDEX, PERCENT

|  | 1990 | 1991 | 1992 | 1993 | 1994 |
|---|---|---|---|---|---|
| Bulgaria | 26.3 | 334 | 85 | 72.9 | 96 |
| Czechoslovakia | NA | NA | NA | NA | NA |
| Czech Republic | 9.7 | 56.7 | 11.1 | 20.8 | 11 |
| Poland | 585.8 | 70.3 | 43 | 35.7 | 30 |

## AVERAGE NOMINAL NET MONTHLY WAGE, DOLLARS

|  | 1990 | 1991 | 1992 | July 1993 | July 1994 | May 1995 |
|---|---|---|---|---|---|---|
| Bulgaria | 139 | 53 | 88 | 85 | 116 | |
| Czechoslovakia | NA | NA | NA | NA | NA | |
| Czech Republic | 183 | 129 | 164 | 195 | 243 | 294* |
| Poland | 108 | 167 | 179 | 222 | 245 | 317 |

*April

## UNEMPLOYMENT RATE, PERCENT

|                | 1990 | 1991 | 1992 | 1993 | 1994 |
|----------------|------|------|------|------|------|
| Bulgaria       | 1.6  | 10.5 | 13.2 | 16.3 | 14.1 |
| Czechoslovakia | NA   | NA   | NA   | NA   | NA   |
| Czech Republic | 0.8  | 4.1  | 2.6  | 3.5  | 3.2  |
| Poland         | 6.3  | 11.8 | 13.6 | 16.4 | 16   |

## BUDGET SURPLUS/DEFICIT, PERCENT OF GDP

|                | 1990 | 1991 | 1992 | 1993  | 1994 |
|----------------|------|------|------|-------|------|
| Bulgaria       | -8.5 | -3.7 | -5.4 | -10.9 | -5.5 |
| Czechoslovakia | NA   | NA   | NA   | NA    | NA   |
| Czech Republic | 1.6  | -0.6 | -0.2 | 0.1   | 1    |
| Poland         | 0.4  | -3.8 | -6   | -2.8  | -2.7 |

## NOMINAL MARKET EXCHANGE RATE, DOMESTIC CURRENCY TO DOLLAR

|                | 1990 | 1991 | 1992 | 1993 | 1994 |
|----------------|------|------|------|------|------|
| Bulgaria       | 2.6  | 17.9 | 23.3 | 28   | 54   |
| Czechoslovakia | 18   | 29.5 | NA   | NA   | NA   |
| Czech Republic | NA   | NA   | 28.3 | 29.2 | 28.8 |
| Poland         | 0.95 | 1.06 | 1.36 | 1.81 | 2.27 |

## ANNUAL GROWTH RATES, PERCENT: EXPORT

|                | 1990  | 1991  | 1992  | 1993  | 1994  |
|----------------|-------|-------|-------|-------|-------|
| Bulgaria       | -21.3 | -34.2 | 5.2   | -13.4 | -16.5 |
| Czechoslovakia | -10.5 | 5.6   | 10.7  | NA    | NA    |
| Czech Republic | NA    | NA    | NA    | 15.5  | 13.7  |
| Poland         | 24.7  | -18.5 | -11.5 | -2.8  | 24.8  |

## ANNUAL GROWTH RATES, PERCENT: IMPORT

|                | 1990  | 1991  | 1992 | 1993 | 1994  |
|----------------|-------|-------|------|------|-------|
| Bulgaria       | -23.5 | -51.5 | 36.1 | 0.2  | -42.1 |
| Czechoslovakia | 0.3   | -7.3  | 45.1 | NA   | NA    |
| Czech Republic | NA    | NA    | NA   | 0.5  | 20.8  |
| Poland         | -2.5  | 24.3  | 2.5  | 17.7 | 13.5  |

## NET EXTERNAL DEBT, $BILLION

|                | 1990 | 1991 | 1992 | 1993 | 1994 |
|----------------|------|------|------|------|------|
| Bulgaria       | 10   | 11.1 | 13   | 13.1 | 9.9  |
| Czechoslovakia | 7    | 6.3  | 7.5  | NA   | NA   |
| Czech Republic | NA   | NA   | NA   | 8.7  | 12   |
| Poland         | 44   | 44.8 | 47   | 45.3 | 44.1 |

## EMPLOYMENT BY ECONOMIC BRANCH, 1980S, PERCENT

|                | Year | Agric. | Man. | Serv. |
|----------------|------|--------|------|-------|
| Bulgaria       | 1985 | 16.5   | 46.6 | 36.9  |
| Czechoslovakia | 1980 | 13.1   | 48.8 | 38.1  |
| Czech Republic | NA   | NA     | NA   |       |
| Poland         | 1984 | 29.6   | 36.1 | 34.3  |

Agric. = Agriculture and forestry.
Man. = Manufacturing and construction.
Serv. = Transportation, trade and other services.

## EMPLOYMENT BY ECONOMIC BRANCH, 1992-93, PERCENT

|                | Year | Agric. | Man. | Serv. |
|----------------|------|--------|------|-------|
| Bulgaria       | 1992 | 18     | 45.7 | 36.3  |
| Czechoslovakia | 1992 | 9.9    | 43.8 | 46.3  |
| Czech Republic | NA   | NA     | NA   |       |
| Poland         | 1993 | 25.2   | 31.6 | 43.2  |

## ESTIMATES OF THE SHARE OF PRIVATE SECTOR IN THE CREATION OF GDP, %

|                | 1988    | 1994 |
|----------------|---------|------|
| Bulgaria       | 0.3[a]  | 40   |
| Czechoslovakia | 0.7     | NA   |
| Czech Republic | NA      | 65   |
| Poland         | 18.8    | 52   |

a = 1970.

## AVERAGE SPACE OF A DWELLING COMPLETED, SQUARE METERS

|                | 1980 | 1985 | 1991 | 1994   |
|----------------|------|------|------|--------|
| Bulgaria       | 59   | 65   | 71   | 77[a]  |
| Czechoslovakia | 76   | 80   | 83   | NA     |
| Czech Republic | NA   | NA   | 79   | 87     |
| Poland         | 64   | 70   | 75   | 90     |

a = 1992.

## CATTLE, PER 100 HECTARES OF AGRICULTURAL LAND

|                | 1979–81 | 1991 | 1994    |
|----------------|---------|------|---------|
| Bulgaria       | 28.8    | NA   | 21.3[a] |
| Czechoslovakia | 72      | 45.1 | NA      |
| Czech Republic | 81.2    | 69.7 | 47.4    |
| Poland         | 65.9    | 43.3 | 38.2    |

a = 1992

**HORSES, PER 100 HECTARES OF AGRICULTURAL LAND**

|                | 1980 | 1990 | 1992 | 1994 |
|----------------|------|------|------|------|
| Bulgaria       | 2    | 1.9  | 1.8  | NA   |
| Czechoslovakia | 0.7  | 0.6  | 0.5  | NA   |
| Czech Republic | 0.6  | 0.6  | 0.5  | NA   |
| Poland         | 9.4  | 4.9  | 4.8  | 3.3  |

**PRODUCTION OF MILK, KILOGRAMS PER CAPITA**

|                | 1980 | 1990 | 1992 | 1994 |
|----------------|------|------|------|------|
| Bulgaria       | 208  | 230  | 173  | NA   |
| Czechoslovakia | 381  | 440  | 339  | NA   |
| Czech Republic | 392  | 466  | 359  | 257  |
| Poland         | 455  | 440  | 343  | 305  |

**USE OF (ARTIFICIAL) FERTILIZERS, KILOGRAMS/HECTARE**

|                | 1980/81 | 1990/91 | 1991/92 |
|----------------|---------|---------|---------|
| Bulgaria       | 134     | 110     | 69      |
| Czechoslovakia | 253     | 193     | 61      |
| Czech Republic | 264     | 122     | 86      |
| Poland         | 186     | 95      | 62      |

# NOTES

## 1. INTRODUCTION

1. Klaus (1992), citing Milton Friedman and Alec Nove, "Market or Plan? An Exposition of the Case for the Market," Centre for Research into Communist Economies, *Occasional Paper,* no.1, London, 1984.
2. "New Democracies Barometer IV," survey by the Paul Lazarsfeld Society, Vienna, cited in *The Economist,* March 2, 1996, pp. 48-49.

## 2. BULGARIA:
### Property Restitution, Privatization, and Market Formation

1. Simeon ruled from 893 to 927; under him "his people made great progress in civilization, literature flourished, and his capital Preslav is reputed as rivaling Constantinople in magnificence." *Encyclopedia Britannica,* 1950 edition, vol. 4, p. 360. Preslav is located in northeastern Bulgaria.
2. Excavations have revealed many relics of the Roman period. Little remains of the Bulgarian settlement under the Ottomans. As Gutkind comments, "As a subject people, under conditions of slavery, the Bulgarians were not allowed to build massive houses and public edifices . . . hence no lasting relics have survived." Gutkind, p. 65.
3. Berend and Ranki, p. 39.
4. Ibid, p. 51.
5. Gutkind, pp. 58, 68.
6. It also bore strong similarity to the law passed in Estonia in 1919. See Lapping, pp. 3-5.
7. Berend and Ranki, pp. 192-195.
8. Raul Hilberg, *The Destruction of the European Jews,* Chicago, Quadrangle Books: 1961, p. 670.
9. Gray (1993), p. 23.
10. *State Gazette,* #56, July 13, 1991.
11. President Zhelev had good personal reason to be antagonistic to the Communists. They had removed him from his position in the political science department at Sofia University for authorship of a book, in the 1960s, thought to be critical of the government. He was banished and spent more than ten years as a farm worker.
12. Frydman et al., pp. 25 and 26.
13. BBC Summary of World Broadcasts, May 17, 1995.
14. "Bulgaria's Four-year Plan," *The Financial Times Limited,* East European Markets, June 9, 1995.
15. Movit, p. 34.

16. Stefan Krause, OMRI, Inc. (online service), August 1, 1995.
17. BBC Summary of World Broadcasts, May 1, 1995.
18. A recent government decision to reemphasize teaching of Russian in the schools on the ground that, of the major languages, it is the easiest for Bulgarians to learn, is one indicator of a resumption of Russian ties.
19. President Suleyman Demirel of Turkey has said that, since the fall of communism, Bulgaria has treated its ethnic Turks well. Stefan Krause, OMRI, Inc., July 5, 1995.
20. Shopov, p. 64.
21. *Bulgarian News,* September 8, 1993.
22. Paul R. Gregory and Robert C. Stuart, *Comparative Economic Systems,* Boston: Houghton Mifflin, 1992.
23. This chapter uses the rate of 26.4 lev per dollar, the rate that was in effect in May of 1993, since much of the data are from that period. The rate fluctuated between 55 and 65 lev per dollar in 1994 and reached 69 lev per dollar in August 1995. The text will note if the more recent rates are used.
24. European Bank for Reconstruction and Development, "The Economics of Transition," vol. 3, #2, Table 2, Oxford University Press, Oxford, England, 1995; Movit, p. 21.
25. *Poland International,* Economic Report, Warsaw: World Economy Research Institute, 1995, pp. 34-37.
26. *The Economist,* April 30, 1994, p. 55; pension spending in the former Czechoslovakia in 1992 was 16.8 percent of GDP and in Poland 24.8 percent.
27. *The Economist,* December 3, 1994.
28. "Bulgarian Economic Monitor: The Economy Is Showing First Signs of a Turnaround," *PlanEcon Report* #20-22, July 18, 1994.
29. National Statistics Institute. The National Statistics Institute was founded in 1991; it is applying uniform classifications consistent with international standards.
30. Bulgarian National Bank, 1993, p. 12.
31. Movit, p. 24.
32. Dikov, p. 4.
33. EAST Database, University of Pennsylvania, Philadelphia.
34. Minassian and Totev, p. 10.
35. *168 Hours BBN,* June 14-16, 1993.
36. *The Economist,* April 30, 1994, p. 55; this compares to 49 percent in the former Czechoslovakia and 74 percent in Poland.
37. "Three-Quarters of Bulgarians Live at Poverty Level," *168 Hours BBN,* November 15-21, 1993, p. 8.
38. *The Transition Newsletter* 4, The World Bank, Washington, D.C., July-August 1993.
39. Movit, p. 31.
40. As calculated by the Economic Commission for Europe. Poland, from 1989 through 1992, received $1.4 billion.
41. Movit, p. 36.
42. "Bulgarian Economic Monitor: The Economy Is Showing First Signs Of a Turnaround," *PlanEcon Report,* #20-22, July 18, 1994, p. 8.
43. "Bulgaria, Russia's Tyumen Plan Joint Ventures," Reuter News Service, CIS and Eastern Europe, June 13, 1995.

44. "Bulgaria, Russia Restore Joint Timber Industry," Reuter News Service, CIS and Eastern Europe, July 15, 1995.
45. "World Bank still frustrated at slow pace of reform," *The Financial Times Limited,* Finance East Europe, July 7, 1995.
46. "Bulgaria Plans to Close State-Owned Lossmakers," Reuter Textline, Reuter News Service, CIS and Eastern Europe, August 29, 1995.
47. *The Financial Times Limited,* Finance East Europe, July 26, 1995.
48. Movit, p. 38; National Statistical Institute.
49. By comparison, also with 1937 as the index year of 100, in 1949 Czechoslovakia had reached 123 and Poland 177. It is important to keep in mind the base of industrial activity from which each of these increases occurred. In 1938 Bulgaria accounted for 0.33 percent of European industrial production, while Czechoslovakia accounted for 3.39 percent and Poland for 2.53 percent. Mitchell, *European Historical Statistics 1750-1970.*
50. Carter, in Dawson, p. 72.
51. Ibid, p. 76.
52. Bozhkov, memorandum to author, January 7, 1994.
53. "State Companies Lose Over BGL 26,000 M in Nine Months," *168 Hours BBN,* December 6-12, 1993, p. 5.
54. Kopeva and Mishev, Dec.1993, p. 7.
55. Crampton, p. 136. The size of farm holdings had declined from twenty years earlier, when 85 percent of total holdings per farmer were 25 acres (10 hectares) or less. "Between 1920 and 1940 the agrarian population increased by 18.4 per cent whilst the number of holdings increased by 38.4 percent. . . . With more and more people subsisting on the land agricultural over-population became increasingly apparent."
56. Interview at the Hisar Land Commission.
57. Crampton, p. 139.
58. Levinson, p. 9.
59. Crampton, p. 195.
60. The World Bank, p. 7.
61. Ibid, p. 8.
62. The World Bank, vol. 2, p. 69.
63. Ibid, vol. 2, p. 74.
64. "Wineries Lost Over 5 M Lev by End March," *168 Hours BBN,* September 13-19, 1993, p. 6.
65. "A World of Wine," *Los Angeles Times,* June 15, 1995.
66. "Agricultural Companies Owe More Than 6,000 Mln. leva," *Bulgarian News,* August 19, 1993.
67. "Agriculture," *Bulgarian News,* August 5, 1993.
68. Council of Ministers, Decree #3, January 18, 1994.
69. Movit, p. 27.
70. Vasil Manovsky, cited in the Reuter European Business Report, June 26, 1995.
71. Hoffman and Koleva, p. 5.
72. Gray and Ianachkov, p. 13.
73. Interview with Theodor Kolarski.
74. Throughout the text we use the ratio of 1:10 rather than the accurate 0.929:10 for conversion of square meters to square feet.

75. Bozhkov, memorandum to author, January 7, 1994.
76. Ravicz, p. 29.
77. Peeva, p. 234.
78. Videlov et al., pp. 7 and 8.
79. "Housing Construction Drops More Than 30 Per Cent," *168 Hours BBN,* December 6-12, 1993, p. 12.
80. Hegedus and Tosics, p. 337.
81. Hoffman and Koleva, p. 5.
82. Ibid.
83. National Centre for Regional Development and Housing Policy, p. 7.
84. "House-Building Factories Restructure Production,"*168 Hours BBN,* June 7-13, 1993.
85. Interview with Theodor Kolarski.
86. Ravicz, pp. 21-23.
87. "Households Spend Close to Half Their Income on Food," *168 Hours BBN,* September 13-19, 1993, p. 8.
88. Hoffman and Koleva, p. 11.
89. "Housing Construction Dropped 10 Per Cent between January and June," *168 Hours BBN,* September 27-October 3, 1993, p. 12.
90. Hoffman and Koleva, p. 9.
91. Act of Amendment and Supplement to Settling the Housing Problems of Long-Term Contract Savers, *State Gazette* #82, 1991, amended by *State Gazette* #62, 1992.
92. Interviews with Genovava Hadjidimitrova and Georgi Petkov.
93. Supported by funding from the U.S. Agency for International Development.
94. Interview with Michael Hoffman and Maya Koleva.
95. Boyan Gjuzelev, Center for the Study of Democracy, at the Boyana Conference on Privatization and Economic Reform, June 3, 1993.
96. Bozhkov, memorandum to author, January 7, 1994.
97. Gray and Ianachkov, p. 2.
98. Under the Expropriation of City Buildings Real Estate Act of 1948 and other subsequent acts.
99. Crampton, p. 166.
100. Berend and Ranki, p. 346.
101. The World Bank, p. 5.
102. Kopeva, letter to author, August 1, 1994.
103. Art. 17, Sections 3, 1, and 5.
104. Art. 15.
105. Art. 18.
106. Art. 21, Sections 1 and 2.
107. Art. 22.
108. Stefan Krause, OMRI, December 17, 1995.
109. Calculated by the Ministry of Agriculture on the assumption that, on average, each landowner as of 1946 or later has three heirs who are represented in a single claim.
110. Anachkova et al., p.83.
111. Gray and Ianachkov, p. 11.
112. Peeva, p. 236.
113. Act of February 5, 1992. This act provides for restitution of real property, taken under the Expropriation of Large Housing Act of 1948 and several other acts, that "exists in the same physical dimensions as when it was expropriated."

114. Ordinance #60 of 1975.

115. The Restitution of Nationalized Real Property Act, February 5, 1992, Art. 10.

116. The National Statistics Institute data are cited in "Close to 31,000 Sites Restituted by June 30th, 1993," *168 Hours BBN,* October 25-31, 1993, p. 12.

117. "Minister Views Housing Problems Caused by Restitution Act," quoting Construction Minister Doncho Konakchiev, BBC Summary of World Broadcasts, July 21, 1995.

118. Interview with Dimiter Kebedjiev.

119. Hoffman and Koleva, p. 2.

120. "Bulgaria to Return 97 Pct of Land by End of 1996," Reuter Textline, Reuter News Service, CIS and Eastern Europe, August 29, 1995.

121. "Bulgaria: Land Restitution to Be Completed By Mid-1996," statement of then Agriculture and Food Minister Vasil Chichibaba, Reuter Textline, BBC Monitoring Service: Eastern Europe, July 13, 1995.

122. Art. 23a, *State Gazette* #34 of 1992.

123. Mikhailov, p. 93.

124. Levinson, p. 9.

125. Georgi Spasov, cited in "Presidential Adviser Says BSP Policy Would be 'End of Land Reform'," BBC World Broadcasts, August 21, 1993.

126. Bozhkov, memorandum to author, January 7, 1994.

127. *State Gazette* #17, March 1, 1991, as amended by *State Gazette* #74, October 9, 1991; *State Gazette* #18, March 2, 1992; and *State Gazette* #28, April 3, 1992.

128. LOUAL Regulations, Art. 60, sec. 5.

129. "Half the Land to Go Private by End-1993," *168 Hours BBN,* September 20-26, 1993, p. 7.

130. Article 10, sec. 1: "Proprietors or their inheritors shall be reinstated in their farm land owned prior to the establishment of Cooperative Farms (TKZS) or State Farms (DZS) and incorporated in them or in other TKZS or DZS-based agricultural organizations."

131. Art. 18g(1) of the regulations under LOUAL governs restoration of former boundaries, while Art. 18g(2) and Art. 27 prescribe how reallotments shall occur.

132. Art. 18i of the LOUAL regulations.

133. Art. 6.

134. The LOUAL, Art. 10b.

135. The LOUAL, Art. 10, (10).

136. Regulations on the Application of the Law of Ownership and Use of Agricultural Land, *State Gazette* #34, April 30, 1991, as amended *State Gazette* #80, September 27, 1991, and *State Gazette* #34, April 24, 1992, Ch. 1, Art. 4.

137. Arts. 4 (1), 4 (2), and 5.

138. Regulations on the LOUAL, Chap. 2, Art. 10.

139. *State Gazette* #63, 1991, amended by *State Gazette* #35 and #55, 1992.

140. "Few Co-ops Handed Back," *168 Hours BBN,* October 25-31, 1993, p. 12.

141. Under the Cooperatives Act, *State Gazette* #63, 1991, amended by *State Gazette* #34 and 55, 1992, Art. 10 (2), a member who contributed land may keep title to his land at its boundaries before entering the coop or "convert it into a share of the joint ownership of the land. . . ."

142. See LOUAL Regulations, especially Arts. 50-52, for further details.

143. "Land Reform Strategy Approved until End-1994," *168 Hours BBN,* October 4-10, 1993, p. 7.
144. Kopeva, Mishev, and Howe, p. 215.
145. We visited Saedinenie on June 17, 1993, in the company of our translators, Ivan Sariev and Andrian Pervasov. We met there with the mayor, Angel Kutsov, and with the chairman of the Liquidation Council, Tsveran Marincheshki, and with Stoyan Enchev, Dimiter Krantov, and Milyo Turgunski, all members of the council.
146. We visited the mayor, town secretary, and members of the Land Commission.
147. The law specifies that ownership may be established by "act of notary, deeds of partition, TKZS protocols, land registers, applications for TKZS membership, rent ledgers, and other evidence in writing." The LOUAL, Art. 12.
148. Where no other source is cited, the data have been provided by Diana Kopeva of the Agricultural Policy Analysis Unit of the Ministry of Agriculture.
149. Kopeva and Mishev, p. 10.
150. Kopeva, letter to author, September 16, 1994.
151. "Final Data Issued On Land Restitution Applications," BBC Summary of World Broadcasts, August 20, 1992.
152. Kopeva, letter to author, September 16, 1994.
153. "Bulgaria: Progress of Land Reform and Restitution," BBC Summary of World Broadcasts, December 28, 1992.
154. "Bulgaria to Return 97 Pct of Land by End of 1996," Reuter Textline, Reuter News Service, CIS and Eastern Europe, August 29, 1995.
155. LOUAL Regulations, Art. 25, secs. 1-6.
156. The number of decisions is far in excess of the number of claims, since the Land Commissions issue a separate decision for each plot.
157. Bulgarian news agency BTA, citing Todor Todorov, head of the parliamentary committee on agriculture and forestry, March 2, 1995.
158. Kopeva, letter to author, August 1, 1994.
159. Kopeva and Mishev, p. 9.
160. *Bulgarian Economic Review,* May 21-June 3, 1993, p. 3.
161. Recorded interview with President Zhelev on "Panorama" program, BBC Summary of World Broadcasts, September 8, 1993.
162. Mikailov, p. 99.
163. *State Gazette* #24, March 26, 1993.
164. Georgy Tanev, Minister of Agriculture, states that there are no such co-ops, since only 742 people hold deeds covering 1,500 acres (612 hectares). "BGL 1,500 M for Autumn, Spring Sowing," *168 Hours BBN,* November 8-14, 1993, p. 7.
165. "Privatisation to Start in 1994," *168 Hours BBN,* September 20-26, 1993, p. 3.
166. Law for Financing Agricultural Practices In 1993-1994, *State Gazette* #54, November 5, 1993.
167. Petranoff (February 1994), p. 8.
168. Petranoff (March 1994), p. 6.
169. "Final Data Issued on Land Restitution Applications," BBC Summary of World Broadcasts, August 20, 1992.
170. Kopeva and Mishev, p. 10.
171. Ibid, p. 14.

172. Diana Kopeva, memorandum to author, November 20, 1995.
173. Ibid.
174. Stefan Krause, OMRI, Inc., April 21, 1995.
175. "Bulgaria Removes Curbs on Small Land Owners," Reuter News Service, CIS and East Europe, August 10, 1995.
176. "Bulgarian Premier Slams President, Constitutional Court," Reuters World Service, July 28, 1995.
177. Gareth Jones, "President Warns Bulgaria Risks Recommunization," Reuters World Service, May 12, 1995.
178. "Bulgarian Court, Government Clash over Eviction," Reuters, Limited, Reuters World Service, August 4, 1995.
179. Art. 10, sec. 5: "Proprietors shall be reinstated in . . . lands incorporated without compensation into the state forestry reserve, with the exception of forest nurseries and forest shelter belts."
180. There is some privatization in agriculture through auction sales of collective farm equipment and buildings.
181. Valentin Karabashev, Deputy Prime Minister, "Privatization and Economic Reform," speech given at the Boyana conference on privatization, June 3, 1993.
182. Yozioldash, p. 41.
183. The Restitution of Nationalized Real Property Act, February 5, 1992, Art. 7.
184. Frydman et al., p. 23.
185. Yozioldash, p. 3.
186. "Former Privatization Chief Alleges Asset Stripping," BBC, Summary of World Broadcasts, September 1, 1993.
187. The World Bank, p. xxiv; see also the Law on the Formation of State Property Sole Proprietorship Companies of June 27, 1991, which prohibited state enterprises from transferring real property to the private sector and which clarified that only the Council of Ministers has the power to transfer real property as part of the privatization process.
188. Ibid, p. 81.
189. *State Gazette,* #38, May 8, 1992.
190. Actually a Privatization Agency was created in 1991, but Ordinance #156 of August 14, 1992, terminated that agency and established the current Privatization Agency.
191. Kovachev, p. 6.
192. The Privatization Agency has proposed to Parliament that it become the owner of all enterprises scheduled for privatization, arguing that this would be more efficient and would avoid foot-dragging by various ministries. "PA Demands Ownership Rights," *168 Hours BBN,* October 18-24, 1993, p. 6.
193. *State Gazette* #38, May 8, 1992, Art. 34, Sec. 6.
194. See Pomeroy for details on participation by enterprise employees, exchange of debt for shares by creditors, and various terms for purchase of enterprises that have not been transformed into limited liability or joint stock companies.
195. *State Gazette* #38, May 8, 1992, Arts. 22-26.
196. Ibid, Sec. 11, Transitional and Final Provisions.
197. Art. 7 ordered creation of the Fund for Covering the Expenditures for Privatization of State-Owned Enterprises; the regulations concerning the Fund are in Decree #187, September 24, 1992, published in the *State Gazette* #81, October 6, 1992.

198. Art. 6 (2).
199. Sec. 7, Transitional and Final Provisions.
200. See Pomeroy for a fuller description.
201. "Bulgaria: Cabinet Approves Mass Privatization Programme," Reuter Textline, BBC Monitoring Service: Eastern Europe, August 10, 1995.
202. "Laggard Bulgaria Pins Hopes on Mass Privatisation," Reuter Textline, Reuter News Service, CIS and Eastern Europe, August 14, 1995.
203. Kovachev, p. 4.
204. "Bulgarian Economic Monitor: The Economy Is Showing First Signs of a Turnaround," *PlanEcon Report,* #s 20-23, July 18, 1994, p. 9.
205. Bozhkov, memorandum to author, January 7, 1994.
206. "80-100 Industrial Units to Initiate Privatisation by End-1993," *168 Hours BBN,* September 6-12, 1993, p. 6.
207. "Foreign Partners to Invest BGL 698 M in Local Industry," *168 Hours BBN,* November 8-14, 1993, p. 5.
208. Comments of Mladen Georgiev, Head of Privatisation and Transformation, Ministry of Construction, at the Boyana Conference on Privatization, June 4, 1993.
209. "Sinit Pays 23.2 M Lev for Service Station," *168 Hours BBN,* September 27-October 3, 1993, p. 8.
210. "Ministry Transacts Just Four Privatisation Deals," *168 Hours BBN,* November 8-14, 1993, p. 7.
211. "Real Privatisation Has Not Started Yet," *168 Hours BBN,* September 20-26, 1993, p. 1.
212. Reneta Indjova, cited in "Real Privatisation Has Not Started Yet," *168 Hours BBN,* September 20-26, 1993, p. 5.
213. "East Europe Faces Main Privatisation Tasks," Reuters European Community Report, January 17, 1996.
214. Gradev and Keremeidchev, p. 3.
215. Human settlement types are specified in "Classifiers for Human Settlements in Republics of Bulgaria."
216. Regulation for the Basic Market Prices of Immovable Property, *State Gazette* #65, August 9, 1991, amended by *State Gazette* #s 77 and 93 of 1991, and #s 51, 54, and 68 of 1992. Sales and leases of state and municipal housing may not be at prices lower than the basic market price.
217. Videlov et al., p. 16. "Housing estates" is assumed to refer to the high-rise Soviet-style apartment blocks that ring the periphery of Sofia. According to an interview with banker Georgi Petkov, in Sofia a 450 square foot (45 square meter) apartment sold for from $9,500 to $76,000 (250,000 to two million lev), depending on location. This opinion supports the data in Tables 2.4 and 2.5.
218. "Construction Costs Rise," *168 Hours BBN,* June 7-13, 1993, p. 8.
219. Kopeva, letter to author, September 14, 1994. The districts include the following locations:

   1. Center city: Large flats in brick buildings with central heat, much in demand for offices.
   2. Lozenets, Chervena Zvezda, Istok, Yavorov, Zone B-5, Ivan Vazov, Beli Brezi, and Hipodrouma: Areas are to the south and east of the center, with good transportation; most buildings have central heat and are in demand both for offices and housing.

3. Lagera, Krasno Selo, Strelbishte, Durvenitsa, Mladost 1, 2, and 3, and Emil Markov: Buildings have all utilities, most flats have telephones, and there is good transportation; the demand is for housing.

4. Hadji Dimiter, Slatina, Podouene, Zapaden Park, Krasna Polyana, Banishora, and Drouzhba 1: Less accessible with demand for housing.

5. Ovcha Koupel, Lyulin, Drouzhba 2, and Mladost 4: Panel construction, difficulties with telephones, transportation, and heating, far from the center of the city.

6. Levski, Nadezhda, Orlandovtsi, Obelya, and all other suburbs.

220. Videlov et al., p. 16.
221. Ibid.
222. *State Gazette* #65, 1993.
223. Ivanka Yanakieva and Maria Rissina, "Experts Set Land Prices," *Bulgarian Economic Review,* June 3-16, 1992.
224. Ibid, p. 7.
225. Kopeva and Mishev, pp. 22 and 23.
226. Kopeva, letter to author, July 26, 1994.
227. Kopeva and Mishev, p. 23.
228. City notaries are public officials. Bulgaria adopted the notarial system as employed in Austria and Germany. As is common in much of Europe, there also are private notaries in Bulgaria. Their records do show actual price paid for property, but these records are private. Recording occurs under the Law for Cadaster and Land Registration.
229. See the definition *supra* under discussion of the urban land market.
230. Interview with Michael Hoffman.
231. Carter, in Dawson, p. 92.
232. Instruction #2 on Building in Agricultural Land, *State Gazette* #47, 1993, and Instruction #3 on Territorial and Town-Planning on the Black Sea Coast, *State Gazette* #57, July 2, 1993.
233. "Bulgaria: Special Report—Bulgaria—Vital Development Role for Varna," Reuter Textline, Lloyds List, August 23, 1995.
234. Interview with Slavtcho Yankov and Georgi Georgiev, National Centre for Regional Development and Housing Policy, Sofia.
235. Carter, in French, p. 439.
236. Interview with Michael Hoffman.

### 3. CZECHOSLOVAKIA
**Land and Housing Privatization in Czechoslovakia / The Czech Republic**

1. Havel , pp. 62-63.
2. Magocsi gives maps that depict these and subsequent changes.
3. Wallace, chs. 11, 12.
4. Večernik; Kornai, e.g. table 13.7; Carter (1979).
5. Bratislava has five districts, each with five municipalities.
6. "NIMBY" ("Not In My BackYard") has entered the Czech vocabulary.
7. Only 34,000 have declared themselves as Gypsies in the recent census: Večernik, pp. 21-22. Also, see Czech Republic, Statistical Office (1993).

8. Svitek et al, p. 12.
9. *The New York Times,* September 30, 1994; *Business Central Europe,* January 1996, p. 27. Also, Table in Appendix.
10. The exchange rate being used is 25 koruna = $1. This was the rate in 1993; by the close of 1994 it was 28 koruna = $1.
11. *The New York Times,* January 1, 1993, February 9, 1995; *The Economist,* September 10, 1994; *Business Central Europe,* January 1996, p. 27.
12. EAST Database, University of Pennsylvania, Philadelphia, PA..
13. *The Wall Street Journal,* December 27, 1992.
14. *The Economist,* November 5, 1994; EAST Database, University of Pennsylvania, Philadelphia, PA.
15. OECD, Committee for Agriculture, Committee for Trade, p. 43; *Business Central Europe,* January 1996, p. 27..
16. *Prognosis,* August 7-20, 1992; Mládek (1993) and interviews in August 1992, May 1993.
17. *The Prague Post,* January 3, 1996. However, one estimate notes loss of 30,000 units annually due to demolition, business conversion, etc. Also, *Economist Intelligence Unit,* March 20, 1995; Czech Statistical Office (1995), p.15.
18. BBC, April, 1995; OECD, Committee for Agriculture, Committee for Trade; Czech Statistical Office (1995), p. 13.
19. Gray (1993) p. 3.
20. Mládek (1993).
21. Berend and Ranki, p. 344.
22. Interview with Jan Mládek, August 1992; Mládek (1994) p. 4.
23. Mládek (1994) p. 4.
24. Ibid.
25. Havel, pp. 109-110.
26. Also Archduchess of Austria and Queen of Hungary (1717-80).
27. Bertaud and Renaud summarize the rationale and the process by which such development took place.
28. Carter (1979) p. 430.
29. Rubenstein and Unger, p.6.
30. Gray (1993), p. 48.
31. In January 1995 a delegation from Ukraine visited the Czech Republic to seek technical aid on the process of transformation from a command to a market economy. Deputy Economics Minister Lada Pavlykovska said at this time that experts from the United States, England, and France did not really comprehend Ukraine's problems, while the Czechs have a better understanding, having gone through the process themselves. Ustina Markus, OMRI (online service), part 2, February 1, 1995.
32. Grime and Duke ; Mládek (1993); Frydman et al (1993). The political context in which "justice" of restitution is defined is discussed in Appel.
33. As of early 1995, about two-thirds of the claims filed have been satisfied: *CTK National News Wire,* March 30, 1995.
34. Deputy Prime Minister Pavel Rychetsky quoted in *The New York Times,* February 26, 1991.
35. The relatively few German and Hungarian Czechoslovak citizens who remained in the republic are covered by special laws: Gray (1992), p. 5. Sudeten German

claims were reopened but, on March 8, 1995, the Czech Constitutional Court rejected the claim, upholding the validity of the 1945 Beneš decree. The court subsequently held that property could be restituted. In particular, in the case where an ethnic German maintained Czechoslovak citizenship, the court decided that restitution claims could be filed for property taken after February 1948. The issue continues to surface into 1996 and rankle Czech-German relations: *The New York Times,* February 9, 1996.

36. In May 1994 a special law on restitution of Jewish-held property, provided seizure specifically noted that the taking had been on grounds of "Aryanization," was signed by President Havel: "Czech Republic," *East European Constitutional Review,* Summer/Fall 1994, p. 7. Jewish communal property was covered under a law passed in October 1994 after earlier parliamentary rejection of the measure: *The Wall Street Journal,* January 14, 1994 and February 22, 1994; *The New York Times,* October 23, 1994. Also, see Appel, p. 10, for a discussion of restitution laws as designed specifically and only to redress injustices of the communist regime.

37. Mládek (1991), p. 5: discussion of Law #298-1990; OMRI, January 8, 1995; *CTK National News Wire,* February 1, 1996..

38. Law #403-1990, the Act Concerning the Transfer of Some State Property to the Ownership of Individual or Juridical Persons, also referred to as the Act on Relieving the Consequences of Some Property Injustice. See Mládek (1993), pp. 123-124; Frydman et al (1994), p. 15.

39. Mládek (1993), pp. 123-124; Also, see Grime and Duke, p. 754.

40. Only with a constitutional court ruling in 1995 were nonresidents entitled to file claims; relatively few have done so: *CTK National News Wire,* May 25, 1995.

41. Grime and Duke, p. 754, citing Mládek (1993). Also Kotrba. The counting game is complex, and there were perhaps as many as 80,000 to almost 100,000 nonagricultural properties. Of these, some 40,000 co-op units were subject to different laws leading to their "transformation." The figure in the text represents the best estimate of the number of cases of successful restitution.

42. Transferred under Law #172-1991.

43. Restitution claims may be filed until November 1, 1995, with some 73,000 filed as of May 1995. The process is slow, with some 10 percent settled as of mid-1995: *CTK National News Wire,* May 10, 1995.

44. The Condominium Law, May 1, 1994.

45. The Czech Constitutional Court, in a 2-1 decision, upheld the validity of an amendment to Sec. 872 of the Civil Code, transforming such leases into lifetime leases. This decision established precedent in the court for minority opinions: "Czech Republic," *East European Constitutional Review,* Summer/Fall 1994, p. 7.

46. Law #871-1991, titled the Extra-Judicial Act, or the Large Restitution Act.

47. Mládek (1993), p.126. A public opinion survey conducted in mid-1995 showed almost three times as many opposed to negotiating such restitution as favoring discussions.

48. According to the Ministry of Justice, relatively few have expressed interest in filing claims: *CTK National News Wire,* May 29, 1995.

49. Mládek (1994), p. 18.

50. Personal communication with Ministry of Privatization, Czech Republic, August and December 1993.
51. *The Financial Times,* April 16, 1995; EAST Database, University of Pennsylvania, Philadelphia, PA.
52. Personal communication with Ministry of Privatization, Czech Republic, August and December 1993.
53. Czech Republic, Ministry of Agriculture; Mládek (1994). Exceptions to restitution possibilities arise in cases where, for example, land had become part of a factory subject to privatization. When such privatization does occur, the Land Fund will guarantee that real estate is not subject to restitution claims: interview with Anna Vitová, May 1993.
54. Czech Republic, Ministry of Agriculture, pp. 8, 43.
55. *CTK National News Wire,* March 30, 1995. The process of such "indirect restitution" has been suspended indefinitely, according to Prime Minister Klaus, as part of steps to shut down the National Property Fund: BBC Monitoring Service, Eastern Europe, June 26, 1995.
56. Czech Republic, Ministry of Agriculture, p. 45.
57. An amendment to the legislation would allow restitution in cases where the state subsequently had sold the land: interview with Stanislav Jelen, May 1993.
58. Gray (1993), p. 49; Mládek (1994), p. 17. Only 10 percent had been co-op members.
59. Czech Republic, Ministry of Agriculture, pp. 32, 39. As of 1991 in Slovakia, restitution had resulted in return of more than one-half of forests, mainly to cooperatives and to individuals: interview with Petr Michalovič, August 1992.
60. Law #42/1991, Law on Regulation of Property in Relations in Cooperatives.
61. Law #229/1991, An Act for the Adjustment of Ownership Rights of Land and Other Agricultural Property.
62. *CTK National News Wire,* March 25, 1991.
63. Mládek (1994), p. 17; Czech Republic, Ministry of Agriculture, p. 43; OECD, Committee on Agriculture, Committee on Trade. The last gives slightly different figures: "From 1,197 collective farms, the results of the transformation process were: 1,233 new cooperatives, 39 shareholding companies, 59 other companies, and 24 remaining collectives facing liquidation proceedings," p. 52. Cochrane, p. 323, asserts "most of the transformed cooperatives retained almost the same internal and management structures they had before their transformation."
64. Major reports on the dominance of real estate value as a portion of all national assets in Czechoslovakia (as well as in the other Central and East European states).
65. Earle et al, p. 300 and passim.
66. Havel, pp. 67-69.
67. Law #427-1990 as amended by Law #541-1990, the Federal Law on Transfers of State Property of Some Goods to Other Legal and Natural Persons.
68. Svítek et al., p. 56. Auction revenues were sequestered in a special fund rather than being treated as general budget income: Gray (1992), p. 4.
69. Sýkora and Šimoničkova.
70. Sýkora and Štepanek (1992).
71. Sýkora (1992).

72. Sýkora and Štepanek.
73. Grime and Duke; Frydman et al.; Kotrba; Hanoušek and Kroch.
74. The Ministry of Privatization has maintained that it would prevent sales where the purpose was even partly to acquire the real property of the enterprise for purposes other than to carry out the activities of the enterprise: interview with Charles Jelínek, August 1992.
75. Law #92-1991, Conditions of Transferring State Property, known as the Act on Large Privatization.
76. EAST Database, University of Pennsylvania, Philadelphia, PA.
77. Hanoušek (1995).
78. *The New York Times,* June 20, 1992.
79. Law #513-1991, effective since January 1, 1992.
80. See Svítek et al. for detailed information.
81. Slay and Tedstrom, p. 5. EAST Database, 7/23/1993, summarizes information on large privatization: Seven-eighths of book value of enterprises was converted into joint stock companies. The Czech model has served as a wider prototype. President Yeltsin of Russia announced a voucher plan following on the Czech plan under which each Russian will receive a voucher worth 10,000 rubles ($40) for investment in state property that is being privatized. Managers and employees may bid for 51 percent of the shares and holders of the vouchers for the other 4 percent: *The New York Times,* August 20, 1992. Poland, as well, approved a plan under which citizens acquire shares: this plan is under way.
82. Czech Republic, Ministry of Privatization, August and December 1993.
83. *The Wall Street Journal,* October 1, 1992.
84. Havel and Kukla, p. 41.
85. Teague, p. 11.
86. *Prognosis,* July 14, 1992.
87. *Hospodařské Noviny,* July 31, 1992, quoting Minister Skalicky.
88. *The Wall Street Journal,* October 1, 1992.
89. EAST Database, University of Pennsylvania, Philadelphia, PA.
90. OECD, Committee on Agriculture, Committee on Trade (1994), pp. 32, 52.
91. Mládek (1994), p. 19, *CSTK Eco Service,* September 18, 1995; *Reuters Textline,* 9/10/95.
92. Interview with Anna Červenková, August 1992. However, while some 35,000 co-op members applied to own their flats, only 500 contracts were concluded: *CTK National News Wire,* December 15, 1995.
93. A survey by the DEMA Company also found that the older population was more likely to own housing: *CTK National News Wire,* August 17, 1995..
94. Kotrba, p. 5; Czech Republic, Ministry of Privatization, August and December, 1993.
95. Mládek (1994), p. 18.
96. In mid-1995, expectations were that of 2 million acres (800,000 hectares) still state owned, 100,000 acres would go to satisfy restitution claims; 500,000 acres would be offered for sale (to Czech citizens only); and some of the remainder given to religious bodies. The privatization would begin in 1996 with local neighbors "given preference" with payment to be spread over twenty years: *CTK National News Wire,* August 9, 1995; *Reuters Textline,* August 10, August 18, 1995.

97. Czech Republic, Ministry of Agriculture (1994), p. 8; Mládek (1994), p. 4.
98. Czech Republic, Ministry of Agriculture (1994), p. 37.
99. Ibid, p. 9.
100. Hanoušek, p. 2.
101. Kotrba. Remaining government ownership, partly as the National Property Fund and also in the form of government shares of privatized industry and banks, remains an issue. As of mid-1995, the government policy was to eliminate such participation by 1997: OMRI, August 9, 1995.
102. Mládek (1994), p. 19.
103. OECD, Committee for Agriculture, Committee on Trade (1994), p. 52.
104. Interview with Ivan Plicka, August 1992.
105. Carter (1979), p. 441.
106. Bertaud and Renaud; the writers stress that there have been no incentives to develop these lands to better and more efficient use.
107. Sýkora (1994).
108. *The Prague Post,* August 18, 1992.
109. Sýkora and Šymoničková.
110. A fledgling Multiple Listing Service (MLS) surfaced in 1993. It was based on the nine agencies of the Prague Real Estate Association, housed at the DATAREAL firm and using in particular its data base. As of August 1993, the listings were on the order of 100 or 200 properties (with about 30 from the DATAREAL company). A similar initiative has been started at the republic level.
111. Sýkora (1995), p. 330. In 1938 there were far fewer: some twenty-two real estate brokers (some of whom were banks) in the greater Prague area: see listings in telephone book, Czechoslovakia, Ředitelství Pošt a Telgrafú v Praze.
112. Interview with Antonin Skružný, August 1992.
113. Interview with Jaroslav Macháček, May 1994.
114. Interview with Antonin Skružný, August 1992.
115. Law #367-1990 regulates nonresidential maximum rents. Under this law, Prague has set different maximum rents based on location and has let some districts of the city to allow rents to float free.
116. Sýkora and Štepanek, p. 99. These are equivalent to New York rents. Also see Sýkora (1995). A given fixed-up unit, when leased to a foreigner for business use in central Prague may yield forty times the monthly rent collected from a controlled tenant. Such leases for top space will yield about 1,000 koruna per square meter (about $4 per square foot): *The Prague Post,* January 3, 1996.
117. *Prague Business Week,* July 17, 1992.
118. Interview with Ivan C. Chadima, August 1992. However, even with new office construction and refurbishment of older properties, some feel that "drop in Prague office rents unlikely": *Estate News: Central and Eastern Europe Property Gazette,* 8 #36, August/September 1994, p. 13.
119. Interview with Antonin Skružný, August 1992.
120. Interview with Ivan C. Chadima, August 1992.
121. Interview with Vavřinec Bodenlos, August 1992.
122. In Western Europe, it is common for fares to cover half or more of operating costs.
123. The city of Olomouc has retained title to land where properties have been auctioned under privatization, placing the land on ninety-nine year lease: Rubenstein and Unger, p. 4.

124. Mládek (1991), p. 30.
125. Prague, City.
126. Telgarsky et al.
127. Law #367-1990 regulates nonresidential maximum rents.
128. *CTK National News Wire,* February 13, 1996.
129. *CTK National News Wire,* October 11, 1995; *The Prague Post,* January 3, 1996; *Business Central Europe,* February 1996.
130. Interview with Anthony Chip Caine, August 1992.
131. Interview with Tomáš Procházka, August 1992.
132. OECD, Committee on Agriculture, Committee on Trade (1994), p. 54.
133. Rubenstein and Unger, pp. 2, 5.
134. The Slovak Republic has a Ministry for Building and Construction which later became the Ministry of Public Works. Its subsidiary research institute encompasses urban design and the economics of building and housing. Neither institute has any command functions; they both act as advisors to ministries and municipalities.
135. Law #262-1992.
136. Bratislava also has regional planning. Its partners are international: Györ, a city of 60,000 in Hungary as well as Vienna in Austria. There is some commuting across borders, and the cities are linked by Danube hydrofoils, trains, and the airports of Vienna and Bratislava. Rapid transit to link the airports, Bratislava and Vienna, is planned.
137. A brief history of planning is in Sýkora (1995).
138. In 1992 the city allocated some funds for roof repair; much more is needed.
139. METROSTAV et al.; Sýkora (1995), pp. 335-339.
140. City Architect's Office of Prague (1992) p.36.
141. Interview with Antonin Skružný, August 1992.
142. Svítek et al., p. 82.
143. Caine.
144. Interview with attorney Bettelheim at Lovell White Durrant, August 1992.
145. Interview with Ivan C. Chadima, August 1992.
146. Law #22-1964.
147. Law #344-1992.
148. Interview with Jan Mládek, August 1992.
149. Interview with Pavel Vorlíček, August 1992.
150. Decree #393-1991 of the Czech Ministry of Finance, On the Prices of Buildings, Land, Forested Land and Compensation for Temporary and Permanent Personal User Rights of Land, Extract appended.
151. Kirke Agentura, p. 2. It should be noted that there is no capital gains tax.
152. RECOM. Prague maps were being prepared in 1993, using methods outlined in Kokoška.
153. Interview with Pavel Vorlíček, August 1992.
154. Interview with Vaclav Zajíček May 1993.
155. Interviews with Jiří Kokoška and Pavel Dvorský, May 1993.
156. Law #393-1991 as amended by Decree #110-1992.
157. Interview with Antonin Götz, August 1993.
158. Decree #393-1991 as amended by Decree #110-1992.

159. Telgarsky et al.
160. Sýkora and Šimoničková.
161. While planning and controls are not in great favor, there is some readiness to respond to assistance from abroad. Several small towns have received help from the New York–based Project for Public Spaces, through the Czech Center for Public Communities. And, as noted earlier, Charter 77 has supported planning initiatives in metropolitan areas.

## 4. POLAND:
### Land and Housing in Transition

1. Data sources used in this chapter: publications of Poland's Main Statistical Office (GUS or *Główny Urząd Statystyczny*), unless otherwise specified; sources of legal acts: *Dziennik Ustaw Rzeczypospolitej Polskiej,* unless otherwise specified. The following abbreviations of currencies are used: $ = US dollars; ZL = Polish zlotys, until December 31, 1994; NZL = new Polish Zlotys, after December 31, 1994 (NZL 1 = ZL 10,000).
2. *The New York Times,* September 30, 1994, reporting on a survey by Gallup Hungary, Ltd. in the Czech Republic, Hungary, and Poland.
3. In August 1995, the corresponding numbers were 25 percent expected improvement and 14 percent expected deterioration *(Nowy Dziennik,* August 28, 1995).
4. In August 1995, 17 percent expected improvement, 21 percent expected deterioration (Ibid).
5. Attitudes in Hungary paralleled those in Poland, while more people in the Czech Republic saw themselves as better off than five years ago and a majority were optimistic about their own and their country's economic future. A majority in the Czech Republic also valued individual freedom over equality. *The New York Times,* September 30, 1994.
6. Personal communication. This statement was also quoted by mass media.
7. *Nowy Dziennik,* June 21, 1994, reporting on a poll by *Gazeta Wyborcza.*
8. There are also 12 million people of Polish ethnicity living outside Poland. The largest concentrations are 5.6 million in the United States, 1.5 million in Germany, and 1 million in France.
9. Warsaw Master Plans.
10. Rural houses are equipped with fewer sanitary facilities and household conveniences, but the difference between urban and rural is diminishing. Rural dwellings are, on average, larger by 150 square feet (15 square meters) than urban dwellings.
11. Fifty-five percent of Poles are "practicing regularly," 30 percent go to church irregularly, and 12 percent are believers who do not practice. *Donosy,* 1994.
12. Weigel, p. 40.
13. In contrast, in Hungary, where the banking system is stronger, those in need of loans could obtain them through the banks. In order to become eligible, they must register, pay taxes, and so on.
14. Residents of the neighboring countries are coming by the millions to buy, in some cases also to sell or to barter commodities and hard currency. Poles make similar shopping and business trips abroad, although less frequently than their neigh-

bors. The price and wage differentials are high. Wages in Germany are eight to twelve times higher than in Poland. Wages in Poland have been slightly lower than in Hungary, slightly higher than in the Czech Republic and Slovakia, and substantially higher (two to fifty times) than those in the Commonwealth of Independent States. Polish prices were in general lower than those in Germany and in the Czech Republic and higher than the prices in the former Soviet Union. The price structures are significantly different. Many Poles work illegally in Germany. At the same time, many inhabitants of the former Soviet Union seek illegal employment in Poland, most frequently in agriculture, which is already overstaffed, and construction.

15. Kornai, p. 72.
16. This increase was partially due to a change in the system of national accounts. The United Nations' NIPA system (national income and product accounts) replaced the old Communist national income accounting. Among other things, the activities of cooperatives were shifted from the socialized (public sector) to the private sector.
17. Among those employed in the private sector, 8.2 percent worked in cooperatives; only 2.3 percent worked in the firms owned by foreigners.
18. By the end of 1993, only 2.3 percent of shops were not privately owned. *Nowy Dziennik,* August 16, 1994.
19. The total value of its operations in 1993 was thirty-four times larger than in 1992 and amounted to $5 billion. In 1993 there were 152 sessions during which 107 million shares were traded. In February 1994 the value of the Warsaw stock exchange index, WIG—the Polish equivalent of the Dow Jones—"crossed the 18,000 mark, shattering all 12-month inflation-adjusted growth records for stock market rallies anywhere in the world in this century" *(PlanEcon Report,* February 14, 1994). Yet in the spring of 1994 this index declined by half and, during summer 1994, it remained at around 10,000. Throughout 1995 it stabilized around the 8,000 level.
20. *The Economist,* August 27, 1994.
21. Kornai, pp.140-145.
22. Pinto and van Wijnbergen.
23. Mieszczankowski, pp. 339-340.
24. At one extreme, there were what amounted to latifundia, as, for example, the Davidgródek estate of Prince Radziwiłł of 383,000 acres (155,000 hectares); at the other extreme, there were small "semiproletarian" plots whose owners had to supplement their income as hired workers or casual laborers. Landau and Tomaszewski, p. 39.
25. The 27 percent of the Polish labor force officially listed as engaged in agriculture contrasts with 18 percent in Bulgaria and 6.4 percent in the Czech Republic.
26. As of summer 1994 in former East Prussia (northeastern Poland), there already were more than a dozen farms each with an area of 5,000 acres (2,000 hectares) or more. *Donosy,* September 14, 1994.
27. Landau and Tomaszewski, p. 42.
28. Ibid, pp. 143-180.
29. During the Nazi occupation, the German Reich treated Poland as a supplier of slave labor and cheap food. The western part of the country was absorbed directly into

NOTES

Germany. All land and all Jewish property (few Jews owned land) in this territory was confiscated without compensation and the owners displaced, often to concentration camps. On the Polish territory that was not directly incorporated into the Reich, the scale of expropriations was smaller and more gradual. However, as of 1942, about three-fifths of all arable land in this part of Poland had been taken over by the Germans. The expropriation of Polish farmers proceeded gradually. Its progress depended on the number of German colonists arriving from the Reich. The Germans were given the best farms, situated on the most fertile soils. All landowners who remained on their property were supervised by appointed district farm "advisors." The whole distribution of food was controlled by the Germans. Under tie-in transactions, authorities compelled the farmers to sell agricultural products to the authorities at official prices (many times lower than black market prices) and in return sold to the farmers, also at low official prices, such products as vodka, kerosene, and textiles. Landau and Tomaszewski, pp. 143-180.

30. This created various situations that could be used as textbook illustrations to well-known arguments used by von Mises and Hayek for the inefficiency or economic infeasibility of socialism because of the impossibility of economic calculations (Bornstein). For example, a profit-maximizing, or loss-minimizing, private farmer in Poland would deliver grain to a state procurement agency, next would purchase a large quantity of bread at low subsidized prices, and then would use this bread to feed his pigs.

31. For a long time, farmers were allowed to sell their produce only within the *voivodship* where they lived. When in the Warsaw *voivodship* there was a so-called crop disaster (too much produce), and there was much more fruit than could be consumed and processed locally, the farmers were not permitted to sell their produce in other *voivodships*. While fruits were expensive and in short supply, say, in the Gdańsk *voivodship*, they were spoiling by the ton in the Warsaw region. The only possibility was illegal shipment from one *voivodship* to another. Another example was the requirement that produce be sold at the farmers' market only by its producer, in order to remove a middleman's profit and speculation. Thus, during the harvest of, say, strawberries, the farmer, instead of working in the field, had to turn into a merchant. It was not possible to seize on the advantages of specialization and division of labor.

32. Thus, for agriculture, the ratio of the share of GDP to the share of total labor was 0.60 in 1938, 0.46 in 1989, and 0.27 in 1993. This means that, in 1993, labor productivity in agriculture was one-fourth the average labor productivity and one-fifth the productivity in the non-farm sectors.

33. Between 1985 and 1991 the prices of agricultural inputs increased 105 times while the prices of agricultural products increased 46 times. If the price scissors (the ratio of agricultural input prices to agricultural output prices) for 1985 are set to 1, they become 0.84 in 1989, 1.69 in 1990, and 2.24 in 1991. During the next two years, they remained in the neighborhood of 2: 1.95 in 1992, and 2.03 in 1993. As a result of all these price adjustments, the price ratio between nonfood consumption goods and food returned to the level of the early 1980s. Before 1980, food was even cheaper.

34. As a result of this decline the reformers lost support of the countryside. This had a strong effect on the outcome of the September 1993 elections (during which the

"post-Communist" parties won) and the December 1995 elections (as a result of which a former Communist became Poland's President).

35. In 1992 the profitability ratio of public sector agriculture was minus 9.4. All other industries in the public sector had a positive profitability ratio that year.

36. The labor absorption capacity is significantly differentiated by location. It is highest in the central and southeastern areas and lowest in northern and western Poland, where large state farms dominate. Therefore, the pains of unemployment are greater in the latter territory.

37. The negligence was such that, for example, the Polish Communist Party did not fulfill the formalities necessary to legalize the ownership of many of its buildings. As a result, after 1989 the new authorities legally evicted the party from these buildings.

38. In a socialist country no person can live off of interest or rent.

39. Gomułka was famous for his dislike of babies and horses. The former made food and housing shortages more painful and disturbed Gomułka's plans of socialist development. The latter ate scarce grain and hampered fast technological progress in agriculture.

40. At the same time, a standard family house in the United States would have cost about $80,000, or an equivalent of roughly forty monthly salaries, and, in most cases, families were eligible for mortgage loans, so the initial cash cost was no larger than eight to twelve monthly salaries.

41. Mayo and Stein. This hypothesis was confirmed by Pogodzinski (1992b) who studied the Polish housing market and furnished evidence for the spillovers from that market into the labor market. He found the relationship between housing queue and labor supply statistically significant and negative.

42. Gorczyca (1993), p. 172.

43. "Own," of course, in the sense of using it rather than being a legal owner.

44. *Polityka,* December 23, 1995. The average size of an apartment built in Warsaw in spring 1994 was 1,000 square feet (100 square meters). *Gazeta Wyborcza,* July 1994.

45. Unfinished houses can be bought at bargain prices, then finished to Western standards and rented. Rent over a few years will recoup the investment since a strong rental market is predicted. An official estimate of the total housing investment needed (expected?) in Poland during the present decade amounts to about $60 billion, or two-thirds of the current Polish GDP (Poland, International).

46. Also, 329,000 persons were registered as waiting for apartments from state enterprises and 160,000 were waiting for municipal apartments.

47. *Home&Market,* December 1993-January 1994.

48. *Estate News,* May 1993.

49. *Home&Market,* December 1993-January 1994.

50. *Życie Warszawy,* July 4, 1994; *Donosy,* August 22, 1994.

51. In 1996 this fund will receive a state subsidy of $19 million (NZL 50 million). *Polityka,* December 23, 1995.

52. *Prawo Lokalowe,* pp. 45-47.

53. *Życie Warszawy,* June 29, 1994.

54. Kornai, pp.55-57.

55. While Venezuela has a similar GNP per capita to Poland's, most of its urban housing stock consists of primitive structures erected in the slums.

56. At the end of 1993 the official unemployment rate in the *voivodships* of Warsaw, Cracow, and Poznań was between 7 and 9 percent. The "true" unemployment rate in these *voivodships* is believed to be much lower. At the same time, the official unemployment rate for several northern voivodships, such as Koszalin, Słupsk, and Olsztyn, was about 30 percent.

57. In Poland, the term "reprivatization" is used. We have chosen, for consistency, to use "restitution," since that is the term in more common use elsewhere.

58. The existing law does not effectively prevent the sale of property for which there may be claims from former owners. Investors are afraid to buy before this is clarified. "Every foreign investor . . . has to be sure that no one is going to take his land away from him in a year or two," said Mirosław Szypowski, president of the PUREO, or the Polish Union of Real Estate Owners *(Polska Unia Właścicieli Nieruchomości). The Christian Science Monitor,* July 26, 1995.

59. *The New York Times,* July 20, 1994; *Polityka,* July 16, 1994.

60. Paradoxically, some ownership titles and related documents were destroyed by their very owners who, for example during the Stalinist terror, decided to liquidate proofs of any property that could qualify them in the category of peoples' enemies.

61. Some claims of the Polish church go back to 1772, when a northern region of Warmia (the so-called Royal Prussia) was annexed by Prussia and, as a result, the church lost most of its property. Warmia was returned to Poland after World War II.

62. Among other things, it covered land, buildings, and assets of companies that before World War I belonged to Russian owners, including the property of the Russian Orthodox Church. Some of it was nationalized in 1939; the remainder was formally taken over by Poland's Communist authorities based on a February 1958 law.

63. *East European Constitutional Review,* Summer 1995.

64. In absolute terms, the Soviet Union had even higher losses in population and wealth, but a large portion was not directly related to the war with Germany. Forced deportations and forced labor camps accounted for millions of human lives. The postwar changes of Soviet borders resulted in a gain in both people and territory.

65. By contrast, the expropriations in many other East European countries (such as the Baltic States, Ukraine, Slovakia, Hungary, Bulgaria, Croatia, Albania, and others) were implemented not only for the sake of "social justice" but also as punishment for the collaboration with native fascist regimes.

66. Obviously there are similar problems with non-Jewish property.

67. A May 1994 poll concerning restitution yielded the following opinions: Sixty-eight percent were for restitution; of these, 45 percent favored restitution in kind, 25 percent favored vouchers, 20 percent favored money compensation. Twenty-two percent were against restitution. Those who tend to favor restitution include the intelligentsia, private entrepreneurs, public administrators, urbanites, and the well off *(Życie Warszawy,* June 29, 1994). In May 1995, the number of supporters of restitution decreased to 59 percent.

68. A law of March 1950 made this land a national (state) property.

69. Drozd and Truszkiewicz.

70. In February 1993 in New York, an agreement was signed between eight Jewish organizations and Avrahan Shohat, minister of finance of Israel. According to this document, the Jewish state (Israel) is a natural heir of the rights to the communal Jewish property, and if there is no individual heir, also of the Jewish private and personal property. *Nowy Dziennik,* February 13, 1993.

71. Jermakowicz, p.11.

72. As mentioned earlier, a new law specifies that tenants may remain until 2005, paying rents set by the *gminas.*

73. Pawlak, pp. 68-76.

74. Landau and Tomaszewski, p. 188

75. In addition to the September 1944 law, the expropriations of land were regulated by a large number of other legal acts that clarified and extended the scope of nationalization, including a December 1944 decree that nationalized all privately owned forested land larger than 25 hectares and a January 1945 decree that extended the expropriations to nonfarm pieces of land. The decrees of November 1945, September 1946, and September 1947 took care of the real estate left behind by persons deported to the Soviet Union and all farms not used by their owners. A July 1947 law expropriated the Evangelical Church. An October 1948 decree nationalized real estate and assets belonging to all banks, except co-op banks. A March 1950 law (on "dead hand" goods) took over most of the farmland owned by the Catholic church. A May 1962 law nationalized all surface waters. Antosiewicz (1993).

76. Kostrowicki, p. 16.

77. In addition, about 900,000 farms were reallotted by assembling a (sometimes very large) number of small plots of land so that each owner obtained acreage similar in character and size to that which he had had before but in one or more larger units.

78. Landau and Tomaszewski, who openly sympathized with this reform, stated: "As a result of land reform, former large land owners ceased to exist as a social group. Some chose other professions, or lived on private savings. Others could barely make a living" (p. 189).

79. Kostrowicki, p.17.

80. Perhaps the major harm from the "agricultural reconstruction" program was psychological. As a result of both the Nazi and Soviet occupations, as well as the post-1944 policies, peasants lost their faith in secure individual ownership and understandably decreased their investments and work effort while focusing on the most important task: how to outsmart the authorities.

81. An amendment affirming the superiority of state farming was formally added to the Polish constitution.

82. Similar dilemmas are faced by other Central and Eastern European countries. The Czechs fear former Sudeten Germans. The Slovenes are afraid of Italians who may wish to buy back their former property in Istrian peninsula (confiscated after the war). Lithuanians, Belarussians, and Ukrainians fear the former Polish owners of land estates.

83. In Stalinist Poland, in many cases, it was dangerous even to file a claim.

84. These agreements were reached with Austria, Belgium, Britain, Canada, Denmark, France, Greece, Ireland, The Netherlands, Norway, Sweden, Switzerland, and the United States.

85. In particular, those who served in the Polish military forces in the West (participated in the military operations of British, American, and other Western Allies) and returned to Poland without the assistance of this office.

86. People were required by this office to provide information about their property, membership in political parties, and other personal information, which later could be used against them. For example, the former real estate owners would be accused of being class enemies.

87. See note 84.

88. *Home&Market,* February 1993. Many East European countries are not honoring claims of noncitizens; a Polish Nobel Prize winner in literature, Czesław Miłosz, who lives in the United States, is seeking return of his Lithuanian estates, arguing that he holds honorary citizenship in Lithuania. *Nowy Dziennik,* June 23, 1994.

89. Jermakowicz, p. 11.

90. *Nowy Dziennik,* September 26, 1994.

91. *Nowy Dziennik,* April 22, 1994.

92. The World Jewish Congress seeks to recover Jewish communal property, such as synagogues, schools, and hospitals, as a way of re-creating Jewish communities. The Czech Republic has passed appropriate legislation, as has Slovakia, which will restitute Jewish property taken after 1938. *The New York Times,* October 23, 1994.

93. The number of claims filed by other churches has been much smaller. The largest number of claims filed, 150, came from Orthodox churches.

94. *Polityka,* July 16, 1994; *Donosy,* March 8, 1996.

95. According to Mirosław Szypowski (*Home&Market,* February 1993), the complete documentation concerning this possession was "borrowed" (checked out) from a record office of Mokotow (a district of Warsaw) in 1985 and never returned.

96. *Nowy Dziennik,* January 24, 1994.

97. For good reason. At that time, in Communist Poland, the ownership title did not bear much practical importance.

98. *Nowy Dziennik,* November 29, 1993.

99. *Nowy Dziennik,* August 1, 1993; *Home&Market,* November 1993.

100. *Nowy Dziennik,* February 2, 1994.

101. "Cutting the trees was like a revolution. The strongest were cutting the most. . . . Police did not intervene." *Gazeta Wyborcza,* March 1994.

102. First of them was submitted on May 17, 1990.

103. *Nowy Dziennik,* December 1, 1992.

104. All the amounts in zlotys are translated into their dollar equivalents at a rate of ZL 20,000 to $1.

105. This proposal follows the Hungarian variant. In Hungary, the restitution was confined to reprivatization vouchers that could be used to buy apartments or shares in privatized enterprises. The Hungarian system was highly regressive. For property valued at $20,000 (200,000 forints), the owner was to receive a full equivalent in vouchers. For higher-valued properties, the compensation was only a fraction of the estimated value. Only former owners were eligible; their heirs were excluded.

106. According to Tadeusz Koss, the spokesman for PUREO: "This draft brings shame to the Polish Republic. It supports the expropriations that were done 50 years ago which violated the rights of owners. The only hope is that the President [Wałęsa]

will never agree to sign it. The draft is being translated in other languages and the whole world will learn about the law violations in Poland. For example, the violation of the European Convention on the Fundamental Rights and Freedoms of People (which will damage the image of Poland abroad; among other things, it will negatively affect foreign investment.") Andrzej Karnkowski, president of the Committee for the Defense of Private Property *(Komitet Obrony Prywatnej Własności)* said: "This bill accepts the extermination of certain social groups because it deprives them forever from the possibility of recovering their property." *Nowy Dziennik,* May 17, 1994.

107. Hence, a question becomes: If this restitution law would treat only some of the past law violations, why is it needed at the first place?

108. *Nowy Dziennik,* March 13, 1993.

109. As Jermakowicz (1992) observes, restitution could " . . . give rise to a feeling of injustice among those who receive low real wages working in an inefficient economy which could result in severe social conflicts especially among the working classes." p. 12.

110. Total number of claims is expected to reach 500,000; cost of compensation, $18.5 billion; if other legal bases for claims are recognized, such as bonds issued by prewar Poland, and the currencies used in Poland during World War II, the cost could rise to $40 billion *(Nowy Dziennik,* September 26, 1993).

111. See the story of Jastarnia in this chapter (subsection on municipalization).

112. According to Mirosław Szypowski, those who before 1989 purchased dwellings bona fide without knowledge of their true owners should not lose their property rights. Yet those who purchased the dwellings after 1989, even despite the fact that the "true" owners made appropriate claims before the transaction was made, should be expropriated. Szypowski maintains that the local administration is still selling someone else's property. This has been the case of the parcels in Warsaw on which Hotel Marriott, Hotel Sobieski, and many other large buildings were built recently *(Home&Market,* February 1993).

113. The World Bank and the PHARE fund have promised to help to cover this cost *(Polityka,* May 1994).

114. The Ministry of Ownership Transformations applied to the World Bank for a special loan to help the former owners get started with their recovered property. Also there is an agreement between the PUREO and the AMERBANK to start mortgage loans for owners who recover their real estate and need money for renovation and reconstruction work. *Home&Market,* February 1993.

115. Kornai, pp.228-301.

116. In the spring of 1994, these two parties merged, adopting the name "the Freedom Union."

117. *The Economist,* September 17, 1994.

118. This is a major criticism of the Czech and Russian mass privatization schemes. In the Czech Republic a large proportion of shares of privatized enterprises are owned by investment funds that in turn are owned by banks, which are owned (at least partly) by the state. In some cases, there occurred a "cross ownership"— an investment fund would purchase shares of the bank that owns the fund.

119. Privatization in Hungary also has been relatively decentralized, while that in Russia and the Czech Republic has been highly centralized.

120. *Prawno-Ekonomiczne,* Vol. 3. (Year unknown).

121. Often referred to as "commercialization."

122. Gray, 1992a, pp. 96 and 97.

123. Firmy Joint Ventures, p. 7.

124. In Communist Poland, there existed a peculiar, nonprofit organization—the "United Economic Ensembles, PAX." The mission of PAX was far from clear. Unclear also was its status. This organization, for some reason, was tolerated and perhaps even sponsored by the Communist authorities. It proclaimed itself as an organization of "progressive Catholics" who wished to cooperate with the Communist regime. Its relationship with the church was mixed: partly antagonistic, partly cooperative. PAX owned real estate, factories, stores, and publishing and printing houses.

125. In 1992, foundations ran 283 businesses.

126. Kornai, pp.140-145.

127. As of July 1995, 413 companies participated in the program; 79 percent of them were industrial firms, 16 percent were construction firms.

128. In the Czech Republic the comparable numbers are $30, or 15 percent of the monthly wage.

129. Milewski.

130. Kodeks.

131. The Management of State-owned Agricultural Real-estate Act of October 19, 1991, #107, Art. 6.

132. Ibid, Art. 25.

133. Claude Blanchi, "Eastern European Report," (New York: International Thompson, January 28, 1992).

134. *Rzeczpospolita,* April 4 and 6, 1993.

135. *The Financial Times,* June 17, 1993; *Nowy Dziennik,* September 21, 1993.

136. *The Warsaw Voice,* September 13 and 20, 1992; interview with Witold Śnieć. In 1992, the average price was $0.003 per square foot (ZL 500 per square meter). *Rzeczpospolita,* April 4, 1993.

137. For example, a German family, the Otto von Bismarcks, filed an application with the Polish Ministry of Internal Affairs to purchase a state farm in the Szczecin *voivodship.* The family declared that it intended to set up a center for technical progress in agriculture. The permit was denied on the ground that the land was classified as a "territory of special importance."

138. Arts. 42-47.

139. Herbst and Muzioł-Węcławowicz, 1993.

140. *Polityka,* April 4, 1995.

141. The whole procedure was helped by the fact that this region belonged to Poland before the war.

142. Poland, International.

143. Hopfer, p. 28.

144. Hopfer, pp. 27 & 28.

145. Dowald and Mikelsons, January 1993.

146. *Zycie Warszawy,* July 8, 1994.

147. *Zycie Warszawy,* June 30, 1993 and *Polityka,* December 9, 1995.

148. Poland, International, 1992, p. 195.

149. By increasing its housing stock by 6 million units, in 1992 Poland would have had 17.44 million units, attaining a level of 2.2 persons per dwelling which would be equal to the one for Sweden, Switzerland, Germany, and France. The GDP per capita in these countries was several times higher than that in Poland.

150. In fact, as we present below, this type of system has been introduced in Poland, but under even more rigid conditions. Obviously, it could accommodate only a small number of families.

151. *Nowy Dziennik,* January 5, 1993.

152. *Home&Market,* March 1993.

153. According to Lech Drągowski, the owner of a large Warsaw real estate agency, the prices of apartments in Warsaw were "low," except for some extreme cases— about $300 to $400 per square meter. Houses sold slowly; apartments sold fast.

154. Around 1990, there were about 800 to 900 phones per 1,000 persons in Switzerland, Sweden, the United States, and Canada; about 700 in France and Germany; 400 to 500 in Spain and Greece; 293 in Bulgaria; 264 in Czechoslovakia; 167 in Hungary; 137 in Poland; and 125 in the Soviet Union.

155. While Poles would pay the rent in zlotys, hard currency, or both, transactions with foreigners almost always would be expressed in U.S. dollars or German marks.

156. *Business Eastern Europe,* January 24, 1994. The rent range for similar apartments affordable primarily by foreigners was $900 to $1,300 in Sofia and $1,500 to $2,500 in Prague.

157. *Home&Market,* June 1993.

158. *Życie Warszawy,* August 18, 1993.

159. Interview with Witold Śnieć.

160. Warsaw's climatic conditions are dominated by western winds. This may partially explain why the west bank was historically the more developed and more expensive part of the city.

161. If a piece of real estate was advertised more than once, the multiple ads were excluded from the sample.

162. A qualification is necessary. The data used in the project have a number of drawbacks. First, the years 1991 and 1992 are not fully compatible and some seasonal bias may be present—they cover an eleven-month period for 1991 (January-November) and a nine-month period for 1992 (April-December). Second, not all the real estate transactions are covered by the advertisements included in the sample and few of these advertisements led to transactions. They do not represent data on actual transactions but only reflect intentions. For example, in 1992, when the market was unusually slow, only one-sixth of advertisements turned into successful transactions. According to Kałkowski, the number of ads amounted to 2 percent of total apartment stock, while the number of transactions amounted to 0.3 percent. It is estimated that the total offer of all real estate in 1992 in Cracow amounted to about $120 million, which is the total value of all new cars purchased by Cracow residents in the same year (16,000 passenger cars).

163. *Rzeczpospolita,* June 28, 1993.

164. At the turn of the nineteenth century and the beginning of the twentieth century this region had a large, poor peasant population in overcrowded rural areas, many of whom emigrated, most often to the United States. In many parts of these *voivodships* almost every family has relatives overseas.

165. *Poland, International* (1992).
166. For comparability, the 1994 figures are expressed in NZL.
167. *Polityka,* January 6, 1996.
168. *Życie Warszawy,* September 14, 1994.
169. *Nowy Dziennik,* February 8, 1996.
170. *Życie Warszawy,* September 14, 1994.
171. *Rzeczpospolita,* April 6, 1993.
172. One could possess two or more housing savings books, but each book could be registered with only one cooperative, and the eligibility of each person (each married couple) was limited to one apartment.
173. Often parents started a housing savings book for a newborn in order to collect enough money that, enlarged by the state contributions, would enable their son or daughter to become a co-op member upon turning eighteen. In this way many "boomers" could move into their own apartment on the day of their marriage.
174. The prices of co-op apartments were not significantly different from the prices of private real estate.
175. Warsaw and many other large cities introduced special regulations barring migrants from moving in. In order to become eligible for such a residence permit, a complex and often lengthy procedure was necessary. Usually the applicant had to be sponsored by a current or prospective employer. This system was essentially similar to that practiced by the United States and other rich countries in processing applications for permanent residence and citizenship.
176. The overall consumer price index between 1970 and 1975 increased by 11 percent, between 1975 and 1980 by 37 percent, between 1980 and 1985 by 296 percent, and between 1985 and 1990 by 5,500 percent.
177. Very few people had any credit records; the trustworthiness of borrowers had yet to be established. It was impossible to decide how solid the income was of those few who made enough money to qualify for a loan.
178. *Życie Warszawy,* June 30, 1993.
179. The rate was a few points above the consumer price index of that time.
180. *Home&Market,* February 1994.
181. Interview with Edward P. Kozłowski.
182. *Home&Market,* December 1993-January 1994.
183. *Życie Warszawy,* June 30, 1993.
184. *Gazeta Bankowa,* February 19, 1993.
185. PHARE has contributed $5 million for work between 1993 and 1997. *Home&Market,* February 1994.
186. Gray (1992), p. 290; interview with Piotr Jaworski.
187. The laws of September 1947 and February 1955.
188. Relevant laws concerning land records during the Communist period were: the law of October 1946, the law of November 1964, transferring the records to the state notary's office, and the law of July 1982.
189. Law of July 1957.
190. The law of February 1991 terminated the state notary system. Notaries must be at least twenty-six years of age, have a spotless reputation, hold a law degree, and pass an examination.
191. Before privatization, notaries earned an average of $400 per month; today they earn between $2,000 and $3,000 per month. *Życie Warszawy,* August 25, 1994.

192. Regulation of October 1989.

193. *Księgi wieczyste,* or land records, are maintained at *Sądy Rejonowe,* or local courts.

194. The cadaster includes type of ownership—for example, individual, corporate—land use, soil quality, location, number of plots, area, and plot geometry.

195. *Życie Warszawy,* June 14, 1994.

196. Hopfer et al., 1994.

197. Law of November 1984.

198. For the first six months of a tax year, it is the price of 125 kilograms of rye during the last quarter of the prior year, while for the second six months, it is the price of 125 kilograms of rye during the second quarter of the current tax year.

199. Brzeziński, pp. 131-135.

200. "Eastern Europe, Poland, Tax Information," Release #426, Matthew Bender & Co., Inc., June 1994, p. 48.

201. Brzeziński, pp. 135-136; the forest tax is regulated by the law of September 1991.

202. Ibid., pp. 149-151.

203. Ibid., pp. 141-142; law of January 1991.

204. "Eastern Europe, Poland, Tax Information," Release #426, Matthew Bender & Co., Inc., June 1994, p. 48.

205. Gray, 1992a, p. 98.

206. Warsaw Master Plans, p. 9.

# BIBLIOGRAPHY

Antosiewicz, Janina. *Reprywatyzacja* [Restitution]. Warszawa: Wydawnictwo Prawnicze, 1993.

Appel, Hilary. "Justice and the Reformulation of Property Rights." *Eastern European Politics and Societies,* 9:1 (winter 1995), pp. 22-40.

Banasiński, C., and P. Czechowski (eds.). *Komentarz do Ustawy o Gospodarowaniu Nieruchomościami Rolnymi Skarbu Państwa Oraz o Zmianie Niektórych Ustaw Wraz z Tekstami Przepisów Wykonawczych i Wzorów Umów* [Commentary to Law on Management of Rural Real Estate Owned by the State Treasury and on the Change of Certain Laws; with the Texts of Executive Instructions and Forms of the Agreements]. Warsaw: International Foundation for Capital Market Development and Ownership Changes in Poland—Centre for Privatization, 1992.

Berend, Ivan, and Gyorgy Ranki. *Economic Development in East-Central Europe in the 19th and 20th Centuries.* New York: Columbia University Press, 1974.

Bertaud, Alain, and Bertrand Renaud. "Cities Without Land Markets." *World Bank Discussion Papers 227.* Washington, D.C.: World Bank, 1994.

Beskid, L. (ed.). *Warunki Zycia i Kondycja Polaków na Początku Zmian Systemowych* [Living Conditions of Poles at the Beginning of Systemic Changes]. Warsaw: Polska Akademia Nauk, Instytut Filozofii i Socjologii, 1992.

Blanchi, Claude. *Eastern European Report.* New York: International Thompson Publishing Corporation, January 28, 1992.

Bornstein, Morris (ed.). *Comparative Economic Systems: Models and Cases.* Boston: Irwin, 1988.

Brzeski, Władysław. Materials of the Cracow Real Estate Institute, 1994.

Brzeziński, Bogumiż. *Prawo Podatkowe* [Tax Law]. Toruń: TNOK Dom Organizatora, 1993.

Buckley, R., P. H. Hendershot, and K. E. Villani. "Rapid Housing Privatization in Reforming Economies; Pay the Special Dividend Now." Ms., 1993.

Bulgaria. National Statistical Institute. *Bulgaria and the World in Figures.* Sofia: National Statistical Institute, 1993.

Bulgaria. National Statistical Institute. "Oblastite i Obshtinite v Republicka Bulgaria" ["Departments and Communes in the Bulgarian Republic"]. Sofia: National Statistical Institute, 1992

*Bulgarian Business News.* "168 Hours BBN," issues from May 3, 1993 to December 30, 1993.

*Bulgarian Economic Review.* Fortnightly Edition of PARI Daily, various issues.

Bulgarian National Bank. "Report January-June 1993." Sofia, 1993.

Bulir, A. "Regional Aspects of Small Scale Privatization." *Privatization Newsletter of Czechoslovakia* 9 (1992).

Caine, Anthony. "Report to Charter 77" [Prague], 1993.

Carter, Frank W. "Bulgaria." In A. H. Dawson (ed.), *Planning in Eastern Europe*. New York: St. Martin's, 1987, pp. 67-101.

Carter, Frank W. "Prague and Sofia: An Analysis of Their Changing Internal Structure." in R. A. French and F. E. I. Hamilton, (eds.). *The Socialist City, Spatial Structure and Urban Policy*. Chichester, UK: Wiley, 1979, pp. 425-459.

Češka, Roman. "Privatization in the Czech Republic." In Andreja Bohm and Marko Simoneti (eds.). *Privatization in Central and Eastern Europe*. Ljublijana: Central and Eastern European Privatization Network, 1993, pp. 84-103.

Ciamaga, L. (ed.). *Polskie Przemiany Transformacja Rynkowa* [Polish Changes, Market Transformation]. Warsaw: Wydawnictwo Naukowe PWN, 1992.

Cochrane, Nancy J. "Farm Restructuring in Central and Eastern Europe." *The Soviet and Post-Soviet Review* 21:2-3 (1994), pp. 219-335.

Comiso, E. "Property Rights, Liberalism, and the Transition from 'Actually Existing' Socialism." *East European Politics and Societies* 5:1, 1991.

Crampton, R. J. *A Short History of Modern Bulgaria*. Cambridge, UK: Cambridge University, 1987.

Czech Republic. Ministry of Agriculture. *Basic Principles of the Agricultural Policy of the Government of the Czech Republic up to 1995 and for a Further Period*. Prague: Czech Republic. Ministry of Agriculture, 1994.

Czech Republic. Statistical Office. *Ročenka Česke Republiky* [Yearbook of the Czech Republic]. Prague: Statistical Office, 1993.

Czech Republic. Statistical Office. *Czech Republic in Figures 1995*. Prague: Statistical Office, 1995.

Czechoslovakia. Ředitelství Pošt a Telegrafú Praze [Directorate of Posts and Telegraphs in Prague], *Seznam Telefonnich Ustředen . . . Sitě Pražske* [Directory of Telephone Subscribers . . . Prague Network]. Prague: Statní Tiskarna, 1938.

Dawson, A. H. (ed.). *Planning in Eastern Europe*. New York: St. Martin's, 1987.

Deliev, Ivan, et al.. "Development of the Credit and Financial Systems in the Housing Sector in the Republic of Bulgaria." National Centre for Regional Development and Housing Policy, Habitat Housing Workshop. Sofia, Bulgaria, November 15-17, 1993.

Dhanji, F., and B. Milanovic. "Privatization in Eastern and Central Europe, Objectives, Constraints and Models of Divestiture." Policy, Research and External Affairs Working Papers. Washington, D.C.: World Bank, 1991.

Dikov, Peter. "The Land Reform in Bulgaria and Registration of Land Ownership." Seminar on Reform of Real Property. Copenhagen, Denmark, October 25-29, 1993.

Dostál, Petr, Michael Illner, Jan Kara and M. Barlow, eds. *Changing Territorial Administration in Czechoslovakia*. Amsterdam: Instituut voor Sociale Geografie Universiteit van Amsterdam, 1992.

Drozd, Edward, and Zygmunt Truszkiewicz. *Gospodarka Gruntami i Wywłaszczanie Nieruchomości-Komentarz*. [Agricultural Land Management and Expropriation of Real Estate], Poznań: Wydawnictwo Stowarzyszenia Notariuszy Rzeczpospolitej Polskiej, 1994.

Earle, J. S. et al. *Small Privatization: The Transformation of Retail Trade and Consumer Services in the Czech Republic, Hungary and Poland*. Prague: Central European University, 1994.

*Eastern Europe and the Commonwealth of Independent States 1994,* 2nd edition. London: Europa Publications Limited, 1994.

EAST Database, Social Science Data Center, University of Pennsylvania.

*Firmy Joint Ventures w Polsce* [Joint-Venture Firms in Poland]. Warsaw: Powszechna Agencja Informacyjna, 1992.

Frydman, Roman A. et al. *The Privatization Process in Central Europe.* Prague: Central European University Press, 1993.

Frydman, Roman A. et al. "Eastern European Experience with Small Scale Privatization." *CFS Discussion Paper Series,* 104. Washington, D.C.: World Bank, 1994.

Gniewek, Edward. *Obrót Nieruchomościami Państwowymi i Komunalnymi.* [State and Municipal Real Estate Transactions]. Kraków: Wydawnictwa Instytutu Prawa Spółek i Inwestycji Zagranicznych, 1994.

Gorczyca, Mirosław. *Przewidywane zmiany sytuacji mieszkaniowej w Polsce do 2010 roku.* [Forecasted Changes in Housing in Poland till the Year 2010], Warszawa: Główny Urząd Statystyczny, Zakład Badań Statystyczno-Ekonomicznych, 1993.

Gorczyca, Mirosław. *Przedsięwzięcia Warunkujące Rozwiązanie Problemu Mieszkaniowego w Polsce.*[Undertakings Necessary for the Solution of Housing Problems in Poland], Warszawa: Główny Urząd Statystyczny, Zakład Badań Statystyczno-Ekonomicznych, 1994.

Gradev, Todor, and Spartak Keremeidchev. "Designing the Reform Scenario: Privatization, Restitution and Perceptions of Equity in Bulgaria," paper presented at the Association of Collegiate Schools of Planning, Philadelphia, PA, October 28, 1993.

Gradev, Todor, and Spartak Keremeidchev, eds., "Privatization in Bulgaria, Analysis and Forecasts" [in Bulgarian]. Sofia: Center for the Study of Democracy, 1993.

Gray, Cheryl W. "Evolving Legal Frameworks for Private Sector Development in Central and Eastern Europe." *World Bank Discussion Papers,* 209. Washington, D.C.: World Bank, 1993.

Gray, Cheryl W. "The Legal Framework for Private Sector Activity in the Czech and Slovak Federal Republics." *WPS 1051.* Washington, D.C.: World Bank, 1992a.

Gray, Cheryl W. et al. "The Legal Framework for Private Sector Development in a Transitional Economy: The Case of Poland." *Georgia Journal of International and Comparative Law,* 22:2, 1992b.

Gray, Cheryl W., and Peter Ianachkov. "Bulgaria's Evolving Legal Framework for Private Sector Development." *WPS 906.* Country Economics Department and Legal Department. Washington, D.C.: World Bank, 1992.

Grime, Keith, and Vic Duke. "A Czech on Privatization." *Regional Studies,* 27:8, 1993, pp. 751-757..

Grozdeva, A. "Privatization Technology in Bulgaria." *Economic Thought,* Institute of Economics, Bulgarian Academy of Sciences, Sofia, 1993, pp. 80-91.

Gutkind, E. A. *Urban Development in Eastern Europe: Bulgaria, Romania, and the U.S.S.R.* Ed. Gabriele Gutkind. with contribution on Bulgaria from Peter Tashev, vol. 8 [International History of City Development]. New York: The Free Press, 1972.

Hanoušek, Jan. "Privatization in the Czech Republic: Winners and Losers."

Ms., University of Pennsylvania, Department of Economics, Philadelphia, January 1995.

Hanoušek, Jan, and Eugene A. Kroch. "Large Scale Privatization in the Czech Republic: A Model of Learning in Sequential Bidding." Ms., University of Pennsylvania, Department of Economics, Philadelphia, December 1994.

Havel, J., and E. Kukla. "Privatization and Investment Funds in Czechoslovakia." *RFE/RL Research Report,* 1:17, 1992, pp. 37-41.

Havel, Václav. *Summer Meditations.* New York: Knopf, 1992.

Herbst, Irena, and Alina Muzioł-Węcławowicz. "Housing Problems and Reforms in Poland." Ms., 1993.

Hoffman, Michael L., and Maya T. Koleva. "Housing Policy Reform in Bulgaria." Sofia: MTK Consultants, 1993.

Hopfer, Andrzej. "Urban Land Development and Valuation System." In Vincent Renard and Rodrigo Acosta (eds.). *Land Tenure and Property Development in Eastern Europe.* Paris: Pirville-CNRS/ADEF, 1993, pp. 25-34.

Hopfer, Andrzej. et al. *Wycena Nieruchomości i Przedsiębiorstw* [Real Estate and Enterprises Evaluation]. Twigger SA, Warszawa, 1994.

Hrůza, Jiří. "Urban Concepts of Prague." *Sborník České Geografické Společnosti* [Journal of the Czech Geographical Society]. 97:2, 1992, pp. 75-87.

Hunter, Brian (ed.). *The Statesman's Year Book 1992-1993.* New York: St. Martin's, 1993.

Information Centre for Technology Transfer. "Privatization, Acts of the National Assembly, Ordinances of the Council of Ministers." Sofia: Information Centre for Technology Transfer, 1992.

Jackson, Marvin, and Diana Kopeva. "Land Markets in Transition Economies: The Case of Bulgaria's Radical Land Reform." Preliminary version, Paper presented to the Agricultural Economics Society, University of Exeter, April 9-11, 1994.

Jermakowicz, W. *Privatization in Poland: Aims and Methods.* Warsaw: International Foundation for Capital Market Development and Ownership Changes in Poland—Centre for Privatization, 1992.

Jędrzejewski, Stanisław. *Nowe Prawo Budowlane.* [New Construction Law]. Branta: Oficyna Wydawnicza.

Kałkowski, L. "Krakowski Rynek Nieruchomości [Cracow's Real Estate Market]." *Swiat Nieruchomości* [Real Estate World], 2, 1992/93.

Kennet, D., and M. Lieberman (eds.). *The Road to Capitalism: Economic Transformation in Eastern Europe.* Fort Worth, TX: Dryden, 1992.

Kidyba, A., and A. Wróbel. *Ustrój i Zadania Administracji Publicznej w Rzeczypospolitej Polskiej* [Systems and Tasks of Public Administration in the Polish Republic]. Warsaw: Friedrich Ebert Foundation Warsaw Office, 1993.

Kingsley T., P. Mayfield, and Roman Rewald. *Poland's Cooperative and State-Enterprise Housing: Options for Privatization.* Washington, D.C.: Urban Institute, 1992.

Kirke Agentura. "The Prague Property Market." Prague: Kirke Agentura, ND.

*Kodeks Cywilny* [Civil Code]. Warszawa: Wydawnictwo Prawnicze, 1991.

Kokoška, Jiří. *Oceňovaní Nemovitosti v Současne Praxi* [Valuation of Real Estate in Contemporary Practice]. Prague: Inforpres, 1993.

Kopeva, Diana, and Plamen Mishev. "Formation of Land Market in Bulgaria and Its Present and Likely Future Impact on Agricultural Activity." *Working Paper 1,* APAU Project D, PHARE Programme, Agricultural Policy Analysis Unit, Ministry of Agriculture. December 1993.

Kopeva, Diana, and Plamen Mishev. "Summary of Land Reform." *Working Paper 2,* APAU Project 92.3, PHARE Programme, Agricultural Policy Analysis Unit, Ministry of Agricultural Development. Sofia, February 1993.

Kopeva, Diana, Plamen Mishev, and Keith Howe. "Land Reform and Liquidation of Collective Farm Assets in Bulgarian Agriculture: Progress and Prospects." *Communist Economies and Economic Transformation,* 6:2, 1994.

Kornai, János. *The Socialist System.* Princeton, NJ: Princeton University, 1992.

Kostrowicki, Jerzy. (ed.). *Przemiany Structury Przestrzennej Rolnictwa Polski, 1950-1970* [Transformation of the Spatial Structure of Polish Agriculture, 1950-1970]. Prace Geograficzne [Geographic Studies] #127. Wrocław: Polska Akademia Nauk, Zakład Narodowy Imienia Ossolińskich, 1978.

Kotrba, Josef. "Privatization in the Czech Republic: An Overview." *Discussion Paper 18.* Prague: CERGE/EI (Centre for Economic Research and Graduate Education/Economic Institute), 1993.

Kovachev, Ivo. "How to Make Privatization Work and How to Make It Work for Good: Implications for and Specifics of Municipal Privatization." Paper presented at the Boyana Conference on Privatization and Economic Reform, Boyana, Bulgaria, June 3-4, 1993.

Landau, Z., and J. Tomaszewski. *The Polish Economy in the Twentieth Century.* New York: St. Martin's, 1985.

Lapping, Mark. "Land Reform in Independent Estonia in the 1920s: A Case Study in Agrarian Reform and the Creation of a Rural Land Market." Paper presented at the Association of Collegiate Schools of Planning. Philadelphia, PA, October 28, 1993.

Legis 168 Hours BBN, "Collection of Bulgarian Laws," 1, 1993.

Levinson, Alfred. "The Impact of Privatization on Settlement Patterns in Southwestern Bulgaria." Paper presented at the European Summer Institute in Regional Science. University of Joensuu, Finland, June 15, 1993.

Łaszek, Jacek. "Co Dalej z Kredytem Hipotecznym? [What's Next with Mortgage Loans?]" *Świat Nieruchomości* [Real Estate World], 2, 1992/1993.

Magocsi, P. R. *Historical Atlas of East and Central Europe.* Seattle: University of Washington Press, 1993.

Majkowski, W. *People's Poland, Patterns of Social Inequality and Conflict.* Contributions in Sociology # 55. Westport, CT: Greenwood, 1985.

Major, Ivan. *Privatization in Eastern Europe: A Critical Approach.* Aldershot, UK: Edward Elgar, 1993.

Manteuffel, Ryszard et al. *Struktura i Ekonomika Polskiego Rolnictwa.*[Polish Agricultural Structure and Economics]. Wrocław: Zakład Narodowy im. Ossolińskich Wydawnictwo Polskiej Akademii Nauk, 1984.

Matras, Hanna. "Structure and Performance of the Housing Sector of the Centrally Planned Economies: USSR, Hungary, Poland, GDR, and Yugoslavia." Discussion Paper. Washington, D.C.: World Bank Infrastructure and Urban Development Department, 1989.

Mayo, Stephen K., and James I. Stein. "Housing and Labor Market Distortions in Poland: Linkages and Policy Implications." *Discussion Paper Report INU 25,* 1988.

METROSTAV et al. "Územní Plán Hlavniho Města Prahy; Prvny Čteni [Land Plan of the Capital City of Prague; First Reading]". Prague: METROSTAV, 1992.

Mieszczankowski, M. *Struktura Agrarna Polski Międzywojennej* [Agrarian Structure in Poland Between the Wars]. Warsaw: PWN, 1960.

Mikhailov, Mikhail. "Problems of the Economic Reform of Agriculture." *Economic Thought.* Sofia: Institute of Economics, Bulgarian Academy of Sciences, 1993, pp. 92-100.

Milewski, R. "Privatization in Poland." Ms., University of Lodz, 1993.

Minassian, Garabed, and Stoyan Totev. "Bulgarian Economy in Transition: The Regional Aftereffect." Paper presented at ACE Conference, Katovice, September 24-27, 1993.

Minassian, Garabed (ed.). *Bulgarian Economy of Today And Tomorrow.* Sofia: Bulgarian Academy of Sciences, Institute of Economics, March 1992.

Mládek, Jan. "The Different Paths of Privatization." In: J. S. Earle et al. (eds.), *Privatization in the Transition to a Market Economy.* London: Pinter, 1993.

Mládek, Jan. "Transformation and Performance of the Czech Agriculture." Prague: Czech Institute of Applied Economics, 1994.

Movit, Charles. "Outlook for Bulgaria." *PlanEcon Review and Outlook for Eastern Europe.* June 1995, pp. 21-44.

Nagorski. Andrew. *The Birth of Freedom.* New York: Simon and Schuster, 1994.

National Centre for Regional Development and Housing Policy. "Evaluation of the Present Condition of Bulgarian Housing Sector." Habitat Housing Workshop, Sofia, Bulgaria, November 15-17, 1993.

*Ochrona Środowiska-Zbiór Przepisów* [Environment Protection-Collection of Laws] Wydawnictwo Prawnicze "Lex", Gdańsk, 1994.

Organization for Economic Cooperation and Development. Committee for Agriculture, Committee for Trade "Agricultural Policies, Markets and Trade in CEEC, the NIS, Mongolia and China: Monitoring and Outlook 1994." Paris: Organization for Economic Cooperation and Development, Directorate for Food, Agriculture and Fisheries. March 1994.

Pańko, Walerian. *Dzierżawa Gruntów Rolnych* [Agricultural Land Lease]. Warszawa: Państwowe Wydawnictwo Naukowe, 1975.

Pawlak, Wiktor. *Polskie Prawo Rolne* [Polish Agricultural Law]. Warszawa: Państwowe Wydawnictwo Naukowe, 1988.

Peeva, Valya. "Property Laws and Land Tenure in Bulgaria." In Vincent Renard and Rodrigo Acosta (eds.). *Land Tenure and Property Development in Eastern Europe.* Paris: ADEF/Pirville-CNRS, 1993, pp. 229-242.

Petranoff, Stefan. "An Evaluation of the Agricultural Credit Center." APAU Project 93.5, Ministry of Agricultural Development, Sofia. March 1994.

Petranoff, Stefan. "State Regulation of the Credit Market: The Law for Financing Agriculture in 1993." APAU Project 93.5, Ministry of Agricultural Development, Sofia. December 1993.

Petranoff, Stefan. "State Regulation of the Credit Market: The Law for Financing the Agricultural Practices in 1993/94." APAU Project 93.5, Ministry of Agricultural Development, Sofia. February 1994.

Pinto, Brian, and Sweder van Wijnbergen, "Ownership and Corporate Control in Poland: Why State Firms Defied the Odds, International Finance Corporation," Washington, D.C., 1994.

Pogłodzińska, Zofia. *Mieszkania w Obrocie Prawnym* [Housing Law]. Zielona Góra: Biuro Prawne Podmiotów Gospodarczych, 1993.

Pogodzinski, J. M. "Reform of the Polish Housing Market: Estimates of Housing and Labor Market Interaction" Ms. San Jose, CA: San Jose State University, Department of Economics, 1992a.

Pogodzinski, J.M. "The Effect of Housing Market Disequilibrium on the Supply of Labor: Evidence from Poland, 1989-1990." Ms. San Jose CA: San Jose State University, Department of Economics, 1992b.

*Poland, International Economic Report 1991/1992*, J. Gołębiowski (ed.). Warsaw: World Economy Research Institute, 1992.

*Poland, International Economic Report 1993/1994*, Jan W. Bossak (ed.). Warsaw: World Economy Research Institute, 1994.

Pomeroy, Harlan. "The Privatization Process in Bulgaria." Center for the Study of Democracy, April 1993.

Prague, City. "Initial Information for Flat Policy." Prague: City Architect's Office, 1992.

*Prawno-Ekonomiczne Podstawy Przekształceń Własnościowych Polskiej Gospodarki* [Legal and Economic Foundations for Property Transformation in the Polish Economy], Fundacja Edukacyjna Przedsiębiorczości, Miscellaneous Publications.

*Prawo Lokalowe* [Housing Law]. Zbiór Przepisów. Lex, Wydawnictwo Prawnicze i Ekonomiczne, Gdańsk, 1993.

Ravicz, R. Marisol. "The Bulgarian Banking System and the Housing Finance Market." U.I. Project 6127-95. Washington, D.C.: Urban Institute, 1991.

RECOM. "Cenova Mapa Karlovy Vary" ["Price Map of Karlovy Vary"]. Karlovy Vary: the Agency, 1992.

Rubenstein, James M., and Bernadette L. Unger. "Planning After the Fall of Communism in Czechoslovakia (The Czech Republic)." *Focus* (American Geographical Society), winter 1992, pp. 1-6.

Shopov, Georgi. "The Social Safety Net." *Economic Thought,* Sofia: Institute of Economics, Bulgarian Academy of Sciences, 1993, pp. 59-70.

Sitarski, Janusz. "Wyjść z Socjalizmu [To Exit Socialism]." *Świat Nieruchomości* [Real Estate World] 7/8, 1994.

Slay, Ben, and John Tedstrom. "Privatization in the Postcommunist Economies . . ." *RFE/RL Research Report,* 1:17, 1992, pp. 1-8.

Stanislavova, Albena. "Housing Stock Privatization and Transition to Market Economy Environments in Central and East-European Countries." International Seminar. Moscow, September 1-5, 1992.

Stark, D. "Privatization Strategies in East Central Europe." Working Papers on Transition from State Socialism. Ithaca, NY: Cornell University, Center for International Studies, 1991.

Strong, Ann L. (ed.). *Designing Markets.* Papers presented at the 35th annual meeting of the Association of Collegiate Schools of Planning, Philadelphia, 1993.

Svítek, Ivan, et al. "Investment 1992-1993." Prague: Lions Share Group, 1992.

Sýkora, Luděk. "City in Transition: Prague's Revitalization." Conference paper, European Cities: Growth and Decline, The Hague, 1992.

Sýkora, Luděk. "City in Transition: The Role of Rent Gaps in Prague's Revitalization." *Tijdschrift voor Economische en Sociale Geografie.* 84:4, (1993), pp. 281-293.

Sýkora, Luděk. "Prague." In James Berry and Stanley McGreal (eds.). *European Cities, Planning Systems and Property Markets.* London: E&FN Spon., 1995.

Sýkora, Luděk and Iva Šimoníčková. "From Totalitarian Urban Economy Managerialism to Liberalized Urban Property Market." In Max Barlow, Petr Dostal, and Martin Hampl (eds.), *Development and Administration of Prague.* Amsterdam: Universiteit van Amsterdam, Instituut voor Sociale Geografie, 1994.

Sýkora, Luděk, and Vit Stepanek. "Prague: City Profile." *Cities,* 9:2, May 1992.

Teague, Elizabeth. "Is Equity Compatible with Efficiency?" *RFE/RL Research Report,* 1:17, (1992), pp. 9-14.

Telgarsky, Jeffrey P. et al. "Housing Allowances and Czechoslovakia's Safety Net." Report for USAID. Washington, D.C.: Urban Institute, 1992.

Turner, Bengt, Josef Hegedus, and Ivan Tosics. *The Reform of Housing in Eastern Europe and the Soviet Union.* London: Routledge, 1992.

Večernik, Jiří. "Changing Income Distribution and Prospects for the Future." Prague: Institute of Sociology Academy of Sciences, Prague, 1993.

Videlov, Mityo et al.. *National Monograph of the Republic of Bulgaria.* Sofia: National Centre for Regional Development and Housing Policy, May 1993.

Wallace, William W. *Czechoslovakia..* Boulder, CO: Westview, 1976.

Warsaw Master Plans, Warszawa, 1990.

Weigel, J. "The Great Polish Experiment." *Commentary* 97:2, (February 1994), pp. 37-42.

Wilkin, Jerzy. "Private Agriculture and Socialism: The Polish Experience." In Roger Clarke (ed.), *The Polish Economy in the 1980's.* Chicago: St. James, 1989.

World Bank. *Bulgaria Crisis and Transition to a Market Economy.* Washington: D.C.: World Bank, 1991.

Yozioldash, Savash. "Private Business and its Stimulation." *Economic Thought.* Sofia: Institute of Economics, Bulgarian Academy of Sciences, 1993, pp. 41-50.

Zgliński, Włodzimierz. *Report of the Council on Agriculture with the President of the Republic of Poland,* 1994.

Zienkowski, L. (ed.). *Polish Economy in 1990-1992, Experience and Conclusions.* Warsaw: Research Centre for Economic and Statistical Studies of the Central Statistical Office and The Polish Academy of Sciences, 1993.

# INDEX